T0212453

Lecture Notes in Computer Science　　　　10164

Commenced Publication in 1973
Founding and Former Series Editors:
Gerhard Goos, Juris Hartmanis, and Jan van Leeuwen

More information about this series at http://www.springer.com/series/7407

Edoardo Di Napoli · Marc-André Hermanns
Hristo Iliev · Andreas Lintermann
Alexander Peyser (Eds.)

High-Performance Scientific Computing

First JARA-HPC Symposium, JHPCS 2016
Aachen, Germany, October 4–5, 2016
Revised Selected Papers

 Springer

Editors
Edoardo Di Napoli
Forschungszentrum Jülich
Jülich
Germany

Marc-André Hermanns
Forschungszentrum Jülich
Jülich
Germany

Hristo Iliev
RWTH Aachen University
Aachen
Germany

Andreas Lintermann
RWTH Aachen University
Aachen
Germany

Alexander Peyser
Forschungszentrum Jülich
Jülich
Germany

ISSN 0302-9743   ISSN 1611-3349   (electronic)
Lecture Notes in Computer Science
ISBN 978-3-319-53861-7   ISBN 978-3-319-53862-4   (eBook)
DOI 10.1007/978-3-319-53862-4

Library of Congress Control Number: 2017932438

LNCS Sublibrary: SL1 – Theoretical Computer Science and General Issues

Printed on acid-free paper

This Springer imprint is published by Springer Nature
The registered company is Springer International Publishing AG
The registered company address is: Gewerbestrasse 11, 6330 Cham, Switzerland

Preface

Current high-performance computing (HPC) systems consist of complex configurations with a massive number of components that are very likely heterogeneous and typically have a limited amount of memory per component. These hardware and software configurations can change dynamically owing to fault recovery or power saving procedures. To make efficient use of such systems, complex software components require programming layers structured in deep hierarchies. Additionally, applications increasingly use HPC systems for data analytics and complex workflows. Therefore, the successful development of software for scientific computations requires collaboration between domain scientists on one hand and computer science/HPC experts on the other.

JARA-HPC is the high-performance computing section of JARA, the Jülich Aachen Research Alliance. This alliance represents a cooperative venture between RWTH Aachen University and Forschungszentrum Jülich. This cooperative relationship goes beyond the mere juxtaposition of university and non-university research and teaching and represents a pioneering model in Germany. Scientists from JARA-HPC combine in-depth knowledge of massively parallel computing architectures with expertise in specific research fields. Within JARA-HPC, distinct research teams embodied by simulation laboratories (SimLabs) provide support to communities in diverse computational science disciplines. At the same time, HPC experts in cross-sectional groups provide support to the SimLabs in the form of services needed by a broader spectrum of scientific communities, such as performance optimization for software codes and visualization of simulation data.

Since its establishment, JARA-HPC has proven that close interdisciplinary mixing of domain-specific knowledge and HPC expertise is a concept that is key for success in scientific software. This success has been substantiated by the in-depth collaborations which have reaped synergies from a diverse knowledge base during the development of complex scientific codes. JARA-HPC established the JARA-HPC Symposium (JHPCS) to pass on its collected experience and complement it with the experience developed by other HPC development teams. In the long term, the aim of the JHPCS is to motivate broader discussion on various aspects of HPC application development among experts at an international scale. Participants in the symposium are given the opportunity for a profound exchange with colleagues from different research fields utilizing HPC systems in their scientific work.

This volume contains the papers presented at the First JHPCS held during October 3–4, 2016 in Aachen, Germany. The JHPCS Program Committee received a total of 26 submissions. Each submission was reviewed by at least two Program Committee members as well as additional external reviewers in a single-blind peer review. Owing to the above-average quality of the submissions, the Program Committee decided to accept 21 papers on diverse topics, such as coupling methods and strategies in computational fluid dynamics (CFD), performance portability and applications in HPC, as well as provenance tracking for large-scale simulations. The symposium program included a keynote talk by Viktor Eijkhout from the Texas Advanced Computing Center (TACC) on "Parallel Programming for the 21st Century." Furthermore, it featured a half-day workshop that focused on CFD-related aeroacoustic research with a mix of invited talks and paper submissions. Overall, the program reflected the anticipated broad spectrum of topics and brought together several communities active in HPC software development.

December 2016

Edoardo Di Napoli
Marc-André Hermanns
Hristo Iliev
Andreas Lintermann
Alexander Peyser

Organization

Program Committee

Edoardo Di Napoli	Forschungszentrum Jülich, Germany
Bernd Hentschel	RWTH Aachen University, Germany
Marc-André Hermanns	Forschungszentrum Jülich, Germany
Hristo Iliev	RWTH Aachen University, Germany
Andreas Lintermann	RWTH Aachen University, Germany
Bernd Mohr	Forschungszentrum Jülich, Germany
Boris Orth	Forschungszentrum Jülich, Germany
Alexander Peyser	Forschungszentrum Jülich, Germany
Herwig Zilken	Forschungszentrum Jülich, Germany

Additional Reviewers

Baumeister, Paul	Plotnikov, Dimitri
Diaz-Piers, Sandra	Roidl, Benedikt
Fabregat-Traver, Diego	Schlimpert, Stephan
Foysi, Holger	Shende, Sameer
Hemchandra, Santosh	Thust, Kay
Meinke, Matthias	Trensch, Guido
Meysonnat, Pascal	Winkelmann, Jan
Nanavati, Sachin	Wortmann, Daniel
Peyser, Alexander	Wylie, Brian

Invited Talk
(Abstract)

Parallel Programming for the 21st Century

Victor Eijkhout

Texas Advanced Computing Center, Austin, TX, USA

Abstract. The dominant parallel programming systems, MPI and OpenMP, are now 20 years old. Computer architectures have become considerably more complicated in this time, and these systems have undergone refinements accordingly, making them ever more complicated to use. Maybe it is time to take a step back and reconsider the nature of parallel programming: is all this complexity necessary at the user level? Our parallel programming systems have a design that is inspired by underlying hardware mechanisms, which introduces considerations in the parallel program that are extraneous to the algorithm being implemented. This raises the question what the minimal specification is of an algorithm that allows for efficient parallel execution. Past experience has shown that a parallelizing compiler is not the right approach. A more interesting approach, writing a sequential program in terms of distributed objects, was tried in High Performance Fortran and failed there.

We argue that this 'sequential semantics' approach can work, if the programmer expresses the algorithm in terms of the right abstractions. We motivate and define these abstractions and show how the IMP (Integrative Model for Parallelism) system implements them, giving essentially the performance behaviour of a hand-written code. To the programmer, a Finite Element program in IMP has the complexity of a sequential code, without any parallel communication explicitly specified. We show results obtained so far, and future directions of research.

Contents

Efficient HPC-Optimized Multi-Physics Coupling Strategies in CFD

Partitioned High Performance Code Coupling Applied to CFD 3
  Florent Duchaine, Sandrine Berger, Gabriel Staffelbach,
  and Laurent Gicquel

Dynamic Load Balancing for Large-Scale Multiphysics Simulations 13
  Niclas Jansson, Rahul Bale, Keiji Onishi, and Makoto Tsubokura

On the Significance of Exposure Time in Computational
Blood Damage Estimation 24
  Lutz Pauli and Marek Behr

A Partitioned Methodology for Conjugate Heat Transfer
on Dynamic Structures. 37
  Miguel Zavala-Aké, Daniel Mira, Mariano Vázquez,
  and Guillaume Houzeaux

Farfield Noise Prediction Using Large-Scale
Lattice-Boltzmann Simulations 48
  Benjamin Duda and Ehab Fares

FEniCS-HPC: Coupled Multiphysics in Computational Fluid Dynamics. 58
  Johan Hoffman, Johan Jansson, Niyazi Cem Degirmenci,
  Jeannette Hiromi Spühler, Rodrigo Vilela De Abreu,
  Niclas Jansson, and Aurélien Larcher

The Direct-Hybrid Method for Computational Aeroacoustics
on HPC Systems. 70
  Michael Schlottke-Lakemper, Hans Yu, Sven Berger,
  Andreas Lintermann, Matthias Meinke, and Wolfgang Schröder

A Novel Approach for Efficient Storage and Retrieval of Tabulated
Chemistry in Reactive Flow Simulations 82
  Sebastian Popp, Steffen Weise, and Christian Hasse

Multi-scale Coupling for Predictive Injector Simulations 96
  Mathis Bode, Marco Davidovic, and Heinz Pitsch

Domain-Specific Applications and High-Performance Computing

Ab Initio Description of Optoelectronic Properties at Defective Interfaces
in Solar Cells   111
   Philippe Czaja, Massimo Celino, Simone Giusepponi, Michele Gusso,
   and Urs Aeberhard

Scale Bridging Simulations of Large Elastic Deformations
and Bainitic Transformations   125
   Marc Weikamp, Claas Hüter, Mingxuan Lin, Ulrich Prahl,
   Diego Schicchi, Martin Hunkel, and Robert Spatschek

Ab Initio Modelling of Electrode Material Properties.   139
   Siaufung O. Dang, Marco Prill, Claas Hüter, Martin Finsterbusch,
   and Robert Spatschek

Overlapping of Communication and Computation in nb3dfft
for 3D Fast Fourier Transformations   151
   Jens Henrik Göbbert, Hristo Iliev, Cedrick Ansorge, and Heinz Pitsch

Towards Simulating Data-Driven Brain Models at the Point Neuron Level
on Petascale Computers.   160
   Till Schumann, Csaba Erő, Marc-Oliver Gewaltig,
   and Fabien Jonathan Delalondre

Parallel Adaptive Integration in High-Performance Functional
Renormalization Group Computations   170
   Julian Lichtenstein, Jan Winkelmann, David Sánchez de la Peña,
   Toni Vidović, and Edoardo Di Napoli

Performance Portability

Performance Optimization of Parallel Applications in Diverse On-Demand
Development Teams   187
   Hristo Iliev, Marc-André Hermanns, Jens Henrik Göbbert, René Halver,
   Christian Terboven, Bernd Mohr, and Matthias S. Müller

Hybrid CPU-GPU Generation of the Hamiltonian and Overlap Matrices
in FLAPW Methods   200
   Diego Fabregat-Traver, Davor Davidović, Markus Höhnerbach,
   and Edoardo Di Napoli

Visualizing Performance Data with Respect to the Simulated Geometry.   212
   Tom Vierjahn, Torsten W. Kuhlen, Matthias S. Müller,
   and Bernd Hentschel

Provenance Tracking

Framework for Sharing of Highly Resolved Turbulence Simulation Data   225
Bastian Tweddell, Jens Henrik Göbbert, Michael Gauding,
Benjamin Weyers, and Björn Hagemeier

UniProv: A Flexible Provenance Tracking System for UNICORE   233
André Giesler, Myriam Czekala, Björn Hagemeier,
and Richard Grunzke

A Collaborative Simulation-Analysis Workflow for Computational
Neuroscience Using HPC   243
Johanna Senk, Alper Yegenoglu, Olivier Amblet, Yury Brukau,
Andrew Davison, David Roland Lester, Anna Lührs, Pietro Quaglio,
Vahid Rostami, Andrew Rowley, Bernd Schuller, Alan Barry Stokes,
Sacha Jennifer van Albada, Daniel Zielasko, Markus Diesmann,
Benjamin Weyers, Michael Denker, and Sonja Grün

Author Index   257

Efficient HPC-Optimized Multi-Physics Coupling Strategies in CFD

High-Performance Computing (HPC) enables the simulation of complex multi-physics phenomena which appear in combustion and reactive flows, in fluid-structure interaction, and in aeroacoustics problems. High temporal and spatial resolutions necessitate massive parallelization of the corresponding simulation software. Finding strategies to efficiently couple methods to solve for the individual physics under the constraints of process load-balance, minimization of communication, and maximization of computational efficiency, also with respect to recent hardware developments, is a challenging task and an active field of research. In particular, regarding upcoming exascale systems, the scalability of such coupled software solutions is key to code sustainability and code applicability to solve even more complex multi-physics problems in the future. To tackle such coupling problems, various strategies exist. While two-stage approaches consecutively simulate different physics and realize a one-way coupling, directly online-coupled methods allow for solving problems in parallel including mutual dependencies. In general, the latter approach is more efficient and solves a global coupled system of equations, a process-local multi-physics problem, or the individual physics on dedicated processes. From these methods new challenges arise, such as how to efficiently parallelize the solution method for the full set of the coupled equations or how to efficiently implement communication between multi-physics domains or between dedicated physic-specific processes.

The present topic covers contributions from the sessions *"Efficient multi-physics coupling strategies in CFD"*, *"Coupling methods for reactive flows and FSI"*, and the mini-workshops *"CFD applications using HPC"* and *"Aeroacoustics coupling methods"* of the JARA-HPC Symposium 2016 (JHPCS'16). All contributions discuss methods to numerically solve multi-physics problems, involve discussions on coupling strategies for large-scale and multi-scale applications, and/or focus on code scalability, decomposition strategies, dynamic load-balancing, and the analysis of the corresponding physical results.

Partitioned High Performance Code Coupling Applied to CFD

Florent Duchaine$^{(\boxtimes)}$, Sandrine Berger, Gabriel Staffelbach,
and Laurent Gicquel

Cerfacs, 42 Avenue Gaspard Coriolis, 31 057 Toulouse, France
`florent.duchaine@cerfacs.fr`

Abstract. Based on in situ observations obtained in the context of multiphysics and multicomponent simulations of the Computational Fluid Dynamics community, parallel performances of code coupling is first discussed. Overloads due to coupling steps are then analyzed with a simple toy model. Many parameters can impact the communication times, such as the number of cores, the communication mode (synchronous or asynchronous), the global size of the exchanged fields or the amount of data per core. Results show that the respective partionning of the coupled codes as well as core distributions on the machine have an important role in exchange times and thus on the total CPU hours needed by an application. For the synchronous communications presented in this paper, two main outcomes independent from the coupler can be addressed by incorporating the knowledge of the coupling in the preprocessing step of the solvers with constraint and co-partitioning as well as process placement. Such conclusions can be directly extended to other field of applications such as climat science where coupling between ocean and atmosphere is of primary importance.

Keywords: Coupled CFD applications · Scalability · Co-partitioning · OpenPALM

1 Introduction

Today, the design of gas turbines requires to consider strong interactions between different physics as well as the components of the engine. As a result, integrated simulations involving multiphysics and multicomponents are performed both at the research level as well as in industries. With the constant increase of computing power, numerical simulations of the interactions between the compressor, combustion chamber and turbine, as well as of the thermal interaction between fluid flows and solids offer new design paths to diminish development costs through important reductions of the number of experimental tests. In these fields, the main idea is to jointly simulate the different parts of the coupled problems with a high level of fidelity limiting hypotheses on the boundary conditions:

- for the interactions between turbomachinery parts and combustor, inlet and outlet models of the component interfaces can be avoided by resolving the full system at once (Fig. 1(a)),

© Springer International Publishing AG 2017
E. Di Napoli et al. (Eds.): JHPCS 2016, LNCS 10164, pp. 3–12, 2017.
DOI: 10.1007/978-3-319-53862-4_1

– to determine mean heat loads on structures, many authors use Conjugate Heat
  Transfer (CHT) where the fluid and solid equations are resolved simultane-
  ously to predict the temperature and heat flux distributions in the system
  (Fig. 1(b)).

Recent works have shown the ability of eddy resolving methods such as Large
Eddy Simulation (LES) to provide reliable results in the contexts of combustors
and turbomachinery [5,6,10,14]. Using an unsteady LES flow solver to resolve
such problems raises several complexities to address in the context of coupled
problems. Indeed, LES requires high mesh resolutions to accurately capture the
flow physics and is more CPU consuming than averaged methods to converge
spatial and temporal statistics. These specificities imply to use high performance
architectures to decrease the restitution times of the simulations.

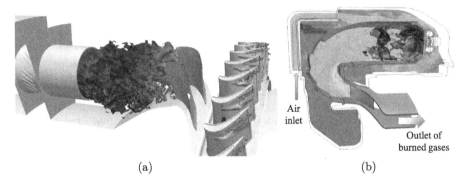

(a)   (b)

Fig. 1. Example of an integrated combustor/turbine simulation [3] (a), view of fluid
and solid models of an industrial combustor Conjugate Heat Transfer simulation [4] (b).

There are two basic approaches to numerically solve coupled problems such
as CHT. The first one is a direct coupling approach where the different physics
are solved simultaneously in a large system of equations by a monolithic solver.
The second approach consists in solving each set of equations separately with
dedicated solvers that exchange interface conditions through a coupler. The last
solution adopted here has the advantage of using existing state-of-the-art codes
to solve fluid and solid equations. Nevertheless, it stresses the tool used to couple
the solvers in terms of parallel computing performances. Several communities
have investigated the use of code coupler in many different areas ranging from
climate studies to industrial applications. These communities are now faced to
the challenge of running the coupled applications with highly loaded codes on
massively parallel machines where the solvers exchange a large amount of data
at a high frequency.

This paper presents a feed-back on the use of coupling libraries on massively
parallel systems for multiphysics and multicomponent simulations with a LES
solver [7]. Based on observations monitored on real applications running on HPC

systems, a toy model is constructed to identify paths of improvements on a simple controlled code.

2 In Situ Observations

The OpenPALM software is used in this study [4]. It is a code coupler, i.e. a library of functionalities that facilitate the scheduling of existing components execution sequentially or concurrently as well as the exchange of data between these components. This is achieved in part via a collection of primitives that are called in the codes as well as with more complex mechanisms for application scheduling. OpenPALM aims at implementing a general tool allowing to easily integrate high performance computing applications in a flexible and evolutive way proposing a solution to the balance among performance, software reuse, and numerical accuracy. OpenPALM is mainly composed of three complementary components, (1) the PALM[1] library [2,11], (2) the CWIPI[2] library [13] and (3) the graphical interface PrePALM [2,11].

Code coupling is an appealing method to develop multiphysics and multi-component applications. However if it is done incorrectly it can become a performance pitfall and render useless the efforts invested to optimize each individual code. There are at least two important aspects to take into account to manage efficient code coupling in a HPC context (Fig. 2): (1) reducing the overhead of data transfer between the solvers and (2) maintaining a global processor idle time low, unless both codes have perfectly equal CPU per iteration times, the fastest code will have to wait the others. Having a good load balancing is the key to maintain a low idle time and thus reduce CPU waste. The first point requires the most attention and a direct point to point communication between each solver's processors is proposed [8]. Also non matching grids being used, a parallel interpolation method is required. The algorithm consists of two parts: the initialization or setup phase, i.e. where the communication routes and the interpolation coefficients are computed, and the run-time phase, or how inter-code synchronization is actually executed. The first phase is done just once per coupled simulation except if the geometries are mobile. Figure 3 presents the time requested for the initialization and the run-time phases for a turbomachinery application [9] performed on Titan[3] until 132,000 cores. Globally, a decrease of both times is observed as the number of cores involved in the coupling increases. Interestingly, there are two order of magnitude difference between the two phases, the initialization being the more time consuming. These times are affected by the location algorithms, machine performance and characteristics as well as by the way external communications between solvers are handled (communication algorithm, interface partitioning).

Focusing on the communication time (run-time phase), Fig. 4 shows the exchange time as a function of the ratio between the number of cores allocated to the fluid and those allocated to the solid (in abscissa) as well as the total number

---

[1] Projet d'Assimilation par Logiciel Multiméthodes.

[2] Coupling With Interpolation Parallel Interface.

[3] Titan: Oak Ridge National Laboratory. No. 1 system of Top500 in November 2012.

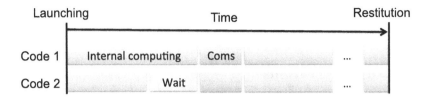

Fig. 2. Time line corresponding to a coupled simulation including two codes.

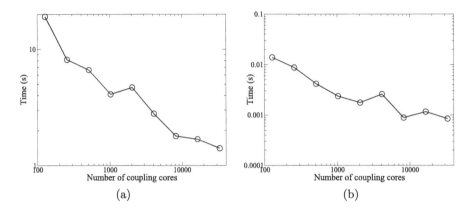

Fig. 3. Time requested for the initialization (a) and the run-time (b) phases as a function of the number of cores involved in the coupling process for a turbomachinery application [9] performed on Titan.

of cores involved in the exchange (which increases with the bubbles size) in the case of a CHT computation on Curie[4] [4]. The total number of exchanging cores (indicated by the bubble size) does not have a leading role in the variation of the communication times. Instead Fig. 4 highlights that the more the ratio of cores increases, the more communications are expensive. This points out that important unbalance in the core distribution between the solvers which may be requested to synchronize to avoid waiting as illustrated on Fig. 2 which can be detrimental for exchange time optimization. Interestingly, two points (colored in red in Fig. 4) exhibit very close core ratios with very different communications times. Neither this switching of ratio nor the corresponding total number of cores can explain by themselves the differences in the communication time between the two cases. Other underlying parameters are involved and next the section intends to give elements in this direction with a controlled toy coupled application.

---

[4] Curie supercomputer, owned by GENCI and operated at the TGCC by CEA.

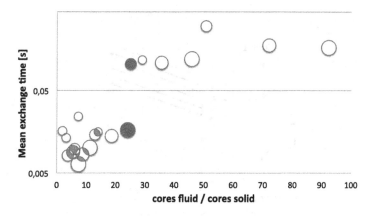

Fig. 4. Evolution of the exchange time as a function of the ratio between the number of cores allocated to the fluid and the number of cores allocated to the solid (abscissa) and the total number of cores involved in the exchange (increasing with the bubbles size). Data extracted from [4]. (Color figure online)

3 Toy Model

The toy model is composed of two identical codes. In the following, quantities referring to the first and second executables are respectively indexed with the subscripts 1 and 2. Each of these entities build a square including $npts_i$ (with i the index of the solver) points distributed on N_i cores where N_i is such that $N_i = m^2$, $m \in \mathcal{N}$. As detailed on Fig. 5, the partitioning is homogeneous, i.e. each square edge is cut in the same way (which justifies the need for a number of cores such that $N_i = m^2$). The codes perform 100 data exchange ping-pongs with the OpenPALM coupler to provide statistically converged exchange times. Both the initialization and the communication phases are recorded separately. Since the initialization time mainly relies on localisation methods, the investigation focus of this study is on communication times.

The results come from computations performed on a Cerfacs-based BULL B510 Supercomputer. Each computational node includes two processors, itself composed of eight cores. The Infiniband interconnection network offers a theoretical $5\,\mathrm{GB.s}^{-1}$ bandwidth between nodes. The MPI latency is lower than 1μs. For the present tests, MPI communications are performed thanks to the IntelMPI library.

The influence of various parameters has been considered. This paper reports cases for synchronous communications first with the same number of cores for each executable and then with a different number of cores. The dependency of exchange time to the global amount of data on the models as well as per core is investigated by changing the number of points on the grid $npts_i$. The number of cores is denoted N_i, and the total amount of data sent by a code (in bytes, B) is denoted $datatot_i$ and the quantity of data per core is given by $dataproc_i$. No placement effort is made and the MPI ranks are distributed among the available

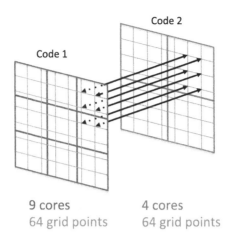

Fig. 5. Schematic of the inter-code communication toy.

cores in a linear way, i.e. the first application is assigned to the first N_1 cores and the second one to the following N_2 cores.

The influence of the total amount of data on the grid is investigated by increasing the number of nodes that composed the grids. Figure 6(a) shows the evolution of the exchange time as a function of the total amount of data on the grid for different values of core numbers $N_1 = N_2$. The curves display the same behavior in logarithmic scale with as expected the exchange time greatly increasing with the number of grid points. On the contrary, for a given number of grid points, increasing of the number of cores on which data are distributed tends to decrease the communication time. This can explain the differences observe between the two red circles on Fig. 4 for which the case with the biggest number of core has the lowest exchange time. Such behavior can be mathematically modeled based on architecture parameters [1]. To explore the effect of the quantity of data per core on communications, Fig. 6(b) shows the communication times arranged here as a function of the data quantity per core. This different representation of the same data highlights three groups of curves:

- $N_1 = N_2 = 1$ and 4
- $N_1 = N_2 = 9$
- $N_1 = N_2 = 16, 25, 36$ and 49.

These gatherings may be explained by the bandwidth variation between the various levels of the supercomputer network. The bandwidth between two computing cores of a given machine depends on their relative positioning on the network as well as on the size of the exchanged message. Three cases can be distinguished that depend on the computer communication networks used by the toy model:

- $N_1 = N_2 = 1$ and 4: the cores are distributed on the two processors of the same node. Communications are thus achieved within the same node but on potentially different processors. They are thus relatively fast but very dependent on the exchanged message size.

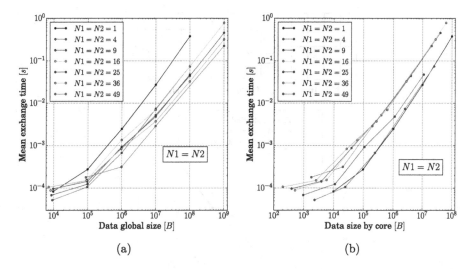

Fig. 6. Evolution of the exchange time as a function of the total amount of data on the grids $datatot_i$, for several values of the number of cores (a), Evolution of the exchange time as a function of the data size per core $dataproc_i$, for several values of the number of cores (b).

- $N_1 = N_2 = 9$: the cores are mainly placed on the same node, only three cores are on a different node due to the use of one process for the coupler's driver. Even though most of the communications are intra-processor or intra-node, some exchanges are made between cores from different nodes.
- $N_1 = N_2 = 16, 25, 36$ and 49, the cores are distributed on several nodes (3 to 7 nodes depending on the case). A large part of the communications (if not all) is made between nodes. Most of the communications are thus made between cores that are quite far from each other on the network resulting in slower exchanges.

These analyses bring to the conclusion that the minimization of exchange times between coupled components can be performed by process placement on the parallel architecture. Such placement algorithm must take into account internal exchanges in the parallel models to minimize the impact on the standalone model performances.

In a real coupled application, the exchange interface between two codes is rarely partitioned in the same way and/or distributed over the same number of computing cores. To investigate this point, the toy is run for cases where the number of allocated cores is different for each executable ($N_1 \neq N_2$). These tests are performed for every possible N_1 and N_2 value combinations. The global tendencies remain the same for all cases. Therefore, for brevity, Fig. 7 presents only the results for the cases where $N_1 = 16$ and $N_2 = 16; 25; 36$. For each of them, the relative positions of the partitioning are indicated on the top of the figure. Exchange times evolve within the same range as those presented for

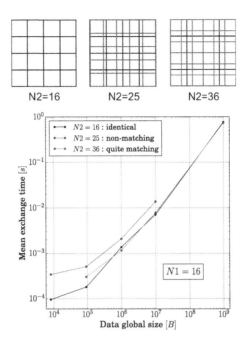

Fig. 7. Evolution of the exchange time as a function of the total amount of data on the grid, for cases where the partitioning of the two executables is either identical, or quite coincident, or totally non-coincident.

the case $N_1 = N_2$ increasing as the total amount of data increases. However, it is worth noting that for every tested case, given a fixed number of cores N_1, every values of N_2 different from N_1 leads to communication times superior or similar to the $N_1 = N_2$ case. Cases with partitionings of the two executable grids that are either identical or quite coincident minimize the number of communications between the two codes leading to lower communication times. A smart partitioning of both domains with respect to each other could lead to lower exchange times and hence better performance of the coupled simulations. According to these observations, future work should focus on the development of co-partitioning techniques able to decrease greatly the communications time between solvers [12].

4   Conclusion

The CPU costs of a coupled simulation are determined both by the internal computational time of each code as well as by the interconnection process and the communication times between solvers. Core repartition between the coupled model to insure a good load balancing is rather trivial. Studying the effect of the data exchange time is much more complex and is examined here via a toy model.

Many parameters can impact the communication times, such as the number of cores, the communication mode (synchronous or asynchronous), the global size of the exchanged fields or the amount of data per core. For the synchronous communications presented in this paper, two main outcomes independent from the coupler can be addressed by incorporating the knowledge of the coupling in the preprocessing step of the solvers with constraint and co-partitioning as well as process placement. Moreover, tests on asynchronous communications show an important improvement of the scalability of the coupler indicating development paths for the future. Finally, many order of magnitude higher than the communication time, the time requested by the interconnection process also depends on several parameters such as core distribution between the coupled components. Nevertheless, the real gain to decrease its CPU cost relies on interconnection algorithms and thus on further development in coupling libraries rather than on the global management of the coupling environment.

References

1. Berger, S.: Implementation of a coupled computational chain to the combustion chamber's heat transfer. Ph.D. thesis, Institut National Polytechnique de Toulouse, June 2016
2. Buis, S., Piacentini, A., Déclat, D.: Palm: a computational framework for assembling high-performance computing applications. Concurr. Comput. Pract. Exp. **18**(2), 231–245 (2006)
3. Duchaine, F., Dombard, J., Gicquel, L., Koupper, C.: Integrated large-eddy simulation of combustion chamber/turbone interactiàons. In: 51st 3AF International Conference on Applied Aerodynamics, Strasbourg, France, 4–6 April 2016 (2016)
4. Duchaine, F., Jauré, S., Poitou, D., Quémerais, E., Staffelbach, G., Morel, T., Gicquel, L.: Analysis of high performance conjugate heat transfer with the openpalm coupler. J. Comput. Sci. Discov. **8**, 015003 (2015)
5. Duchaine, F., Maheu, N., Moureau, V., Balarac, G., Moreau, S.: Large eddy simulation and conjugate heat transfer around a low-mach turbine blade. J. Turbomach. **136**(5), 051015 (2013)
6. Gicquel, L.Y.M., Staffelbach, G., Poinsot, T.: Large eddy simulations of gaseous flames in gas turbine combustion chambers. Prog. Energy Comb. Sci. **38**(6), 782–817 (2012)
7. Gicquel, L., Gourdain, N., Boussuge, J.F., Deniau, H., Staffelbach, G., Wolf, P., Poinsot, T.: High performance parallel computing of flows in complex geometries. C. R. Mécanique **339**(2–3), 104–124 (2011)
8. Jauré, S., Duchaine, F., Staffelbach, G., Gicquel, L.: Massively parallel conjugate heat transfer solver based on large eddy simulation and application to an aeronautical combustion chamber. Comput. Sci. Disc **6**(1), 015008 (2013)
9. de Laborderie, J., Duchaine, F., Vermorel, O., Gicquel, L.: Application of an overset grid method to the large eddy simulation of a high-speed multistage axial compressor. In: ASME Turbo Expo 2016: Turbomachinery Technical Conference and Exposition. No. GT2016-56344, Seoul, Korea, 13–17 June 2016 (2016)
10. Gourdain, N., Sicot, F., Duchaine, F., Gicquel, L.: Large eddy simulation of flows in industrial compressors: a path from 2015 to 2035. Philos. Trans. A **372**(2022), 20130323 (2014)

11. Piacentini, A., Morel, T., Thévenin, A., Duchaine, F.: O-palm: an open source dynamic parallel coupler. In: Proceedings of the IV International Conference on Computational Methods for Coupled Problems in Science and Engineering-Coupled Problems (2011)
12. Predari, M., Esnard, A.: Coupling-aware graph partitioning algorithms: Preliminary study. In: IEEE International Conference on High Performance Computing, Goa India, December 2014
13. Refloch, A., Courbet, B., Murrone, A., Villedieu, P., Laurent, C., Gilbank, P., Troyes, J., Tessé, L., Chaineray, G., Dargaud, J., Quémerais, E., Vuillot, F.: Cfd platforms and coupling - cedre software. Onera J. Aerosp. Lab (2) (2011)
14. Tucker, P., Eastwood, S., Klostermeier, C., Xia, H., Ray, P., Tyacke, J., Dawes, W.: Hybrid les approach for practical turbomachinery flows - part 2: further applications. J. Turbomach. **134**(2), 021024 (2012)

Dynamic Load Balancing for Large-Scale Multiphysics Simulations

Niclas Jansson[1]($\boxtimes$), Rahul Bale[1]($\boxtimes$), Keiji Onishi[1], and Makoto Tsubokura[1,2]

[1] RIKEN Advanced Institute for Computational Science, Kobe, Japan
{leifniclas.jansson,rahul.bale}@riken.jp
[2] Department of Computational Science, Graduate School of System Informatics,
Kobe University, Kobe, Japan

Abstract. In parallel computing load balancing is an essential component of any efficient and scalable simulation code. Static data decomposition methods have proven to work well for symmetric workloads. But, in today's multiphysics simulations, with asymmetric workloads, this imbalance prevents good scalability on future generation of parallel architectures. We present our work on developing a general dynamic load balancing framework for multiphysics simulations on hierarchical Cartesian meshes. Using a weighted dual graph based workload estimation and constrained multilevel graph partitioning, the required runtime for industrial applications could be reduced by 40% of the runtime, running on the K computer.

Keywords: HPC · Load balancing · Multiphysics · BCM

1 Introduction

Load balancing is an essential component in today's large scale multiphysics simulations. With an ever increasing amount of parallelism in modern computer architecture, it is essential to remove even the slightest workload imbalance. As it could severely impact application's scalability. Traditionally, load balancing is seen as a static problem, closely related to the fundamental problem of parallel computing, namely data decomposition. Data is often decomposed either offline by a preprocessor or online in the initial steps of a simulation. This decomposition is typically performed with respect to the underlying discretization of the computational domain, with the aim of evenly distributing the cells, for example tetrahedra or hexahedra in unstructured meshes, or blocks in the case of Cartesian block structured meshes.

However, such a decomposition assumes that the workload for each cell is uniform. For certain problems this is true, but for a large class of problems it is not, for example, reactive flows, where the cost of computing the chemical reactions is different depending on the species concentration in a cell. Another example is when immersed boundary methods are employed. There, the cost of computing one cell will be different depending on whether the cell is cut by a surface or not, and also whether the geometry is stationary or moving through the domain.

© Springer International Publishing AG 2017
E. Di Napoli et al. (Eds.): JHPCS 2016, LNCS 10164, pp. 13–23, 2017.
DOI: 10.1007/978-3-319-53862-4_2

In this paper we present our work on developing a generic dynamic load balancing technique for the Building Cube Method (BCM) [5], suitable for large-scale multiphysics problems. Our method is based on the load balancing framework used in DOLFIN HPC [3], a framework for automated scientific computing. The rest of this paper is organized as follows. In Sect. 2, we present the theory for static load balancing and discuss its limitations. Section 3 extends this theory to dynamic load balancing, with the introduction of workload modeling and re-partitioning schemes. In Sect. 4 we evaluate the performance. We present a discussion of the predictivity of the load balancing framework in Sect. 5 and, lastly, give conclusions and outline future work in Sect. 6.

2   Static Load Balancing

In parallel computing, the idea of data decomposition or static load balancing is simple, namely divide the workload evenly across all the workers. This can be formulated as a partitioning problem.

Given a set of cells $\mathcal{C}$ from a domain $\mathcal{T}$, the partitioning problem for p workers can be expressed as, find p subsets $\{\mathcal{T}^i\}_{i=1}^p$ such that:

$$\mathcal{T} = \cup_{i=1}^p \mathcal{T}^i \quad \text{and} \quad \mathcal{T}^i \cap \mathcal{T}^j = \emptyset, \quad i \neq j \tag{1}$$

with the constraint that the workload:

$$W(\mathcal{T}^i) = |\{\mathcal{C} \in \mathcal{T} \mid \mathcal{C} \in \mathcal{T}^i\}|$$

should be approximately equal for all subsets.

Solving Eq. 1 can be done in several ways. The least expensive, geometric methods, such as space filling curves [1] only depend on the geometry of the domain. These methods are fast, but do not take into account the topology, hence the data dependencies between different cells in the domain are not optimized. For Cartesian meshes such as BCM, neglecting the consideration of data dependencies is less severe. All the cells have the same amount of neighbors, and if the decomposition method tries to assign cells which are close to each other to one worker (in the geometrical sense), data dependencies will automatically be approximately balanced. However, if woarkload is not uniform across cells, or if data dependencies between the cells are assymetric, we have to resort to graph methods in order to solve Eq. 1.

Graph methods do not solve Eq. 1 directly, instead the following k-way partitioning problem is considered: Given an undirected graph $G = (V, E)$ with nodes V and edges E, split V into k subsets $\{Q_j\}_{j=1}^k$ with the constraint that the number of nodes in each subset should be roughly equal, and the number of edges cut should be minimized. If we model the computational work by V and the data dependencies in the domain by E, we see that this method will balance both the computational work and the dependencies. Furthermore, if we instead consider a weighted graph G and add the constraint that the sum of all weights should be roughly equal in all subsets Q_j, the method can then, by allowing multiple weights in the graph, handle a non uniform workload.

3   Dynamic Load Balancing

In order to perform dynamic load balancing, two components are needed: First, a way to evaluate the workload, and second, a way to decompose the data with the constraint to even out the workload. Using the graph based methods from Sect. 2 we can compute new constrained partitions of our computational domain. But the challenge is to be able to evaluate the current and future workloads, and decide if load balancing is needed.

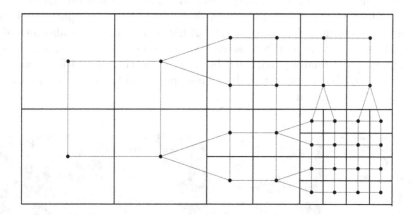

Fig. 1. Example of the dual graph of a BCM mesh.

3.1   Workload Modeling

We model the workload by a weighted dual graph of the underlying Building Cube mesh (see Fig. 1). Let $G = (V, E)$ be the dual graph of the mesh, with nodes V (one for each cube) and edges E (connecting two nodes if their respective cubes share a common face), q be one of the partitions, and let w_i be the computational work (weights) assigned to the graph. The workload of partition $q \in T$ is then defined as:

$$W(q) = \sum_{w_i \in w_q} w_i$$

Let W_{avg} be the average workload and W_{max} be the maximum, then the graph is considered imbalanced if:

$$W_{\mathrm{max}}/W_{\mathrm{avg}} > \kappa \tag{2}$$

where κ is the threshold value determined depending on the current problem and/or machine characteristics.

To model a simulation's workload, we finally have to assign appropriate values to the graph's weights w_i. In order to have a fine-grained control over the workload, we let each node have j weights $w_i^{v_j}$, representing the computational work for the given node, and each edge k weights $w_i^{e_k}$, representing the communication cost (data dependencies between graph nodes). The total weight for a given graph node is then given by

$$w_i = \sum_j w_i^{v_j} + \sum_k w_i^{e_k}$$

For a typical simulation, we always assign the number of grid points in each cube to $w_i^{v_1}$ and the size of the halo (number of grid points to exchange) to $w_i^{e_k}$ for each of the graph edges connecting to node V_i. One or several more weights are later added to the graph node to model the additional computational cost of chemical reactions or immersed bodies. Additional weights can also be added to the edges, but we limit the present study to model only the halo exchange cost. The graph is finally partitioned by a graph partitioner, with the weights as an additional balancing constraint. Thus, new load-balanced partitions are obtained, as illustrated in Fig. 2.

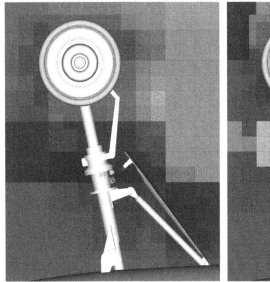 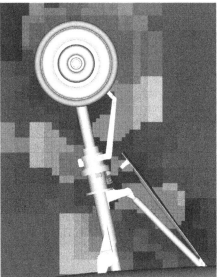

(a) Unbalanced (Z-ordering).   (b) Balanced wrt. geometry.

Fig. 2. Load balancing wrt. immersed geometry and fluid cells, colored by MPI rank.

3.2   Intelligent Remapping

For transient problems where the computational cost changes rapidly, it might not be feasible to load balance as soon as the workload changes. Therefore, the framework tries to minimize the data flow in two different ways. First, it uses the threshold value κ to filter out small workload fluctuations. Second, if load balancing is necessary, the algorithm tries to minimize data movement as much as possible.

Given a set of new partitions T' from an already partitioned domain T, if the new partitions are assigned such that a minimal amount of data has to be moved from T to form T', we have achieved our goal of minimizing data movement. This can be solved using a method referred to as intelligent remapping.

Given an imbalanced workload. New partitions T' are computed using a constrained graph method. The result is then placed in a matrix S, where each entry S_{ij} is the number of graph vertices in a partition T^i which would be placed in the new partition T'^j. The goal is to keep as much data local as possible, hence the maximum row entry in S is kept local. This can be achieved by transforming S into a bipartite graph (Fig. 3), with edges e_{ij} weighted with S_{ij}, and solving the maximally weighted bipartite graph problem (MWBG) [6].

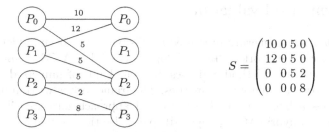

Fig. 3. Example of a weighted bipartite graph and its corresponding matrix S.

Solving this problem is known to be expensive with a cost of $O(V^2 \log(V) + VE)$, where V and E refer to nodes and edges in the bipartite graph. In [6] it was shown that the bipartite graph problem can be solved in time $O(E)$ using a heuristic algorithm based on sorting the matrix S and using a greedy algorithm to reassign the partitions. But in the worst case $E \sim P^2$, where P is the number of processes used to run the simulation, this linear heuristic also quickly becomes too expensive to solve. In [4] we decreased complexity of the heuristic algorithm to $O(P)$ using parallel binary radix sort.

The heuristic algorithm assigns the largest (unassigned) partition from a sorted list generated from the similarity matrix S (row-wise). In [6], S was gathered onto single core and sorted in serial using a binary radix sort. Since the matrix is of size P x P, where P is the number of cores, sorting quickly becomes a bootlneck at scale. Therefore, in [4] the heuristic was modified to perform the sorting in parallel using byte sorting parallel radix sort.

When we combine graph-based data decomposition methods, workload modeling using a weighted dual graph and intelligent remapping, we arrive at the general dynamic load balancing framework, as expressed in Algorithm 1.

Algorithm 1. Dynamic load balancing framework.

---

for *each partition $q \in \mathcal{T}$* **do**

$$W(q) = \sum_{w_i \in w_q} \left(\sum_j w_i^{v_j} + \sum_k w_i^{e_k} \right)_{w_i}$$

end
$W_{\max} \longleftarrow ComputeGlobalMax(W)$
$W_{\mathrm{avg}} \longleftarrow ComputeGlobalAverage(W)$
if $W_{max}/W_{avg} > \kappa$ **then**
    $\mathcal{T}' \longleftarrow ComputeNewPartitions(\mathcal{T})$
    $S \longleftarrow ConstructMatrix(\mathcal{T}')$
    $\mathcal{G} \longleftarrow SolveMWBG(\mathcal{T}')$
    $\mathcal{T} \longleftarrow RedistributeData(\mathcal{G})$
end

---

4   Performance Evaluation

The load balancing framework presented in this paper has been implemented in the multiphysics framework CUBE, developed at RIKEN AICS. CUBE is based on the Building Cube Method and uses different kinds of immersed boundary methods to represent complex geometries. The framework is written in Fortran 2003, and uses a light-weight object-oriented approach for extensibility. The framework uses a hybrid MPI + OpenMP parallelization, in which each rank is assigned a set of cubes and thread parallelization is performed on per cube level basis, with two-dimensional slices in the z-direction of each cube. For scalability CUBE uses parallel I/O in the form of MPI-I/O, and ParMETIS for graph partitoning.

To evaluate the performance of the load balancer, we used CUBE to solve two different incompressible flow problems on the K computer and compared the total execution time for performing a fixed number of time steps for both an unbalanced (no load balancing) and a balanced case (using load balancing) on various numbers of cores. For both problems we used the QUICK scheme for the convective terms and an unsteady multigrid solver for the pressure. Time integration was performed using a second-order Crank–Nicolson method.

4.1   Immersed Boundary Method

A distributed Lagrange multiplier immersed boundary method [2,7] in CUBE was used to represent the complex geometries (Fig. 4) in the numerical experiments. A Lagrangian-Eulerian approach is used in the implementation of the immersed boundary method because Lagrangian description is a very accurate method of representing complex, mobile immersed bodies (IB). In this approach, an Eulerian description is used to solve the equations governing the fluid motion, whereas a Material or Lagrangian description is used to represent the immersed body. The immersed body is discretized in to a discrete set of Material or Lagrangian points. The interaction between the fluid and the immesrsed

(a) Nose landing gear geometry.   (b) Full car model.

Fig. 4. Geometries used to evaluated the performance of the load balancing framework.

body is enabled through interpolation operators such as the smoothed Dirac delta function, inverse distance interpolation, or trilinear interpolation. In this work we use the smoothed Dirac delta function for the interpolation between Lagrangian-Eulerian domains.

A spatial decomposition approach is employed to discretize the combined Lagrangian-Eulerian system, wherein the Lagrangian domain is discretized on the basis of the Eulerian domain decomposition. For a given rank, this ensures data locality between Lagrangian and Eulerian domains, avoiding MPI communication for Lagrangian-Eulerian interpolation.

4.2   IB Workload Modeling

In the load balancer, the weights were assigned as described in Sect. 3.1, with the additional immersed boundary cost added to $w_i^{v_2}$, modeled as $\gamma \cdot n_{\text{particles}}$, where $n_{\text{particles}}$ is the number of Lagrangian particles. The choice of the parameter γ is not trivial and it depends on the relative number of Lagrangian-Eulerian interpolation operations for a given purely Eulerian stencil operation. The interpolation between Lagrangian and Eulerian meshes involves $\sim 2n^3$ operations for a given Lagrangian particle. Here, n depends on the type discrete delta function, e.g., for a 3-point delta function $n = 4$. n^3 could be a good candidate for the cost parameter γ. But, Lagrangian-Eulerian interpolation is required only once every time step, whereas purely Eulerian stencil operations depend on iterative processes such as solution of the Poisson equation. If N_{p-iter} is the number of Poisson solver iterations in one time step, then one could choose $\gamma = n^3/N_{p-iter}$. Therefore, γ would depend on the type of discrete delta function and the type of Poisson solver, but for most cases $n^3/N_{p-iter} \sim \mathcal{O}(1)$. Thus, we choose γ in the range of 1–4 for immersed body applications. It is to be noted that γ is application dependent, and a informed choice has to be made for its value.

4.3 Load Balancing Threshold κ

For the present analysis, a load imbalance threshold, $\kappa = 1.05$, is chosen, i.e. the load balance is triggered if there is an imbalance of 5% or more. In the two applications we consider, flow around a vehicle and nose landing gear, the immersed geometries are stationary, so load balancing is triggerd only once during the simualtion. Thus, κ only determines when load balancing and data redistribution is triggered; it has no influence on how the balanced or unbalanced cases perform, consequently it does not affect the overall runtime of the simulation. In more dynamic cases, such as applicaitons with rapidly moving IBs, the simulation runtime will be affected by the choice of κ. A small value of κ will frequently trigger data redistribution. Which will increase the overall simulation runtime. Thus, for dynamic applications, a parameteric study of the effect of κ would be necessary in order to choose an optimal value of κ.

4.4 Nose Landing Gear

The first problem is based on the nose landing gear (Fig. 4a) case from AIAA's BANC series of benchmark problems. Our setup uses a mesh consisting of 48255 cubes, subdivided into 16 cells in each axial direction, and the landing gear consists of $0.5M$ surface triangles.

In Fig. 5a we present the time required to perform one timestep for the unbalanced case and for the balanced case when γ is set to 3 and 4, respectively. From the results we can observe that using the load balancer results in approximately 60% resuction in the unbalanced runtime. As the number of cores increases, the gains of load balancing diminishes. This is most likely due to the fact that when using a relative small model, such as the landing gear, and few cubes in the mesh, the initial data decomposition will (for large core counts) will result in more partitions around to the geometry and indirectly balance the workload automatically. A value of $\gamma = 1$ resulted in a runtime that was approximaltely equal to the unbalanced case. This indicates that values of 3 and 4 for γ are reasonable choices for load balancing nose landing gear type geometries. The lack of Lagrangian communication cost in the model could also affect the result. Figure 5a shows the relative runtime of both load balanced cases normalized by the unbalanced runtime.

4.5 Full Car Model

As a second example we simulate the flow past a full car model (Fig. 4b). The numerical methods used for this problem are exactly the same as for the landing gear benchmark. We use a mesh consisting of 38306 cubes with 16^3 cells per cube and a car model consisting of 12.5 M surface triangles.

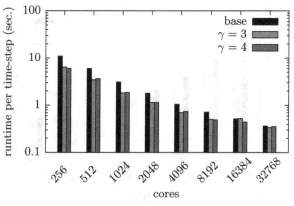

(a) Runtime per time-step.

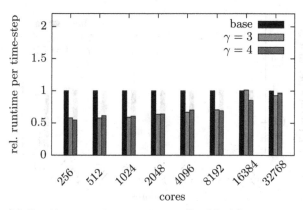

(b) Runtime per time-step normalized by the runtime of the unbalanced case.

Fig. 5. Runtime per time-step and relative runtime for the nose landing gear.

The runtime per timestep presented in Fig. 6a shows the results of the balanced case with $\gamma = 3$ & $\gamma = 4$ and the unbalanced case. The trends for the runtime in all the cases are similar to those of the nose landing gear case. We can see that for all the tested core counts the runtime is improved except for the 16384 core case. In the best case, which is 256 cores, the runtime of the balanced case reduced to 40% of the unbalanced case. The relative runtime is also plotted in Fig. 6a.

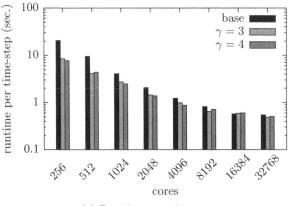

(a) Runtime per time-step.

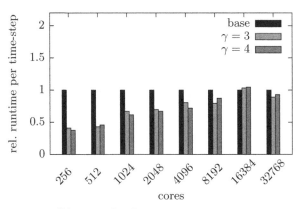

(b) Normalized runtime per time-step.

Fig. 6. Runtime per time-step and relative runtime for the full car model.

5   Discussion

A key aspect of dynamic load balancing techniques is the prospect of load balancing not just current workloads, but future workloads as well. The evaluation of future workloads and ability of the load balancer to address such workloads depends of the type of applications. The applications considered in our work have static workload. The evaluation of future workloads is relevant to dynamic applications. For some dynamic applications it may be possible to evaluate, predict and address a future imbalance. Examples of such applications are simulations with moving geometries, simulations of spray dynamics, and others. When the velocity of an immersed geometry is known, the future location of the geometry and its workload can be evaluated in advance and addressed when necessary. In applications of spray dynamics, the rate of new spray particle injection and the average trajectory of the bulk particles can be used to predict the future workload and balance it accordingly. If these dynamic applications are coupled with adaptive mesh refinement (AMR), the ability to predict the future workload will be all the more useful. When AMR is in use, the overall workload of the system changes with time. In cases where the workload increases due to creation of new mesh cells, the ability to predict the future workload can reduce the cost of data redistribution. When the location of new mesh cells is known, the future workload can be evaluated in advance and the data redistribution can be carried out before the creation of cells to reduce the data redistribution cost. Conversely, when location of mesh cells to be destroyed, resulting in workload reduction, is known, the data redistribution can be deferred until after the cell destruction to reduce the redistribution cost [6].

6   Summary and Future Work

In this work we have investigated the feasibility of using dynamic load balancing techniques to improve the performance of multiphysics simulation using the Building Cube Method. Our results show that the runtime could be reduced by almost a factor of two fifth when using the load balancer. In the current study we have limited ourselves to flow problems, but we want to stress that the load balancing framework is generic and could be applied to any type of workload, as demonstrated when we incorporated the cost of Lagrangian particles in the workload modeling. Future work includes fine tuning of the workload modeling, especially focusing on the computational and communcation cost of, e.g., chemical reactions and Lagrangian particles.

Acknowledgments. This work was supported through the computing resources provided on the K computer by RIKEN Advanced Institute for Computational Science.

References

1. Bader, M.: Space-Filling Curves. Texts in Computational Science and Engineering, vol. 9. Springer, Heidelberg (2013)
2. Bhalla, A.P.S., Bale, R., Griffith, B.E., Patankar, N.A.: A unified mathematical framework and an adaptive numerical method for fluid-structure interaction with rigid, deforming, and elastic bodies. J. Comput. Phys. **250**, 446–476 (2013)
3. Jansson, N.: High performance adaptive finite element methods: with applications in aerodynamics. Ph.D. thesis, KTH Royal Institute of Technology (2013)
4. Jansson, N., Hoffman, J., Jansson, J.: Framework for massively parallel adaptive finite element computational fluid dynamics on tetrahedral meshes. SIAM J. Sci. Comput. **34**(1), C24–C41 (2012)
5. Nakahashi, K.: Building-cube method for flow problems with broadband characteristic length. In: Armfield, S.W., Morgan, P., Srinivas, K. (eds.) Computational Fluid Dynamics 2002, pp. 77–81. Springer, Heidelberg (2003)
6. Oliker, L.: PLUM parallel load balancing for unstructured adaptive meshes. Technical report RIACS-TR-98-01, RIACS, NASA Ames Research Center (1998)
7. Shirgaonkar, A.A., MacIver, M.A., Patankar, N.A.: A new mathematical formulation and fast algorithm for fully resolved simulation of self-propulsion. J. Comput. Phys. **228**(7), 2366–2390 (2009)

On the Significance of Exposure Time in Computational Blood Damage Estimation

Lutz Pauli[(✉)] and Marek Behr

Chair for Computational Analysis of Technical Systems (CATS),
RWTH Aachen University, 52056 Aachen, Germany
pauli@cats.rwth-aachen.de

Abstract. The reliability of common stress-based power law models for hemolysis estimations in blood pumps is still not satisfying. Stress-based models are based on an instantaneous shear stress measure. Therefore, such models implicitly assume that red blood cells deform immediately due to the action of forces. In contrast, a strain-based model considers the entire deformation history of the cells. By applying a viscoelastic tensor equation for the stress computation, the effect of exposure time is represented as a biophysical phenomenon. Comparisons of stress-based and strain-based hemolysis models in a centrifugal blood pump show very significant differences. Stress peaks with short exposure time contribute to the overall hemolysis in the stress-based model, whereas regions with increased shear and long exposure time are responsible for damage in the strain-based model.

Keywords: Computational hemodynamics · Hemolysis modeling · Ventricular assist device · Finite element method · Blood damage

1 Introduction

Computational fluid dynamics (CFD) has become a very prominent development tool for the virtual design of various devices exposed to flow. For the design of blood-handling medical devices, the acceptance of CFD is, however, not as broad as in the traditional engineering disciplines. The complex micro-macro interaction of blood, as the flowing medium, can be identified as the main reason for the limited acceptance. Therefore, specialized numerical tools are necessary, which are not yet sufficiently implemented in available commercial CFD software.

The development of reliable blood damage models is a key issue for the virtual design of ventricular assist devices (VADs). The mechanical hemolysis in VADs is an example for a microscale effect that can only be measured on the macroscale. Therefore, hemolysis is usually modeled as a bulk phenomenon and based on a simple power law, depending on scalar shear-stress and exposure time. In the commonly used stress-based model, the scalar shear stress depends solely on the precomputed flow field according to the Navier-Stokes equations. The stress-based model is only able to account for macroscale phenomena and

© Springer International Publishing AG 2017
E. Di Napoli et al. (Eds.): JHPCS 2016, LNCS 10164, pp. 24–36, 2017.
DOI: 10.1007/978-3-319-53862-4_3

therefore, it implicitly assumes that red blood cells (RBCs) deform instantaneously. A different approach is a simulation by means of a strain-based model. Here, the viscoelastic deformation of RBCs is computed by a tensorial evolution equation. The tensor results are used to estimate a distortion of RBCs in the flow field. With the distortion, an effective shear stress can be computed, which is acting on the RBC itself. As a consequence, microscale effects are considered in the simulation, even though the overall result is on the macroscale.

In the present study, the stress-based and the strain-based models are introduced in Eulerian frame. Both formulations are discussed and classified according to other modeling approaches existing in the literature. The differences of the stress-based and strain-based models are evaluated in a CFD simulation of a centrifugal blood pump.

2   Methods

Accurate and reliable modeling of hemolysis in large scale flow situations like in blood pumps is an open research issue. On the one hand, the microscale effects leading to mechanical hemolysis are, up to now, not fully understood and on the other hand, models that resolve the microscale behavior of single RBCs in complex flows would be computationally too expensive. Therefore, a compromise between accuracy and computational efficiency has to be considered already in the modeling. In the following, we present two approaches to model hemolysis as a macroscale phenomenon. In both cases, blood flow is modeled with the Navier-Stokes equations, using the mass and momentum balance for an isothermal, incompressible liquid. Blood itself is assumed to be a Newtonian liquid with constant viscosity.

Stress-Based Hemolysis. Motivated by the early findings by Blackshear *et al.* [5], Giersiepen *et al.* [16] have been the first to relate shear stress and exposure time to the index of hemolysis by using a simple power law of the form

$$IH = A_{\mathrm{Hb}}\, \sigma_s^{\alpha_{\mathrm{Hb}}}\, t^{\beta_{\mathrm{Hb}}}. \tag{1}$$

The three parameters in Eq. (1) were fitted to the experimental data by Wurzinger *et al.* [29]. Due to the secondary blood damage effects in Wurzinger's experiments, Giersiepen's parameters are known to overestimate hemolysis. Therefore, there exist several other regressions of the parameters in Eq. (1). Within this thesis, we will only use the proposed parameter set by Zhang *et al.* [30], which is the most recent regression and covers a wide range of shear stress and exposure times.

The power law is a one-dimensional model equation. In order to apply the model to three-dimensional flow problems, the scalar shear stress σ_s is derived from the instantaneous stress tensor $\boldsymbol{\sigma}$ of the Navier-Stokes equations [6]. The scalar shear stress becomes

$$\sigma_s = \mu G_{\mathrm{f}} = \mu \sqrt{2\mathbf{E} : \mathbf{E}}, \tag{2}$$

where $\mathbf{E} = \frac{1}{2} \left(\nabla \mathbf{u} + \nabla \mathbf{u}^\top \right)$ is the rate-of-strain tensor.

To integrate the power law in time and space, we use the Eulerian approach. In the Eulerian approach, a convection-diffusion-reaction equation is used to compute a linearized free plasma hemoglobin ratio f_{Hb} as a field variable in the flow domain. The governing equation reads

$$\frac{\partial f_{\mathrm{Hb}}}{\partial t} + \mathbf{u} \cdot \nabla f_{\mathrm{Hb}} - \nabla \cdot (\nu_{\mathrm{Hb}} \nabla f_{\mathrm{Hb}}) - r_{\Delta_{\mathrm{Hb}}} = 0, \tag{3}$$

where $\nu_{\mathrm{Hb}} = 6 \times 10^{-7} \mathrm{cm}^2/\mathrm{s}$ is the self diffusion coefficient for hemoglobin [26]. Following Farinas et al. [11,12], the reaction or source term can be expressed by

$$r^a_{\Delta_{\mathrm{Hb}}} = (A_{\mathrm{Hb}} \, \sigma_s^{\alpha_{\mathrm{Hb}}})^{1/\beta_{\mathrm{Hb}}} \quad \text{(without saturation effect), or} \tag{4}$$

$$r^b_{\Delta_{\mathrm{Hb}}} = (A_{\mathrm{Hb}} \, \sigma_s^{\alpha_{\mathrm{Hb}}})^{1/\beta_{\mathrm{Hb}}} (1 - f_{\mathrm{Hb}}) \quad \text{(with saturation effect).} \tag{5}$$

Thus, the reaction term is the power law (Eq. (1)) linearized in time, so that the index of hemolysis can be computed by $IH = f_{\mathrm{Hb}}^{\beta_{\mathrm{Hb}}}$ or by

$$IH_{\mathrm{out}} = \frac{\int_\Gamma (\mathbf{u} \cdot \mathbf{n}) f_{\mathrm{Hb}}^{\beta_{\mathrm{Hb}}}(\mathbf{x}) \, d\Gamma}{\int_\Gamma \mathbf{u} \cdot \mathbf{n} \, d\Gamma} \tag{6}$$

for a velocity-weighted spatial averaging at an outflow boundary.

A major limitation of the stress-based hemolysis modeling is the fact that the model implicitly assumes an instantaneous deformation of RBCs, which in reality show very complex viscoelastic deformation under shear flow.

Strain-Based Hemolysis. An alternative to the stress-based model is the strain-based hemolysis model by Arora et al. [2], which has been introduced in 2004. They used the model for hemolysis estimations in the GYRO centrifugal blood pump and found good agreement with experimental data [1,3]. In contrast to Arora, who used a Lagrangian approach, we will apply the hemolysis model to the Eulerian approach.

The basic idea of the model is that instead of an instantaneous shear rate G_{f} (compare Eq. (2)) an effective shear rate G_{eff} is computed, based on the deformation (or straining) of an RBC. In flows with high shear rates, RBCs are known to behave similar to droplets [8,14,27]. Both RBCs and droplets have ellipsoidal shape with their long axis aligned parallel to the flow direction and both have the ability to relax to their original form, once the stress is released [10,13]. This analogy is used in the modeling of the RBC deformation. Maffettone and Minale [20] published a partial differential equation to represent droplets in viscous flow with the aid of a symmetric and positive-definite shape tensor $\mathbf{S}$ (also called *morphology* tensor). The droplet model has been extended by Arora et al. in order to account for the motion of the RBC membrane. The following equation is obtained for the shape tensor $\mathbf{S}$ [23]:

$$\frac{\partial \mathbf{S}}{\partial t} + \mathbf{u} \cdot \nabla \mathbf{S}$$

$$= - f_1 \left[\mathbf{S} - g(\mathbf{S})\mathbf{I} \right] \qquad \text{(relaxation)} \qquad (7)$$
$$+ f_2 \left[\mathbf{ES} + \mathbf{SE} \right] \qquad \text{(elongation)}$$
$$+ f_3 \left[\mathbf{WS} - \mathbf{SW} \right] \qquad \text{(rotation)}$$

The tensors $\mathbf{E}$ and $\mathbf{W}$ are the rate-of-strain and vorticity tensors, respectively. The function $g(\mathbf{S}) = 3I\!I\!I_\mathbf{S}/I\!I_\mathbf{S}$ ensures that Eq. (7) preserves the volume of the droplet, where $I\!I_\mathbf{S}$ and $I\!I\!I_\mathbf{S}$ are tensor invariants of $\mathbf{S}$. The three mechanism (relaxation, elongation and rotation) of the droplet model are illustrated in Fig. 1(a). Mechanical properties of an RBC are introduced to Eq. (7) by the three parameters f_1, f_2 and f_3, based on experimental findings in the literature. As shown in Reference [2], the parameter f_1 behaves like the inverse of the relaxation time. The relaxation time of the RBC membrane is approximately 200 ms [7,17] and thus,

$$f_1 = 5.0 \text{s}^{-1}. \qquad (8)$$

The parameter f_2 is matched with the surface area of a hemolyzing RBC. Rand [25] and Blackshear and Blackshear [4] found 6% increase in surface area before membrane rupture occurs and Leverett et al. [19] found a critical shear stress of $\sigma_s^{\text{crit}} = 150$ Pa (which corresponds to a shear rate of $G_f^{\text{crit}} \approx 42000 \text{s}^{-1}$ if a viscosity $\mu = 3.6 \times 10^{-3}$ Pa s is assumed) for such catastrophic hemolysis. As an RBC has 40% excess surface area with respect to a droplet of the same volume, the modeled ellipsoidal droplet should stretch to 1.4×1.06 times its original surface area at catastrophic hemolysis [2]. The two conditions (critical shear rate and critical surface area) can be used with a convergent series for the area of a general ellipsoidal droplet by Keller and Skalak [18] to obtain an optimization problem for the parameter f_2. The finally computed parameter reads (see also References [24] for details)

$$f_2 = 4.2998 \times 10^{-4}. \qquad (9)$$

Due to oscillatory eigenvalues of the shape tensor $\mathbf{S}$ at transient shear flows, Arora et al. [2] restricted $f_3 = f_2$.

In order to use Eq. (7) for hemolysis approximations, the computed shape tensor is coupled to the power law, or more precisely to the reaction term of Eq. (3). The distortion of the ellipsoidal droplet can be computed with the following formula [9]:

$$D \equiv \frac{L - B}{L + B}, \qquad (10)$$

with lengths of the longest and smallest semi-axes of the droplet, L and B (compare Fig. 1(b)). Both values can be evaluated by the largest and smallest eigenvalue of tensor $\mathbf{S}$, respectively. In case of steady, simple shear flow, the strain-based model should estimate the same amount of hemolysis as the stress-based model if the exposure time is long enough. In such a situation, shape tensor $\mathbf{S}$ and its eigenvalues can be computed analytically, so that the distortion D is expressed by [24]

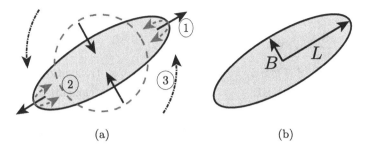

Fig. 1. (a) A droplet deformation model in analogy to an RBC. The droplet can be elongated due to straining (1). Without tension, the droplet relaxes to a spherical shape (2). Vortices are able to rotate the droplet (3) (adopted and modified from Reference [24]). (b) Distortion of a droplet is computed by the longest and smallest semi-axes, L and B.

$$D = \frac{\sqrt{f_1^2 + f_2^2 G_f^2} - f_1}{f_2 G_f}. \tag{11}$$

Equation (11) can be rearranged to define an effective shear rate G_{eff}, that is,

$$G_{\text{eff}} = \frac{2 f_1 D}{(1 - D^2) f_2}. \tag{12}$$

The effective shear rate G_{eff} can be used in any situation, including transient and inhomogeneous flows; but in contrast to the instantaneous shear rate G_f, it is able to express the straining that is acting on the RBC itself. By using G_{eff} for the definition of the scalar shear stress σ_s, the coupling to Eq. (3) is accomplished. Therefore,

$$\sigma_s = \mu G_{\text{eff}} = \frac{2 \mu f_1 D}{(1 - D^2) f_2} \tag{13}$$

if the strain-based model is used.

All the above equations are implemented in an in-house CFD code, which is based on stabilized space-time finite element methods. The code is fully parallelized using MPI and OpenMP and runs on several state-of-the-art supercomputers. Scalability has been shown for more then 6×10^4 MPI tasks on a Blue Gene/Q (JUQUEEN).

3   Results

In this section, we compare the stress-based and the strain-based hemolysis modeling in a centrifugal blood pump. The geometry of the pump is based on a benchmark blood pump by the FDA. The blood pump is used to assess the state of the art in CFD-based blood damage estimation. As the FDA study on the benchmark blood pump is still in progress, we will use a slightly modified pump geometry in our comparison, shown in Fig. 2. The pump is characterized by a long inlet tube, which is curved at the beginning. The shape of the impeller is characterized by four straight blades and a shaft at the center. The outlet is designed as a small throat connected to the upper part of the chamber. The throat is attached to a diffuser, which in turn is connected to a straight tube with constant diameter. Exact dimensions with technical drawings of the pump are provided in the documentation by the FDA [28]. In this study, the impeller and the pump chamber are reduced by approximately 10%, compared to the original pump. The inflow and outflow tubes are not changed.

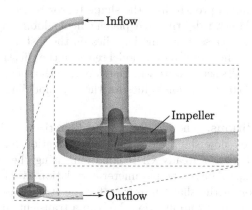

Fig. 2. Geometry of a modified benchmark blood pump. Compared to the original pump provided by the FDA, impeller and pump chamber are reduced by 10%.

3.1 Blood Flow Simulations

We simulate blood flow in the pump for two hydraulic parameter sets: 2.5 L/min, 2777 rpm and 6 L/min, 3888 rpm. Blood density and dynamic viscosity are chosen as $\rho = 1054 \text{kg/m}^3$ and $\mu = 3.5 \times 10^{-3}$ Pa s, assuming a Newtonian material model. The volume mesh consists of approximately 4.1×10^6 mainly unstructured tetrahedral elements and 1.5×10^6 space-time nodes. For the boundary layer, a structured, tetrahedral mesh with twelve layers is used next to the housing and the impeller. The rotation of the impeller is treated by the MRF method [22]. Therefore, it is sufficient to choose an unstructured triangular surface mesh as the interface. For the inflow boundary of the pump, we apply a constant parabolic velocity profile. The velocity magnitude is determined by the given flow rate. At the outflow, a Neumann boundary condition with $p = 0$ is assumed. No-slip boundary conditions are applied at the walls and at the rotating impeller. We use transient computations with a time step size $\Delta t_1 = 5 \times 10^{-4}$s for the first operating condition and $\Delta t_2 = 5 \times 10^{-5}$s for the second operating condition. For both conditions, we apply the σ-model [21] (LES turbulence model) with $\kappa = 1.5$.

We perform the flow simulations for 350 and 750 time-steps, respectively. Afterwards, time-averaged flow solutions are generated using the last 50 time-steps for the first operating condition and the last 100 time-steps for the second operating condition.

3.2   Hemolysis Simulations

The hemolysis predictions are based on the time-averaged flow solutions of the blood pump. For the stress-based modeling approach, only Eq. (3) needs to be solved to obtain the concentration of the free plasma hemoglobin ratio. For the strain-based modeling approach, first the shape tensor $\mathbf{S}$ needs to be computed by using Eq. (7). Afterwards, the free plasma hemoglobin ratio can be computed. Therefore, the stress-based model relies on the instantaneous shear rate G_f (Eq. (2)), whereas the strain-based model relies on the effective shear rate G_{eff} (Eq. (12)). In the results section, we will first compare the shear rate distribution and afterwards, the concentration values for the two modeling approaches.

Simulation Conditions. The blood pump is discretized with the same mesh as used for the blood flow simulations. The concentration for the stress-based model is computed with a steady CDR equation, using the source term with saturation effect (Eq. (5)) and the parameter correlation by Zhang *et al.*

The computation of the shape tensor $\mathbf{S}$, for the strain-based model, is very challenging for this complex application. We run a transient simulation in order to reach the steady-state deformation of the RBCs for the given flow field. For the first operating condition, we choose a time step size of $\Delta t_1 = 1 \times 10^{-4}$s. For the second operating condition, the time step size is reduced to $\Delta t_2 = 5 \times 10^{-5}$s. The computation of the free plasma hemoglobin ratio is based on similar settings as used for the stress-based model. Only the power law parameters are exchanged with optimized parameters as given in Reference [15].

Results for the Shear Rate Distribution. For the shape tensor computation, we run 620 time steps for the first operating condition and 900 time steps for the second operating condition, in order to reach a steady-state deformation in the entire flow domain. With the shape tensor solution, a distortion D and an effective shear rate G_{eff} is computed by using Eqs. (10) and (12).

The effective shear rate G_{eff} shows a completely different distribution than the instantaneous shear rate G_f. A comparison of the two different shear rates on the impeller surface is shown in Fig. 3 for both operating conditions. The instantaneous shear rate G_f has very high peaks at the edges of the impeller blades, whereas the effective shear rate G_{eff} shows increased values in a wide ring around the inflow tube. Overall, the magnitude of the effective shear is much lower than the instantaneous shear.

A similar behavior is visible at the bottom of the outer housing, as shown in Fig. 4 for the second operating condition. The instantaneous shear rate G_f has a very high peak at the fillet between the throat and the housing rim, which is also

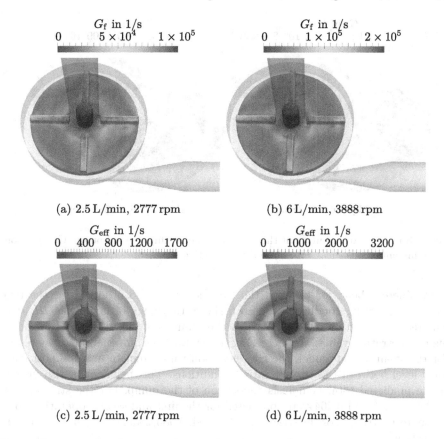

Fig. 3. Shear rate distribution at the impeller of a centrifugal blood pump. Comparison of the instantaneous shear rate G_f and the effective shear rate G_{eff}.

the highest shear value in the entire domain. In the distribution of the effective shear rate G_{eff} such a peak is not observed. Increased values of G_{eff} are again much more dispersed and appear in the gaps between impeller and the housing, the outer rim and next to the jet in the outflow tube. The highest values of G_{eff} occur at the upper housing wall above the impeller blades (not visible in Fig. 4). The magnitudes of the effective shear rate G_{eff} are again much lower than for the instantaneous shear rate G_f.

Based on the shear rate distribution, the free plasma hemoglobin ratio is computed for the stress-based and the strain-based model.

Results for the Hemoglobin Concentration. As the stress-based and the strain-based models both rely on the same velocity field, the overall distribution of the free plasma hemoglobin ratio is similar between the two models. However, the magnitude is very different. For the stress-based model, the concentrations are more than an order of magnitude higher, compared to the strain-based model.

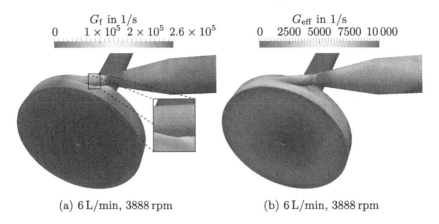

G_{f} in $1/\mathrm{s}$

0   1×10^5 2×10^5 2.6×10^5

G_{eff} in $1/\mathrm{s}$

0   2500 5000 7500 10 000

(a) 6 L/min, 3888 rpm   (b) 6 L/min, 3888 rpm

Fig. 4. Shear rate distribution at the bottom of a centrifugal blood pump. Comparison of the instantaneous shear rate G_{f} and the effective shear rate G_{eff}.

A different behavior between the two models is also observed for the two different operating conditions. Figure 5 shows the index of hemolysis IH at a centered cross section ($z = 0.7$ cm) in the pump. For the stress-based model, the concentration values are increasing if flow rate and impeller speed increase. For the strain-based model, the concentration values remain at an almost constant level between the two operating conditions. This behavior is also visible in the predicted total hemolysis generation of the pump. For the stress-based model 0.202% and 0.364% are predicted for the first and second operating condition, respectively. For the strain-based model, 0.080% and 0.082% are obtained, respectively.

Figure 5 also reveals some high concentration regions at the inner tips of the impeller blades. These regions are observed for both operating conditions.

4   Discussion

The comparison of stress-based and strain-based models shows major differences in the estimated critical shear rates. The stress-based model predicts localized high shear peaks at the impeller tips and at the fillet between the outflow and the rim. However, the exposure time is very short if the impeller is passing by an RBC or if an RBC approaches the fillet. As the strain-based model tries to predict the viscoelastic (time dependent) deformation of the RBCs on their way through the pump, these localized high shear peaks are not visible. Stresses have to act for a certain amount of time in order to be able to significantly deform the RBCs in the flow. Therefore, high shear areas for the strain-based model are more dispersed and located at different positions compared to the stress-based model. For example, the inner ring of the impeller is identified as a critical region. The highest shear rates for the strain-based model appear at the upper wall of the pump chamber above the impeller blades. Increased shear rates are also visible at the bottom of the pump and next to the outflow jet.

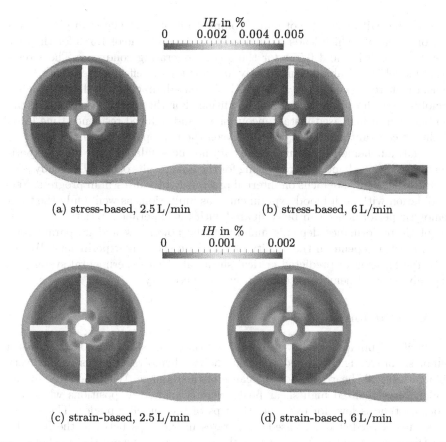

(a) stress-based, 2.5 L/min   (b) stress-based, 6 L/min

(c) strain-based, 2.5 L/min   (d) strain-based, 6 L/min

Fig. 5. Index of hemolysis at a centered cross section in a centrifugal blood pump. Comparison of the stress-based and the strain-based models for different operating conditions.

In order to reduce hemolysis, critical shear rates are usually the most important indicator for shape optimizations of the pump geometry. Computation of the free plasma hemoglobin ratio is mainly used to predict the total hemolytic performance, which can be compared to in vitro measurements with blood. However, if the free plasma hemoglobin ratio is computed with an Eulerian approach, a side benefit is the fact that recirculation and stagnation areas can be identified very easily. Of course, this information is already contained in the flow solution, but a visualization would require several postprocessing steps. For example, the high concentration areas next to the inner tips of the impeller, shown in Fig. 5, indicate a poor transition of blood flow from the inlet tube to the pump chamber. This observation is supported by the increased effective shear rate G_{eff} at the inner impeller surface, shown in Fig. 3.

Stress-based and strain-based models also predict very different hemolytic performance. These differences can be mainly explained with the effect of exposure or residence time. The average residence time of RBCs in a blood pump can be estimated with the ratio of pump volume to flow rate. The pump has a volume of 56.64cm^3, which leads to an average residence time of $1.38\,$s for the first operating condition and $0.57\,$s for the second operating condition. The stress-based model is not able to sufficiently account for the effect of residence time. Thus, the increased shear rates, due to the increased impeller speed, cause higher hemolysis for the second operating condition. For the strain-based model, the combination of increased instantaneous shear and reduced residence time leads to almost constant hemolysis levels between the two operating conditions.

So far, our hemolysis estimations could not be validated with blood experiments. On the one hand, we are waiting for the final results of the FDA study [28]. On the other hand, we focus on internal projects, which are still in progress. Yet, a validation with such blood experiments has limitations as well. Only the total hemolytic performance can be compared with the experimental data. The total hemolytic performance depends mainly on the power law and its parameters, which in turn depend on the quality of the blood shearing experiments. To validate the location of predicted critical shear rates, an experimental system for spatially resolved hemolysis testing would be necessary.

5   Conclusion

A centrifugal pump geometry was used to study stress-based and strain-based hemolysis modeling. It turned out that the two hemolysis models predict very different critical shear rates for the cause of the damage. With the stress-based model, very localized high shear peaks were estimated at positions where the exposure time is low, for example, the tips of the impeller blades. The strain-based model predicted increased shear-rates in the gaps between the impeller and the housing and next to a jet in the outflow pipe, where the combination of instantaneous shear and exposure time is high. It was shown that the total hemolytic performance significantly differs for the two models and that the effect of exposure or residence time is visible in this case as well.

Acknowledgments. We like to thank Jaewook Nam and Matteo Pasquali for their contributions to previous implementations of the hemolysis models. In addition, we gratefully acknowledge the support by the DFG program GSC 111 (AICES Graduate School). Computing resources were provided by the RWTH Aachen University IT Center and by the Forschungszentrum Jülich John von Neumann Institute for Computing under the Jülich Aachen Research Alliance (JARA).

References

1. Arora, D., Behr, M., Coronado-Matutti, O., Pasquali, M.: Estimation of hemolysis in centrifugal blood pumps using morphology tensor approach. In: Bathe, K. (ed.) Proceedings of 3rd MIT Conference on Computational Fluid and Solid Dynamics, pp. 578–582. Elsevier Ltd. (2005)
2. Arora, D., Behr, M., Pasquali, M.: A tensor-based measure for estimating blood damage. Artif. Organs **28**, 1002–1015 (2004). errata in Artificial Organs 36(5), 500 (2012)

3. Arora, D., Behr, M., Pasquali, M.: Hemolysis estimation in a centrifugal blood pump using a tensor-based measure. Artif. Organs **30**(7), 539–547 (2006)
4. Blackshear, P., Blackshear, G.: Mechanical hemolysis. In: Skalak, R., Chien, S. (eds.) Handbook of Bioengineering, p. 15.1–15.19. McGraw-Hill, New York (1987)
5. Blackshear, P., Dorman, F., Steinbach, J.: Some mechanical effects that influence hemolysis. ASAIO J. **11**(1), 112–117 (1965)
6. Bludszuweit, C.: Three-dimensional numerical prediction of stress loading of blood particles in a centrifugal pump. Artif. Organs **19**(7), 590–596 (1995)
7. Bronkhorst, P., Streekstra, G., Grimbergen, J., Nijhof, E., Sixma, J., Brakenhoff, G.: A new method to study shape recovery of red blood cells using multiple optical trapping. Biophys. J. **69**(5), 1666–1673 (1995)
8. Chien, S.: Shear dependence of effective cell volume as a determinant of blood viscosity. Science **168**(3934), 977–979 (1970)
9. Chien, S.: Red cell deformability and its relevance to blood flow. Annu. Rev. Physiol. **49**, 177–192 (1987)
10. Evans, E., LaCelle, P.: Intrinsic material properties of the erythrocyte membrane indicated by mechanical analysis of deformation. Blood **45**, 29–43 (1975)
11. Farinas, M., Garon, A.: Fast three-dimensional numerical hemolysis approximation. Artif. Organs **28**(11), 1016–1025 (2004)
12. Farinas, M., Garon, A., Lacasse, D., N'dri, D.: Asymptotically consistent numerical approximation of hemolysis. J. Biomed. Eng. **128**, 688–696 (2006)
13. Fischer, T.M.: Shape memory of human red blood cells. Biophys. J. **86**, 3304–3313 (2004)
14. Fischer, T., Stohr-Lissen, M., Schmid-Schönbein, H.: The red cell as a fluid droplet: tank tread-like motion of the human erythrocyte membrane in shear flow. Science **202**(4370), 894–896 (1978)
15. Gesenhues, L., Pauli, L., Behr, M.: Strain-based blood damage estimation for computational design of ventricular assist devices. Int. J. Artif. Organs **39**(4), 166–170 (2016)
16. Giersiepen, M., Wurzinger, L., Opitz, R., Reul, H.: Estimation of shear stress-related blood damage in heart valve prostheses - in vitro comparison of 25 aortic valves. Int. J. Artif. Organs **13**(5), 300–306 (1990)
17. Hénon, S., Lenormand, G., Richert, A., Gallet, F.: A new determination of the shear modulus of the human erythrocyte membrane using optical tweezers. Biophys. J. **76**(2), 1145–1151 (1999)
18. Keller, S., Skalak, R.: Motion of a tank-treading ellipsoidal particle in a shear flow. J. Fluid Mech. **120**, 27–47 (1982)
19. Leverett, L., Hellums, J., Alfrey, C., Lynch, E.: Red blood cell damage by shear stress. Biophys. J. **12**, 257–273 (1972)
20. Maffettone, P., Minale, M.: Equation of change for ellipsoidal drops in viscous flow. J. Non-Newton. Fluid Mech. **78**, 227–241 (1998)
21. Nicoud, F., Toda, H., Cabrit, O., Bose, S., Lee, J.: Using singular values to build a subgrid-scale model for large eddy simulations. Phys. Fluids (1994-present) **23**(085106), 1–12 (2011)
22. Pauli, L., Both, J., Behr, M.: Stabilized finite element method for flows with multiple reference frames. Int. J. Numer. Meth. Fluids **78**, 657–669 (2015)
23. Pauli, L., Nam, J., Pasquali, M., Behr, M.: Transient stress-based and strain-based hemolysis estimation in a simplified blood pump. Int. J. Numer. Meth. Biomed. Eng. **29**(10), 1148–1160 (2013)
24. Probst, M.: Robust Shape Optimization for Incompressible Flow of Shear-Thinning Fluids. Ph.D. thesis, RWTH Aachen University, Aachen, Germany (2013)

25. Rand, R.: Mechanical properties of the red cell membrane: II. viscoelastic breakdown of the membrane. Biophys. J. **4**(4), 303–316 (1964)
26. Riveros-Moreno, V., Wittenberg, J.: The self-diffusion coefficients of myoglobin and hemoglobin in concentrated solutions. J. Biol. Chem. **247**(3), 895–901 (1972)
27. Schmid-Schönbein, H., Wells, R.: Fluid drop-like transition of erythrocytes under shear. Science **165**(3890), 288–291 (1969)
28. Stewart, S., Hariharan, P.: Computational round robin #2 (model blood pump), October 2013. https://fdacfd.nci.nih.gov/interlab_study_2_blood_pump
29. Wurzinger, L., Opitz, R., Eckstein, H.: Mechanical blood trauma: an overview. Angeiologie **38**, 81–97 (1986)
30. Zhang, T., Taskin, M., Fang, H., Pampori, A., Jarvik, R., Griffith, B., Wu, Z.: Study of flow-induced hemolysis using novel couette-type blood-shearing devices. Artif. Organs **35**(12), 1180–1186 (2011)

A Partitioned Methodology for Conjugate Heat Transfer on Dynamic Structures

Miguel Zavala-Aké[(⊠)], Daniel Mira, Mariano Vázquez,
and Guillaume Houzeaux

Barcelona Supercomputing Center (BSC), Barcelona, Spain
miguel.zavala@bsc.es

Abstract. A partitioned coupling approach for conjugate heat transfer applications is presented. The coupling scheme is based on the extension of the parallel algebraic domain composition method already validated in fluid-structure interactions problems for thermal coupling. The method alters the original Dirichlet-Neumann approach enforcing the boundary conditions over the subdomains through matrix operations. The algorithm is tested on two benchmark cases with conjugate heat transfer: flow over a heated cylinder and flow over a flat-plate. The results indicate good agreement with previous research and encourages its application for large-scale problems.

Keywords: Parallel coupling · Multiphysics · Conjugate heat transfer

1 Introduction

How a fluid interacts with its environment is interesting on a great variety of applications. The cooling of a turbine blade or the mechanical vibrations of a gas turbine engine are examples where different physics interact through a common interface. The interactions must be modelled taking into account appropriate numerical methods for every component. The coupling could be attempted by using different approaches for every physical zone, or even with simulation codes written in different languages or used at different architectures. Furthermore, the physics of the system could define the numerical method to be used, for instance, while the heat transfer in a solid is a diffusive processes, a fluid is usually dominated by convection, which could lead to differences of orders of magnitude between the temporal scales, i.e. the temporal perturbations in the fluid are almost negligible in the solid. Numerically, it means that the fluid might require several time steps to generate a change in the solid. The interaction between two transient fluids is almost instantaneous so that the temporal scales are practically equal.

The main goal of this study is to introduce and validate the parallel algebraic domain composition method (DCM) [1], previously used on fluid-structure interactions, against benchmarks examples of conjugate heat transfer. The main idea

© Springer International Publishing AG 2017
E. Di Napoli et al. (Eds.): JHPCS 2016, LNCS 10164, pp. 37–47, 2017.
DOI: 10.1007/978-3-319-53862-4_4

in the domain composition method is to modify the original Dirichlet-Neumann approach enforcing the boundary conditions over the subdomains through matrix operations. In the case of fluid-structure interaction problems, rather than computing the total force exerted by a fluid along boundary integrating the pressure and viscous stresses, the force is obtained as an algebraic force given by the residual of the momentum equation [2].

This paper is focused on describing a method to address conjugate heat transfer problems which can be used to resolve dynamic structures. The work starts describing the mathematical details related to solving the coupling interface, Sect. 2. Section 3, deals with the numerical approach used to solve the coupling, while the Sect. 4 describes briefly the results achieved using the proposed coupling method. Furthermore, a parallel performance analysis of the coupling implementation is also considered. Finally, Sect. 5 discusses conclusions and directions of future work.

2   Mathematical Modelling

This section deals with the mathematical details related to the coupling of a low-Mach approximation of the Navier-Stokes equations with a heat conduction solver.

2.1   Governing Equations

The governing equations describing the flow field correspond to the low Mach number equations given by the zeroth-order Navier-Stokes equations

$$\frac{\partial \rho}{\partial t} + \nabla \cdot (\rho \mathbf{u}) = 0$$

$$\frac{\partial \rho \mathbf{u}}{\partial t} + \nabla \cdot (\rho \mathbf{uu}) + \nabla p = \nabla \cdot \boldsymbol{\tau} \tag{1}$$

$$\frac{\partial \rho E}{\partial t} + \nabla \cdot (\rho H \mathbf{u}) = \nabla \cdot (-\boldsymbol{q})$$

where t, ρ, $\mathbf{u}$, p are the time, density, velocity field, pressure, respectively. The total energy E and the enthalpy H are given by

$$E = e = \frac{1}{\gamma - 1} T \tag{2}$$

$$H = E + \frac{p}{\rho} = \rho c_p T \tag{3}$$

Moreover, $\boldsymbol{\tau}$ indicates the sum of the molecular and Reynolds stress tensor components. According to the Boussinesq approximation, one has:

$$\boldsymbol{\tau} = \mu(\nabla u + (\nabla u)^T) - \frac{2}{3}\mu \nabla \cdot \mathbf{uI} \tag{4}$$

The heat flux vector components, $\boldsymbol{q}$, are given by the Fourier law

$$\boldsymbol{q} = -\kappa \nabla T \tag{5}$$

The transport properties are expressed in terms of the molecular viscosity μ and the conductivity κ with the Sutherland law

$$\mu = C_1 \frac{T^{3/2}}{T + C_2}$$
$$\kappa = C_3 \frac{T^{3/2}}{T + C_4} \tag{6}$$

where $C_1 - C_4$ are constants for a given gas. For air at moderate temperatures, $C_1 = 1.458 \times 10^{-6} kg/(ms K^{1/2})$, $C_2 = 110.4K$, $C_3 = 2.495 \times 10^{-3}(kgm)/(s^3 K^{3/2})$, $C_4 = 194K$. Finally, the system is closed by the equation of state, which relates the pressure p with the temperature T through a pressure and temperature of reference p_0 and T_0 respectively

$$p = (p_0/T_0)T \tag{7}$$

2.2 Conjugate Heat Transfer

The term conjugate heat transfer (CHT) is generally used when the physical systems of heat transfer (convection and diffusion) are considered interacting with each other. It requires the continuity between the energy equation of the fluid and the heat conduction equation, given as

$$\frac{\partial T}{\partial t} + \nabla \cdot (-\alpha \nabla T) = Q \tag{8}$$

where $\alpha_f = \kappa_f/(\rho_f c_p)$ and Q are the thermal diffusivity of the material and the external heat source, respectively. The CHT approach imposes the heat flux from the fluid into the solid domain throughout Neumann boundary conditions, while the solid imposes a surface temperature onto the fluid domain through Dirichlet boundary conditions

$$T_S = T_F$$
$$\kappa_S \frac{\partial T_S}{\partial n} = \kappa_F \frac{\partial T_F}{\partial n} \tag{9}$$

3   Numerical Methodology

This section briefly describes the numerical details related to the finite element and coupling approaches, Sects. 3.1 and 3.2, respectively. The coupling approach section introduces the main concepts involved in the solution of partitioned subdomains: the domain composition method, the residual flux and some details related to the coupling tool.

3.1 Finite Element Method

The governing equations are solved using the Finite Element method with the Variational Multiscale Stabilization (VMS) approach [3] and with a second order Crank-Nicholson scheme for the time integration. The discretization of the low Mach number equations, Eq. (1), yields a coupled algebraic system

$$\begin{pmatrix} A_{nn} & A_{nt} \\ A_{tn} & A_{tt} \end{pmatrix} \begin{pmatrix} U_n \\ U_t \end{pmatrix} = \begin{pmatrix} b_n \\ b_t \end{pmatrix} \tag{10}$$

which is converged through a Gauss-Seidel method at each linearization step within a time loop. The diagonal submatrix A_{nn} is related to the discretization of continuity and momentum (fluid motion), while the submatrix A_{tt} is associated to the energy equation. The off-diagonal submatrices A_{nt} and A_{tn} take into account the coupling between the terms of the fluid motion and the energy equation. The vectors $[U_n \ U_t]^T$ and $[b_n \ b_t]^T$ represent the unknowns and right-hand side terms of the individual subsystems, respectively. The momentum and continuity equations are solved independently, applying the iterative Orthomin solver for the pressure-Schur complement [4].

3.2 Coupling Approach

The multi-physics coupling approach is based on the parallel algebraic domain composition method [1]. This methodology has been validated in fluid rigid body interaction [2] and fluid structure interaction (FSI) problems [5]. Furthermore, this coupling approach has also been applied to reproduce experimental results of a bladeless wind-driven generator prototype [6].

Domain Composition Method. In the classical Dirichlet-Neumann coupling scheme [7,8], the total physical domain is divided in small regions, each of them characterized by a specific type of physics, see Fig. 1. Each of this disjoint sub-domain can be solved by itself using suitable boundary conditions. Through two different strategies, we can reconstruct the solution of the whole domain at each time step from the solution of each subdomain. In the Jacobi (parallel) strategy both domains could be solved at the same time while in the Gauss-Seidel (sequential) strategy, the domains are solved one after the other. In order to achieve a suitable solution at each time step, a number of extra iterations between the sudomains may be required.

In the Gauss-Seidel approach, the solution of the whole domain is obtained by imposing suitable boundary conditions alternately to each subdomain. The most common method to perform that is the iterative Dirichlet-Neumann algorithm. It consists on imposing Dirichlet boundary conditions at the coupling boundary of one subdomain and solving it. After that, the solution obtained at this coupling boundary is employed to calculate the derivative associated to the Dirichlet condition. This derivative is used to solve the subdomain with the Neumann boundary condition.

The domain composition method (DCM) modifies the original Dirichlet-Neumann approach enforcing the boundary conditions over the subdomains through matrix operations [1]. The main idea of DCM is to use the residual of the Dirichlet subdomain as an approach of the normal derivative on the coupling boundary. Once calculated, the normal derivative (residual flux), it could be used as an approach of the total flux going through the coupling boundary on the Neumann subdomain. One of the characteristics of the total flux is that it could be used directly to assemble the Neumann condition on the right hand side of the equation system given by the Neumann subdomain. This procedure ensures the continuity of the coupling variable and its associated flux on the coupling interface.

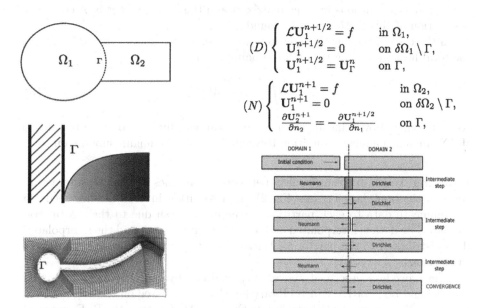

$$(D)\begin{cases} \mathcal{L}U_1^{n+1/2} = f & \text{in } \Omega_1, \\ U_1^{n+1/2} = 0 & \text{on } \delta\Omega_1 \setminus \Gamma, \\ U_1^{n+1/2} = U_\Gamma^n & \text{on } \Gamma, \end{cases}$$

$$(N)\begin{cases} \mathcal{L}U_1^{n+1} = f & \text{in } \Omega_2, \\ U_1^{n+1} = 0 & \text{on } \delta\Omega_2 \setminus \Gamma, \\ \dfrac{\partial U_2^{n+1}}{\partial n_2} = -\dfrac{\partial U_1^{n+1/2}}{\partial n_1} & \text{on } \Gamma, \end{cases}$$

Fig. 1. (a) The whole physical domain is divided on disjoint subdomains. (b) Iterative Dirichlet-Neumann approach.

Residual Flux. Without loss of generality, it could be demonstrated that there is a direct relation between the residual $\mathbf{r} = \mathbf{A}\mathbf{u} - \mathbf{b}$ of the energy equation of the the zeroth-order Navier-Stokes equations and the heat conduction equation with the normal derivative on the boundary Γ. The demonstration is based on the fact that the variational form of the continuity, momentum and energy equations written in a conservative form:

$$\frac{\partial U}{\partial t} + \nabla \cdot \mathbf{F} = Q \tag{11}$$

where $\mathbf{F}$ is a flux related to the conserved quantity U and Q represent a source term, could be expressed as

$$\underbrace{\int_{\Gamma} \frac{\partial \mathbf{F}}{\partial n} W dS}_{\mathbf{r}} = \underbrace{\int_{\Omega} \mathbf{F} \cdot \nabla W d\Omega - \int_{\Omega} \frac{\partial U}{\partial t} W d\Omega}_{\mathbf{Au}} - \underbrace{\int_{\Omega} Q W d\Omega}_{\mathbf{b}} \qquad (12)$$

where W represent the test function which must vanish on the Dirichlet interface Γ with the unity normal vector $\mathbf{n}$ [2,9]. From here, an approximation of the normal derivative λ could be associated to the residual $\mathbf{r}$ when we replace the exact solution of the conservative law in the right hand side of finite element discretization of Eq. (12) [10]. The solution $\mathbf{u}$ is achieved after the assignment of the boundary conditions into the matrix $\mathbf{A}$ and the source vector $\mathbf{b}$. A complete description of this method can be found in [1].

In the case of the energy equation, we associate the normal derivative λ_Γ to the total heat flux going through the boundary Γ

$$\lambda_\Gamma = \int_\Gamma (-\kappa \frac{\partial \mathbf{T}}{\partial n}) W dS \qquad (13)$$

As mentioned above, this approach of the total heat flux can be used to enforce the Neumann boundary condition through Γ on the Neumann subdomain.

Coupling Tool. To transfer data between two meshes Ω_i and Ω_j interacting through the boundary Γ_{ij} (see Fig. 2), each partition in both meshes needs to communicate data to each partition in the other mesh due to their geometric overlap. The data is interpolated and set to the target mesh and the interpolated data distributed to the partitions. With this data, the source code performs its calculations.

The procedure described above, is carried out by the coupling tool named Parallel and Locator Exchange Library++ (PLE++) based on the original PLE tool from Yvan Fournier (Électricité de France). At the start, the PLE was used to couple the CFD code Code_Saturne with the Heat transfer code Syrthes and several instances of the same code. In order to include more flexibility to the PLE

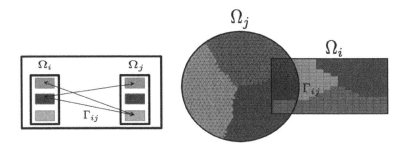

Fig. 2. Partition into two overlapping subdomains.

library, a C++ environmental library was developed to extend the capability of PLE to an easy communication between application codes written in C/C++, Fortran or Python.

4   Numerical Results

This section briefly describes the results achieved using the coupling methodology introduced above. Furthermore, it includes the validation of two benchmark cases and the analysis of the parallel performance of the proposed method.

4.1   Heated Cylinder

This test case corresponds to a heated cylinder placed in a fluid coupled to a annular ring Fig. 3(a).

The problem was originally proposed under of assumption of a steady laminar incompressible fluid flow with a Reynolds number of 40 constant fluid properties and at Prandtl number of 0.71 [11]. The cylinder is situated at a distance of $L_u/D = 4.28$ from the inlet and $L_d/D = 10$ from the outflow boundary while the cross flow is set to $H/D = 7.14$. The internal and external diameters are $d = 5 \times 10^{-3}$ and $D = 7 \times 10^{-3}$, respectively. The inlet temperature of the fluid is fixed at 303 K while the internal tube surface temperature is fixed at 373 K. The temperature at the interface between the fluid and the solid is considered the coupled boundary and is resolved using a conjugate heat transfer approach.

The effect of the thermal conductivity ratio k_s/k_f on the local Nusselt number Nu and the non-dimensional fluid-solid surface temperature T^* is depicted in Fig. 3(b). While the local Nusselt number is directly proportional to k_s/k_f at $\theta = 0$, the temperature difference between the forward ($\theta = 0$) and backward

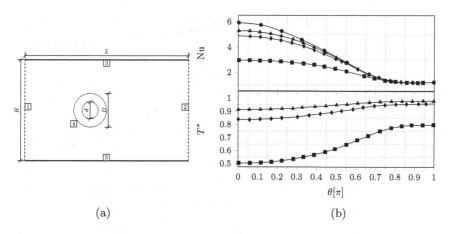

(a)   (b)

Fig. 3. (a) Computational domain for the flow around a cylinder. (b) The local Nusselt number and the reduced temperature at the interface for the isothermal case $k_s/k_f = \infty$ (circle), $k_s/k_f = 10$ (triangle), $k_s/k_f = 5$ (diamond), $k_s/k_f = 1$ (quad).

($\theta = \pi$) stagnation point is inversely proportional to k_s/k_f. A good agreement between the presented results and those obtained from [11] is observed at all locations.

4.2   Flat-Plate

Here, we present the validation results for the conjugate heat transfer benchmark proposed in [8]. This benchmark constitutes a severe test case since it comprises high velocities along with real material properties for the solid.

The test case corresponds to the cooling of a flat plate. The geometry is depicted in the Fig. 4(a). At the inlet (region 0) the temperature is $273\,K$ with a Prandlt number of $Pr = 0.71$. The initial velocity corresponds to $Ma_\infty = 0.8$ and Reynolds of $Re_L = 9 \times 10^5$ (based on the vertical dimension $L = 4.5$ mm). At the bottom, there are four succeeding regions. In region 1, symmetry boundary conditions are applied, while in the next region, a constant wall temperature of $300\,K$ and no-slip conditions are specified so that the boundary layer can be developed. The region 3 is the contact interface with the solid, while the rest of the walls are assumed adiabatic. Finally, the domain is closed by a region with symmetry boundary conditions. Once converged, the simulation can be validated using the temperature evolution at two points in the coupling interface.

Figure 4(b) shows the temperature evolution at the beginning and the end of the coupling interface. The fluid and solid meshes consist of 119529 and 9728 quadrilateral elements, ensuring sufficient resolution near the wall ($y^+ < 1$). The time step size is set to 5×10^{-2} s. The fixed-point iteration is set to 1×10^{-5}, being necessary less than 10 iterations for the first three time steps. The rest of the simulation only uses one fixed point iteration per time step. A good agreement with the reference data is observed for the entire time history of the two interface points.

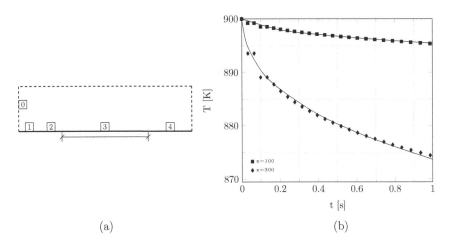

(a)   (b)

Fig. 4. (a) Computational domain for flat plate. (b) Temperature evolution at the beginning and the end of the coupling interface.

4.3   Parallel Efficiency

In order to apply the CHT approach described in Sect. 3.2 to large-scale problems, two factors must be taken into account: (1) the performance of the computations for each individual subdomain and (2) the performance associated to the coupling scheme. This section addresses the parallel implementation of the coupling scheme for the CHT approach. In particular, it is limited to show the availability of the subdomains to achieve a good performance, and also to show the possible limitations of the coupling performance.

In general, a reduction in parallel performance when computing single physics usually leads to a full breakdown of the performance of the coupling scheme, despite the algorithm can be very efficient. Because of that, the analysis of the parallel performance of the code without coupling is the first step to be verified. Figure 5(a) shows the strong-scaling curve performed on the supercomputer Vesta at the Argonne National Laboratory. The curve shows an excellent performance of the code up to 16384 MPI processes on the modelling of the expansion of a turbulent jet on a confined geometry. The speedup achieved for this problem was around 91% with 16384 MPI processes. As the solid subdomain uses the same numerical framework as the fluid, the focus can now be restricted to the features of the coupling scheme.

The parallel implementation of the coupling scheme as described in the Sect. 3.2 is now considered. In particular, the analysis performed corresponds to the CHT approach of the flat-plate experiment presented above. The coupling execution consisted of 64 MPI processes divided between the fluid and solid subdomains (60 and 4, respectively), while the number of time steps performed were limited to six. It is important to note that both the number of cores used to simulate the coupling and the mesh size of the solid subdomain were arbitrary selected to highlight the parallel details of the coupling.

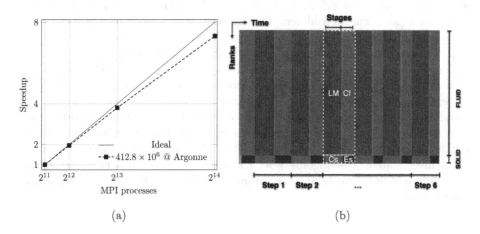

(a)   (b)

Fig. 5. (a) Strong-scaling curve for the fluid subdomain (without coupling) and (b) Trace of coupling case (flat-plate experiment).

Figure 5(b) shows the parallel execution of the flat-plate case unfolds over time (the trace) obtained by the parallel performance tool HPCToolkit [12]. The figure shows the time line of each MPI process with colours in the vertical direction showing different computing stages. In the case of the fluid, the first stage (LM) represents the solution of the low Mach equations, while the second stage (C_f) corresponds to the coupling. At the same time, there are also two stages in the solid case, the coupling (C_s) and the solution of the energy equation (E_s).

In the sequential strategy (Sect. 3.2) the domains are solved one after the other, which can be clearly seen on the trace. Each time step sequence starts with the solution of the low Mach equations in the fluid subdomain (LM), while the solid subdomain is waiting for the solution (C_s). Once the solution of the fluid subdomain is achieved, the solid subdomain performs its own solution (E_s). It should be noted that between the solution stages LM and E_s no overheads due to the exchange of information were introduced into the algorithm. This approach requires that both subdomains wait during the calculation stage of the other subdomain introducing a limitation in the maximum performance that can be achieved when the number of MPI processes are not selected appropriately. This is the topic of our current investigation.

5   Conclusions and Future Work

A partitioned coupling approach based on the parallel algebraic domain composition method (DCM) has been validated for conjugate heat transfer applications. The method is based on computing the total heat flux through matrix operations, specifically through the residual flux of the energy equation and use it as Neumann boundary condition. As the partitioned Dirichlet-Neumann approach, the DCM ensures the continuity of the coupling variable and its associated flux on the coupling interface. In order to validate this proposed approach two benchmark cases were considered. The first case corresponds to a heated cylinder placed in a steady laminar incompressible fluid flow coupled to an annular ring. The second case considers the cooling of a flat plate with an inlet velocity corresponding to Mach number 0.8 and Reynolds number 9×10^5. The results indicate good correlation with the reference data for both cases and encourages the extension to larger problems. Regarding the parallel implementation of the coupling scheme, it shows no overheads due to the exchange of information. Nevertheless, because of the features of the coupling scheme, limitations exist in the maximum performance that can be achieved. These limitations are currently being investigated. The ongoing work considers the use of this methodology in the solution of problems taking into account the thermal effect on fluid-structure interactions.

References

1. Houzeaux, G., Cajas, J.C., Eguzkitza, B., Vázquez, M.: Parallel implementation of domain composition methods (2015)
2. Samaniego, C., Houzeaux, G., Samaniego, E., Vázquez, M.: Parallel embedded boundary methods for fluid and rigid-body interaction. Comput. Methods Appl. Mech. Eng. **290**, 387–419 (2015)
3. Houzeaux, G., Principe, J.: A variational subgrid scale model for transient incompressible flows. Int. J. Comput. Fluid Dyn. **22**(3), 135–152 (2008)
4. Houzeaux, G., Aubry, R., Vázquez, M.: Extension of fractional step techniques for incompressible flows: The preconditioned orthomin (1) for the pressure schur complement. Comput. Fluids **44**(1), 297–313 (2011)
5. Uekermann, B., Cajas, J.C., Gatzhammer, B., Houzeaux, G., Mehl, M., Vázquez, M.: Towards partitioned fluid-structure interaction on massively parallel systems. In: Proceedings of WCCM XI/ECCM V/ECFD VI, Barcelona (2014)
6. Cajas, J.C., Houzeaux, G., Yáñez, D.J., Mier-Torrecilla, M..: Shape project vortex bladeless: parallel multi-code coupling for fluid-structure interaction in wind energy generation (2016)
7. Küttler, U., Wall, W.A.: Fixed-point fluid-structure interaction solvers with dynamic relaxation. Comput. Mech. **43**(1), 61–72 (2008)
8. Birken, P., Quint, K.J., Hartmann, S., Meister, A.: A time-adaptive fluid-structure interaction method for thermal coupling. Comput. Vis. Sci. **13**(7), 331–340 (2010)
9. Kuzmin, D.: A guide to numerical methods for transport equations. University Erlangen-Nuremberg (2010)
10. Toselli, A., Widlund, O.B.: Domain Decomposition Methods: Algorithms and Theory, vol. 34. Springer, Heidelberg (2005)
11. Vessakosol, P., Charoensuk, J.: Numerical analysis of heat transfer and flow field around cross-flow heat exchanger tube with fouling. Appl. Therm. Eng. **30**(10), 1170–1178 (2010)
12. Adhianto, L., Banerjee, S., Fagan, M., Krentel, M., Marin, G., Mellor-Crummey, J., Tallent, N.R.: HPCTOOLKIT: Tools for performance analysis of optimized parallel programs. Concurrency Comput. Pract. Experience **22**(6), 685–701 (2010)

Farfield Noise Prediction Using Large-Scale Lattice-Boltzmann Simulations

Benjamin Duda[1(✉)] and Ehab Fares[2]

[1] Exa GmbH, Landshuter Allee 8, 80637 Munich, Germany
bduda@exa.com
[2] Exa GmbH, Curiestraße 4, 70563 Stuttgart, Germany

Abstract. In order to predict farfield noise created by the flow over complex geometries, high-fidelity flow simulations based on the Lattice-Boltzmann solver PowerFLOW are used in conjunction with the acoustic analogy solver PowerACOUSTICS. Since the flow needs to be spatially and temporally well resolved, the simulations are usually carried on a large number of computational cores for adequate turnaround times. This paper provides the background on the two-step methodology and gives an overview on aero-acoustics computations in aerospace, ranging from an isolated airframe component to the entire aircraft system.

Keywords: Lattice-Boltzmann methods · Large-Scale CFD · Farfield aeroacoustics

1 Introduction

Accurate farfield noise predictions in the aerospace industry are becoming more and more important due to the continuous growth in air travel, which has led to an increase in community noise exposure around airports and thus to stricter airport regulations. The difficulty of numerically capturing noise generation and the propagation of sound to the farfield leads to a multi-scale problem. Turbulent scales and noise generating mechanisms are usually orders of magnitudes smaller than the distance between noise source and observer, which rules out the direct numerical propagation. The approach followed here consists in the coupling of a high-fidelity flow solver, which can spatially and temporally resolve pressure fluctuations of the flow field generated by very small turbulent scales, with a farfield solver that relies on an acoustic analogy. This approach is schematically shown in Fig. 1.

© Springer International Publishing AG 2017
E. Di Napoli et al. (Eds.): JHPCS 2016, LNCS 10164, pp. 48–57, 2017.
DOI: 10.1007/978-3-319-53862-4_5

PowerFLOW   **PowerACOUSTICS**

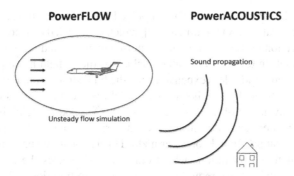

Fig. 1. Coupling of high-fidelity flow simulation in the near field with acoustic post-processing tool for farfield sound propagation

2   Numerical Method

In a first step, the flow around the body is simulated with PowerFLOW, which is a compressible flow solver based on the three dimensional 19 state (D3Q19) Lattice-Boltzmann model (LBM) [1–4]. LBM is a computational fluid dynamics (CFD) technology, which has been developed and gained popularity over the last decades due to the advent of high performance computing. It has been extensively validated for a wide variety of applications and the reader is referred to these publications for more information [5–8].

In contrast to more traditional methods like those based on the Navier-Stokes equations, LBM uses a simpler and more general physics formulation at a microscopic level. Nonetheless, the macroscopic behavior of the Navier-Stokes equations are recovered from the LBM equation via the Chapman-Enskog expansion [4, 8]. Characteristics of the numerical scheme include low dissipation and dispersion properties. LBM being an inherently unsteady simulation, the results are thus similar to a Direct Numerical Simulation (DNS). Since DNS of high Reynolds number flows usually encountered for aerospace applications require unattainable computational resources, a turbulence modelling strategy is adopted which relies on modelling the effect of turbulence where possible, e.g. attached boundary layers, and resolving turbulence where necessary, e.g. free shear layers, flow separations and wakes. This approach is called Lattice-Boltzmann Very Large Eddy Simulation (LB-VLES) and is used throughout this work [3].

Geometrical details of real applications tend to influence broad-band noise characteristics. Therefore, the actual geometry should be represented numerically as accurately as possible. Since this LB method is solved on Cartesian meshes with a cut-cell approach and an accurate surface representation, complex geometry handling is ensured. Variable refinement regions can be defined to allow for local mesh refinement of the volume mesh size by successive factors of two.

Throughout the simulation, unsteady pressure data is sampled on the geometry or on porous permeable surfaces inside the fluid. In a second step, an acoustic analogy approach based on the Ffowcs Williams and Hawkings (FWH) formulation is used to evaluate the perceived noise at a farfield location based on the near field pressure data recorded during the simulation [9]. The employed FWH formulation is based on the retarded-time formulation 1A by Farassat [10], which is extended to account for uniform mean flow convection effects to simulate the noise generated and measured in an ideal infinite wind tunnel. In terms of computational costs, the farfield noise propagation is usually orders of magnitudes less expensive than the fluid simulation. For an acceptable turnaround time for large datasets however, parallel FWH computations are necessary.

Another key advantage of the Lattice-Boltzmann Method is the high efficiency of computations on modern compute clusters with hundreds or thousands of interconnected nodes and tens of computational cores per node. This is due to the predominantly local nature of computational operations which dramatically reduces the core-to-core and node-to-node communications requirements compared to traditional RANS methods. Simulations were performed recently up to 16000 cores on a large Linux cluster with Infiniband interconnect. Parallel scalability of PowerFLOW is documented in Fig. 2 demonstrating the high efficiency of the simulations of real industrial cases for simulations on as many as 16,000 of cores.

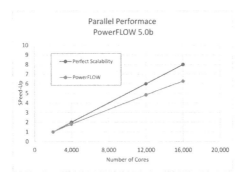

Fig. 2. Average parallel scalability for large industrial case

3   Simulations

In this section two aerospace related cases will be discussed: an isolated simplified nose landing gear in model-scale and an installed high fidelity main landing gear in full-scale installed on an aircraft in landing configuration.

3.1   Isolated Nose Landing Gear

Firstly, LBM-VLES results of the unsteady flow about the ONERA–The French Aerospace Lab/Airbus SAS LAGOON landing gear are shown. The simulations were part of an aeroacoustic benchmark and are discussed in detail in refs [11, 12]. The geometry consists of a simplified two-wheel landing gear, including a segmented cylindrical leg, a cylindrical axle, and two rims with inboard annular cavities and a closed outboard face with mounting tires. It is shown in Fig. 3. The flow simulation was conducted for a Mach number of 0.23 and a Reynolds number of $1.541 \cdot 10^6$ based on the wheel diameter.

Fig. 3. Isolated landing gear tested in wind tunnel [11].

Figure 4 gives a snapshot of the resolved turbulent structures by iso-surfaces of λ_2 with the flow coming from the top right. Flow separation occurs at the rims and downstream of the strut and the wheels. A variety of small and large scale structures are resolved in the near field of the landing gear. Due to the mesh coarsening in downstream direction the structures start dissipating. The simulation has been run for a physical time of 0.8s but only the second half of the run has been used for obtaining time statistics and farfield acoustics.

Fig. 4. Resolved turbulent structures in the wake of the landing gear.

The top part of Fig. 5 shows comparisons between the PIV in-plane time averaged streamwise velocity component in the wake of the gear and the predicted value. Regions affected by the presence of the shadow of the laser sheet due to the wheel have no value in the database and are therefore blanked in the figures. A fairly good quantitative agreement between prediction and measurements can be observed. The bottom part of Fig. 5 shows comparisons between the LDV in-plane standard deviation of the streamwise velocity components in the wake of the gear and the predicted ones. The numerical results have been obtained by adding the square root of 2/3 k to the standard deviations computed using the resolved LBM fluctuation field. This allows one to take into account the effect of the unresolved (modeled) scales of motion in the computation of the standard deviation, by considering the modeled fluctuations to be isotropic.

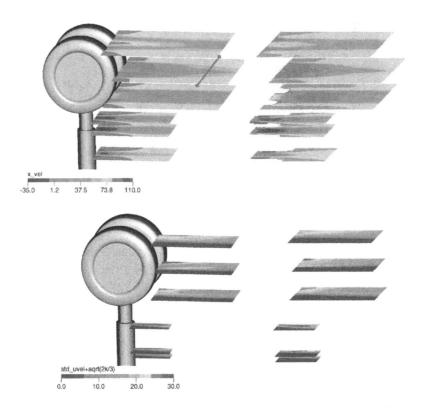

Fig. 5. Mean (top) and std. deviation (bottom) of streamwise velocity component. Comparison between simulation (left) and experiment (right) [12].

The FWH computation is carried out by integrating the unsteady pressure field on the gear surface which was sampled at a frequency of 100 kHz for 0.4s. This yields a file size of already about 325 GB for the isolated landing gear, which needs to be processed. Figure 6 shows a good comparison between the numerically and experimentally obtained noise spectrum for an overhead microphone. The discrepancies for low frequencies can be attributed to the experimental setup in the wind tunnel, which was not replicated in the simulation.

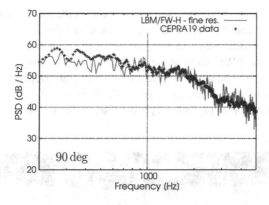

Fig. 6. Farfield noise results from 200 Hz to 5000 Hz for an overhead microphone. Comparison between simulation and experiment [12].

3.2 Full-Scale Aircraft in Landing Configuration

Secondly, LBM-VLES results are shown for the flow around a full-scale Gulfstream aircraft approaching an airport. The computations were conducted in the scope of NASA's Environmentally Responsible Aviation (ERA) project and the complete study can be found in refs. [13–15]. The simulations shown here correspond to a landing configuration with main gear and flaps deployed. The Mach number was 0.2 and the Reynolds number $10.5 \cdot 10^6$ based on the mean aerodynamic chord. The simulation with a fine resolution consisted of 8.4 billion volume elements and was carried out on 12,000 cores.

Figure 7 shows again the wide variety of resolved turbulent flow structures, highlighting the unsteady flow around the landing gear, the flap side edges and brackets connecting wing and flap. It is crucial that the turbulence modelling approach in LB-VLES is capable of resolving turbulent fluctuations in areas of detached flow because only the time accurate prediction of these features will allow a correct farfield noise assessment.

Fig. 7. Resolved turbulent structures at the flap and main landing gear [13].

The pressure dilatation field displayed in Fig. 8 allows identifying noise sources. The flap side edge vortices and the main landing gear (including the gear cavity) are the most dominating ones but additional noise is generated by the flow around the flap brackets. Also for this case, the FWH computation is carried out by integrating the unsteady pressure field but this time on the entire surface of the aircraft. Depending on the desired frequency range, the input files can easily reach 10 TB in size. An efficient handling and a fast parallel computation of the farfield pressure signal is thus indispensable for large, full-scale applications.

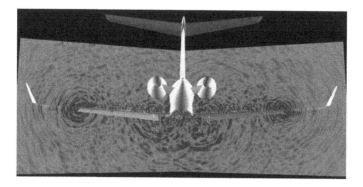

Fig. 8. Pressure field showing flap tips and main landing gears as dominant noise sources [13].

In order to quantify the strength of the noise sources in various frequencies a beamforming calculation is carried out in time domain. Farfield pressure signals are computed for an array of hundreds of microphones and correlating the microphone data then allows pinpointing the sources. Figure 9 shows the beamforming maps for frequencies of 879 Hz and 1270 Hz. The images on the left are results from a flight test using the same microphone array and the images on the right are simulation results. The contours have been normalized so that the peak level in each map is zero. Very good agreement is achieved and both the flap side edges and the main landing gear are confirmed to be dominant noise sources. The discrepancies, especially near the center of the aircraft, can be attributed to the fact that the simulation only had flow-through nacelles whereas the real aircraft was flown with engines close to idle but still generating noise.

Figure 10 shows a comparison between the numerically and experimentally obtained sound pressure level spectra in one third octave bands for the flyover microphone. Three simulations were conducted with two different grid resolutions and two different flap brackets geometry. The original flap brackets geometry contained a variety of small geometrical details. These holes and gaps, which are probably closed on the real aircraft, generated additional noise, which explains the discrepancies seen for high frequencies. Closing these features leads to a much better agreement with flight test data, cf. [14]. Generally, a very good agreement in the mid frequency range can be observed with larger deviations in the low frequency range. This can be attributed to the noise generated by the main landing gear cavity and to sources not captured in the simulation such as the almost idly running engines.

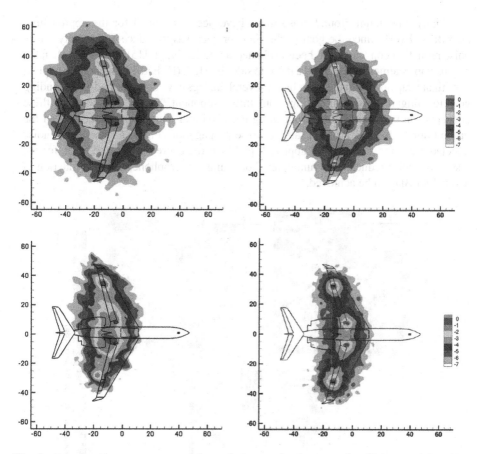

Fig. 9. Beamforming contour maps of sound pressure levels comparing flight test (left) with simulation (right) for a frequency of 879 Hz (top) and 1270 Hz (bottom) [13].

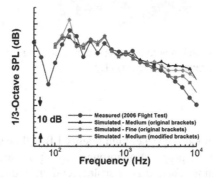

Fig. 10. Farfield noise results for a flyover microphone. Comparison between simulation and flight test [13].

Finally, maximum ground noise maps have been calculated for the approaching aircraft by FWH. Since the goal of the ERA project was to reduce community noise, noise reduction concepts have been evaluated numerically, cf. [15]. On the one hand, a porous flap treatment (APM) and a flexible side edge link (FLEXSEL) have been applied to mitigate flap noise. On the other hand, several fairings have been applied to the landing gear to mitigate noise originating from this component. The performance of these concepts can be quantified by calculating the maximum perceived noise level on the ground during landing through farfield noise propagation. Figure 11 shows the noise affected areas for a prescribed approach path and the decrease of these areas for the respective noise reduction technologies. For a single microphone, a noise reduction of about 1.6 dBD can be achieved.

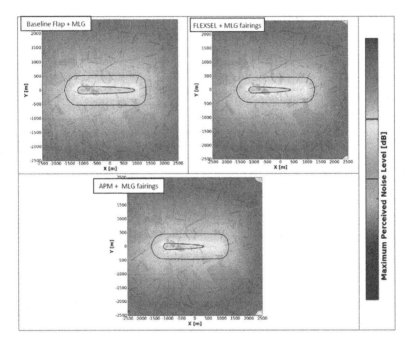

Fig. 11. Ground map of maximum perceived noise during landing for standard aircraft and for aircraft equipped with noise reduction concepts [15].

4   Conclusion

Results of a two-step methodology, i.e. high fidelity LBM flow simulations for sound generation followed by noise propagation through acoustic analogy, are presented for a model-scale isolated landing gear and a full-scale aircraft in landing configuration. Good agreement between simulation and experiments is achieved. The quality of the numerical results can be attributed to the accuracy and efficiency of both the underlying flow solver, which allows the high temporal and spatial resolution of turbulent structures in detached flow regions, and the acoustic analogy approach, which allows handling of very large data. In order to address even larger scale industrial applications, efficient parallelization remains an important aspect not only for the flow simulation itself, but also for the volume mesh generation as well as for near and farfield post-processing.

References

1. Chen, H.: Volumetric formulation of the lattice-boltzmann method for fluid dynamics: basic concept. Phys. Rev. E **58**(3), 3955–3963 (1998)
2. Chen, H., Texeira, C., Molvig, K.: Realization of fluid boundary condition via discrete boltzmann dynamics. Int. J. Mod. Phys. C **09**, 1281–1292 (1998)
3. Chen, H., Kandasamy, S., Orszag, S., Shock, R., Succi, S., Yakhot, V.: Extended boltzmann kinetic equation for turbulent flows. Science **301**, 633–636 (2003)
4. Chen, H., Chen, S., Matthaeus, W.: Recovery of the navier-stokes equations using a lattice-gas boltzmann method. Phys. Rev. A **45**(8), 5339–5342 (1992)
5. Li, Y., Shock, R., Zhang, R., Chen, H.: Numerical study of flow past an impulsively started cylinder by lattice boltzmann method. J. Fluid Mech. **519**, 273–300 (2004)
6. Fares, E., Jelic, S., Kuthada, T., Schroeck, D.: Lattice boltzmann thermal flow simulation and measurements of a modified SAE model with heated plug. In: Proceedings of FEDSM 2006-98467 (2006)
7. Fares, E.: Unsteady flow simulation of the ahmed reference body using a lattice boltzmann approach. J. Comput. Fluids **35**, 940–950 (2006)
8. Qian, Y., d'Humieres, D., Lallemand, P.: Lattice BGK models for the navier-stokes equation. Europhys. Lett. **17**, 479–484 (1992)
9. Williams, J.E.F., Hawkings, D.L.: Sound generated by turbulence and surfaces in arbitrary motion. Philos. Trans. R. Soc. **264**(1151), 321–342 (1969)
10. Farassat, F., Succi, G.P.: The prediction of helicopter discrete frequency noise. Vertica **7**(4), 309–320 (1983)
11. Airbus SAS: LAGOON Simplified (2-Wheel) Nose Landing Gear Configuration #1 - Experimental Database. TR-R12, Toulouse, France, April 2011
12. Casalino, D., Ribeiro, A., Fares, E., Noelting, S.: Lattice-boltzmann aeroacoustic analysis of the LAGOON landing-gear configuration. AIAA J. **52**(6), 1232–1248 (2014)
13. Khorrami, M., Fares, E.: Simulation-based airframe noise prediction of a full-scale, full aircraft. In: Aeroacoustics Conference, Lyon, France, AIAA 2016–2706 (2016)
14. Fares, E., Duda, B., Khorrami, M.: Airframe noise prediction of a full aircraft in model and full scale using a lattice boltzmann. In: Aeroacoustics Conference, Lyon, France, AIAA 2016–2707 (2016)
15. Khorrami, M., Duda, B., Hazir, A., Fares, E.: Computational evaluation of airframe noise reduction concepts at full scale. In: Aeroacoustics Conference, Lyon, France, AIAA 2016–2711 (2016)

FEniCS-HPC: Coupled Multiphysics in Computational Fluid Dynamics

Johan Hoffman[1,2(✉)], Johan Jansson[1,2], Niyazi Cem Degirmenci[1],
Jeannette Hiromi Spühler[1], Rodrigo Vilela De Abreu[1], Niclas Jansson[1],
and Aurélien Larcher[3]

[1] Department of Computational Science and Technology,
KTH Royal Institute of Technology, Stockholm, Sweden
{jhoffman,jjan,ncde,spuhler,rvda,njansson}@kth.se
[2] Basque Center for Applied Mathematics (BCAM), Bilbao, Spain
[3] Norwegian University of Science and Technology, Trondheim, Norway
aurelien.larcher@math.ntnu.no

Abstract. We present a framework for coupled multiphysics in computational fluid dynamics, targeting massively parallel systems. Our strategy is based on general problem formulations in the form of partial differential equations and the finite element method, which open for automation, and optimization of a set of fundamental algorithms. We describe these algorithms, including finite element matrix assembly, adaptive mesh refinement and mesh smoothing; and multiphysics coupling methodologies such as unified continuum fluid-structure interaction (FSI), and aeroacoustics by coupled acoustic analogies. The framework is implemented as FEniCS open source software components, optimized for massively parallel computing. Examples of applications are presented, including simulation of aeroacoustic noise generated by an airplane landing gear, simulation of the blood flow in the human heart, and simulation of the human voice organ.

Keywords: FEniCS · Unicorn · Eunison · High-performance computing · Multiphysics · Computational fluid dynamics · Adaptive finite element method

1 Introduction

Computational fluid dynamics (CFD) is becoming a standard tool in many areas of science and engineering, and finds new applications every day. Increasingly, it is now also possible to study complex systems where different physics models interact, so called multiphysics. Multiphysics CFD poses a number of challenges with respect to numerical approximation, in particular in the context of high performance computing (HPC).

CFD is based on the computation of numerical approximations of the Navier-Stokes equations, possibly including a turbulence model when direct numerical simulation (DNS) is not feasible due to the high computational cost of resolving

© Springer International Publishing AG 2017
E. Di Napoli et al. (Eds.): JHPCS 2016, LNCS 10164, pp. 58–69, 2017.
DOI: 10.1007/978-3-319-53862-4_6

all turbulent scales in the simulation. The price of turbulence modelling, e.g. RANS or LES, is the introduction of model parameters that may need tuning to a particular problem, which requires calibration data that is not always available.

In recent years, CFD approaches have been developed for finite element approximation with turbulence models based on the residual of the Navier-Stokes equations, without any physics based turbulence models, see e.g. [3,10]. Together with goal-oriented mesh adaption and slip boundary conditions we refer to this approach as *direct finite element simulation* (DFS), which has proven to be a highly efficient method for turbulent flow simulation without model parameters that need tuning [8].

In this paper we present the FEniCS-HPC framework for multiphysics CFD simulations. We emphasise high Reynolds number flow, including turbulence, where we present examples ranging from classical engineering to clinical medicine. The framework is based on DFS, a monolithic coupling strategy for fluid-structure interaction with implicit contact models [1,9], and computational aeroacoustics (CAA) by solving the CFD and the acoustic wave propagation on the same mesh with the same time step. The framework builds on the generality of the FEniCS open source software, with a number of key components optimized for massively parallel computing.

2   The FEniCS-HPC Framework

FEniCS-HPC is a high-level problem solving environment for automated solution of partial differential equations (PDEs) by the finite element method. To manage the complexity of multiphysics problems FEniCS-HPC takes the weak form of a PDE as input in a near-mathematical notation and automatically generates low-level source code, abstracting away implementation details and HPC concepts from domain scientists.

Besides the code generation part, a key component of FEniCS is the Object-Oriented finite element library DOLFIN [17], from which we have developed a high performance branch DOLFIN-HPC [12], optimized for distributed memory architectures. DOLFIN handles mesh representation and assembly of weak forms but relies on external libraries for solving the linear systems. Our high performance branch extends DOLFIN with a fully distributed mesh, parallel adaptive mesh refinement, and predictive dynamic load balancing capabilities [14].

The parallelization strategy within DOLFIN-HPC is based on an element wise distribution, given from the dual graph of the underlying computational mesh. To minimize data dependencies during finite element assembly, whole elements is assigned to each processing elements (PE), and the overlap between PEs are represented as ghosted entities. Thus, assembling the stiffness matrix in every time-step can be performed in a straightforward way. Each PE computes the local stiffness matrix of its elements, and add them to the global matrix. For the linear solvers, a row-wise distribution of matrices is assumed, which directly maps to our element wise distribution.

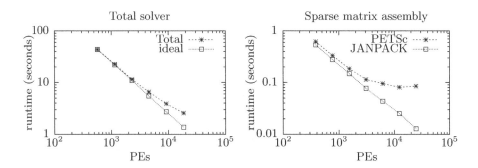

Fig. 1. Strong scalability test on a Cray XC40 for a full incompressible Navier-Stokes solver (left) and sparse matrix assembly in DOLFIN-HPC (right), using two different linear algebra backends and programming models, PETSc (MPI based) and JANPACK (PGAS based).

DOLFIN-HPC is written in C++, and is parallelized using either flat MPI or hybrid MPI + PGAS [13]. The framework has proven to scale well on a wide range of architectures, even for very latency sensitive kernels with the addition of the hybrid parallelization (Fig. 1).

3   Mathematical Model and Numerical Methods

3.1   Conservation Equations

We apply the conservation equations for an incompressible continuum to model our applications presented in this paper. Let Ω be a three-dimensional domain in $\mathbb{R}^3$ with boundary Γ over a time interval $I = [0, \hat{t}]$. We seek a velocity $\boldsymbol{u}(x,t) : \Omega \times [0, \hat{t}] \to \mathbb{R}^3$, a pressure $p(x,t) : \Omega \times [0, \hat{t}] \to \mathbb{R}$ and a phase function $\theta(x,t) : \Omega \times [0, \hat{t}] \to \mathbb{R}$ such that

$$\begin{aligned}
\rho(\partial_t \boldsymbol{u} + (\boldsymbol{u} \cdot \nabla)\boldsymbol{u}) + \nabla \cdot \tau &= \boldsymbol{g} \quad \text{in } Q, \\
\nabla \cdot \boldsymbol{u} &= 0 \quad \text{in } Q, \\
\partial_t \theta + (\boldsymbol{u} \cdot \nabla)\theta &= 0 \quad \text{in } Q, \\
\hat{\boldsymbol{u}}(\cdot, 0) &= \hat{\boldsymbol{u}}^0 \quad \text{in } \Omega,
\end{aligned} \tag{3.1}$$

with $\tau(\boldsymbol{u}, p)$ the stress tensor, $\hat{\boldsymbol{u}} \equiv (\boldsymbol{u}, p)$ and $Q = \Omega \times I$.

3.2   Fluid-Structure Interaction

With the aim of establishing a framework that allows for a general formulation and implementation of different models while applying adaptive error control for realistic 3D applications in continuum mechanics, a so-called *unified continuum model* for fluid-structure interaction problems was developed [9]. The problem is described by the fundamental conservation laws for a unified continuum (Eq. 3.1), where the Cauchy stress τ is kept general, allowing for different constitutive laws in different parts of the continuum. The phase function θ is defined to mark the solid ($\theta = 0$) and fluid ($\theta = 1$) domain respectively and is used to choose constitutive law,

$$\tau = \tau_D - pI, \tag{1}$$
$$\tau_D = \theta \tau_f + (1 - \theta)\tau_s, \tag{2}$$
$$\tau_f = 2\mu_f \epsilon(u), \tag{3}$$
$$D_t \tau_s = 2\mu_s \epsilon(u) + \nabla u \tau_s + \tau_s \nabla u^T. \tag{4}$$

The subscript indicates whether the variable is defined in the solid or in the fluid part. A convection equation for θ is formulated, however in this setting we track the fluid-structure interface with the mesh, and the phase convection equation becomes trivial and can be eliminated. The kinematic constraint on the velocity $u_S = u_f$ at the fluid-structure interface is fulfilled by the continuity of the velocity field for the whole domain, and a weak version of the continuity constraint on the normal stresses $\tau_s \cdot n = \tau_f \cdot n$ can be shown to be implicitly enforced by using an integration by parts argument.

3.3   Finite Element Approximation for the Pure Fluid Case

Our computational approach is a standard Galerkin finite element discretization with least squares stabilization using adjoint based adaptive algorithms and residual based implicit turbulence modeling. Here we give the formulation for the pure fluid case where the phase function $\theta = 1$. For the full method for the general FSI case we refer to [1,9].

Let $0 = t^0 < t^1 \cdots < t^N = \hat{t}$ be a sequence of discrete time steps, with associated time intervals $I^n = (t^{n-1}, t^n]$ and space-time slabs $S^n := \Omega \times I^n$ over which we define space-time finite element spaces based on a spatial finite element space W^n and spatial mesh T^n [11].

In a cG(1)cG(1) method [6,7] we seek an approximate solution $\hat{U} = (U, P)$ which is continuous piecewise linear in space and time. This time-stepping formulation is equivalent to the implicit Crank-Nicolson method in time.

With W^n a standard finite element space of continuous piecewise linear functions, and W_0^n the functions in W^n which are zero on the boundary Γ, the cG(1)cG(1) method for constant density incompressible flow with homogeneous Dirichlet boundary conditions for the velocity takes the form: for $n = 1, ..., N$, find $(U^n, P^n) \equiv (U(t_n), P(t_n))$ with $U^n \in V_0^n \equiv [W_0^n]^3$ and $P^n \in W^n$, such that

$$((U^n - U^{n-1})k_n^{-1} + (\bar{U}^n \cdot \nabla)\bar{U}^n, v) + (2\nu\epsilon(\bar{U}^n), \epsilon(v)) - (P^n, \nabla \cdot v) + (\nabla \cdot \bar{U}^n, q)$$
$$+ SD_\delta^n(\bar{U}^n, P^n; v, q) = (f, v), \forall \hat{v} = (v, q) \in V_0^n \times W^n, \tag{5}$$

where $\bar{U}^n = 1/2(U^n + U^{n-1})$ is piecewise constant in time over I_n, with the stabilizing term

$$SD_\delta^n(\bar{U}^n, P^n; v, q) \equiv (\delta_1(\bar{U}^n \cdot \nabla \bar{U}^n + \nabla P^n - f), \bar{U}^n \cdot \nabla v + \nabla q) +$$
$$(\delta_2 \nabla \cdot \bar{U}^n, \nabla \cdot v),$$

where

$$(v, w) = \sum_{K \in \mathcal{T}_n} \int_K v \cdot w \, dx,$$

$$(\epsilon(v), \epsilon(w)) = \sum_{i,j=1}^{3} (\epsilon_{ij}(v), \epsilon_{ij}(w)),$$

with the stabilization parameters

$$\delta_1 = \kappa_1 (k_n^{-2} + |U^{n-1}|^2 h_n^{-2})^{-1/2}$$
$$\delta_2 = \kappa_2 |U^{n-1}| h_n$$

where κ_1 and κ_2 are positive constants of unit size. For turbulent flow we choose a time step size

$$k_n \sim \min_{x \in \Omega}(h_n/|U^{n-1}|).$$

We note that the least squares stabilization omits the time derivative in the residual, which is a consequence of the test functions being piecewise constant in time [7]. We apply the Arbitrary Lagrangian-Eulerian formulation of (5) when deforming the mesh.

3.4   Turbulent Flow

To simulate turbulent flow we rely on a Direct Finite Element Simulation (DFS) methodology with residual based turbulence modeling. DFS is based directly on the Navier-Stokes equations without any physics based explicit turbulence model, which provides a mathematical foundation for the method and opens for quantitative a posteriori error estimation, and efficient goal-oriented adaptive algorithms [7,8,10].

3.5   Contact Model

Our approach to model contact is derived from the idea to simulate the fluid-structure interaction as a unified continuum.

We model contact implicitly by switching fluid cells to solid cells when contact is detected based on a distance criterion. The distance between solid surfaces is computed by using an Eikonal equation. Since both the contact and the distance are modeled by partial differential equations, they can be solved in our automated software framework.

3.6   Mesh Smoothing Algorithms

When deforming the mesh, it is important to keep the quality of the cells in the mesh. Our numerical solvers can apply two smoothing algorithms.

The linear smoother solves a linear elasticity equation for the mesh velocity. It is a fast and simple method to enhance the quality of a mesh where the vertices are diffusively relocated over the domain. However, since no information about the quality of the cells in the mesh is included in the equation, there is no guarantee that the mesh quality is improved.

In the nonlinear smoother, the deformation of the mesh is formulated as a time-dependent nonlinear elasticity equation. The stiffness of the model is weighted by the quality of the cell element. By advancing the partial differential equation in time and approaching a stationary solution, the quality of the mesh is enhanced towards its goal of optimal shape.

4   Multiphysics in Computational Fluid Dynamics

To illustrate the capabilities of the FEniCS-HPC framework we present three CFD multiphysics examples, from classical engineering to clinical medicine.

4.1   Heart Biomechanics

The purpose of our research is to establish a simple and robust framework for modeling and simulation of the blood flow in the heart. We aim for a simulation model that is patient-specific, and both easy to modify and flexible to extend. In [18], we focus on the aspect of fluid mechanics of the blood flow in the left ventricle (LV) of the heart. The motion of the endocardial wall is extracted from images using medical imaging techniques and we apply the incompressible Navier-Stokes equations to simulate the hemodynamics within the chamber. We set time-dependent boundary conditions to model the opening and closing of the mitral and aortic valves. The goal is to ultimately apply this simulation model in a clinical setting, for which we have established a semi-automated pathway from ultrasound measurements to patient-specific flow simulations of the LV [16]. The robustness, validation, and the clinical feasibility of the model is currently under development.

To enhance the LV model, prototypes are being developed of both a natural and a mechanical aortic valve, embedded in the left ventricle and the aorta. The fluid-structure interaction is formulated as a unified continuum problem as described in (Sect. 3.2). A stabilized local ALE space-time finite element discretization is used for the unified continuum with the mesh moved according to the solid deformation and with mesh smoothing in the fluid part of the domain [9].

A CAD model of an idealized natural aortic root is developed based on a small set of parameters, proposed by [19]. Even though the material properties of the valve leaflets have no anatomical foundation yet, the opening and closing characteristics as observed in e.g. [15] can be identified.

Fig. 2. Vortex generation in the left ventricle during diastole (left), and the velocity field around an embedded mechanical (middle) and a natural (right) aortic valve during systole.

Our model of a bileaflet mechanical heart valve is reduced to the leaflets only, and is embedded in an idealized aorta. Contrary to the natural valve, we simulate the fluid-structure interaction of the leaflets and the hemodynamics of the left ventricle conjointly.

Figure 2 depicts the vortex generation during diastole, and the velocity field around the embedded mechanical and natural aortic valves during systole.

4.2   Human Phonation

The goal of the EUNISON project [2] is to develop a simulation model of the human voice from first principles, including vocal folds and vocal tract. The fluid-structure-contact-acoustics model is solved in a realistic geometry, where a constant inflow velocity is given upstream of the vocal folds to drive the model, simulating the airflow from the lungs, which causes the vocal folds (VF) to start to self-oscillate which leads to phonation.

To resolve the VF contact zone and the glottal jet well enough to initiate the self-oscillation a mesh with ca. 500 k mesh points is necessary, with most of the mesh points in these zones. The fine mesh limits the timestep, here ca. 10 k timesteps are needed per oscillation cycle, requiring ca. 6 h of computation time with 640 cores on the Beskow supercomputer at KTH. Adaptive time-stepping is used which allows significantly larger timesteps when the glottis is closed and there is no high velocity jet, but the average timestep is still small.

In Fig. 3 a detailed visualization of the contact region is given showing the characteristic "glottal wave" contact pattern throughout the oscillation cycle. A qualitative match to 8 schematic steps of the glottal wave can be made with clearly identifiable divergent and convergent angles of the folds, and contact starting in the upstream part of the vocal folds and traveling downstream, giving high confidence in the validity of the FSI model.

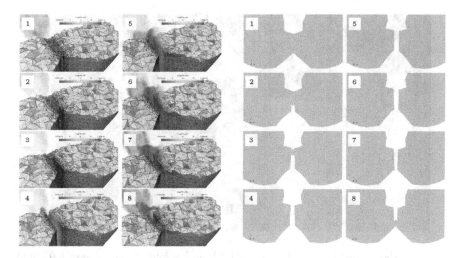

Fig. 3. FEniCS-HPC parallel simulation of realistic human vocal folds with turbulent fluid-structure interaction and contact demonstrating the characteristic "glottal wave" contact pattern in the oscillatory cycle in human phonation. Slice through the center of the vocal folds (left), and a clip through the solid phase together with volume rendering of the magnitude of the velocity (right). The contact model functions by switching the phase function from fluid to solid determined by a geometric predicate computed by solving an Eikonal equation.

4.3 Aeroacoustics

This is an ongoing work and the first results were presented at the 4th AIAA Workshop on Benchmark Problems for Airframe Noise Computations (BANC-IV), in June 2016. For the workshop, the aeroacoustic sound generated by a scaled model of a nose landing gear of a Gulfstream commercial jet was computed, and comparisons were performed with wind tunnel measurements [20].

In airframe noise computations, the standard practice is a hybrid approach where the Ffowcs Williams-Hawkings (FWH) integral equation [5] is solved to compute the noise in the far-field, and compressible LES is used to compute the source terms for the integral formulation. One uncertainty with this approach is to define the surfaces at which the LES sources should be integrated. Here, there are two choices: "solid surfaces", which are the physical boundaries of the object being studied, or "permeable surfaces", which are arbitrary, virtual surfaces surrounding the object of interest, away from its boundaries. The problem with the former approach is that no quadrupole sources (fluctuations of stress in the turbulent wake) are taken into account; permeable surfaces were therefore created to remedy this problem by including quadrupole sources in the solution of the FWH equation. However, there is no precise way of choosing permeable surfaces and the choice could vary dramatically depending on the application.

Here, we propose an alternative hybrid approach where the incompressible NSE are used together with a space-time discretization of Lighthill's equation,

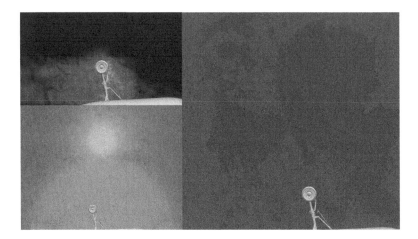

Fig. 4. Snapshot of adjoint velocity (upper left), and adjoint density (lower left), and cells marked for refinement in the adaptive algorithm in red (right). (Color figure online)

as seen previously in [4]. The advantage is that there is no need for choosing between permeable or solid surfaces, since all source terms are included in the space discretization of Lighthill's wave equation. The novelty of this work is that adaptive mesh refinement based on a posteriori error estimation is used for both

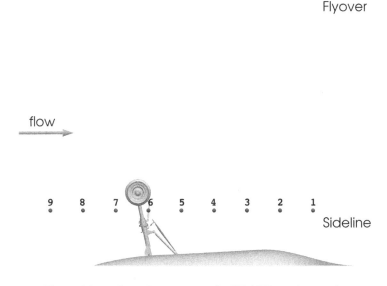

Fig. 5. Microphone locations in the UFAFF wind tunnel.

NSE and Lighthill's wave equation (Fig. 4), and that the equations are solved together for each time step in FEniCS-HPC, avoiding expensive I/O operations and the need of a software communication interface. Moreover, there is no need for using interpolation schemes nor filtering since both the flow and the acoustic problems are solved on the same, fixed mesh.

The present simulations were run on 4,096 cores on the supercomputer Beskow at PDC Center for High Performance Computing for 4 days, and the mesh used for sampling of results had 12 million vertices (66 million cells).

Sound pressure levels were measured at 20 different locations in the University of Florida Aeroacoustic Flow Facility (UFAFF), Fig. 5. A selection of 6 representative microphones are compared with measured values in Fig. 6. The signals compare well, especially in the frequency range of 800–2000 Hz for the flyover microphones, and 1000–9000 Hz for the sideline ones. The sideline microphones show, in general, better agreement, which may be a consequence of lack of resolution in the mesh, causing dispersion of waves as they travel a longer distance (flyover microphones are ca. 1 m further away from the gear than sideline ones).

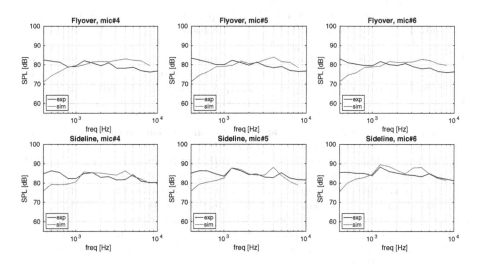

Fig. 6. Far field Sound Pressure Level (SPL) for selected microphones.

Acknowledgments. This research has been supported by the European Research Council, the EU-FET grant EUNISON 308874, the Swedish Research Council, the Swedish Foundation for Strategic Research, the Swedish Energy Agency, the Basque Excellence Research Center (BERC 2014-2017) program by the Basque Government, the Spanish Ministry of Economy and Competitiveness MINECO: BCAM Severo Ochoa accreditation SEV-2013-0323 and the Project of the Spanish Ministry of Economy and Competitiveness with reference MTM2013-40824. We acknowledge the Swedish National Infrastructure for Computing (SNIC) at PDC – Center for High-Performance

Computing for awarding us access to the supercomputer resources Beskow. Initial volume meshes have been generated with ANSA from Beta-CAE Systems S. A., who generously provided an academic license for this project.

References

1. Deliverable d2.4 incompressible flow model for fluid-structure-acoustic coupling. EUNISON FP7 FET project documentation
2. Eunison - extensive unified-domain simulation of the human voice, eu-fet project. http://eunison.eu
3. Bazilevs, Y., Calo, V., Cottrell, J., Hughes, T., Reali, A., Scovazzi, G.: Variational multiscale residual-based turbulence modeling for large eddy simulation of incompressible flows. Comput. Meth. Appl. Mech. Eng. **197**(1), 173–201 (2007)
4. Escobar, M.: Finite element simulation of flow-induced noise using lighthills acoustic analogy. Ph.D. thesis, Universität Erlangen-Nürnberg (2007)
5. Williams, J.E.F., Hawkings, D.: Sound generation by turbulence and surfaces in arbitrary motions. Phil. Trans. Roy. Soc. **A264**, 321–342 (1969)
6. Hansbo, P.: A crank-nicolson type space-time finite element method for computing on moving meshes. J. Comput. Phys. **159**, 274–289 (2000)
7. Hoffman, J., Jansson, J., de Abreu, R.V.: Adaptive modeling of turbulent flow with residual based turbulent kinetic energy dissipation. Comput. Meth. Appl. Mech. Eng. **200**(37–40), 2758–2767 (2011)
8. Hoffman, J., Jansson, J., Jansson, N., De Abreu, R.V.: Towards a parameter-free method for high reynolds number turbulent flow simulation based on adaptive finite element approximation. Comput. Meth. Appl. Mech. Eng. **288**, 60–74 (2015)
9. Hoffman, J., Jansson, J., Stöckli, M.: Unified continuum modeling of fluid-structure interaction. Math. Mod. Meth. Appl. S. **21**(3), 491–513 (2011)
10. Hoffman, J., Johnson, C.: A new approach to computational turbulence modeling. Comput. Meth. Appl. Mech. Eng. **195**(23), 2865–2880 (2006)
11. Hoffman, J., Johnson, C.: Computational Turbulent Incompressible Flow. Applied Mathematics: Body and Soul, vol. 4. Springer, Heidelberg (2007)
12. Jansson, N.: High performance adaptive finite element methods: with applications in aerodynamics. Ph.D. thesis, KTH Royal Institute of Technology (2013)
13. Jansson, N.: Optimizing sparse matrix assembly in finite element solvers with one-sided communication. In: Daydé, M., Marques, O., Nakajima, K. (eds.) VECPAR 2012. LNCS, vol. 7851, pp. 128–139. Springer, Heidelberg (2013). doi:10.1007/978-3-642-38718-0_15
14. Jansson, N., Hoffman, J., Jansson, J.: Framework for massively parallel adaptive finite element computational fluid dynamics on tetrahedral meshes. SIAM J. Sci. Comput. **34**(1), C24–C41 (2012)
15. Labrosse, M.R., Lobo, K., Beller, C.J.: Structural analysis of the natural aortic valve in dynamics: from unpressurized to physiologically loaded. J. Biomech. **43**(10), 1916–1922 (2010)
16. Larsson, D., Spuhler, J.H., Nordenfur, T., Hoffman, J., Colarieti-Tosti, M. Gao, H., Larsson, M.: Patient-specific flow simulation of the left ventricle from 4d echocardiography - feasibility and robustness evaluation. In: 2015 IEEE International Ultrasonics Symposium (2015)
17. Logg, A., Wells, G.N.: DOLFIN: automated finite element computing. ACM Trans. Math. Softw. **37**(2), 1–28 (2010)

18. Spühler, J.H., Jansson, J., Jansson, N., Hoffman, J.: A finite element framework for high performance computer simulation of blood flow in the left ventricle of the human heart. Technical report 34, KTH, Computational Science and Technology (CST) (2015)
19. Thubrikar, M.: The Aortic Valve. CRC Press, Boca Raton (1990)
20. Zawodny, N., Liu, F., Yardibi, T., Cattafesta, L., Khorrami, M., Neuhart, D., Van de Ven, T.: A comparative study of a 1/4-scale gulfstream g550 aircraft nose gear model. In: Proceedings of 15th AIAA/CEAS Aeroacoustics Conference (30th AIAA Aeroacoustics Conference) (2009)

The Direct-Hybrid Method for Computational Aeroacoustics on HPC Systems

Michael Schlottke-Lakemper[1,2]([⊠]), Hans Yu[1,2], Sven Berger[2],
Andreas Lintermann[1,2], Matthias Meinke[2], and Wolfgang Schröder[1,2]

[1] JARA-HPC, RWTH Aachen University,
Kopernikusstraße 6, 52074 Aachen, Germany
[2] Institute of Aerodynamics, RWTH Aachen University,
Wüllnerstraße 5a, 52062 Aachen, Germany
m.schlottke-lakemper@aia.rwth-aachen.de

Abstract. Classic hybrid methods for computational aeroacoustics use different solvers and methods to predict the flow field and the acoustic pressure field in two separate steps, which involves data exchange via disk I/O between the solvers. This limits the efficiency of the approach, as parallel I/O usually does not scale well to large numbers of cores. In this work, a highly scalable direct-hybrid scheme is presented, in which both the flow and the acoustics simulations run simultaneously. That is, all data between the two solvers is transferred in-memory, avoiding the restrictions of the I/O subsystem. Results for the simulation of a pair of co-rotating vortices show that the method is able to correctly predict the acoustic pressure field and that it is suitable for highly parallel simulations.

Keywords: Direct-hybrid method · Computational aeroacoustics · Hierarchical Cartesian grid · In-memory coupling · Parallel efficiency · Discontinuous Galerkin method

1 Introduction

In hybrid computational aeroacoustics (CAA) simulations, the flow solution and the aeroacoustic pressure fields are obtained with two independent methods, which allows the use of optimized algorithms and grids specifically adapted to the respective physical system [9,10,18]. After the flow field is obtained with, e.g., a large-eddy simulation (LES), noise-generating source terms are extracted and used in a second step, where only the propagation of acoustic waves is simulated. As the LES and the CAA simulation are executed consecutively, the relevant source term information needs to be stored persistently on disk between the two steps. Modern supercomputers allow to run simulations on hundreds of thousands of cores with a high efficiency. However, the I/O bandwidth of such systems does not scale in the same manner as the computational power [35] and thus the overall parallel efficiency of the classic hybrid approach is limited by the large volume of data that has to be exchanged.

© Springer International Publishing AG 2017
E. Di Napoli et al. (Eds.): JHPCS 2016, LNCS 10164, pp. 70–81, 2017.
DOI: 10.1007/978-3-319-53862-4_7

The restrictions of the I/O subsystem can be avoided by running both the LES and the CAA simulation concurrently. This way the two solvers can exchange all necessary data directly in memory. The partitioned approach, in which two separate solvers are coupled and executed simultaneously, has already been used successfully, e.g., for the simulation of fluid-structure interaction (FSI) problems [3,8,16,17,36]. However, in this ansatz the differences in grid topology or memory structure between the LES and the CAA solver create an additional overhead and make it difficult to obtain a load-balanced domain decomposition. This problem is further exacerbated by the large amount of source term data that needs to be exchanged in hybrid LES-CAA simulations at each time step, which is significantly increased in comparison to surface-coupled multiphysics problems such as FSI.

To avoid the need to exchange source term data using costly I/O operations or transfers via the Message Passing Interface (MPI), a direct-hybrid method combining large-eddy simulation with computational aeroacoustics for large-scale aeroacoustics simulations has been proposed in [34], which scales efficiently to thousands of cores. In this scheme, both solvers are executed simultaneously on a joint hierarchical Cartesian grid, allowing to exchange all data in memory. A similar strategy for hybrid CAA has been used by Kornhaas et al. [22,23], where the linearized Euler equations are solved on different levels of a hierarchical multigrid solver. However, their approach is limited to uniformly coarsened CAA grids and the same numerical method is employed for the CFD and the CAA simulation. While in [34] intermediate results were shown for the direct-hybrid method that still involved disk I/O, here, the direct-hybrid method is used for the first time to simulate a pair of co-rotating vortices with in-memory data transfers. Furthermore, scaling experiments are conducted to show how the direct-hybrid approach performs in comparison to classic hybrid methods.

The direct-hybrid method is described in Sect. 2. After the governing equations are introduced in Sect. 3, the discretizations schemes for the LES and CAA are described in Sect. 4. In Sect. 5, the direct-hybrid scheme is used for the simulation of a pair of co-rotating vortices and the parallel efficiency of the proposed method is evaluated. Finally, conclusions are drawn in Sect. 6.

2   The Direct-Hybrid Method

In contrast to classic hybrid LES-CAA schemes, in the direct-hybrid method the LES and the CAA simulations run simultaneously and are both performed on a joint hierarchical Cartesian mesh within a single simulation framework [34]. This grid topology simplifies the spatial coupling of the two solvers, since its hierarchical structure allows to efficiently transfer source term information from the LES to the CAA simulation. As both solvers are executed concurrently, data can be exchanged directly in memory.

The cells of the shared Cartesian grid are organized in a so-called octree structure, with parent-child relationships between different levels and neighbor relationships within a level. The grid generation process follows the method described in [27] and starts with a single cubic cell which encloses the whole computational domain. This zero-level cell is then refined uniformly until the desired refinement level is reached. Individual regions of the mesh can be further refined to meet resolution requirements, e.g., in areas with small-scale physical features such as wall-bounded shear layers or to accurately resolve boundaries. The coupling between the flow and the acoustics simulations is performed at each time step. To be aligned in time, the same time step size is used in both solvers. Then, the source term data is transferred from the LES to the acoustic grid. Since both simulations typically operate on different levels of the same grid, identification of corresponding cells is necessary, which is possible by traversing the octree constituting the hierarchical Cartesian mesh. The source term information is then exchanged by interpolating the data from the LES mesh to the CAA mesh. In this paper, however, the area, in which source information is exchanged, is refined to the same level for both solvers. This means that there is a one-to-one mapping between LES and CAA cells, making the interpolation operations trivial.

During grid generation, the zero-level cell is homogeneously refined to a minimum level l_α and all coarser cells or cells outside the computational domain are discarded. These cells at level l_α become the roots of their subtrees (Fig. 1) and are further subdivided until the demanded refinement level is reached. To obtain a load-balanced domain decomposition, a Hilbert space-filling curve [33] is used to map the grid at level l_α to the interval $[0, 1]$, i.e., grid partitioning occurs on a coarser level than computation. Each cell at level l_α is assigned a load that depends on the cumulative computational weight of all cells in its respective subtree. Load balancing is achieved by taking into account these load values when distributing the cells among the processes. For each l_α cell, the entire subtree is placed on the same rank. This means that no additional inter-rank communication for the exchange of data between LES and CAA cells is necessary. All information is available in local memory, even if the cells are at different refinement levels. By consecutively placing l_α cells and their subtrees on the MPI ranks according to their position on the Hilbert curve, spatial locality is ensured, reducing the overall communication cost.

Cells of the subtrees are assigned different computational weights w_{LES} and w_{CAA}, depending on whether they are used by the LES solver, by the CAA solver, or by both. These weights are based on the computational cost per cell and time step and are determined a priori. The weights also need to take into account, e.g., whether acoustic source terms are calculated and the chosen approximation order of the numerical method (see Sect. 4). Figure 1, where a quadtree is used to simplify the representation, shows an example with two subtrees. The left subtree has 9 pure LES cells, 10 pure CAA cells, and 9 cells used for both LES and CAA. Thus, the cumulative load of the entire subtree is $18w_{\text{LES}} + 19w_{\text{CAA}}$. Similarly, the right subtree has a load value of $16w_{\text{LES}} + 16w_{\text{CAA}}$.

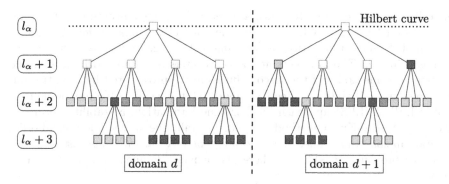

Fig. 1. Domain decomposition of a hybrid quadtree grid with LES cells (●), CAA cells (○), and cells used for both LES and CAA (◉).

3   Governing Equations

Two sets of governing equations are used in hybrid methods for CAA. The first set models the physics of the underlying flow field, while the second set describes only the sound propagation. In this paper, the Navier-Stokes equations are used for the LES, which are given in, e.g., [12,34,37]. For the sound propagation, the acoustic perturbation equations (APE) [5] are solved and are used to predict the acoustic field for flow-induced noise. Derived from the linearized conservation equations, they are modified to retain only acoustic modes without generating vorticity or entropy modes. After neglecting all viscous, non-linear and entropy-related contributions, the APE-4 system can be written as [5]

$$\frac{\partial \boldsymbol{u}'}{\partial t} + \boldsymbol{\nabla}\left(\bar{\boldsymbol{u}} \cdot \boldsymbol{u}'\right) + \boldsymbol{\nabla}\left(\frac{p'}{\bar{\rho}}\right) = \boldsymbol{q}_m, \tag{1}$$

$$\frac{\partial p'}{\partial t} + \bar{c}^2 \boldsymbol{\nabla} \cdot \left(\bar{\rho}\boldsymbol{u}' + \bar{\boldsymbol{u}}\frac{p'}{\bar{c}^2}\right) = 0. \tag{2}$$

The source term $\boldsymbol{q}_m$ is the linearized Lamb vector

$$\boldsymbol{q}_m = -(\boldsymbol{\omega} \times \boldsymbol{u})' \approx -(\boldsymbol{\omega}' \times \bar{\boldsymbol{u}} + \bar{\boldsymbol{\omega}} \times \boldsymbol{u}'), \tag{3}$$

where $\boldsymbol{\omega}$ is the vorticity vector. The unknowns of the APE are perturbed quantities, which are denoted by prime $(\cdot)'$ and are defined by $\phi' := \phi - \bar{\phi}$, where the bar $(\bar{\cdot})$ indicates time-averaged quantities. The source term $\boldsymbol{q}_m$ is calculated using data from the flow simulation, i.e., the perturbed and mean vectors for velocity and vorticity in (3) are based on hydrodynamic quantities.

4   Numerical Methods

For the LES, the unsteady Navier-Stokes equations for compressible flow are discretized by a strictly conservative finite-volume method. State variables on the cell surfaces are computed with a monotonic upstream-centered scheme for conservation laws (MUSCL) [26]. For the convective fluxes, a low-dissipation version of the advection upstream splitting method [28] is used, which was first proposed in [29]. The gradients at the cell centers are obtained by a weighted least-squares method and the viscous fluxes are approximated by a central difference scheme. Turbulence effects are modeled implicitly with a monotone integrated LES (MILES) approach [2]. For time integration, a stability-optimized five-stage Runge-Kutta method is used. Overall, the method is second-order accurate in space and time. It has been extensively validated and used for various flow problems [11–14,37], where also a more detailed description can be found.

To solve the acoustic perturbation equations, a discontinuous Galerkin spectral element method (DGSEM) is used. The DGSEM was proposed by Kopriva et al. [21] and has been used extensively in [6,7,15,34]. It was developed for quadrilateral/hexahedral mesh elements and is thus well-suited for the use on hierarchical Cartesian grids. The scheme yields a semi-discrete formulation for the time derivative of the solution, which is integrated by a five-stage fourth-order Runge-Kutta method [4]. More details on the use of the DGSEM to discretize the APE are given in [34]. To support non-conforming meshes, which for hierarchical Cartesian grids arise from local cell refinement, a mortar element method is employed. Kopriva [19] describes a general framework for the mortar method, which is later extended to discontinuous Galerkin spectral element methods in [20]. It expands the DGSEM formulation to non-conforming meshes by introducing an intermediate interface between non-conforming elements, called mortar, on which conformity is restored.

5   Results

The direct-hybrid method is used to predict the sound generated by a pair of co-rotating vortices in a quiescent medium in 2D. Two point vortices, each with circulation Γ, are separated by a distance of $2r_0$, as illustrated in Fig. 2. According to potential flow theory, the vortices reciprocally induce a tangential velocity of $u_\theta = \Gamma/(4\pi r_0)$, which results in corotation of the vortices with the rotational Mach number $M_r = \Gamma/(4\pi r_0 c_0)$ on a circle with radius r_0. The angular frequency of the spinning vortex configuration is $\omega = \Gamma/(4\pi r_0^2)$, corresponding to a rotation period of $T_r = 8\pi^2 r_0^2/\Gamma$. The initial conditions for the LES solver are based on analytical solutions [25]. To avoid the singularity at the center of the vortices, the vortex-core model proposed by Scully [38] is used. The density is assumed constant and set to the stagnation value $\rho = \rho_0$, while the hydrodynamic pressure is determined by the steady Bernoulli's equation. For the remaining parameters, the same values are used as in [1]: the rotational Mach number is $M_r = \frac{1}{9}$, the core radius is $r_c/r_0 = \frac{2}{9}$, and the Reynolds number $Re = \Gamma/\nu$ is $1.14 \cdot 10^5$. In the CAA solver, all perturbed quantities are initially set to zero. The LES solver uses a computational domain of size $(x/r_0, y/r_0) \in [-60, 60] \times [-60, 60]$. Around the origin, a circular area with

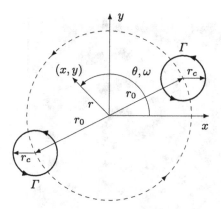

Fig. 2. Flow setup for two co-rotating vortices.

$r/r_0 = 5$ is refined to a cell length of $\Delta/r_0 = 7.32 \cdot 10^{-3}$. The grid resolution is consecutively reduced to $\Delta/r_0 = 5.86 \cdot 10^{-2}$ for $r/r_0 > 20$, resulting in a total of 7.5 million LES cells. In the area of overlap with the LES domain, the CAA solver uses the same resolution as the LES solver. That is, the solvers use the same cells of the shared quadtree representation, which avoids the need to interpolate source term data from one grid to the other. The square CAA domain with a side length of $270r_0$ encloses the LES domain and further reduces the grid resolution to $\Delta/r_0 = 1.17 \cdot 10^{-1}$ for $r/r_0 > 85$, with a total of 13.6 million CAA cells. A polynomial degree of $N = 1$ is used for the discontinuous Galerkin approximation of the acoustic perturbation equations.

Before predicting the acoustic pressure field, mean values for the hydrodynamic velocities and vorticity are determined (see also Sect. 3). They are obtained by a pure LES simulation setup. The acoustic field generated by a pair of co-rotating vortices is that of an acoustic quadrupole [32]. Due to rotation symmetry, the acoustic frequency is twice the rotation frequency of the vortices, resulting in an acoustic period of $T_a c_0/r_0 = 28.3$. Figure 3 shows the acoustic pressure contours for the direct-hybrid simulation at $t = 7T_a$. The double spiral pattern associated with a rotating quadrupole source is clearly recognizable.

In Fig. 4(a), the solution obtained with the direct-hybrid method for the spinning vortex simulation is compared to the reference solution from [25]. The results are normalized by the largest amplitude since the use of the vortex-core model reduces the energy introduced by the source terms into the acoustic system in comparison to the analytical flow field. The results of the direct-hybrid simulation closely match the exact solution, confirming the validity of the overall scheme. Figure 4(b) further shows a strong scaling experiment from 192 to 3,072 cores and one MPI rank per core on the Cray XC 40 system at HLRS Stuttgart. The Cray XC 40 "Hazel Hen" system consists of 7,712 dual-socket nodes, each equipped with two Intel Haswell E5-2680v3 12-core processors at 2.5 GHz and 128 GiB of main memory. In the figure, the parallel efficiency of the direct-hybrid method is compared to a classic hybrid method, where source term data

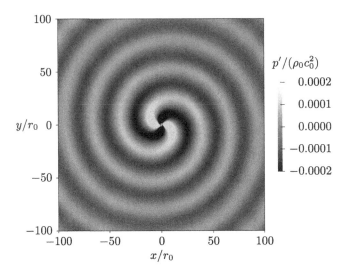

Fig. 3. Pressure contours at $t = 7T_a$.

is exchanged at each time step, i.e., without interpolation in time. The results show that with 75% efficiency on 3,072 cores the direct-hybrid method scales very well, especially given the low number of cells that remain on each core, and that it outperforms the classic hybrid approach, whose scalability is limited by the available parallel I/O bandwidth.

In practice, classic hybrid methods are usually employed in combination with a time interpolation scheme. That is, during the CAA simulation, a source term file is read every n_{CAA} steps and the source term information is interpolated to the intermediate time steps. This approach is motivated by the fact that for explicit time integration schemes, the maximum stable time step size as determined by the grid resolution and the wave propagation speed is typically smaller than what is required to resolve the smallest acoustic wave lengths. Similarly, during the LES simulation, source term data is stored to disk every n_{LES} time steps. Higher values of n decrease the influence of I/O operations on the numerical efficiency and $n \rightarrow \infty$ represents a case without any I/O operations at all. Typical values for n are in the range of 5 to 100, e.g., $n_{LES} = 8$ and $n_{CAA} = 10$ for the CAA analysis of turbulent jets [18] or $n_{LES} = 100$ and $n_{CAA} = 60$ for combustion noise prediction [30]. While the scaling results for the classic hybrid scheme in Fig. 4(b) correspond to $n_{LES} = n_{CAA} = 1$, the influence of higher values of n on the scalability is further analyzed individually for the LES part (Fig. 5(a)) and for the CAA part (Fig. 5(b)). Compared to the LES part of a classic hybrid simulation in Fig. 5(a), the direct-hybrid method scales better up to $n_{LES} \approx 100$. Due to the small size of the scaling problem, the pure flow solution experiences super-scalar speedup due to caching effects, which can be seen for $n_{LES} = \infty$. When looking at the speedup results for the CAA

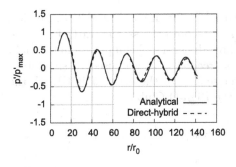

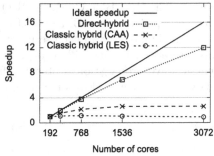

(a) Comparison of pressure signal to analytical solution along $y = -x$ at $t = 7T_a$.

(b) Parallel efficiency compared to a classic hybrid simulation.

Fig. 4. Results obtained by the direct-hybrid method for the spinning vortex simulation.

component in Fig. 5(b), the direct-hybrid method exhibits superior scalability compared to a classic hybrid simulation even beyond $n_{CAA} = 100$. To conclude, the parallel efficiency of the direct-hybrid approach surpasses the classic hybrid method for $n < 100$, which is well within the typical value range for large-scale aeroacoustics simulations.

While the moderate size of the spinning vortex setup restricts the maximum number of cores, which can be used efficiently, to 3,072, other scaling experiments have been conducted with the LES and the CAA solvers individually. In [31], a three-dimensional FV-LES simulation with one billion cells was scaled from 5,472 to 91,872 cores with 86% efficiency. Similarly, two DG-CAA setups with different polynomial degrees $N = 3$ and $N = 7$ were scaled to 93,600 cores with 98% efficiency on the same system and to 458,752 cores with 80% efficiency on the IBM Blue Gene/Q system at Jülich Supercomputing Centre (JSC), respectively

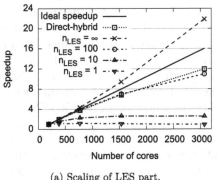

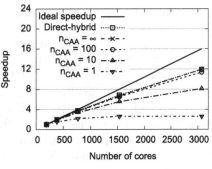

(a) Scaling of LES part.

(b) Scaling of CAA part.

Fig. 5. Parallel efficiency in comparison to classic hybrid scheme with different I/O frequencies.

(Fig. 6). The IBM Blue Gene/Q "JUQUEEN" system consists of 28,672 nodes, each equipped with an IBM PowerPC A2 16-core processor at 1.6 GHz and 16 GiB of main memory. In each setup, a three-dimensional computational domain was discretized by one billion degrees of freedom and was used to simulate a generic wave propagation problem. After scaling to the entire JUQUEEN, the DG-CAA solver was also inducted into the High-Q Club of the JSC[1].

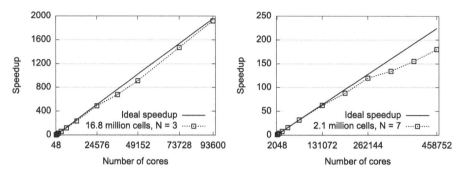

Fig. 6. Strong scaling results for a three-dimensional DG-CAA simulation with one billion degrees of freedom on a Cray XC 40 (left) and an IBM Blue Gene/Q [39] (right).

6   Conclusions

Hybrid LES-CAA methods have been successfully used to predict the acoustic pressure field for a multitude of problems. It was demonstrated that for massively parallel simulations, the data exchange between the LES and the CAA solvers via files becomes a major bottleneck and limits the scalability of the approach. In this paper, a new direct-hybrid method for large-scale aeroacoustics simulations is described. Both the LES and the CAA solvers use the same hierarchical Cartesian grid, simplifying the efficient data exchange between the two methods. A pair of co-rotating vortices is simulated in two dimensions to validate the novel approach. The numerical results for the pressure field are evaluated and closely match the analytical solution. Furthermore, it is shown that the direct-hybrid method scales well from 192 to 3,072 MPI ranks, achieving more than 70% efficiency. Additionally, scaling experiments for the DG-CAA method were conducted and demonstrated good scalability to 93,600 cores and 458,752 cores with 98% and 80% efficiency, respectively.

Overall, the proposed method has shown to be a good candidate for efficient, highly parallel CAA simulations. As a next step, spatial and temporal interpolation schemes need to be examined to lessen the restriction on the resolution requirements in time. In addition, the effects of the interpolation schemes on achieving a load-balanced domain decomposition are to be investigated.

---

[1] http://www.fz-juelich.de/ias/jsc/EN/Expertise/High-Q-Club/ZFS/_node.html.

Acknowledgments. The authors would like to thank Ansgar Niemöller and Vitali Pauz for their helpful contributions. Furthermore, the authors gratefully acknowledge the allocation of supercomputing time as well as the technical support by the High Performance Computing Center Stuttgart (HLRS) of the University of Stuttgart, Germany. They also gratefully acknowledge the computing time granted on the supercomputer JURECA [24] and the Gauss Centre for Supercomputing (GCS) for providing computing time for a GCS Large-Scale Project on the GCS share of the supercomputer JUQUEEN [39] at the Jülich Supercomputing Centre (JSC) of the Forschungszentrum Jülich, Germany.

References

1. Bogey, C., Bailly, C., Juvé, D.: Computation of flow noise using source terms in linearized Euler's equations. AIAA J. **40**(2), 235–243 (2002)
2. Boris, J.P., Grinstein, F.F., Oran, E.S., Kolbe, R.L.: New insights into large eddy simulation. Fluid Dyn. Res. **10**(4–6), 199–228 (1992)
3. Bungartz, H.J., Benk, J., Gatzhammer, B., Mehl, M., Neckel, T.: Partitioned simulation of fluid-structure interaction on cartesian grids. In: Bungartz, H.J., Mehl, M., Schäfer, M. (eds.) Fluid Structure Interaction II. LNCSE, vol. 73, pp. 255–284. Springer Science + Business Media, Heidelberg (2010). doi:10.1007/978-3-642-14206-2_10
4. Carpenter, M.H., Kennedy, C.: Fourth-order 2N-storage Runge-Kutta schemes. NASA Report TM 109112, NASA Langley Research Center (1994)
5. Ewert, R., Schröder, W.: Acoustic perturbation equations based on flow decomposition via source filtering. J. Comput. Phys. **188**, 365–398 (2003)
6. Fechter, S., Munz, C.D.: A discontinuous Galerkin-based sharp-interface method to simulate three-dimensional compressible two-phase flow. Int. J. Numer. Meth. Fluids **78**(7), 413–435 (2015)
7. Flad, D., Frank, H., Beck, A.D., Munz, C.D.: A discontinuous galerkin spectral element method for the direct numerical simulation of aeroacoustics. In: AIAA Paper 2014–2740 (2014)
8. Gatzhammer, B., Mehl, M., Neckel, T.: A coupling environment for partitioned multiphysics simulations applied to fluid-structure interaction scenarios. Procedia Comput. Sci. **1**(1), 681–689 (2010)
9. Geiser, G., Schlimpert, S., Schröder, W.: Thermoacoustical noise induced by laminar flame annihilation at varying flame thicknesses. In: AIAA Paper 2012–2093 (2012)
10. Gröschel, E., Schröder, W., Renze, P., Meinke, M., Comte, P.: Noise prediction for a turbulent jet using different hybrid methods. Comput. Fluids **37**(4), 414–426 (2008)
11. Günther, C., Meinke, M., Schröder, W.: A flexible level-set approach for tracking multiple interacting interfaces in embedded boundary methods. Comput. Fluids **102**, 182–202 (2014)
12. Hartmann, D., Meinke, M., Schröder, W.: An adaptive multilevel multigrid formulation for Cartesian hierarchical grid methods. Comput. Fluids **37**, 1103–1125 (2008)
13. Hartmann, D., Meinke, M., Schröder, W.: Differential equation based constrained reinitialization for level set methods. J. Comput. Phys. **227**(14), 6821–6845 (2008)

14. Hartmann, D., Meinke, M., Schröder, W.: A strictly conservative Cartesian cut-cell method for compressible viscous flows on adaptive grids. Comput. Meth. Appl. Mech. Eng. **200**, 1038–1052 (2011)

15. Hindenlang, F., Gassner, G.J., Altmann, C., Beck, A., Staudenmaier, M., Munz, C.D.: Explicit discontinuous Galerkin methods for unsteady problems. Comput. Fluids **61**, 86–93 (2012)

16. Jaure, S., Duchaine, F., Staffelbach, G., Gicquel, L.Y.M.: Massively parallel conjugate heat transfer methods relying on large eddy simulation applied to an aeronautical combustor. Comput. Sci. Discov. **6**(1) (2013)

17. Joppich, W., Kürschner, M.: MpCCI - a tool for the simulation of coupled applications. Concurr. Comput. **18**(2), 183–192 (2005)

18. Koh, S.R., Schröder, W., Meinke, M.: Turbulence and heat excited noise sources in single and coaxial jets. J. Sound Vibr. **329**, 786–803 (2010)

19. Kopriva, D.A.: A conservative staggered-grid chebyshev multidomain method for compressible flows. II. A semi-structured method. J. Comput. Phys. **128**(2), 475–488 (1996)

20. Kopriva, D.A., Woodruff, S.L., Hussaini, M.: Computation of electromagnetic scattering with a non-conforming discontinuous spectral element method. Int. J. Numer. Meth. Eng. **53**, 105–222 (2002)

21. Kopriva, D., Woodruff, S., Hussaini, M.: Discontinuous spectral element approximation of Maxwell's Equations. In: Cockburn, B., Kariadakis, G., Shu, C.W. (eds.) Proceedings of the International Symposium on Discontinuous Galerkin Methods. LNCSE, vol. 11, pp. 355–361. Springer, Heidelberg (2000). doi:10.1007/978-3-642-59721-3_33

22. Kornhaas, M., Schäfer, M., Sternel, D.C.: Efficient numerical simulation of aeroacoustics for low Mach number flows interacting with structures. Comput. Mech. **55**(6), 1143–1154 (2015)

23. Kornhaas, M., Sternel, D.C., Schäfer, M.: Efficiency investigation of a parallel hierarchical grid based aeroacoustic code for low Mach numbers and complex geometries. In: Pereira, J.C.F., Sequeira, A. (eds.) V European Conference on Computational Fluid Dynamics, ECCOMAS CFD 2010. Lisbon, Portugal (2010)

24. Krause, D., Thörnig, P.: JURECA: general-purpose supercomputer at Jülich supercomputing centre. J. Large Scale Res. Facil. **2** (2016). Article No: A62

25. Lee, D.J., Koo, S.O.: Numerical study of sound generation due to a spinning vortex pair. AIAA J. **33**(1), 20–26 (1995)

26. van Leer, B.: Towards the ultimate conservative difference scheme. V. A second-order sequel to Godunov's method. J. Comput. Phys. **32**(1), 101–136 (1979)

27. Lintermann, A., Schlimpert, S., Grimmen, J.H., Günther, C., Meinke, M., Schröder, W.: Massively parallel grid generation on HPC systems. Comput. Meth. Appl. Mech. Eng. **277**, 131–153 (2014)

28. Liou, M.S., Steffen, C.J.: A new flux splitting scheme. J. Comput. Phys. **107**(1), 23–39 (1993)

29. Meinke, M., Schröder, W., Krause, E., Rister, T.: A comparison of second- and sixth-order methods for large-eddy simulations. Comput. Fluids **31**, 695–718 (2002)

30. Pausch, K., Schlimpert, S., Koh, S.R., Grimmen, J.H., Schröder, W.: The effect of flame thickening on the acoustic emission in turbulent combustion. In: AIAA Paper 2016–2745 (2016)

31. Pogorelov, A., Meinke, M., Schröder, W.: Cut-cell method based large-eddy simulation of tip-leakage flow. Phys. Fluids **27**(7), 075–106 (2015)

32. Powell, A.: Theory of vortex sound. J. Acoust. Soc. Am. **36**(1), 177 (1964)

33. Sagan, H.: Space-Filling Curves, 1st edn. Universitext - Springer, New York (1994)
34. Schlottke, M., Cheng, H.J., Lintermann, A., Meinke, M., Schröder, W.: A direct-hybrid method for computational aeroacoustics. In: AIAA Paper 2015–3133 (2015)
35. Schlottke-Lakemper, M., Klemp, F., Cheng, H.-J., Lintermann, A., Meinke, M., Schröder, W.: CFD/CAA simulations on HPC systems. In: Resch, M.M., Bez, W., Focht, E., Patel, N., Kobayashi, H. (eds.) Sustained Simulation Performance 2016, pp. 139–157. Springer, Cham (2016). doi:10.1007/978-3-319-46735-1_12
36. Schlüter, J., Wu, X., van der Weide, E., Hahn, S., Alonso, J., Pitsch, H.: Multi-code simulations: a generalized coupling approach. In: AIAA Paper 2005–4997 (2005)
37. Schneiders, L., Hartmann, D., Meinke, M., Schröder, W.: An accurate moving boundary formulation in cut-cell methods. J. Comput. Phys. **235**, 786–809 (2013)
38. Scully, M.: Computation of helicopter rotor wake geometry and its influence on rotor harmonic airloads. Technical report ARSL TR 178–1, Massachusetts Institute of Technology, Cambridge, MA (1975)
39. Stephan, M., Docter, J.: JUQUEEN: IBM Blue Gene/Q supercomputer system at the Jülich supercomputing centre. J. Large Scale Res. Facil. **1** (2015). Article No: A1

A Novel Approach for Efficient Storage and Retrieval of Tabulated Chemistry in Reactive Flow Simulations

Sebastian Popp[✉], Steffen Weise, and Christian Hasse

Numerical Thermo-Fluid Dynamics, TU Bergakademie Freiberg, Freiberg, Germany
sebastian.popp@iec.tu-freiberg.de

Abstract. Turbulent combustion is a typical example of a multi-scale problem, coupling different ranges of time and length scales of the flow field and the chemical reactions. Due to scale separation and the availability of suitable coupling procedures, tabulated chemistry approaches have emerged as an effective method for describing turbulence-chemistry interaction (TCI). However, different flame configurations, complex fuels and multiphase flows, among other things, increase both the number of tabulated variables and the dimension of the database, and thus the overall size. With larger database sizes, the requirements for computing time and memory management have become a crucial issue for CFD applications. In the present study, the novel flatkernel approach for efficient memory management at reduced computational cost is developed. This new software-library-based approach uses polynomial fitting to represent the database. The resulting functions are generated as source code and compiled in a shared library, taking advantage of automatic compiler optimization. Since the shared library is also memory managed by the operating system, the flatkernel approach leads to reduced memory and computing time requirements in the coupled CFD application. The approach developed is applied for scale-resolving Large Eddy Simulations (LES), coupled with the flamelet-progress variable approach (LES-FPV) for combustion modeling of a reactive jet in a cross flow configuration. The evaluation of the simulations is focused on a comparison between the novel method and an existing approach, with respect to memory and computing time requirements.

Keywords: Memory management · Tabulated chemistry · Flamelet · CFD · Polynomial

1 Introduction

Reactive flow simulations of practically relevant systems are a classical multi-scale problem in the field of Computational Fluid Dynamics (CFD). Since turbulence plays a significant role in these flow configurations, the coupling to molecular mixing and chemical reactions has to be accounted for. In principle, Direct Numerical Simulations (DNS) could be used to resolve the whole range of

© Springer International Publishing AG 2017
E. Di Napoli et al. (Eds.): JHPCS 2016, LNCS 10164, pp. 82–95, 2017.
DOI: 10.1007/978-3-319-53862-4_8

time and length scales. However, this is computationally expensive when using detailed reaction mechanisms, since a partial differential equation (PDE) has to be solved for each species involved and the number of species increases strongly along with the fuel complexity. Thus, instead of fully resolving the flow and mixing field, scale-resolving Large Eddy Simulations (LES) have become the de-facto standard for academic research. Furthermore, Reynolds-Averaged Navier-Stokes (RANS) approaches are still widely used in applied and industrial research. Both approaches require a suitable model for turbulence-chemistry interaction (TCI), since the chemistry is strongly coupled to molecular mixing, which is not or not fully resolved in RANS and LES, respectively.

The most prominent regime in combustion is the flamelet regime, where the chemistry is fast and reactions take place in thin layers. Many technical applications such as engines and gas turbines fall into this regime. Thus, a number of flamelet-based tabulation strategies such as flamelet-progress variable (FPV), flamelet-generated manifolds (FGM) and flame prolongation of ILDM (FPI) have been developed and applied [1,5,10]. A recent overview of flamelet-based methods (among others) is given in [2].

These tabulated chemistry approaches are efficient methods which allow for the application of detailed reaction mechanisms at reduced computational cost in combustion simulations. Using tabulated chemistry basically means that instead of computing the thermo-chemical state φ based on the full set of reactive PDEs, φ is retrieved from a database, in the following referred to as flamelet look-up table (FLUT), using suitable quantities for parametrization (ψ). For turbulent combustion, these parameters are at least the mixture fraction Z, describing the local mixture of fuel and oxidizer and the progress variable Y_C, characterizing the conversion from fresh to burnt gases, i.e. the reaction progress. Thus, the thermo-chemical state can be parameterized as $\varphi = \varphi_{\text{FLUT}}(Z, Y_C)$. Based on the particular application the FLUT is built using different canonical one-dimensional flame calculations. An overview of applied database generation strategies for premixed, non-premixed and multi-regime combustion is given in [2]. Additionally, existing approaches for the coupling of LES and tabulated chemistry are described in the aforementioned publication.

In the present study the LES-FPV approach [9] is used and the corresponding coupling procedure between tabulated chemistry and the CFD solver is shown in Fig. 1. Based on the solution of one-dimensional flame configurations, the FLUT is generated using the flamelet look-up table generator (FLUG) and parameterized by a suitable number of quantities ψ. During the coupled CFD calculation, the set of quantities ψ is directly computed, for instance using transport or algebraic equations. The FLUT access is handled by a generic interface, called flameletConfig [11], using an n-dimensional interpolation scheme to retrieve the corresponding solutions from the FLUT.

Depending on the number of quantities used for parametrization and the number of stored solutions, the size of a FLUT can range from several hundred MB to several GB. This can exceed the available RAM in parallel simulations, taking into account the memory requirements of the CFD solver and the

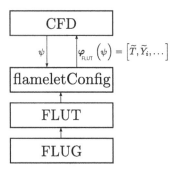

Fig. 1. Retrieving pre-tabulated solutions (φ) during a CFD simulation, using the FPV approach. The FLUT generation is done using the Flamelet Look-up Table Generator (FLUG), while the look-up and interpolation procedure is handled by a generic interface called "flameletConfig" [11].

operating system, since each process requires its own copy of the FLUT in the RAM. Thus, an efficient memory management is crucial for HPC applications. Recently, this issue has been addressed in the review papers by Fiorina et al. [2] and van Oijen et al. [8], emphasizing the need for efficient memory handling. In previous studies, the authors proposed such methods for combustion modeling based on tabulated chemistry. A Memory Abstraction Layer (MAL) has been developed that handles requested FLUT entries efficiently by splitting the database file into several smaller blocks [12]. It keeps the total memory usage at a minimum by using thin allocation methods and compression to minimize file system operations. This method has also been extended to share memory between parallel simulation processes (PMAL). In a more recent investigation a Memory Map (MMAP) technique was applied for reactive flow simulations [11]. The contents of a FLUT are loaded into the virtual address space (VAS) of each parallel process using a function provided by the operating system, which also manages the memory. This mapped memory can be accessed efficiently by multiple processes. The functionality of the MMAP is identical to the PMAL implementation. Applying both approaches in turbulent and laminar flames revealed similar memory requirements, with PMAL allowing for fine grained adaptation to the underlying binary database. However, a significant speedup of the database look-up could be observed with MMAP.

While the previously mentioned methods are based on n-dimensional interpolation to access requested FLUT entries, this study presents a novel approach for efficient memory management at reduced computational cost. Section 2 summarizes the flatkernel approach and in Sect. 3 it is applied to a practically relevant benchmark case for hydrogen combustion in gas turbines, using scale-resolving LES. Additionally, the new approach is compared to the previous memory management implementations.

2   Flatkernel Approach

The previously employed data access scheme for the aforementioned MAL and MMAP approach is an n-dimensional multi-component recursive interpolation. Therefore, the database contains all data and locality information, while the algorithm, which is built into the software, does not contain any data. While this method is numerically stable, it requires a large amount of data to be transferred. The n-dimensional database is linearized in memory to allow for an efficient description, which is a common method when dealing with multi-dimensional data. However, this reduces the efficiency of the algorithm, since the data is not optimally aligned in memory. The importance of both issues increases when the database has a high dimensionality.

The flatkernel approach aims to minimize data movement by reducing the amount of data that has to be transferred and by optimizing the way that the required data is placed in memory. The approach makes use of the imbalance between the computational speed of a CPU and the bandwidth of the memory system, by favoring computation over memory transfer. The data information is moved into the algorithm by generating a set of polynomial functions that contain every information required to execute the algorithm. These functions are then generated in source code, so that they can be optimized in terms of execution speed by the compiler. They are stored in a shared library which is automatically memory managed by the operating system. The locality information, that describes which function is to be executed, is stored in a reduced database.

2.1   Flatkernel Generation

The flatkernel generation is based on a FLUT database, storing the data of the thermo-chemical state on an n-dimensional orthogonal grid. The dimensionality of this grid is based on the number parameters ψ and the resolution of the grid depends on the number of points used for discretization of each parameter. During the flatkernel generation an interval grid is constructed, creating central points from the original FLUT grid, as shown for a one-dimensional example in Fig. 2. Every component field, such as the temperature, of a FLUT database is then fitted using a polynomial expression as illustrated in Fig. 2. Each fit is evaluated using a blend of absolute and relative tolerances. This error criterion is given in Eq. 1, where φ_i' is the original value of a FLUT component i and φ_i is the value from the polynomial evaluation. Thus, the accuracy of the flatkernel method, compared to the original FLUT, depends on the fitting tolerances.

$$|\varphi_i - \varphi_i'| \leq absTol + relTol \cdot |\varphi_i'| \tag{1}$$

The fitted function is only valid for a certain region described by a point-set on the overall interval grid. Ideally this region is as large as possible, to reduce the number of functions that have to be generated and compiled later on. A region is grown incrementally in every dimension as long as the error criterion is met.

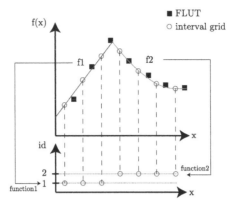

Fig. 2. FLUT points are fitted to polynomial expressions, which are valid on a range described by the associated point-sets.

The combination of a function and point-set is called a kernel. The locality information, which contains the function number that has to be evaluated when accessing a given part of the database, is stored on the interval grid. Switching to an interval grid reduces the addressing effort in the flatkernel approach to a nearest-neighbor algorithm. Addressing is reduced by transferring only one data point from the binary database, while regular interpolation requires 2^d data points (d - number of dimensions) to be transferred. An example of this type of locality information is shown for the temperature component in Fig. 3, based on a FLUT parameterized by the mixture fraction (Z) and the normalized progress variable (C). Every block represents a region on the interval grid where one function is valid, described by the corresponding function number. The dimensions of the interval grid are based on the discretization of the FLUT.

After the fitting procedure, kernels for all individual components are merged into larger sum-kernels, which contain the functions to calculate all components in one function call. They are valid on a sum-kernel point-set constructed from

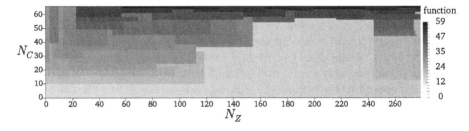

Fig. 3. Example of the locality information for the temperature. Domain dimensions (N number of points) are defined by the discretization of the FLUT, parametrized by Z and C. Each block represents a region on the interval grid where one function is valid.

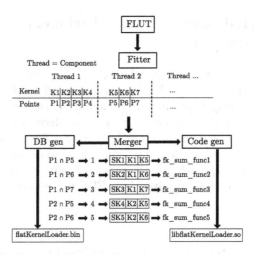

Fig. 4. Flatkernel process: after fitting, each kernel is valid for a certain set of points (P1, P2, etc.) but only for one component, i.e. one quantity of the thermo-chemical state φ. These kernels (K1, K2, etc.) for individual components are then merged into sum-kernels (SK1, SK2, etc.), which are valid for the whole thermo-chemical state. These sum-kernels are compiled in a shared library "libflatKernelLoader.so". The associated locality information is stored in the "flatKernelLoader.bin".

the locality information of each component. This merging process takes all combinations of component function numbers and generates new unique sum-function numbers. These sum-function numbers are stored in the database "flatKernel-Loader.bin" to be used as the locality information. The process of building the point-sets and the sum-kernels is illustrated in Fig. 4. Sum-functions are then generated as source code and compiled into a shared library called "libflatKer-nelLoader.so". The source code is structured to allow for automatic compiler optimization resulting in generated binary code that uses vector extensions (AVX) and Fused Multiply Add (FMA). The efficiency of the flatkernel generation process and thus the amount of generated sum-functions depends on the original structure of the FLUT data, including both the number and the individual profiles of the components.

2.2 Flatkernel Access

A request is made by passing the look-up coordinates ψ to the handling library. The "flatKernelLoader.bin" is opened and the appropriate sum-function number is retrieved. The corresponding sum-function from "libflatKernelLoader.so" is now called with the original request coordinates. All polynomial expressions which calculate all individual components are evaluated and the results are written to a pointer location which is provided by the calling application.

3 Reactive Hydrogen Jet in a Turbulent Vitiated Cross Flow

In this section, the proposed flatkernel method is applied to a jet in a cross flow (JICF) configuration for turbulent non-premixed combustion. The JICF configuration is primarily found in combustion systems, where rapid mixing is required, e.g. aircraft and stationary gas turbines. Recently, this fuel injection method has started to be used in micro gas turbines for hydrogen combustion [4]. In the following, the case is described and a detailed comparison and analysis of the novel flatkernel approach and the previously developed MMAP approach is performed, based on highly resolved LES-FPV computations of the JICF.

3.1 Case Description

The setup of the investigated JICF is mainly based on the configuration proposed in [6], with minor changes concerning the cross flow composition. Since dimensionless quantities, e.g. the momentum ratio and Reynolds numbers of the jet and cross flow, are kept identical for direct comparability, the boundary conditions differ slightly from [6]. An overview of the jet and cross flow properties are shown in Table 1. The setup of the case is shown in Fig. 5. A transverse laminar hydrogen/helium jet, with a jet diameter $d_{jet} = 1.37$ mm, enters the computational domain and develops typical vortical structures due to the interaction with a turbulent cross flow. The turbulent cross flow (Re = 9480) consists of hot reaction products from a lean hydrogen/air flame, with an equivalence ratio of $\phi = 0.45$. The overall computational domain is 35 mm × 35 mm × 30 mm in streamwise, transverse and spanwise directions, respectively. To generate the turbulent inflow boundary conditions of the cross flow, an incompressible channel flow LES is performed. Instantaneous velocity distributions are stored for each time step and provided as instationary boundary conditions in the reactive JICF simulations, using the same constant time step for both LES. This approach was previously used to generate boundary data for turbulent jet flames [3, 10].

As mentioned before, an LES-FPV approach is used for combustion modeling. Therefore, the flow field is described by the Favre-filtered Navier-Stokes equations. The sub-filter turbulence is modeled by applying the eddy viscosity hypothesis, and the eddy viscosity μ_t is evaluated using the Sigma model [7].

Table 1. Properties of the jet and cross flow with the corresponding dimensionless quantities: Reynolds number (Re), momentum ratio (J) and density ratio (S).

	Composition (X_i)	T [K]	u_{bulk} [m/s]	Re	J	S
Jet	70% H_2 30% He	400	345	2420	9	0.37
Cross flow	Products of an H_2/air flame ($\phi = 0.45$)	1519	70	9480		

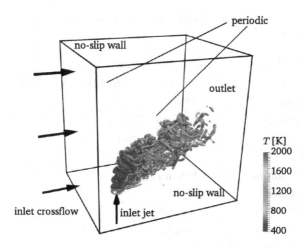

Fig. 5. Setup of the JICF computations, with an iso-surface of the Q-criterion for vortex visualization. The domain size shown here is reduced to allow for an improved view of the jet region.

For combustion modeling, additional transport equations are solved for the Favre-filtered mixture fraction ($\widetilde{Z}$) and Favre-filtered progress variable ($\widetilde{Y}_C$). To account for the unresolved turbulence chemistry interaction, the sub-filter distribution of the mixture fraction is described by a presumed β-shaped filtered density function (FDF) depending on the mixture fraction. Through this procedure the dimensionality of the FLUT is increased by one additional parameter, the sub-filter mixture fraction variance ($\widetilde{Z''^2}$). Within the applied LES-FPV approach, the Favre-filtered mixture fraction variance is computed using an algebraic equation, based on scale similarity [9]. To consider the effects of differential diffusion on hydrogen combustion, the mixture-averaged approach is used for diffusion modeling during the FLUT and flatkernel generation, respectively. The final FLUT for the LES-FPV computations is parameterized by the Favre-filtered quantities mixture fraction ($\widetilde{Z}$), normalized progress variable[1] ($\widetilde{C}$) and mixture fraction variance ($\widetilde{Z''^2}$) with a discretization of 281, 68 and 21 points, respectively. For this analysis, the minimum number of 10 required solution quantities for an LES-FPV calculation are tabulated, including the temperature, enthalpy, thermodynamic and transport properties such as density, specific heat capacity, viscosity and thermal diffusivity, as well as quantities for the transport equation of the progress variable, e.g. the source term and the Lewis number of the progress variable. The flatkernel constructed from the FLUT, applying the absolute and relative tolerances with $absRel = 1 \cdot 10^{-6}$ and $relTol = 1 \cdot 10^{-3}$, includes 374,636 sum-kernels representing all the tabulated quantities.

---

[1] $\widetilde{C} = \dfrac{\widetilde{Y}_C - \widetilde{Y}_{C,\min}}{\widetilde{Y}_{C,\max} - \widetilde{Y}_{C,\min}}$, while the minimum and maximum values of the progress variable are also tabulated.

Table 2. Hardware and software specification of a cluster node used for the LES-FPV computations of the JICF.

Hardware	
CPU	2x Xeon E5-2680v2 (Ivy Bridge-EP)
RAM	128 GB
Interconnect	Infiniband FDR 4x
Interconnect	Gigabit ethernet
Software	
Operating system	Debian 7.0
Kernel	3.2.0
MPI	OpenMPI 1.8.7
Compiler	gcc-4.7.2
OpenFOAM®	2.1.x

For the following analyses, simulations of the JICF are conducted for two different mesh resolutions, 2.2 million cells and 25.2 million cells, respectively. Therefore, a coupled LES-FPV solver based on OpenFOAM® 2.1 is used, applying second-order discretization in time and space. The simulations were run on identical cluster nodes, described in Table 2, using 2 nodes (40 cores) for the case with 2.2 million cells and 6 nodes (120 cores) for the simulations with 25.2 million cells.

3.2 Results and Discussion

In the following, the results are presented from the LES-FPV computations applying the novel flatkernel approach and the interpolation-based approaches with and without memory management [11]. At first, the memory and compute time requirements of both approaches are investigated. Finally, the physical solutions of both applied look-up strategies are compared.

Memory Profiling. For the memory profiling the kernel memory mapping information provided by the operating system (`/proc/<pid>/smaps`) is evaluated. Figure 6(a) shows the memory usage for three simulations on the 25.2 million cell mesh, using the interpolation-based look-up strategy with memory management (MMAP) and without it (NOMM) and the flatkernel method (FK). For every process in the parallel CFD application, one instance of the FLUT has to be loaded if no memory management technique is applied, see detailed discussion in [11]. This results in high memory usage for the NOMM case, which is used as a reference of 100%. Applying the MMAP approach, the memory requirements are significantly reduced to only 2% of the previously required memory. Also the novel flatkernel method reduces the required memory to 16%. Although this reduction is not as efficient as the MMAP method, it is a significant improvement compared to no memory management. Basically, the achievable memory reduction of the flatkernel method depends on the number of functions generated during the fitting and merging process. A reduced number of sum-functions would result in reduced memory usage and thus the memory reduction depends on the particular problem and is related to the data of the underlying FLUT.

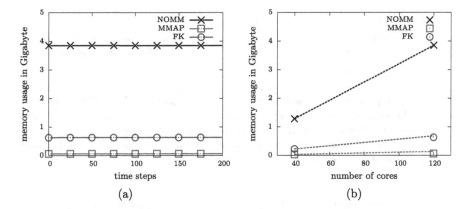

Fig. 6. (a) Comparison of memory usage for the simulations with 25.2 million cells using the interpolation-based approach with memory management (MMAP) and without it (NOMM) and the flatkernel method (FK). (b) Memory scaling from the computations using the 2.2 million cell mesh to the 25.2 million cell mesh. The dashed lines represent linear scaling behavior.

In Fig. 6(b) the averaged memory usage is shown with respect to the cores used for the simulations on the coarse and refined computational grids. In the case of no memory management (NOMM), the memory consumption scales linearly with the number of used cores, since one instance of the FLUT is loaded per core. For the flatkernel and MMAP methods, the memory used remains under the line of linear scaling, indicating a good scalability of the proposed method for highly parallel simulations.

Timing Analysis. Another aspect of the different look-up strategies, is the required access time to retrieve the data from the FLUT and flatkernel, respectively. The specific time consumption, for every single process, is evaluated by using a standard system time (`gettimeofday()`). The measured time includes the required time for the processes to get the parameters for each cell, perform the interpolation (NOMM,MMAP) or evaluate the sum-kernel (FK), and update the cell values for each solution. Figure 7(a) shows the required access time of the simulations with 25.2 million cells for the three previously investigated methods. For both interpolation-based methods, with and without memory management, the timing is almost identical. Instead, when the flatkernel method is applied,

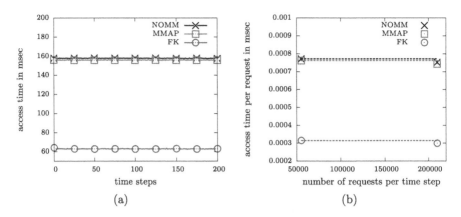

Fig. 7. (a) Comparison of access time for the simulations with 25.2 million cells using the interpolation-based approach with memory management (MMAP) and without it (NOMM) and the flatkernel method (FK). (b) Access time scaling from the computations using the 2.2 million cell mesh to the 25.2 million cell mesh. The dashed lines represent linear scaling behavior.

the access time is reduced by a factor of 2.5. The scaling of the averaged access time per request is shown in Fig. 7(b) with respect to the number of requests per time step, for the simulations on the coarse and fine mesh. Due to the number of used compute nodes, the number of requests per time step increases from simulations on the coarse grid to the simulations on the refined grid. However, the access time per request remains almost constant, again indicating the good scalability of the flatkernel method.

Physical Solutions of the JICF Computations. Finally, the physical solutions of the interpolation-based approach and the flatkernel method are compared. Figure 8 shows instantaneous solutions of the temperature field from simulations of the refined mesh (25.2 million cells) applying the flatkernel (a) and MMAP (b) methods. A qualitative comparison of the two temperature distributions shows no differences between the results from the two look-up strategies.

For a more detailed comparison, temperature and mixture fraction profiles are evaluated on two lines, one near the jet inlet (I) and the other further downstream (II). These profiles are shown in Fig. 9 for both locations. While the solution for the temperature is directly retrieved from the look-up, the mixture fraction is computed during the LES-FPV computations, using a transport equation but still depends on tabulated properties, e.g. the density. The flatkernel method and the FLUT interpolation yield nearly identical profiles for the temperature and the mixture fraction at both locations. Minor differences in the temperature could be observed at the windward side of the jet in Fig. 9(a). Furthermore, the mixture fraction profile at the leeward side of the jet is slightly shifted in the downstream direction. These minor differences occur, since the flatkernel method is not completely lossless. During the flatkernel generation,

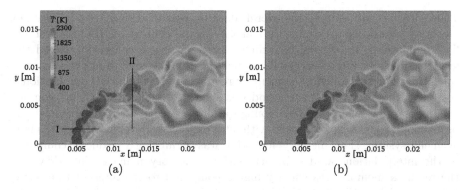

Fig. 8. Instantaneous temperature distribution on plane through the center of the jet in downstream direction, from simulations using the flatkernel method (a) and the interpolation-based approach with MMAP (b).

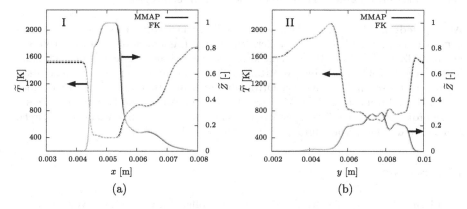

Fig. 9. Temperature and mixture fraction profiles near the jet inlet (a) and further downstream (b) from the simulations using the flatkernel method and the interpolation-based approach with MMAP.

distinct fitting tolerances are applied for the fitting procedure of each component of the FLUT. However, the overall agreement between the physical solutions from the flatkernel method and from the FLUT look-up is very good.

4   Summary

The present study introduced a novel approach for data storage and retrieval in large chemistry databases, applied in reactive flow simulations. Compared to previously applied interpolation-based look-up strategies using n-dimensional interpolation schemes, the interpolation was substituted by an efficient function-based approach. The novel flatkernel approach combines the data and algorithm by representing the discrete database using set polynomial expressions, which are generated in source code and evaluated during the coupled CFD simulation.

Thus, this method reduces the overall data movement during the look-up and favors computations over memory transfer. In the context of HPC for reactive flow simulations, the size of high-dimensional databases can easily exceed the available memory per core. The flatkernel approach provides a method to overcome this issue by reducing the memory requirements at reduced computational cost. The application of this method was shown for coupled LES-FPV computations of a jet in a cross flow configuration and compared to interpolation-based look-up strategies with and without a previously developed memory management system. The memory footprint was significantly reduced compared to the interpolation-based approach without memory management. However, the required memory was slightly higher compared to the interpolation-based method, which applies the MMAP approach for the memory management. Nevertheless, the access time to retrieve the data was significantly reduced by applying the flatkernel method. Finally, a comparison of the physical solutions showed very good overall agreement between the look-up strategies.

Acknowledgments. Financial support is kindly acknowledged from the Federal Ministry of Education and Research of Germany in the framework of Virtuhcon (project number 03Z2FN11), from the Federal Ministry of Food and Agriculture of Germany in the project "BiOtto - Bildung von Rußpartikeln und katalytische Filterregeneration bei der motorischen Nutzung von Ottokraftstoffen aus Biomasse" (project number 22041111) and from the Federal Ministry of Economic Affairs and Energy of Germany in the project "Wasserstoffkleingasturbine als neuartiges Antriebskonzept: Numerische Simulation der der Verbrennung" (project number 03ET7026B).

References

1. Fiorina, B., Vicquelin, R., Auzillon, P., Darabiha, N., Gicquel, O., Veynante, D.: A filtered tabulated chemistry model for LES of premixed combustion. Combust. Flame **157**(3), 465–475 (2010)
2. Fiorina, B., Veynante, D., Candel, S.: Modeling combustion chemistry in large eddy simulation of turbulent flames. Flow Turbul. Combust. **94**(1), 3–42 (2015)
3. Hunger, F., Zulkifli, M.F., Williams, B.A.O., Beyrau, F., Hasse, C.: A combined experimental and numerical study of laminar and turbulent non-piloted oxy-fuel jet flames using a direct comparison of the rayleigh signal. Flow Turbul. Combust. **97**, 231–262 (2016)
4. Jeschke, P., Penkner, A.: A novel gas generator concept for jet engines using a rotating combustion chamber. ASME J. Turbomach. **137**(7), 071010-1–071010-8 (2015)
5. Kuenne, G., Ketelheun, A., Janicka, J.: LES modeling of premixed combustion using a thickened flame approach coupled with FGM tabulated chemistry. Combust. Flame **158**(9), 1750–1767 (2011)
6. Lyra, S., Wilde, B., Kolla, H., Seitzman, J.M., Lieuwen, T.C., Chen, J.H.: Structure of hydrogen-rich transverse jets in a vitiated turbulent flow. Combust. Flame **162**(4), 1234–1248 (2015)
7. Nicoud, F., Toda, H.B., Cabrit, O., Bose, S., Lee, J.: Using singular values to build a subgrid-scale model for large eddy simulations. Phys. Fluids **23**(8), 085106 (2011)

8. van Oijen, J., Donini, A., Bastiaans, R., ten Thije Boonkkamp, J., de Goey, L.: State-of-the-art in premixed combustion modeling using flamelet generated manifolds. Prog. Energy Combust. Sci. **57**, 30–74 (2016)
9. Pierce, C.D., Moin, P.: Progress-variable approach for large-eddy simulation of non-premixed turbulent combustion. J. Fluid Mech. **504**, 73–97 (2004)
10. Popp, S., Hunger, F., Hartl, S., Messig, D., Coriton, B., Frank, J.H., Fuest, F., Hasse, C.: LES flamelet-progress variable modeling and measurements of a turbulent partially-premixed dimethyl ether jet flame. Combust. Flame **162**(8), 3016–3029 (2015)
11. Weise, S., Hasse, C.: Reducing the memory footprint in large eddy simulations of reactive flows. Parallel Comput. **49**, 50–65 (2015)
12. Weise, S., Messig, D., Meyer, B., Hasse, C.: An abstraction layer for efficient memory management of tabulated chemistry and flamelet solutions. Combust. Theory Model. **17**(3), 411–430 (2013)

Multi-scale Coupling for Predictive Injector Simulations

Mathis Bode$^{(\boxtimes)}$, Marco Davidovic, and Heinz Pitsch

Institute for Combustion Technology, RWTH Aachen University,
Templergraben 64, 52062 Aachen, Germany
m.bode@itv.rwth-aachen.de

Abstract. Predictive simulations of full fuel injection systems for e.g. diesel engines could be very important for reducing emissions of current engines but are still rare. Beside the numerical issues arising from discontinuities across the liquid-gas-interface, different scales relevant for the nozzle internal flow, primary breakup in the vicinity of the nozzle, and secondary breakup and evaporation further downstream make efficient simulation of the full injection system challenging. This paper introduces a multi-scale coupling approach for overcoming this issue leading to efficient and predictive injector simulations. After a brief description of the numerical methods used in this study, the coupling among nozzle internal flow, primary breakup, and secondary breakup with evaporation is introduced and analyzed with respect to computing efficiency and physical accuracy. Finally, the simulation framework is applied to the "Spray A" case of the Engine Combustion Network.

Keywords: Large-Eddy Simulation · Direct Numerical Simulation · Multi-scale coupling · High-Performance Computing · Multiphase flows

1 Introduction

Conventional internal combustion engines burning non-renewable fossil fuels in liquid form provide a large fraction of today's transportation energy. Since alternative technologies such as electric mobility are not able to substitute conventional engine technology within the next decades, conventional engines need to be improved in order to deal with stricter emission regulations and the finiteness of fossil fuels. Especially in diesel engines, the combustion and consequently the pollutant formation is highly influenced by the fuel injection typically composed of nozzle internal flow, primary breakup in the vicinity of the nozzle orifice, secondary breakup further downstream, and evaporation. However, details of the fuel injection process are still not completely understood due to its complexity and the difficulties of performing experiments characterizing the atomization process outside of the nozzle [1].

The performance of a particular injector design depends on a cascade of physical processes, originating from the nozzle internal flow driven by the injector

© Springer International Publishing AG 2017
E. Di Napoli et al. (Eds.): JHPCS 2016, LNCS 10164, pp. 96–108, 2017.
DOI: 10.1007/978-3-319-53862-4_9

geometry and operating conditions, potential cavitation, turbulence, and the mixing of the coherent liquid stream with the gaseous ambient environment during the atomization process outside of the injector orifice [2]. The transfer occurring between liquid and gas has to be governed by an interface topology [4]. It is well known that the primary breakup, the first phase of the atomization process, is especially critical for the overall diesel engine performance in terms of emission and pollutant formation [3]. In this regard, the objective of an injector design could be to maximize the interface surface density in order to ensure homogeneous mixing, small droplets, and fast evaporation within the engine. However, how design parameters influence surface density and ultimately drop size distribution is not clear, and predictive models do not exist.

The importance of this topic is emphasized by the work of the Engine Combustion Network (ECN) [5], which is an open forum for international collaboration among experimental and computational researchers in engine combustion and was founded in 2011. The first target case specified by the ECN was the "Spray A" case, which corresponds to the conditions in a single hole diesel injector. Although the ECN has made significant progress on the experimental side, highly-resolved full simulations of the nozzle internal flow and the atomization process are still rare and often lack either sufficient temporal or spatial resolution. Beside the numerical problems of such simulations descending from the discontinuities at the interface, the large range of scales within a simulation is a major issue avoiding the realization of simulations governing both nozzle internal flow and atomization process on currently available High-Performance Computing (HPC) systems.

The typical way to deal with the computational limitations is to focus only on the secondary breakup assuming already formed droplets as result of the primary breakup process. This approach neglects the impact of the injector geometry and instead tunes the breakup model parameters in a way that simulation results match the experimental data. Since, moreover, the cone angle must be known from measurements and the initial droplet size distribution has to be guessed empirically, this approach is not predictive and therefore only useful to a limited extent for fundamental spray research.

This article presents an alternative approach of simulating complete injectors by coupling three different simulation types addressing different scales: Simultaneously, a Large-Eddy Simulation (LES) of the nozzle internal flow and a Direct Numerical Simulation (DNS) of the primary breakup are performed and coupled for studying the processes inside and close to the nozzle. Droplet information in the vicinity of the nozzle is collected and used for initializing a Lagrange-Particle based LES of the secondary breakup with evaporation. This results in a complete and consistent data set for the full injector. Corresponding challenges with respect to the coupling and the simultaneous execution of the simulations on HPC systems will be discussed and the simulation framework with respect to experimental results of the "Spray A" case validated. Load-balancing issues occurring from the underlying numerical methods such as the level set approach are not in the scope of this paper and will not be discussed.

The remainder of this article is organized as follows. The general numerical methods and models employed with respect to injector simulations in the utilized code framework are described in the next section. Then, the application setup and coupling approach are presented and analyzed with respect to computational efficiency and physical accuracy. Afterwards, the introduced approach is applied to the "Spray A" case and results are discussed. The paper finishes with conclusions.

2   Numerical Framework

The low-Mach flow solver arts of the in-house code framework CIAO was used for all simulations within this work. Arts solves the Navier-Stokes equations in the low-Mach limit along with multi-physics effects and employs a Crank-Nicolson type time advancement along with a predictor-corrector update scheme. It is a structured, arbitrary order, finite difference code [6–9], which enables the coupling of multiple domains and their simultaneous computation in general. The momentum equations are discretized by central difference resulting in low numerical dissipation. All scalars are discretized by WENO5 schemes ensuring bounded solutions. Spatial and temporal staggering of flow variables are used in order to increase the accuracy of stencils. For LES, a dynamic Smagorinsky model is used as subfilter stress model [10] employing weighted averaging backward in time along Lagrangian trajectories of fluid particles [11].

In order to enable interface resolving simulations in the vicinity of injector orifices, a second-order monotonicity preserving Lagrange-Remap solver in combination with centered discretization [12] is used within CIAO's general flow-solver. This hybrid approach addresses numerical stability issues often encountered in flows with very high density and momentum ratios. In particular, consistency between density and momentum is maintained even at sharp interfaces when the hybrid discretization is applied to the convective transport term and the pressure-projection. The numerical framework features low artificial dissipation, which is essential for computing turbulent flow structures with a wide range of scales. For highly accurate time integration of the interfacial flow with respect to mass conservation, geometric accuracy, and surface tension effects, a 3D unsplit forward/backward Volume-of-Fluid (VOF) method coupled to a Level Set (LS) method (3DU-CLSVOF) [13] is used.

For simulating the secondary breakup as well as the evaporation of droplets further downstream of the nozzle, a Lagrangian Particle Tracking (LPT) formulation is available for modeling the liquid phase. It applies a standard Kelvin-Helmholtz/Rayleigh-Taylor model [14] for the secondary breakup, while the evaporation model of Miller et al. [15] is used for describing the transition of liquid droplets to the gas phase.

The code framework uses the message passing interface (MPI) standard. The scaling potential of the code has been recently demonstrated in a range of large-scale DNS studies [16,17].

3 Application Setup and Coupling

3.1 "Spray A" Case

The "Spray A" case of the ECN is chosen as demonstration case for introducing the coupling approach, which is the scope of this paper. It will be briefly described within this subsection to introduce the different scales occurring during the injection process and the performed simulations.

Details of the "Spray A" flow conditions are given in Table 1. Using Bernoulli's formula at these conditions, setting the ambient gas velocity to $0\,\frac{m}{s}$ in the simulation, and applying the velocity coefficient defined as ratio between real and theoretical velocity, the steady nozzle bulk exit velocity can be estimated as $614\,\frac{m}{s}$. This already indicates the wide range of occurring length scales knowing that the resulting droplets are of the order of $1\,\mu m$. In order to efficiently handle this wide range of scales, the simulation is cut into three domains as sketched in Fig. 1: Within the left domain, the nozzle internal flow is computed as LES (NIF-LES) resolving the exact nozzle geometry with constant velocity boundary condition at the inlet. Beside resolving the geometry driven flow features, the resolution in this area must be sufficient to give the right amount of Turbulent Kinetic Energy (TKE) at the nozzle exit since turbulence is known to strongly impact the primary breakup in the vicinity of the nozzle. Figure 2(a) shows that the TKE at the nozzle exit converges at a mesh resolution of $5\,\mu m$. Therefore, a non-uniform mesh with a maximum resolution of $5\,\mu m$ is chosen for the NIF-LES. Next to the nozzle internal flow domain follows the primary breakup domain. These are coupled via the Coupling Interface Nozzle Internal Flow/Primary Breakup (CINP). Within the primary breakup domain, a primary breakup DNS (PB-DNS) with interface tracking is performed. A uniform mesh with a resolution of $1\,\mu m$ is chosen as result of a mesh sensitivity study with respect to the resulting total Surface Density (SD) plotted in Fig. 2(b). Finally, a LES using a LPT method (LPT-LES) for representing liquid particles is employed in the third simulation domain. The resolution of the uniform mesh is chosen as 0.25 mm. As can be seen in Fig. 2(c) the Penetration Length (PL) was found to be underpredicted due to an overprediction of the drag force on individual particles for coarser grids. The interface between PB-DNS and LPT-LES is denoted as Coupling Interface Primary Breakup/Secondary Breakup (CIPS). Due to CFL number restrictions, the grid resolutions of the individual simulations imply also different time step sizes. More precisely, it was found that the time step size of the NIF-LES is ten times larger than that of the PB-DNS, while that of the LPT-LES is about 500 times larger than that of the PB-DNS.

Considering the required resolutions within each domain, a complete data set for the "Spray A" case can be computed by coupling a NIF-LES with about 900M grid cells, a PB-DNS with about 900M grid cells, and a LPT-LES with about 12M grid cells. This results in computational cost for NIF-LES, PB-DNS, and LPT-LES of 5M core-h, 8M core-h, and 0.05M core-h, respectively, on Intel Sandy Bridge cores. Due to the big simulation size of the NIF-LES and the PB-DNS, these simulations are run simultaneously in order to avoid the storage

Table 1. Details of the "Spray A" flow conditions [18–20]

Outlet diameter	0.09 mm
Nozzle length	1.03 mm
Velocity coefficient	0.96
Fuel	n-dodecane
Fuel temperature at nozzle	363 K
Fuel injection pressure	150 MPa
Fuel density	703.82 $\frac{kg}{m^3}$
Fuel dynamic viscosity	6.09×10^{-4} kg/ms
Ambient gas temperature	900 K
Ambient gas pressure	6 MPa
Ambient gas dynamic viscosity	3.81×10^{-5} kg/ms
Ambient gas velocity	Near-quiescent
Surface tension	0.09 $\frac{kg}{s^2}$

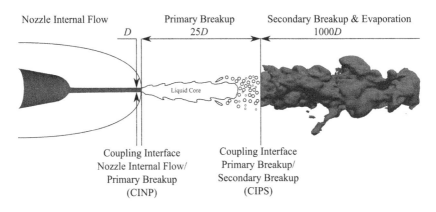

Fig. 1. Resulting simulation domains for "Spray A" case

of large amount of data at the CINP. This is especially important, if the coupling is performed by enforcing a boundary conditions not only at a boundary face but in a boundary volume for capturing complex flow features. Due to the smaller amount of coupling information and overall smaller simulation size, the LPT-LES is run separately using stored droplet information. Details about the CINP and the CIPS are given within the next two subsections.

3.2 Coupling Interface Between Nozzle Internal Flow and Primary Breakup

In this subsection, details of the CINP are described, which enables the simultaneous realization of the NIF-LES and the PB-DNS. A sketch of the work load

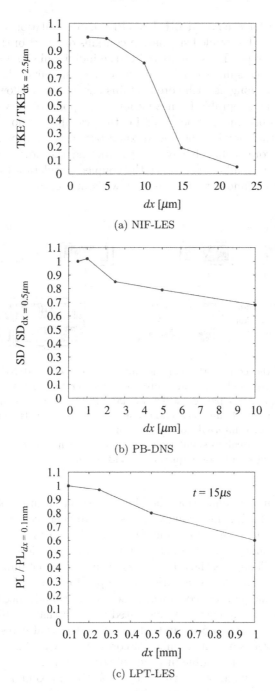

(a) NIF-LES

(b) PB-DNS

(c) LPT-LES

Fig. 2. For each simulation type, the minimum mesh resolution is determined by employing a mesh convergence study with respect to a target quantity. TKE at the nozzle exit, total SD, and PL after 15 μs are used for NIF-LES, PB-DNS, and LPT-LES, respectively.

per compute core for a coupled LIF-LES/PB-DNS simulation is illustrated in Fig. 3. Each core in the coupled simulation contains one part of the flow domain of each simulation type. Thus, compared to the individual simulations, the flow domain per core per simulation is halved. Having in mind that typical flow solvers scale well as long as each core contains enough active flow cells, halving the domain sizes is acceptable from a performance point of view as long as the resulting domains become not too small. I.e. the available memory per core must be large enough that halving the flow domain per simulation per core does not affect the single core scaling behavior. Distributing the flow domains of both simulations equally to all cores enables the coupled simulation to advance both flow domains with a different time step size without methodically idling cores.

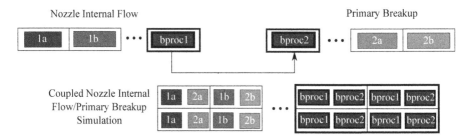

Fig. 3. Sketch of the core work load distribution for a coupled NIF-LES/PB-DNS simulation. Outer rectangles indicate cores, while inner rectangles indicate memory domains corresponding to a particular flow domain. Bold rectangles denote cores partly containing the coupling boundary. These cores are denoted with 'bproc'. Domains belonging to the nozzle internal flow simulation are denoted with '1$\{a, b, ...\}$', while those of the primary breakup simulation are denoted with '2$\{a, b, ...\}$'. In the shown example, the coupled simulation requires two additional cores.

Additionally, it was found that the high-order spatial interpolation schemes used for coupling both simulations with respect to their velocity fields require about 15% additional computing time. Since only few cores contain parts of the coupling domain, many cores are idle during the interpolation resulting in poor scaling behavior. Therefore, the domain size of the cores containing coupled cells was halved in order to hide the additional interpolation cost. More precisely, the interpolation is done on these cores while the others still advance the flow solver due to their larger domain sizes. As indicated in Fig. 3 that doubles the number of cores containing coupled cells and adds some additional cores to the overall simulation. However, since the number of cores at the CINP is small, the extra cores were found to be negligible in terms of code scaling.

Running both simulations with their respective maximum time step size t^{max} is desirable in terms of computational performance, however, consistency of both simulations is not longer guaranteed. Particularly, the local amount of TKE transferred from the NIF-LES to the PB-DNS is critical because it mainly impacts the local Reynolds number, which is the breakup dominating parameter close to the nozzle orifice. Since the coupling velocity for time steps, which were not explicitly solved for in the NIF-LES, is typically interpolated linearly, no subtime fluctuations occur, which leads to slower droplet formation during the primary breakup. Figure 4 shows the resulting droplet size distribution for different time step coupling approaches. The distribution denoted with "DNS" results from a coupled simulation run with the same time step size for NIF-LES and PB-DNS. This ensures consistency between both simulations and can be seen as the correct result. However, the computational cost increases for the NIF-LES of the order of

$$\frac{\Delta t_{\text{NIF-LES}}^{\max}}{\Delta t_{\text{PB-DNS}}^{\max}} - 1 \tag{1}$$

compared to a coupled simulation run with maximum time step size for each simulation. The resulting droplet size distribution of such an maximum time step simulation is denoted with "LES" in Fig. 4. A shift in the droplet size distribution to larger droplets is obvious. To overcome this issue, subtime perturbation is introduced at the CINP, which adds local perturbation to the interpolated velocities based on the average TKE. The droplet size distribution result of such a simulation with maximum time steps and subtime perturbation is denoted as "Perturbated LES" in Fig. 4 and gives the same result as the "DNS" case by adding negligible computational cost.

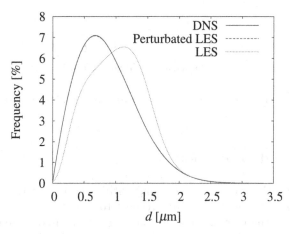

Fig. 4. Droplet size distribution 1 mm downstream from the nozzle orifice for different time step coupling approaches

3.3 Coupling Interface Between Primary Breakup and Secondary Breakup

In contrast to the CINP, which works with the simulation runtime data stored in the memory, the CIPS uses HDD-stored droplet information. The droplet information is recorded time resolved in a rectangular flow domain about $22D$ away from the nozzle exit in the PB-DNS. Regardless of the actual shape of the droplets or ligaments in the PB-DNS, all particles are transferred to the LPT-LES as spheres preserving only the correct volume. In order to validate the coupling location, the Sauter Mean Diameter (SMD) was compared to experimental data obtained by Alan Kastengreen, Argonne National Laboratory, that have been presented on the last ECN workshop [21]. The resulting relative errors at several downstream locations and for different coupling locations are shown in Fig. 5. While the error for coupling after $22D$ is even smaller than the measurement uncertainties, coupling at $15D$ lead to wrong results. This indicates that at $15D$ a liquid core still exists, which dominates the spray statistics and cannot be described by disperse Lagrangian particles. Interface resolved methods are still necessary.

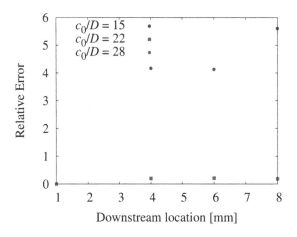

Fig. 5. Relative error of the SMD with respect to experimental data for different coupling locations

4   Results and Discussion

After introducing the multi-scale coupling within the last section, this chapter shows selected simulation results with respect to the "Spray A" case. It briefly demonstrates how the new multi-scale coupling can be used to generate a complete predictive data set with reasonable computational cost.

Figure 5 already showed that using the right location for the CIPS, experimental results with respect to the SMD are matched with the code framework without particular tuning of initial conditions or model parameters. More precisely, it has been seen that the SMD computed only with the coupled NIF-LES/PB-DNS simulations at 1 mm matches the experimental data very well, while the completely coupled results of the LPT-LES further downstream are still in good agreement with the measurements. These results can be further analyzed by looking at e.g. the PL over time or the droplet size distribution at different downstream locations. Both are plotted in Fig. 6. Remarkably, the peak of the droplet size distributions does not shift to smaller droplet diameters

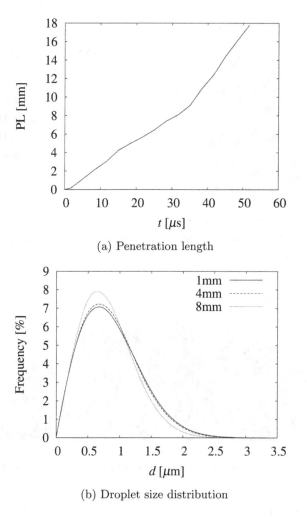

(a) Penetration length

(b) Droplet size distribution

Fig. 6. Liquid penetration and droplet size distribution results for the "Spray A" case

but only increases its amplitude, which means that equilibrium between secondary breakup and evaporation is already reached.

As pointed out in the introduction, fast and constant evaporation of the droplets is often beneficial for a homogeneous combustion process. In order to improve that, the information of the coupled NIF-LES/PB-DNS simulation such as the resulting velocity profile at the nozzle exit, which is plotted in Fig. 7, or the resulting interface during the primary breakup shown in Fig. 8 can be analyzed with respect to its impact on the spray characteristics further downstream. Since the multi-scale approach presented in the work leads to data sets resolving all relevant processes, it is highly usable for model development and spray improvement.

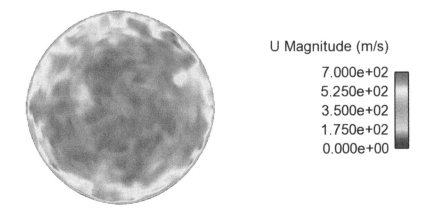

Fig. 7. Resulting velocity profile of the "Spray A" case at the nozzle exit

Fig. 8. Resulting interface of the "Spray A" case during primary breakup

5   Conclusions

This work presented a multi-scale coupling approach for predictive spray simulations. It was shown how the introduction of two different coupling interfaces can significantly reduce the required amount of computation cost for resolving all relevant scales during the fuel injection process. In order to show the completeness of the resulting data sets, the multi-scale coupling was applied to the "Spray A" case specified by the ECN and various results representing different scales were discussed.

Acknowledgment. The authors gratefully acknowledge funding by Honda R&D and the Cluster of Excellence "Tailor-Made Fuels from Biomass", which is funded by the Excellence Initiative of the German federal and state governments to promote science and research at German universities. Also the authors gratefully acknowledge computing time granted for the project JHPC18 by the JARA-HPC Vergabegremium and provided on the JARA-HPC Partition part of the supercomputer JUQUEEN [22] at Forschungszentrum Jülich and under grant 2013092005 of the Partnership for Advanced Computing in Europe (PRACE). Experimental data for validation has been provided by Alan Kastengren, Argonne National Laboratory, and are gratefully acknowledged, too.

References

1. Lasheras, J.C., Hopfinger, E.J.: Liquid jet instability and atomization in a coaxial gas stream. Annu. Rev. Fluid Mech. **32**, 275–308 (2000)
2. Marmottant, P., Villermaux, E.: On spray formation. J. Fluid Mech. **498**, 73–111 (2004)
3. Shinjo, J., Umemura, A.: Detailed simulation of primary atomization mechanisms in diesel jet sprays (isolated identification of liquid jet tip effects). Proc. Combust. Inst. **33**, 2089–2097 (2011)
4. Gorokhovski, M., Herrmann, M.: Modeling primary atomization. Ann. Rev. **40**, 343–366 (2008)
5. Engine Combustion Network. http://www.sandia.gov/ecn
6. Desjardins, O., Blanquart, G., Balarac, G., Pitsch, H.: High order conservative finite difference scheme for variable density low Mach number turbulent flows. J. Comput. Phys. **227**, 7125–7159 (2008)
7. Desjardins, O., Moureau, V., Pitsch, H.: An accurate conservative level set/ghost fluid method for simulating turbulent atomization. J. Comput. Phys. **227**, 8395–8416 (2008)
8. Desjardins, O., Pitsch, H.: Detailed numerical investigation of turbulent atomization of liquid jets. Atomization Sprays **20**, 311–336 (2010)
9. Bode, M., Falkenstein, T., Pitsch, H., Kimijima, T., Taniguchi, H., Arima, T.: Numerical study of the impact of cavitation on the spray processes during gasoline direct injection. In: ICLASS 2015, 13th Triennial International Conference on Liquid Atomization and Spray Systems, Tainan, Taiwan (2015)
10. Germano, M., Piomelli, U., Moin, P., Cabot, W.H.: A dynamic subgrid scale eddy viscosity model. Phys. Fluids A **3**, 1760–1765 (1991)
11. Meneveau, C., Lund, T.S., Cabot, W.H.: A Lagrangian dynamic subgrid-scale model of turbulence. J. Fluid Mech. **319**, 353–385 (1996)
12. Le Chenadec, V., Pitsch, H.: A monotonicity preserving conservative sharp interface flow solver for high density ratio two-phase flows. J. Comput. Phys. **249**, 185–203 (2013)
13. Le Chenadec, V., Pitsch, H.: A 3D unsplit forward/backward volume-of-fluid approach and coupling with a level set method. J. Comput. Phys. **233**, 10–33 (2013)
14. Patterson, M.A., Reitz, R.D.: Modeling the effects of fuel spray characteristics on diesel engine combustion and emissions. SAE Trans. **107**, 27–43 (1998)
15. Miller, R.S., Harstad, K., Bellan, J.: Evaluation of equilibrium and non-equilibrium evaporation models for many-droplet gas-liquid flow simulations. Int. J. Multiph. Flow **24**, 1025–1055 (1998)
16. Bode, M., Falkenstein, T., Le Chenadec, V., Pitsch, H., Arima, T., Taniguchi, H.: A new Euler/Lagrange approach for multiphase simulations of a multi-hole GDI injector. SAE Paper 2015–01-0949 (2015)
17. Bode, M., Deshmukh, A., Kirsch, V., Reddemann, M.A., Kneer, R., Pitsch, H.: Direct numerical simulations of novel biofuels for predicting spray characteristics. In: ICLASS 2015, 13th Triennial International Conference on Liquid Atomization and Spray Systems, Tainan, Taiwan (2015)

18. Saddix, C.R., Zhang, J., Schefer, R.W., Doom, J., Oefelein, J.C., Kook, S., Pickett, L.M.: Understanding and prepredict soot generation in turbulent non-premixed jet flames. Report in Sandia National Laboratories (2010)
19. Kastengren, A.L., Tilocco, F.Z., Powell, C.F., Manin, J., Pickett, L.M., Payri, R., Bazyn, T.: Engine Combustion Network (ECN): measurements of nozzle geometry and hydraulic behalvior. Atomization Sprays **22**, 1011–1052 (2012)
20. National Institute of Standards and Technology. http://www.nist.gov/
21. Engine Combustion Network Workshop 4 (2015). http://www.sandia.gov/ecn/workshop/ECN4/ECN4.php
22. Jülich Supercomputing Centre: JUQUEEN: IBM Blue Gene/Q Supercomputer system at the Jülich supercomputing centre. J. Large-Scale Res. Facil. **1**, A1 (2015). http://dx.doi.org/10.17815/jlsrf-1-18

Domain-Specific Applications and High-Performance Computing

In the last decade, the computational science and engineering community has witnessed an increasing interest in collaborations between High-Performance Computing (HPC) experts and computational scientists working in diverse application-specific domains. At the base of such a trend there are two simple observations. First and foremost, scientific computing is recognized as the de facto third pillar of scientific investigation, alongside theory and experiment. Secondly, the advent of computing architectures in and beyond the Petaflop range has made evident the need for expertise in parallel and high-performance computing; such expertize is fundamental in order to be able to exploit the potential of current and future computing platforms. In fact, it is in the best interest of the scientific community to maximize the use of computational resources in simulating physical systems. The realization that scientific computing and HPC should go hand in hand is driving the necessity for a coordinated effort to close the gap between experts in numerical algorithms and computer science, and scientists working in applied disciplines. Researchers from both sides are compelled to closely interact and capitalize on their respective expertise.

The papers presented in this section provide a typical example of the advantages an interdisciplinary approach to HPC can deliver to scientific computing. As an added value, the contributed papers represent a broad sample of distinct domain-specific applications. The wide breath of the domains illustrates quite effectively how HPC can positively affect diverse fields within the realm of scientific computing. Despite the fact that each topic is based on a number of heterogeneous algorithms, they all require to effectively incorporate techniques and best practices borrowed from methods developed within applied mathematics and computer science. Among the represented subjects, the reader can find topics ranging from ab initio methods, to computational mechanics, and neuroscience.

Ab Initio Description of Optoelectronic Properties at Defective Interfaces in Solar Cells

Philippe Czaja[1](✉), Massimo Celino[2], Simone Giusepponi[2], Michele Gusso[3], and Urs Aeberhard[1]

[1] IEK-5 Photovoltaik, Forschungszentrum Jülich, 52425 Jülich, Germany
p.czaja@fz-juelich.de
[2] ENEA, C.R. Casaccia, 00123 Rome, Italy
[3] ENEA, C.R. Brindisi, 72100 Brindisi, Italy

Abstract. In order to optimize the optoelectronic properties of novel solar cell architectures, such as the amorphous-crystalline interface in silicon heterojunction devices, we calculate and analyze the local microscopic structure at this interface and in bulk a-Si:H, in particular with respect to the impact of material inhomogeneities. The microscopic information is used to extract macroscopic material properties, and to identify localized defect states, which govern the recombination properties encoded in quantities such as capture cross sections used in the Shockley-Read-Hall theory. To this end, atomic configurations for a-Si:H and a-Si:H/c-Si interfaces are generated using molecular dynamics. Density functional theory calculations are then applied to these configurations in order to obtain the electronic wave functions. These are analyzed and characterized with respect to their localization and their contribution to the (local) density of states. GW calculations are performed for the a-Si:H configuration in order to obtain a quasi-particle corrected absorption spectrum. The results suggest that the quasi-particle corrections can be approximated through a scissors shift of the Kohn-Sham energies.

Keywords: Amorphous silicon · Molecular dynamics · Electronic structure · Optical properties

1 Introduction

The silicon hetero-junction (SHJ) technology holds the current efficiency record of 26.33% for silicon-based single junction solar cells [20] and shows great potential to become a future industrial standard for high-efficiency crystalline silicon (c-Si) cells.

One of the key elements of this technology is the passivation of interface defects by thin layers of hydrogenated amorphous silicon (a-Si:H), and the physical processes at the so-formed c-Si/a-Si:H interface largely influence the macroscopic characteristics of the cell. In particular the cell performance depends critically on the optimization of transport and the minimization of recombination

© Springer International Publishing AG 2017
E. Di Napoli et al. (Eds.): JHPCS 2016, LNCS 10164, pp. 111–124, 2017.
DOI: 10.1007/978-3-319-53862-4_10

across the interface, which requires a profound understanding of the underlying mechanisms. Special regard has to be given to the role of localized tail and defect states in a-Si:H and at the interface, which behave substantially different from bulk states and thus prohibit a treatment in terms of bulk semiconductor physics. An accurate and physically meaningful description of the local microscopic structure is therefore an essential step in understanding and predicting the macroscopic device characteristics, which gave rise to a growing interest in ab initio approaches [8,17,26].

In our investigation presented here, we use ab initio molecular dynamics to generate atomic configurations of defective a-Si:H and c-Si/a-Si:H interfaces, and subsequently perform electronic structure calculations to obtain and characterize the electronic states. The electronic structure at the interface is analyzed with respect to the existence of localized defect states which have an impact on the device performance due to their role as recombination centers in non-radiative recombination [33]. The density of these defect states is an important parameter in the Shockley-Read-Hall model for calculating capture cross sections, and should therefore attain realistic values in the generated structures. The states of the bulk a-Si:H are further used for calculating the absorption coefficient from ab initio, which is a first step towards linking the global device characteristics to the local microstructure in a comprehensive multi-scale simulation approach [1]. As the optical properties of any materials depend crucially on their band gap this quantity is of essential importance for obtaining physically relevant results. Unfortunately the independent-particle approximation, which is at the heart of standard first-principles methods, is unable to correctly predict its value [28], which is why so-called quasi-particle corrections [16] need to be applied. The exact calculation of these corrections is however computationally expensive, a heuristic approach – termed *scissors shift* (SS) [10] –, where the electron energies are simply shifted to fit the experimental band gap, is therefore often favored. Since a distinct experimental value of the band gap of a-Si:H does however not exist, a set of shifting parameters can only be determined from a quasi-particle calculation. In this paper we present the results of such a calculation for an a-Si:H configuration.

2   Method

2.1   Atomic Structure Calculations

The ab initio PWscf (Plane-Wave Self-Consistent Field) code of the Quantum ESPRESSO suite is used [9,31] to perform Born-Oppenheimer Molecular Dynamics (BOMD) simulations of the a-Si:H and the a-Si:H/c-Si interface. PWscf performs many different kinds of self-consistent calculations of electronic structure properties within Density-Functional Theory (DFT) [14,22], using a plane-wave (PW) basis set and pseudopotentials (PP). We use the Si and H ultrasoft pseudopotentials with Perdew-Burke-Ernzerhof (PBE) [29] approximant GGA exchange-correlation potential, available in the Quantum ESPRESSO library [31]. To mimic infinitely extended systems, a supercell approach with periodic boundary conditions (PBC) is used.

To generate an a-Si:H system, a random starting configuration is produced with a percentage of H atoms of about 11%, which is the nominal concentration set in experimental materials optimized for PV performance [18]. Initially, a small system of 64 Si + 8 H atoms in a cubic supercell with size L= 11.06 Å (the volume is chosen to fix the density to the experimental value of 2.214 g/cm^3 [21]) is used to perform calculations with a wide range of quench rates. This is due to the fact that the resulting amorphous configuration is largely dependent on the quench rate used to produce the amorphous structure from the melt configuration. Experimental results indicate that the amorphous phase contains a very low number of defects and that the majority of Si atoms have coordination four. To this end we select a small amorphous configuration (Fig. 1) that minimizes both the total value of defects and the deviation from the four-fold coordination of the Si atoms. Then, this configuration, is used as starting configuration for a BOMD simulation on the electronic ground state at constant volume and constant temperature for 6.5 ps, controlling the ionic temperature (T = 300 K) by using an Andersen thermostat [2].

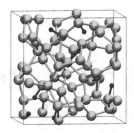

Fig. 1. Snapshot of the a-Si:H in the simulation box. Hydrogen atoms and bonds with Silicon atoms are blue, Silicon atoms and their bonds are yellow. (Color figure online)

The final configuration is then used to produce a large system by replicating it in all directions. The resulting large system is thus composed of 512 Si + 64 H atoms and has a size of L = 22.12 Å. Due to the high computational costs required by PWscf, BOMD simulations on this large system are performed with the Quickstep code of the CP2K suite [4]. CP2K is a quantum chemistry and solid state physics software package that can perform atomistic simulations with different modelling methods (such as DFT) using a mixed Gaussian and plane wave approach. Norm conserving Goedecker-Tetter-Hutter pseudopotentials with PBE exchange-correlation and an optimized TZV2P gaussian basis set are used [11,12,23]. Self consistency at each MD step is achieved using the orbital transformation method [34]. An annealing process from T = 300 K up to T = 600 K, and then back to T = 300 K for 60 ps was then used to thermalize the whole atomic configuration, and minimize the defects at the internal interfaces. After the annealing, a simulation run at T = 300 K was performed for about 20 ps.

The a-Si:H/c-Si interface is built by putting nearby two free surfaces obtained cutting both the crystalline silicon and the hydrogenated amorphous silicon. The relaxed p(2×1) symmetric reconstruction of the Si(001) surface constitutes the c-Si side of the interface. It is formed by 192 Si atoms: 12 layers of silicon each of them with 16 atoms. The a-Si:H side of the system is generated using a simulated-annealing quench-from-the-melt simulation protocol and is composed of 128 Si atoms and 16 H atoms. A void region of about 10 Å is added to suppress the interaction between the external surfaces due to PBC. This distance was checked by convergence tests. The total length of the system is $L_z = 38.70$ Å, while in the x and y direction the system has $L_x = L_y = 15.48$ Å. Total energy calculations of the system at different distances between c-Si and a-Si:H, were performed to find the interface configuration corresponding to the lowest total energy. The configurations were built moving rigidly by hand the a-Si:H part and keeping fixed the c-Si one.

The interface shown in Fig. 2(a), is used as starting configuration for MD simulation on the electronic ground state at constant volume and constant temperature (NVT). The ionic temperature is fixed at T = 300 K and is controlled

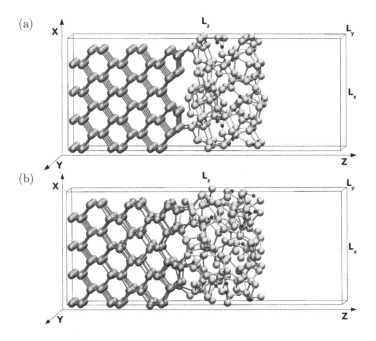

Fig. 2. Snapshots of the a-Si:H/c-Si interface in the simulation box. The structure is infinitely extended in both x and y directions. A void region is considered to suppress the interaction between the external surfaces due to periodic boundary conditions. Free surfaces and a-Si:H/c-Si interface are perpendicular to the y axis. Hydrogen atoms are blue, silicon atoms are dark yellow in the c-Si part and light yellow in the a-Si:H part. (a) Initial configuration. (b) Configuration at 35 ps of the MD simulation. The Si atoms near the interface have moved to form bonds between the c-Si and the a-Si:H layer. (Color figure online)

using an Andersen thermostat [2]. The first four layers of c-Si atoms on the left are kept fixed to impose a bulk like behavior to the crystalline silicon part of the system. The MD simulation is performed for more than 35 ps, the initial part of the simulation (20 ps) was used to thermalize the system and reach a stable configuration. Figure 2(b) displays the configuration of the a-Si:H/c-Si interface at 35 ps.

2.2   Electronic Structure Calculations

We use density functional theory (DFT) [14,22] with periodic boundary conditions to self-consistently calculate the electronic structure of the a-Si:H and the interface configurations described above. The interface configuration is enclosed in a super cell that includes an additional vacuum layer to avoid self-interaction. All calculations are done with the PW-PP code Quantum ESPRESSO [9,31] using the PBE-GGA exchange-correlation functional [29]. For the c-Si/a-Si:H interface a k-point grid of size $4 \times 4 \times 1$ and a plane-wave cut-off of 28 Ry is used, for the a-Si:H a $4 \times 4 \times 4$ (72 atom configuration) and a $2 \times 2 \times 2$ grid (576 atom configuration) respectively, together with a cut-off energy of 52 Ry.

Subsequent to the electronic structure calculation the wave functions and electronic density of states (DOS) of the c-Si/a-Si:H interface are analyzed to obtain information about its local microscopic properties, which are relevant for the mesoscopic dynamics and macroscopic device characteristics. In particular the wave function localization is analyzed qualitatively and quantitatively to allow for the distinction of localized states and the identification of their origins. In combination with the local DOS the contribution of dangling bonds and interfaces to the important mid-gap states can be determined.

As a quantitative measure for the localization of the wave function ψ we use the spread S, which is calculated as the square root of the variance of $|\psi|^2$ with respect to the super cell:

$$S_z = \sqrt{12 \left(\langle z^2 \rangle - \langle z \rangle^2 \right)} = \sqrt{12} \cdot \sqrt{\int_\Omega d\mathbf{r} \, |\psi(\mathbf{r})|^2 z^2 - \left(\int_\Omega d\mathbf{r} \, |\psi(\mathbf{r})|^2 z \right)^2},$$

where we assume that ψ is normalized. It can be easily seen that a maximally localized ψ (i.e., a delta function) gives $S_z = 0$, whereas a wave function that is maximally delocalized over the super cell (i.e., a plane wave) will result in $S_z = L$, where L is the length of the super cell. This explains the factor $\sqrt{12}$ in the definition. The integration volume Ω is naturally chosen such that the boundaries lie inside the vacuum layer where $\psi \approx 0$, such that shifting the integration volume does not affect S. This also provides an unambiguous definition of the wave function center

$$\langle z \rangle = \int_\Omega d\mathbf{r} \, |\psi(\mathbf{r})|^2 z,$$

which can be interpreted as the position where the wave function is localized. This definition allows us to identify localized states (i.e., states with small spread), and to locate them both in real and in energy space.

In order to relate the electronic properties of the interface to the atomic structure, and in particular investigate the effect of structural defects, we use the electron localization function (ELF) [3], which enables us to determine the coordination of each atom, and to identify dangling bonds and weakly bond atoms. For that purpose the ELF is computed along the axes between neighboring atoms, where it shows a characteristic behavior for covalent bonds [32]. This is performed with the Quantum ESPRESSO package.

2.3   Optical Calculations

The calculation of the absorption coefficient for the 72-atom a-Si:H configuration is carried out within the random phase approximation (RPA) [6] as implemented in the BerkeleyGW code [5], using the non-interacting Kohn-Sham states on a $2 \times 2 \times 2$ k-point grid. The same code is used for calculating the quasi-particle (QP) corrections to the Kohn-Sham energies with the GW formalism [13]. In order to reduce the computational costs we perform a single-shot G_0W_0 calculation together with the plasmon-pole approximation [15,25,27]. This has the advantage of requiring the dielectric tensor $\epsilon(\omega)$ only in the static limit $\omega \to 0$, as opposed to a full-frequency calculation, while offering similar accuracy for many semiconductors, including c-Si [24]. The band gap is converged with respect to the cut-off energy E_{cut}^ϵ used in the calculation of ϵ, for which we find a value of 10 Ry, and with respect to the number of unoccupied bands N_{bands}^ϵ and N_{bands}^Σ included in the calculation of ϵ and of the self energy Σ. We find that a large number of roughly 3000 bands is needed to reach convergence of both quantities (Fig. 3). The absorption coefficient is recalculated with the corrected energies E^{QP}, and compared to calculations where scissors shifts with different sets of parameters are used. These parameters are obtained by applying a linear fit $E_{v/c}^{QP} = a_{v/c} \cdot E_{v/c} + b_{v/c}$, where $E_{v/c}$ are the uncorrected energies, both to the valence and the conduction band. The absorption calculation for the 576-atom configuration is carried out on a $2 \times 2 \times 2$ k-point grid as well, using uncorrected and scissors shift energies.

3   Results

3.1   A-Si:H

Figure 4 shows the quasi-particle corrected electron energies as obtained from the GW calculation for the 72-atom a-Si:H structure described above. The results show that the effect of the corrections consists mainly in a spreading of valence and conduction band by approximately 0.26 eV. This suggests that the costly GW calculation can be substituted by a simple scissors shift in further calculations of a-Si:H structures. The choice of the right set of parameters depends

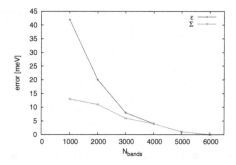

Fig. 3. Convergence of band gap with respect to the number of bands included in the calculation of ϵ and Σ respectively.

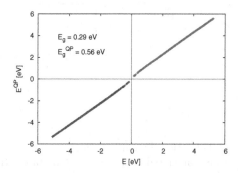

Fig. 4. Quasi-particle corrected vs. uncorrected electron energies. E_g refers here to the energy difference between the lowest unoccupied and the highest occupied state.

on the energy range of interest. By applying a linear fit in the energy range from -1 to 1 eV we obtain $a_v = 1.088$, $b_v = -1.097$ eV, $a_c = 1.146$, and $b_c = -1.228$ eV.

Figure 5 shows the imaginary part of the dielectric function and the absorption coefficient calculated within the independent-particle approximation, that is, with the uncorrected Kohn-Sham energies, the GW approximation, and the scissors-shift approximation. The GW correction modifies the absorption spectrum only in terms of a shift and a slight stretch. This correction can be very well approximated by a scissors shift with the parameters given above, which reproduce almost exactly the GW absorption spectrum.

Using the scissors shift approximation enables us to calculate a quasi-particle-corrected absorption spectrum also for the 576-atom structure, which is shown in Fig. 6. Comparison of the spectra for the two different configurations shows an increase of the optical band gap in the larger structure, along with a decrease of the sup-gap absorption peaks. Even though this represents an improvement, the band gap is still small compared to the experimental value of 1.7 eV, which suggests that one might have to go to even larger structures in order to eliminate

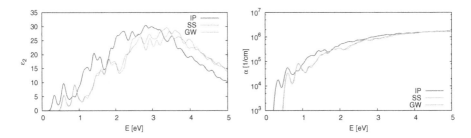

Fig. 5. Imaginary part of dielectric function (left) and absorption coefficient (right) for the 72-atom configuration, calculated with uncorrected states (IP), and with quasiparticle corrected states in GW and scissors shift (SS) approximation.

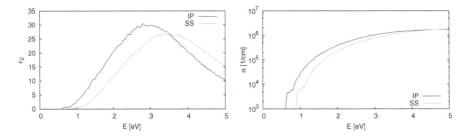

Fig. 6. Imaginary part of dielectric function (left) and absorption coefficient (right) for the 576-atom configuration, calculated with uncorrected states (IP), and with quasiparticle corrected states in scissors shift (SS) approximation.

finite-size effects that artificially reduce the band gap, like the overestimation of the defect density and interactions with periodic images.

3.2   C-Si/a-Si:H Interface

In Fig. 7 the spread in z-direction (i.e., in growth direction) S_z is shown as a function of the wave function energy together with the total DOS around the Fermi energy for the above described interface configuration. The figure shows that there is a dense distribution of strongly localized states inside the c-Si band gap, which can be clearly distinguished from the more extended tail and bulk states.

The origin of these states can be investigated further by looking at the local DOS and the wave function centers as shown in Fig. 8. In the top subfigure, the layer-resolved DOS is displayed as a function of the z-coordinate, which is obtained by integrating the local DOS over layers parallel to the interface. The figure shows that near the interface, which is marked by the dotted line, the band gap starts filling up with states, and completely vanishes in the a-Si:H region. That these mid-gap states are indeed localized can be seen in the bottom figure, where S_z is plotted as a function of the energy and the z-component of the center of the wave functions. Each dot marks the energy and the position of one wave

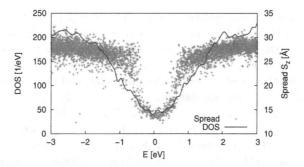

Fig. 7. DOS and wave function spread (in direction perpendicular to the interface) in the energy region around the Fermi energy at 0 eV.

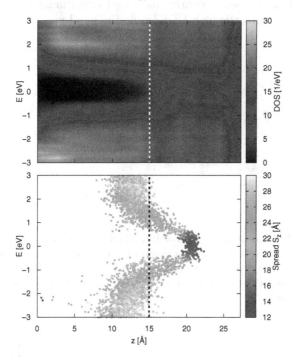

Fig. 8. Top: Local DOS integrated over layers parallel to the interface as a function of the z-coordinate. Bottom: Wave function spread in z-direction. Each dot marks the energy and the position of the center of one wave function, whereas the color represents its spread. The dotted line shows the approximate position of the interface.

function, that is, where along the z-direction it is centered. The color of each dot represents the spread of the wave function. This representation indicates that the contribution to the mid-gap states comes mainly from localized states in the a-Si:H layer, whereas the interface region hardly contributes at all.

The emergence of localized states in the a-Si:H region can be better understood in terms of the atomic structure. For that purpose all the bonds are analyzed by means of the ELF in order to identify dangling and weak bonds. This is shown exemplarily in Fig. 9 for a three-fold bond Si atom. By investigating the ELF between this atom and its nearest neighbors one can clearly distinguish one H bond, two Si bonds, and one dangling Si bond. Applying this analysis to all atoms yields a coordination map as shown in Fig. 10. This reveals that there is a large number of low-coordinated atoms in the a-Si:H layer whereas the atoms at the interface itself (represented by a dotted line) are mostly four-fold coordinated. While supporting the conclusions from the localization analysis, this result also indicates that the quality of the amorphous layer is rather poor. In fact the defect density is of the order of $10^{22}/\,\mathrm{cm}^3$, and thus four orders of magnitude higher than the defect density measured experimentally for thin a-Si:H films [7], which explains the high DOS inside the band gap.

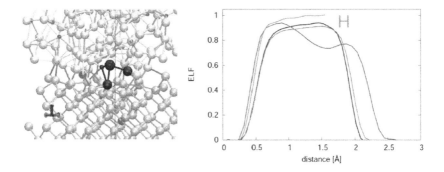

Fig. 9. Left: 3-fold bond atom at the a-Si:H/c-Si interface (purple) and its three bonding partners (magenta). Right: ELF between the atom shown on the left and its four nearest neighbors. The orange curve represents a bond with an H atom, the blue and purple curve represent Si-Si bonds, and the green curve represents a dangling bond. (Color figure online)

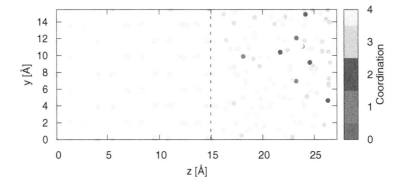

Fig. 10. Coordination numbers for all atoms in the a-Si:H/c-Si configuration.

4 Computational Costs

Table 1 lists the computational costs of typical sets of calculations with converged parameters for all three structures considered in this paper. As self-consistent field (scf) calculations with DFT scale with $\mathcal{O}(N^2 \log N)$ in the number of atoms, the computational costs increase by two orders of magnitude when going from 72 to 576 atoms. This is however only the theoretical scaling behavior and does not yet take into account I/O and communication costs, as well as the non-ideal scaling with respect to the number of cores. These effects become visible especially in the non-self consistent (nscf) calculation of unoccupied bands, where larger matrices have to be handled. Altogether the numbers indicate that the current limit for performing DFT calculations with conventional plane-wave approaches on reasonable time-scales is of the order of a few thousand atoms.

Regarding GW, a full calculation for the small structure requires about 2400 core-h, making it obvious that GW calculations for the larger systems are currently out of range. The most costly part here is the DFT calculation of a large number of unoccupied bands, which are needed exclusively in the GW calculations and not for any other of the calculations we performed. In addition it has to be pointed out once again that the numbers given here refer to an already converged calculation. The convergence process itself is computationally much more challenging, which is due to the fact that three interdependent parameters have to be converged simultaneously, resulting in a total cost of about 80000 core-h.

For the large a-Si:H and the interface configuration the vast majority of the computational time is spent on the BOMD simulations which is due to the fact that the electronic ground state is computed at every time step by an scf calculation. The high computational demand for the interface generation

Table 1. Computational costs for typical sets of calculations for all three structures investigated within this work. MD and DFT calculations were done using Quantum ESPRESSO, except for the 576-atom system, where CP2K was used. GW and absorption calculations were done using BerkeleyGW. For the MD calculations also the simulation time is provided in brackets.

Calculation		Computational costs [core-h]		
		a-Si:H (72)	a-Si:H (576)	a-Si:H/c-Si
MD		2300	190000	220000
		(6.5 ps)	(80.0 ps)	(35.0 ps)
DFT	scf	20	1940	200
	nscf	15	5450	750
GW	unoccupied bands	1800		
	ϵ	380		
	Σ	180		
Absorption		1	320	

motivated the use of the CP2K Quickstep code for the large a-Si:H system, which allowed us to reduce the computational cost by using a mixed Gaussian and plane wave approach.

5 Conclusions

We presented an ab initio description of the atomic and electronic properties of the a-Si:H/c-Si interface, which is at the heart of the technologically relevant silicon-heterojunction solar cells. We introduced and applied different methods for analyzing the electronic structure, in particular with respect to the role of defects and localized states, which have an influence on the cell performance via non-radiative recombination.

Furthermore, we generated configurations of a-Si:H and calculated the electronic structure, including GW corrections. As a first step towards the extraction of macroscopic material properties from the local microscopic structure for use in multiscale models of solar cells, we calculated the absorption spectrum of an a-Si:H structure. As an important result we found that the expensive GW corrections can be replaced by a linear approximation, which makes calculations for larger – and, thus, physically more representative – configurations possible.

Acknowledgments. This project has received funding from the European Commission Horizon 2020 research and innovation program under grant agreement No. 676629. The authors gratefully acknowledge the computing time granted on the supercomputer JURECA [19] at Jülich Supercomputing Centre (JSC) and on the supercomputer CRESCO [30] on the ENEA-GRID infrastructure.

References

1. Aeberhard, U., Czaja, P., Ermes, M., Pieters, B., Chistiakova, G., Bittkau, K., Richter, A., Ding, K., Giusepponi, S., Celino, M.: Towards a multi-scale approach to the simulation of silicon hetero-junction solar cells. J. Green Eng. **5**(4), 11–32 (2016)
2. Andersen, H.C.: Molecular dynamics simulations at constant pressure and/or temperature. J. Chem. Phys. **72**(4), 2384–2393 (1980)
3. Becke, A.D., Edgecombe, K.E.: A simple measure of electron localization in atomic and molecular systems. J. Chem. Phys. **92**(9), 5397–5403 (1990)
4. CP2K. http://www.cp2k.org/
5. Deslippe, J., Samsonidze, G., Strubbe, D.A., Jain, M., Cohen, M.L., Louie, S.G.: BerkeleyGW: a massively parallel computer package for the calculation of the quasiparticle and optical properties of materials and nanostructures. Comput. Phys. Commun. **183**(6), 1269–1289 (2012)
6. Ehrenreich, H.: The Optical Properties of Solids. Academic, New York (1965)
7. Favre, M., Curtins, H., Shah, A.: Study of surface/interface and bulk defect density in a-Si: H by means of photothermal de ection spectroscopy and photoconductivity. J. Non-Cryst. Solids **97**, 731–734 (1987)

8. George, B.M., Behrends, J., Schnegg, A., Schulze, T.F., Fehr, M., Korte, L., Rech, B., Lips, K., Rohrmüller, M., Rauls, E., Schmidt, W.G., Gerstmann, U.: Atomic structure of interface states in silicon heterojunction solar cells. Phys. Rev. Lett. **110**, 136803 (2013)
9. Giannozzi, P., Baroni, S., Bonini, N., Calandra, M., Car, R., Cavazzoni, C., Ceresoli, D., Chiarotti, G.L., Cococcioni, M., Dabo, I., Corso, A.D., de Gironcoli, S., Fabris, S., Fratesi, G., Gebauer, R., Gerstmann, U., Gougoussis, C., Kokalj, A., Lazzeri, M., Martin-Samos, L., Marzari, N., Mauri, F., Mazzarello, R., Paolini, S., Pasquarello, A., Paulatto, L., Sbraccia, C., Scandolo, S., Sclauzero, G., Seitsonen, A.P., Smogunov, A., Umari, P., Wentzcovitch, R.M.: QUANTUM ESPRESSO: a modular and open-source software project for quantum simulations of materials. J. Phys.: Condens. Matter **21**(39), 395502 (2009)
10. Godby, R.W., Schlüter, M., Sham, L.J.: Self-energy operators and exchange-correlation potentials in semiconductors. Phys. Rev. B **37**, 10159–10175 (1988)
11. Goedecker, S., Teter, M., Hutter, J.: Separable dual-space Gaussian pseudopotentials. Phys. Rev. B **54**, 1703–1710 (1996)
12. Hartwigsen, C., Goedecker, S., Hutter, J.: Relativistic separable dual-space Gaussian pseudopotentials from H to Rn. Phys. Rev. B **58**, 3641–3662 (1998)
13. Hedin, L.: New method for calculating the one-particle Green's function with application to the electron-gas problem. Phys. Rev. **139**, A796–A823 (1965)
14. Hohenberg, P., Kohn, W.: Inhomogeneous electron gas. Phys. Rev. **136**, B864–B871 (1964)
15. Hybertsen, M.S., Louie, S.G.: Electron correlation in semiconductors and insulators: Band gaps and quasiparticle energies. Phys. Rev. B **34**, 5390–5413 (1986)
16. Hybertsen, M.S., Louie, S.G.: First-principles theory of quasiparticles: calculation of Band gaps in semiconductors and insulators. Phys. Rev. Lett. **55**, 1418–1421 (1985)
17. Jarolimek, K., de Groot, R.A., de Wijs, G.A., Zeman, M.: First-principles study of hydrogenated amorphous silicon. Phys. Rev. B **79**, 155206 (2009)
18. Johlin, E., Wagner, L.K., Buonassisi, T., Grossman, J.C.: Origins of structural hole traps in hydrogenated amorphous silicon. Phys. Rev. Lett. **110**, 146805 (2013)
19. Jülich Supercomputing Centre: JURECA: general-purpose supercomputer at Jülich supercomputing centre. J. Large-Scale Res. Facil. 2, A62 (2016)
20. Kaneka Corporation. http://www.kaneka.co.jp/kaneka-e/images/topics/1473811995/1473811995_101.pdf
21. Khomyakov, P.A., Andreoni, W., Afify, N.D., Curioni, A.: Large-scale simulations of α-Si: H: the origin of midgap states revisited. Phys. Rev. Lett. **107**, 255502 (2011)
22. Kohn, W., Sham, L.J.: Self-consistent equations including exchange and correlation effects. Phys. Rev. **140**, A1133–A1138 (1965)
23. Krack, M.: Pseudopotentials for H to Kr optimized for gradient-corrected exchange-correlation functionals. Theoret. Chem. Acc. **114**(1), 145–152 (2005)
24. Larson, P., Dvorak, M., Wu, Z.: Role of the plasmon-pole model in the GW approximation. Phys. Rev. B **88**, 125205 (2013)
25. Lundqvist, B.I.: Single-particle spectrum of the degenerate electron gas. Physik der Kondensierten Materie **6**(3), 193–205 (1967)
26. Nolan, M., Legesse, M., Fagas, G.: Surface orientation effects in crystalline-amorphous silicon interfaces. Phys. Chem. Chem. Phys. **14**, 15173 (2012)
27. Overhauser, A.W.: Simplified theory of electron correlations in metals. Phys. Rev. B **3**, 1888–1898 (1971)

28. Perdew, J.P.: Density functional theory and the band gap problem. Int. J. Quantum Chem. **28**(S19), 497–523 (1985)
29. Perdew, J.P., Burke, K., Ernzerhof, M.: Generalized gradient approximation made simple. Phys. Rev. Lett. **77**, 3865–3868 (1996)
30. Ponti, G., Palombi, F., Abate, D., Ambrosino, F., Aprea, G., Bastianelli, T., Beone, F., Bertini, R., Bracco, G., Caporicci, M., Calosso, B., Chinnici, M., Colavincenzo, A., Cucurullo, A., Dangelo, P., Rosa, M.D., Michele, P.D., Funel, A., Furini, G., Giammattei, D., Giusepponi, S., Guadagni, R., Guarnieri, G., Italiano, A., Magagnino, S., Mariano, A., Mencuccini, G., Mercuri, C., Migliori, S., Ornelli, P., Pecoraro, S., Perozziello, A., Pierattini, S., Podda, S., Poggi, F., Quintiliani, A., Rocchi, A., Sció, C., Simoni, F., Vita, A.: The role of medium size facilities in the HPC ecosystem: the case of the new CRESCO4 cluster integrated in the ENEAGRID infrastructure. In: 2014 International Conference on High Performance Computing Simulation (HPCS), pp. 1030–1033 (2014)
31. QuantumESPRESSO. http://www.quantum-espresso.org
32. Savin, A., Jepsen, O., Flad, J., Andersen, O.K., Preuss, H., von Schnering, H.G.: Electron localization in solid-state structures of the elements: the diamond structure. Angew. Chem. Int. Ed. Engl. **31**(2), 187–188 (1992)
33. Shockley, W., Read, W.T.: Statistics of the recombinations of holes and electrons. Phys. Rev. **87**, 835–842 (1952)
34. VandeVondele, J., Hutter, J.: An efficient orbital transformation method for electronic structure calculations. J. Chem. Phys. **118**(10), 4365–4369 (2003)

Scale Bridging Simulations of Large Elastic Deformations and Bainitic Transformations

Marc Weikamp[1](✉), Claas Hüter[1], Mingxuan Lin[2], Ulrich Prahl[2], Diego Schicchi[3], Martin Hunkel[3], and Robert Spatschek[1,4](✉)

[1] Institute for Energy and Climate Research,
Forschungszentrum Jülich GmbH, 52425 Jülich, Germany
{m.weikamp,r.spatschek}@fz-juelich.de
[2] Department of Ferrous Metallurgy,
RWTH Aachen University, 52056 Aachen, Germany
[3] IWT Stiftung Institut für Werkstofftechnik, 28359 Bremen, Germany
[4] JARA-ENERGY, 52056 Aachen, Germany

Abstract. The multiscale process of bainitic microstructure formation is still insufficiently understood from a theoretical and simulation perspective. Production processes of press hardened bainitic steels lead to large deformations, and as a particular aspect we investigate the role of large elastic strains, starting from *ab initio* methods, bridging them to phase field crystal continuum approaches and connecting the results to macroscopic deformation laws. Our investigations show that the phase field crystal model covers large deformations in the nonlinear elastic regime very well. Concerning the microstructure evolution we use a multi phase field model including carbon diffusion, carbide formation and elastic effects. For all the covered aspects we use efficient numerical schemes, which are implemented on GPUs using CUDA.

Keywords: Multi phase field · Bainite transformation · Phase field crystal · *ab initio* Calculations · Nonlinear elasticity · GPU implementation

1 Introduction

The process of press hardening, also known as hot stamping, has become an important tool for the production of high strength steels. Its main application is in the automotive industry, where the demand for high crash safety and simultaneously reduced weight of the automotive parts increases steadily [1]. Major parts of car manufacturing are already produced by press hardening, e.g. A- and B-pillars, bumpers and roof rails.

The manufacturing process of steel parts can be summarised as a sequence of heating, forming, and cooling. This leads to desired shapes while the steel is simultaneously strengthened, as a result of microstructural transformations. Hot stamping manufacturing usually involves synchronous forming and quenching, i.e. cooling, of the heated blanks. This fabrication method can be altered by various techniques, for example cold pre-forming or partial press hardening. The former means shaping at lower temperatures while a necessary calibration is done

© Springer International Publishing AG 2017
E. Di Napoli et al. (Eds.): JHPCS 2016, LNCS 10164, pp. 125–138, 2017.
DOI: 10.1007/978-3-319-53862-4_11

in later steps after heating the sample. Partial press hardening uses different temperature zones during forming, influencing the microstructure transformation locally. The differences in the resulting material properties are significant. Hence the prediction and modeling of the emerging microstructures is important for the design of new steels. From a modeling perspective, the microstructure formation during steel production is very demanding, as multiple scales and hierarchies of structures appear. Therefore, an adequate treatment requires a chain of simulation tools and large scale modeling, which calls for high performance computing and parallelisation strategies.

As large deformations play a significant role during the industrial process of steel manufacturing, we investigate the nonlinear elastic behaviour of materials with the phase field crystal method. Using density functional theory calculations as well as continuum mechanics, we bridge this model to different scales. Considering different strain tensors, we come up with a compact description of the nonlinear elastic behaviour in three dimensions using a Eulerian strain tensor. Taking into account the results of DFT calculations we also show, that the phase field crystal model correctly predicts the nonlinear elastic behaviour of various bcc materials.

Bainite is a particular phase in carbon steels, which consists of ferrite, austenite and carbides [2]. This non-equilibrium phase can be obtained by interrupted cooling plus isothermal holding above the martensite temperature. Fast cooling retains the non-equilibrium structure of bainite and leads to very appealing properties of the steel [3]. The formation of bainite starts with pre-strained austenite. At lower temperatures, the bainite is forming, while it is still under stress due to the applied load during the press hardening process. These stresses significantly affect the transformation and it is therefore important to understand their role. Additionally, the transformation of bainite during press hardening is influenced by carbon and its diffusion. The question whether the process of bainite formation is dominated by diffusion or displacive transformations is still an ongoing debate [4].

In the present work, bainite formation is simulated by a multi phase field model. The model is implemented as a C++ code in a GPU environment, using the advantages of parallel computing. The carbon diffusion is included via a Cahn-Hilliard formalism, which features a decomposition process, leading to the formation of carbides. Additionally, the role of elasticity is examined by the introduction of the (hydrostatic) eigenstrain of bainite during the transformation. Furthermore, we investigate the near-tip segregation at a crack under tension. Analytical results for the equilibrium concentration near the crack tip are compared to finite element simulations and show good agreement.

2   Nonlinear Elasticity in Phase Field Crystal Models and Comparison to *ab initio* Simulations

In order to understand and develop new materials, it is mandatory to identify their elastic response. A full parametrisation describing this response becomes challenging for *large* deformations and can lead to the appearance of many parameters. To reduce this complexity we use the phase field crystal (PFC) model and derived amplitude equations, which naturally contains an intrinsic description of nonlinear elasticity [5]. The predictions of these models, which are validated through *ab initio* calculations, allow a drastic reduction of the complexity of nonlinear deformations by suggesting a proper representation using Eulerian strain tensors.

2.1 Modeling Approach

The investigation of nonlinear elasticity benefits from a multiscale approach using three different models in combination. On the lowest scale is the electronic structure density functional theory, giving the highest accuracy while suffering from expensive calculations. The phase field crystal model is a mesoscale model, which still features atomic resolution. It is implemented as a GPU code, similar to the phase field model, which is discussed later. The macroscale is described by continuum mechanics with different strain tensors.

On the mechanical level one starts with a deformation field, which describes the deformation of a point relative to its initial position $\mathbf{X}$ to a point at the current position $\mathbf{x}$. This defines both the referential ("Lagrangian") displacement field $\mathbf{u}^r = \mathbf{u}^r(\mathbf{X})$ and the current ("Eulerian") displacement field $\mathbf{u}^c = \mathbf{u}^c(\mathbf{x})$. Both descriptions are valid and physically correct but depending on the physical interest and ansatz, a different frame of reference may be more suited than the other. This allows to define different strain tensors, starting with the Green strain tensor

$$\epsilon_{kl} = \frac{1}{2}\left(\frac{\partial u_k^r}{\partial X_l} + \frac{\partial u_l^r}{\partial X_k}\right) + \frac{1}{2}\frac{\partial u_m^r}{\partial X_k}\frac{\partial u_m^r}{\partial X_l}, \tag{1}$$

which formulates the deformation in the referential or Lagrangian frame of reference. The next one is the Almansi strain tensor

$$e_{kl} = \frac{1}{2}\left(\frac{\partial u_k^c}{\partial x_l} + \frac{\partial u_l^c}{\partial x_k}\right) - \frac{1}{2}\frac{\partial u_m^c}{\partial x_k}\frac{\partial u_m^c}{\partial x_l}, \tag{2}$$

describing the elastic response in the current or Eulerian frame of reference. The last tensor is another Eulerian strain measure called Clayton's D tensor,

$$\bar{e}_{kl} = \frac{1}{2}\left(\frac{\partial u_k^c}{\partial x_l} + \frac{\partial u_l^c}{\partial x_k}\right) - \frac{1}{2}\frac{\partial u_k^c}{\partial x_m}\frac{\partial u_l^c}{\partial x_m}. \tag{3}$$

These tensors all agree up to the level of linear elasticity and are only distinguishable in the nonlinear elastic case. In the following we call this nonlinear behaviour *geometric nonlinearity* in order to classify, that the elastic strain is no longer linear in displacements. Additionally, we define the term *physical nonlinearity*, covering effects that lead to an elastic energy, which is no longer quadratic in the (nonlinear) strain.

The phase field crystal model uses a conserved order parameter Ψ to describe the atom density. It is not spatially constant but has a periodic profile in a crystalline phase. The energy functional is defined as

$$F = \int_V d\mathbf{r} \left\{ \Psi \left[(q_0^2 + \nabla^2)^2 - \varepsilon \right] \frac{\Psi}{2} + \frac{\Psi^4}{4} \right\}, \tag{4}$$

with the system's volume V, a dimensionless temperature ε and the wave number q_0, which depends on the lattice spacing of the crystalline structure. In the following we set $q_0 = 1$.

The electronic structure density functional theory results have been performed with the Vienna *ab initio* simulation package (VASP) [6,7]. The calculations have been done at $T = 0$ K and magnetic contributions are not considered [5].

2.2   One-Dimensional Nonlinear Elasticity

The phase field crystal analysis is illustrated here for one dimension. To describe the atom density in the phase field crystal model, we use the one-mode approximation $\Psi(x) = A\cos(qx) + \bar{\Psi}$, with an average density $\bar{\Psi}$. This approximation leads to the free energy density of the system when averaged over $a = 2\pi/q$, which is the "unit cell":

$$f = \frac{\bar{\Psi}^2}{2} \left(-\varepsilon + 1 + \frac{3A^2}{2} + \frac{\bar{\Psi}^2}{2} \right) + \frac{A^2}{4} \left[-\varepsilon + (1 - q^2)^2 + \frac{3A^2}{8} \right]. \tag{5}$$

The energy is minimised, when $q = 1$, as long as the amplitude A is kept constant. We can identify the Eulerian displacement field as $u(x) = (1 - q)x$ from Eq. (5), which gives a Eulerian strain $e_{xx} = \bar{e}_{xx} = \frac{1}{2}(1 - q^2)$. In the one-dimensional case, the strain tensors (2) and (3) coincide. Subsequently, we can write the elastic energy density as $f_{el} \sim \bar{e}_{xx}^2$, indicating, that only a *geometrical nonlinearity* is present. Allowing the system to reduce its energy with respect to the amplitude, $\partial f(A, q, \epsilon, \bar{\Psi})/\partial A = 0$, gives an additional degree of freedom and introduces the *physical nonlinearity* (at finite temperatures). In the linear elastic regime, near $q = 1$, the amplitude is unaffected by the strain of the system but appears at larger strains as melting precursor. The results of the one-dimensional analysis are plotted in the left panel of Fig. 1. The nonlinear behaviour of the system's free energy is clearly visible. Under compression the elastic energy rises faster compared to the case of tension, as one would expect physically.

2.3   Three-Dimensional Nonlinear Elasticity for bcc Materials

Following the one-dimensional case, we can write the free energy density of the phase field crystal system in three dimensions. The one-mode approximation then leads to a lengthy expression; its derivation is omitted for brevity, but can be found in [5]. As a result, one can express the elastic energy density as a

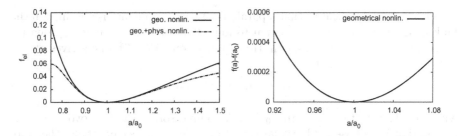

Fig. 1. *Left:* Elastic energy per unit cell as a function of the lattice constant normalised by its equilibrium value a_0 for the 1D case. Parameters are $\bar{\Psi} = 0$, $\epsilon = 0.6$. *Right:* Elastic energy per unit cell of a 3D bcc system as a function of the lattice constant normalised by its equilibrium value a_0. Parameters are $\bar{\Psi} = -0.18$, $\epsilon = 0.1$.

function of the strain in a compact form. The result reads for low temperatures (i.e. constant amplitude $A = A_0$)

$$f_{el} = 4\bar{\Delta}|A_0|^2, \tag{6}$$

with

$$\bar{\Delta} = \bar{e}_{xx}^2 + \bar{e}_{yy}^2 + \bar{e}_{zz}^2 + 2(\bar{e}_{xy}^2 + \bar{e}_{yz}^2 + \bar{e}_{xz}^2) + \bar{e}_{xx}\bar{e}_{yy} + \bar{e}_{yy}\bar{e}_{zz} + \bar{e}_{xx}\bar{e}_{zz}. \tag{7}$$

All amplitudes have the same magnitude in this calculation, which is strictly only valid for an isotropic deformation $\bar{e}_{ij} = \bar{e}\delta_{ij}$. Significant is the fact that only Clayton's D tensor, presented in Eq. (3), is able to express the elastic energy in such a compact form through $\bar{\Delta}$. The right panel of Fig. 1 shows the elastic energy density plotted versus the lattice constant. Similar to the one-dimensional case we can recognise the (geometrical) nonlinearity, leading to a difference between compression and tension.

2.4 Comparison with *ab initio* Simulations and Continuum Modeling

The Birch-Murnaghan equation $E = E_{BM}(V)$ is an energy-volume relation often used to fit *ab initio* data [8]. It is defined for isotropic deformations and reads

$$E_{BM} = E_0 + \frac{9V_0 K}{16}\left\{\left[\left(\frac{V_0}{V}\right)^{\frac{2}{3}} - 1\right]^3 K' + \left[\left(\frac{V_0}{V}\right)^{\frac{2}{3}} - 1\right]^2\left[6 - 4\left(\frac{V_0}{V}\right)^{\frac{2}{3}}\right]\right\}.$$

V_0 is the equilibrium volume, V the actual volume, K the zero pressure bulk modulus and K' the derivative of the bulk modulus with respect to the pressure evaluated at zero pressure. The Birch-Murnaghan equation can be expressed through a Eulerian strain. The differences of the Almansi tensor and the Clayton's D tensor vanish, as we only discuss isotropic deformations here. This gives $e_{xx} = e_{yy} = e_{zz} = (a^2 - a_0^2)/2a^2$. With $V = a^3$ and $V_0 = a_0^3$ we get the compact form

$$E_{BM}(e_{xx}) = \frac{9}{2}KV_0 e_{xx}^2\left[1 + (4 - K')e_{xx}\right]. \tag{8}$$

This equation indicates, that a parabolic strain dependence is obtained, if the bulk modulus derivative K' is equal to four. If we take the free energy density of the phase field crystal model in three dimensions, Eq. (6), one arrives at

$$f_{\text{PFC}}(e_{xx}) = \frac{9}{2} K e_{xx}^2, \qquad (9)$$

with the identification $K = 16|A_0|^2/3$. A comparison of the last two equations shows, that the phase field crystal model predicts a perfect parabola, therefore implying for bcc materials $K' = 4$. We investigate this further using *ab initio* simulations of multiple non-magnetic bcc materials at $T = 0$. The elastic energy as a function of the lattice constant is plotted in the left panel of Fig. 2. If these results are plotted as function of the Eulerian strain, the elastic energies collapse on a Master curve, $E = 9/2V_0 e_{xx}^2$, see right panel of Fig. 2. This result shows, that for many bcc materials the bulk modulus derivative is indeed $K' = 4$. Such a behaviour of the elastic energy is automatically predicted by the phase field crystal model, and can further conveniently be used for large scale modeling.

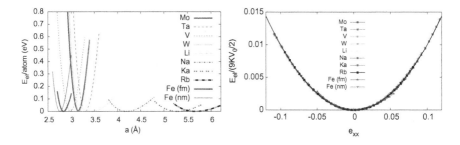

Fig. 2. *Left:* *ab initio* results of various bcc materials at $T = 0$ plotted as function of the lattice constant. *Right:* Elastic energy as a function of the Eulerian strain. All curves fall on one Master curve, see Eq. (9) [5].

3   Phase Field Model of Bainite Formation

Phase field models are a powerful method to describe the formation of microstructures, especially in coupled systems. Using a non conserved order parameter, the tracking of fronts is not necessary, and the transformation of different phases is promoted by chemical and mechanical driving forces. Bainite formation is such a problem. The capturing of diffusion of carbon, precipitation of carbides and the kinetics of phase propagation are significant in order to understand the problem in its full scope. Furthermore, a displacive transformation of austenite to bainitic ferrite in the low temperature regime is considered. This leads to the formation of lower bainite where carbides form between plates of bainite. As elasticity plays a major role in the formation kinetics of bainite, a mechanical solver including the (hydrostatic) eigenstrain of the bainitic phase is implemented. The simulation software has been developed using a finite difference scheme in a GPU framework for three dimensional systems.

3.1   Multi Phase Field Modeling

The multi phase field model is based on [9] and originally formulated in [10], covering the austenite, the bainitic ferrite and the carbide phase. From an energy description of interfacial and gradient energy densities, one arrives at the variational evolution equation of the different phases,

$$\dot{\phi}_i = \sum_{j=1, j \neq i}^{N} \mu_{ij} \left[\sigma_{ij} \left((\phi_j \nabla^2 \phi_i - \phi_i \nabla^2 \phi_j) - \frac{36}{\eta_{ij}^2} \phi_i \phi_j (\phi_j - \phi_i) \right) - \frac{6 \Delta G_{ij}}{\eta_{ij}} \phi_i \phi_j \right], \quad (10)$$

with the interface mobility μ_{ij}, the interface energy σ_{ij}, the interface thickness η_{ij} and the change of Gibbs energy as driving force ΔG_{ij}. Additionally, the symmetry of the phases implies $\mu_{ij} = \mu_{ji}$, $\sigma_{ij} = \sigma_{ji}$, $\eta_{ij} = \eta_{ji}$, and $\Delta G_{ij} = -\Delta G_{ji}$. The parameters are taken from [9]. The three phases, which are considered in this model, are ϕ_1 - bainitic ferrite, ϕ_2 - austenite and ϕ_3 - carbide.

In order to simulate the carbide precipitation, we need to consider the carbon diffusion in the steel. Here we use a Cahn-Hilliard model featuring spinodal decomposition [9],

$$\mathbf{J} = -\phi_1 D \nabla \eta, \quad (11)$$

$$\eta = -b \nabla^2 c + d \cdot f'(c), \quad (12)$$

$$f(c) = (X_{LL} - c)^2 (X_{UL} - c)^2. \quad (13)$$

The flux $\mathbf{J}$ depends on the chemical potential η, the diffusion coefficient D and the phase field order parameter ϕ_1, which leads to diffusion only in the bainitic region. This is reasonable, as we are mainly interested in carbide precipitation for lower bainite. Evolution of the concentration is covered by $\dot{c} = -\nabla \mathbf{J} = \phi_1 D \nabla^2 \eta + \nabla \phi_1 D \nabla \eta$. Phase separation is driven by a double well potential $f(c)$ in the expression for the chemical potential. Thus, the concentration of carbon is either accumulating up to a value X_{UL}, which is the upper limit of carbon concentration in this model, or the carbon diffuses such that a lower limit X_{LL} is reached. The value X_{LL} is the maximum carbon concentration that bainitic ferrite can contain. If the upper limit of X_{UL} is reached, carbide formation is possible. This is expressed through the phase field mobility μ_{13}, which is a function of the carbon concentration, reading

$$\mu_{13} = \mu_{13}^0 \cdot \begin{cases} 0 & \text{if } c < X_{UL} - \beta, \\ 1 & \text{if } c > X_{UL}, \\ \frac{1}{2} + \frac{1}{2} \sin(\frac{\pi}{\beta} c + \frac{\pi}{2} - \frac{\pi}{\beta} X_{UL}) & \text{else.} \end{cases} \quad (14)$$

The parameter β controls the continuous transition of μ_{13}, if nonzero.

Furthermore, a mobility anisotropy is added in order to achieve sheave like structures. For this, the phase field mobility μ_{12} is modified depending on the orientation of the transformation front [9].

In order to get a complete picture of the transformation kinetics, especially if one considers the manufacturing process involving pressing, elastic effects have to be incorporated. The first step is the consideration of the bainitic eigenstrain in isotropic approximation. The linear elastic energy densities for bainite and austenite then read

$$f_\gamma^{el} = \frac{1}{2}\lambda\varepsilon_{ii}^2 + \mu\varepsilon_{ik}^2 \quad \text{for austenite,} \tag{15}$$

$$f_{\alpha B}^{el} = \frac{1}{2}\lambda\left(\varepsilon_{ii} - \varepsilon_{ii}^0\right)^2 + \mu\left(\varepsilon_{ik} - \varepsilon_{ik}^0\right)^2 \quad \text{for bainitic ferrite,} \tag{16}$$

with the Lamé pararmeter λ, the shear modulus μ, the strain tensor ε_{ik} and the eigenstrain $\varepsilon_{ik}^0 = \delta_{ik}\chi\phi_1$. χ is Vegard's coefficient and controls the strength of the eigenstrain, with the limit $\chi = 0$, for which the elastic contributions are absent. Equations (15) and (16) contribute to the total free energy and have to be considered in the phase field evolution equations.

3.2   Results

We first discuss results without elastic effects, hence $\chi = 0$. The carbon is initially distributed randomly, similarly for the order parameter ϕ_3 of the carbide phase. The simulation starts with a small nucleus of bainite on the left side. The grid spacing is defined as $dx = 0.0234\ \mu\text{m}$. Figures 3 and 4 show the results for an initial average carbon concentration of 2.0 wt.%. The bainite nucleus is clearly visible on the left side and grows in a finger like structure in the x-y plane of the simulation box. The results are obtained via a grid of size $128 \times 128 \times 8$ to ensure a quasi two dimensional system, which saves simulation time. In the bainitic region, carbon diffusion is taking place, showing a decomposition process. This is prohibited in the austenite region. If a sufficiently high concentration of carbon is reached, the formation of carbides is enabled according to Eq. (14). These carbides form in a shape similar to the carbon distribution and spherical structures become visible. This result can be influenced by increasing the initial carbon concentration. Then the circles grow in size and eventually touch, forming lamellar structures.

Further results are presented in Fig. 5, where the hydrostatic eigenstrain of the bainitic phase is taken into account. Note that the results here are produced using a plane strain setup, $u_z = 0$, $\varepsilon_{zz} = \varepsilon_{xz} = \varepsilon_{yz} = 0$. The comparison between $\chi = 0.01$ and $\chi = 0$, the nonelastic case, shows, that the bainite phase is forming at a slower rate and the shape of the sheave like structure is changing as well. These results indicate, that the role of elasticity has a major impact on the formation of bainite. Further investigations are planned to examine the role of elasticity. We expect the appearance of transformation plasticity, which describes length changes of the system due to transformations under stress.

4   Near-Tip Segregation at a Mode I Crack

Crack formation and the resulting physical consequences are a very important topic in material science. Catastrophic failure often arise due to crack nucleation

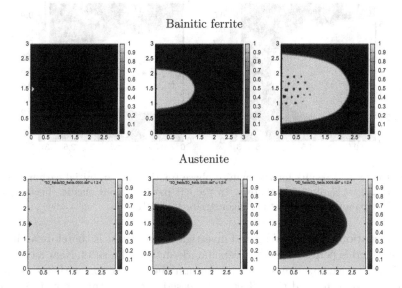

Fig. 3. Phase field results showing the bainite and austenite phase fractions for an initial carbon concentration of 2.0 wt.% at 0, 5000 and 10000 steps with timestep $dt = 0.5 \cdot 10^{-3}$ s, without elasticity.

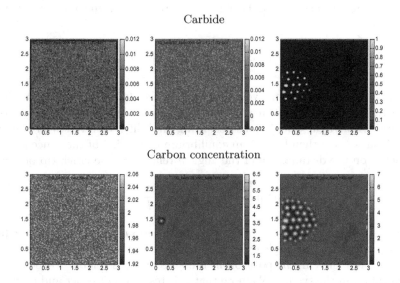

Fig. 4. Phase field results showing the carbide phase fraction and carbon concentration for an initial carbon concentration of 2.0 wt.% at 0, 5000 and 10000 steps with timestep $dt = 0.5 \cdot 10^{-3}$ s, without elasticity.

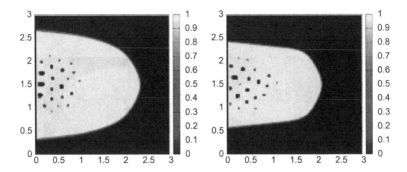

Fig. 5. Phase field results for the bainite phase fraction, for an initial carbon concentration of 2.0 wt.% after 10000 steps. In the left panel without elastic effects, $\chi = 0$, in the right panel with hydrostatic eigenstrain, $\chi = 0.01$.

and propagation. The modeling and investigation of cracks is therefore an important topic and is here also used to benchmark analytical results. Near a crack, tip impurities like carbon can segregate through the interaction with the inhomogeneous stress state, and this effect is discussed here. Starting point is Vegard's law, which expresses the widening of the lattice due to interstitial or substitutional atoms, reading $\varepsilon_{ij}^0 = \chi \cdot c \cdot \delta_{ij}$, if expressed through an eigenstrain. In this case χ is Vegard's coefficient and c the local concentration. The chemical part of the problem has to be linked to a mechanical model, here linear elasticity. Using several simplifications, we can express the relevant total free energy of the system, consisting of the elastic and chemical contribution, in the low concentration regime as

$$F = \left[\mu \left(\varepsilon_{ij} - \varepsilon_{ij}^0 \right)^2 + \frac{1}{2}\lambda \left(\varepsilon_{kk} - \varepsilon_{kk}^0 \right)^2 \right] \cdot \Omega + k_B T \cdot c \ln(c). \qquad (17)$$

The parameter Ω is an atomic volume and k_B is the Boltzmann constant. Simultaneously, the elastic problem with the eigenstrain similar to Eq. (15) has to be solved. Analytical calculations regarding the different stresses in the two-dimensional system then lead to an equilibrium expression of the concentration. It depends on the distance r and the angle θ relative to the crack tip position,

$$c = c_0 \exp \left[\frac{\Omega \chi (1 + \nu) 2 K_I \cos (\theta/2)}{(2\pi r)^{1/2} k_B T} \right], \qquad (18)$$

with the stress intensity factor K_I, the Poisson ratio ν and the distance r from the sharp crack tip. The angle θ is measured between the x-axis, where the crack is located, and the current position in the system; c_0 is related to the average concentration in the system. We note that this result is not exact and only valid in a near-tip regime, where the segregation is still weak, such that the problem can be treated in first order perturbation theory.

In order to verify this analytical result we performed finite element simulations, using the basic model sketched above. The results are presented in Fig. 6, showing very good agreement for the concentration behaviour at various points in the simulation box in regions of low concentration increase.

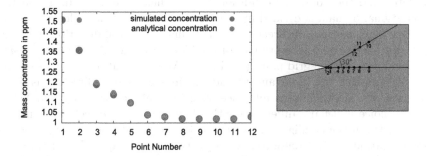

Fig. 6. *Left:* Comparison of analytical and simulation results of the concentration for the segregation near a mode I crack. *Right:* Sketch of the crack model with points at which simulation results and analytical outcomes are compared.

5   GPU Implementation

GPGPU implementations for solving partial differential equations with explicit integration schemes on regular grids are very useful, as they offer a significant acceleration of a code at low costs especially when consumer graphics cards are used. One main advantage in our specific case is, that the porting from the serial CPU code to the GPU implementation is rather straightforward, and even without major optimization efforts a significant speedup can be reached on a single GPU. Practically, the implementation of the phase field model does not take significantly more time than for a corresponding serial CPU code. For our purposes we use CUDA (Compute Unified Device Architecture) for Nvidia graphics cards, which is based on a C++ like language [11]. The key point is that the simulations have to be designed such that they run entirely on the GPU, which avoids slow data transfer to and from the CPU. Still, in most cases, only a relatively low fraction of the theoretical peak performance is reached, as further acceleration would require significant efforts. Nevertheless, it is usually the time to develop suitable physical models for materials science applications, which limits the entire process. For this reason, the numerical acceleration helps significantly to accelerate the model development through a reduction of the runtime from several days to a few hours. For the phase field crystal and amplitude equations simulations, which we used for the analysis of large deformations, semi-implicit pseudospectral methods are used, which benefit from the efficient fast Fourier transformations in CUDA; we have reported a significant speedup in comparison to a serial CPU code, see [13] for details. For phase field simulations with several coupled evolution equations we usually use operator splitting techniques and finite difference forward Euler schemes on regular lattices. An entire integration step in time is subdivided into different kernels, to ensure synchronization of the parallel executions and to avoid race conditions. For example, the integration of one field (e.g. the phase field) is completed before a concentration field is updated and the boundary conditions for the fields are invoked. The entire computational domain is divided into (up to three-dimensional) blocks of equal size. Each block consists of threads, such that in each spatial direction the number of grid points equals the product of the block and thread dimensions, using one thread per physical grid point (see Fig. 7). An optimization of the execution speed by adjusting the block and thread size in each spatial direction is done, which typically has significant influence on the overall performance [12]. Notice that the choice is usually different for the different spatial directions, which is related to the memory alignment of the fields in the global memory. For the time integration it is advantageous to copy a stencil of required field values to the registers of the multiprocessors for accelerated access. Altogether, this allows to keep the fields entirely on the GPU. Only occasionally, for additional evaluations and intermediate storage, the fields are copied to the computer's main memory. For many applications this requires only a negligible fraction of the entire simulation time. Finally, the entire computational domain is surrounded by a halo, where the boundary conditions are applied in a separate CUDA kernel. The width of this halo depends on the order of the underlying differential equations.

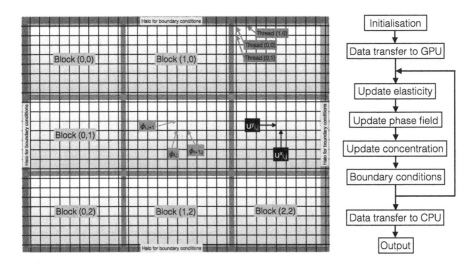

Fig. 7. Sketch of the implementation geometry and program flow of the bainite phase field model using CUDA, shown here in two dimensions. The information is stored on a regular lattice, where the elastic displacements are shifted by half a lattice unit with respect to concentrations and phase fields (staggered grid). The entire system is divided into blocks, at the outer layers boundary conditions are applied.

6 Conclusions

In the first section we presented a phase field crystal model using amplitude equations in combination with mechanical effects. Different strain tensors are presented and the proper choice leads to a reduction of the complex description of nonlinear elasticity. Our findings show, that the Eulerian description is best suited to describe the nonlinearity in the phase field crystal model. Additionally, only Clayton's D tensor is able to express the elastic energy in a three dimensional case of bcc properly. Comparison to the Birch-Murnaghan equation predicts, that the bulk modulus derivative K' is equal to four for bcc materials. *Ab initio* calculations confirm this prediction. The phase field crystal approach achieves this result intrinsically. Hence, the investigations indicate, that the phase field crystal model is an excellent technique to describe nonlinear elasticity from a modelling standpoint. Such a description of nonlinear elasticity can then subsequently be used for large scale microstructure evaluations under large strains, e.g. bainitic press hardening.

The second part of this paper is devoted to a phase field model, which describes the displacive transformation of austenite to bainite. During this formation carbon diffusion is important and therefore taken into account. This results in the formation of carbides, a third phase contained in the multi phase field model. Shape and amount of carbides are strongly connected to the average carbon concentration. An increase of the amount of carbon leads to a transition from localized carbides to lamellar structures. Additionally, the influence of the eigenstrain of the bainitic transformation is taken into account. The results show, that the formation of the bainite is obstructed by elastic effects. Finally, we benchmarked our analytical results of near-tip segregation of a mode I crack. The results show very good agreement with an analytical approximation.

The models are implemented in a GPU framework using CUDA. Finite differences are used for the phase field model as a numerical approach, and a staggered grid is used for the calculation of elasticity. It turns out that for phase field applications like the example demonstrated here, the use of graphics cards for code acceleration is highly useful. Even without major efforts a significant acceleration of the code can be reached, without seriously increasing the complexity of the code. This is particularly useful not only for data production, but also for the stage of model development, as the cycles for simulations and model adjustments are drastically shortened.

Acknowledgements. This work has been supported by the Deutsche Forschungsgemeinschaft via the priority program SPP 1713.

References

1. Karbasian, H., Tekkaya, A.E.: A review on hot stamping. J. Mater. Proc. Technol. **210**(15), 2103–2118 (2010)
2. Bhadeshia, H.K.D.H.: Bainite in Steels, 2nd edn. Institute of Materials, London (2001)

3. Naderi, M.: Hot stamping of ultra-high strength steels. Ph.D. thesis, RWTH Aachen (2007)
4. Fielding, L.: The bainite controversy. Mater. Sci. Technol. **29**(4), 383–399 (2013)
5. Hüter, C., Friák, M., Weikamp, M., Neugebauer, J., Goldenfeld, N., Svendsen, B., Spatschek, R.: Nonlinear elastic effects in phase field crystal and amplitude equations: comparison to ab initio simulations of bcc metals and graphene. Phys. Rev. B **93**(21), 214105 (2016)
6. Kresse, G., Hafner, J.: Ab initio molecular dynamics for liquid metals. Phys. Rev. B **47**(1), 558–561 (1993)
7. Kresse, G., Furthmüller, J.: Efficient iterative schemes for ab initio total-energy calculations using a plane-wave basis set. Phys. Rev. B **54**(16), 11169–11186 (1996)
8. Birch, F.: Finite elastic strain of cubic crystals. Phys. Rev. **71**(11), 809–824 (1947)
9. Düsing, M., Mahnken, R.: Simulation of lower bainitic transformation with the phase-field method considering carbide formation. Comput. Mater. Sci. **111**, 91–100 (2016)
10. Steinbach, I.: Phase-field models in materials science. Model. Simul. Mater. Sci. Eng. **17**(7), 073001 (2009)
11. Nvidia CUDA Programming Guide Ver. 7.0, 21 June 2016. http://docs.nvidia.com/cuda/cuda-c-programming-guide/index.html
12. Monas, A.: Modeling of phase change materials for nonvolatile data storage using GPU simulations. Master's thesis, Ruhr-Universität (2012)
13. Hüter, C., Nguyen, C.-D., Spatschek, R., Neugebauer, J.: Scale bridging between atomistic and mesoscale modelling: applications of amplitude equation descriptions. Model. Simul. Mater. Sci. Eng. **22**, 034001 (2014)

Ab Initio Modelling of Electrode Material Properties

Siaufung O. Dang[1,2(✉)], Marco Prill[1], Claas Hüter[1(✉)],
Martin Finsterbusch[1], and Robert Spatschek[1,3]

[1] Institute for Energy and Climate Research,
Forschungszentrum Jülich GmbH, 52425 Jülich, Germany
{s.dang,c.hueter}@fz-juelich.de
[2] Batterielabor und Methodenentwicklung,
Brunel GmbH im Auftrag der Deutsche ACCUMOTIVE GmbH & Co. KG,
73230 Kirchheim unter Treck, Germany
[3] JARA-ENERGY, 52056 Aachen, Germany

Abstract. We discuss elastic and thermodynamic aspects of $LiCoO_2$ in the context of fracture propagation and hot spot formation. Approaching the problem via ab initio modelling, we can access the delithiated states which is difficult experimentally. Application of density functional theory in the quasi-harmonic approximation provides good agreement in the range of experimentally available data for isobaric heat capacities, suggesting to complement thermodynamic databases required for the modelling of heat flows. The results for the mechanical characteristics suggest a brittle-to-ductile transition with varying lithium contents and crack orientations perpendicular to the basal plane, as indicated by the obtained elastic tensors experimentally.

Keywords: Battery · Cathode · Phonon calculations · Elastic constants

1 Introduction

Advanced lithium-ion batteries have established as preferred energy storage system for many mobile devices, though still critical aspects of mechanical and electrochemical loading pose challenging physical questions. Longer lifetime (cyclability), improved energy density and kinetics of the employed battery materials are still of major interest. In the majority of commercial batteries only about 50% of the theoretical capacity is used, since phase transformations of the lithium transition metal oxides upon further discharge lead to irreversible capacity losses and ultimately to the destruction of the battery module. Another aspect that merits further improvement is the inherent safety of the material. In this respect knowing the heat capacities of the material is of importance for the accurate evaluation of the thermal behaviour in order to properly design thermal management systems. Poor design increases the risk of thermal runaway, a process triggered at the onset of a certain temperature due to improper battery

© Springer International Publishing AG 2017
E. Di Napoli et al. (Eds.): JHPCS 2016, LNCS 10164, pp. 139–150, 2017.
DOI: 10.1007/978-3-319-53862-4_12

operation or inhomogeneity during cell fabrication, with the onset temperature of thermal runaway depending on the electrolyte composition. Because obtaining thermodynamic properties for delithiated compounds presents a major obstacle for caloric measurements over wide temperature ranges, we use a computational approach by means of atomistic modelling. This enables us to explore the thermodynamic properties of cathode materials in the delithiated states, which from a practical point of view represent higher states of charge that are most susceptible to failure by thermal runaway.

Apart from thermodynamic properties, also mechanical properties of lithium ion-based systems are of high importance. The cyclability of the material depends on its ability to maintain its structural integrity. Many lithium ion-based batteries exhibit volume changes accompanying lithium concentration changes in the host material. Graphite as very common negative electrode for these systems shows a volume increase of 10% upon lithium intercalation between the carbon atom sheets [4]. While silicon can store an order of magnitude more lithium ions, the associated volume expansion reaches up to 300% [1]. Apart from the volume expansion due to intercalation, also phase transitions can cause diffusion-induced stresses. The resulting detrimental effects in the electrode materials lead to battery capacity loss and eventually to power fade. However, there has been substantial progress toward the prediction of diffusion induced stresses and the increase of mechanical durability of lithium-ion-based batteries [2,3,5,8,15]. For the important class of $LiCoO_2$ based batteries, several investigations have focused on structural and morphological changes in heavily cycled materials and indicate fracture of the active material particles due to the stresses induced by the volume changes associated with lithium ion intake and removal. It was stated by Huggins et al. that the critical size of the $LiCoO_2$ particles is a function of fracture toughness, elastic modulus and strain. For a better understanding of the fracturing mechanism and the evaluation of the critical particle size we believe that detailed knowledge about the elastic properties of Li_xCoO_2 in dependence of lithium content will help to elucidate this aspect.

On the other hand, there is ongoing research into alternative anode materials. In theory, lithium-metal alloys can exhibit a much higher volumetric energy density compared to the established graphite anode as implemented in all state-of-the art lithium-ion batteries. While commercially available graphite anodes can host 1 lithium ion per 6 carbon atoms (LiC_6), metals like germanium, tin, silicon and lead can host more than 4 lithium atoms per metal atom forming $Li_{22}M_5$ [17]. Silicon-containing alloys have been investigated due to their favorable voltage profile and their reversible capacity [21]. The magnesium-silicon system gets reinforced attention as potential material system for anodes in lithium-ion-batteries. Within the ternary lithium-magnesium-silicon system many of the thermodynamically stable phases have been identified for temperatures from room temperature to liquidus temperature and provide a solid basis for further directed investigations [11]. Mg_2Si was discovered to be actually a solid solution with the formula Li_xMg_2Si [9,16,17,19]. Extended investigations into silicon based compounds may prove fruitful in the near future.

2   Methods

We employ the ab initio code VASP (Vienna ab initio simulation package) [12] to obtain properties at the atomic scale in conjunction with the code phonopy [27] to deal with dynamic properties based on the temperature dependent collective atomic motions (phonons).

VASP is a density-functional theory (DFT) code and as such approximates the solution of the many-body Schroedinger equation of the considered system. The free energy of the system is described depending as a function of the electron density instead of the external potential. This corresponds to a type of Legendre transformation, and the resulting functional is termed Hohenberg-Kohn free energy. The numerical implementation of DFT requires the explicit construction of the Hohenberg-Kohn free energy functional, typically split into three contributions, the noninteracting kinetic energy, the electrostatic energy and the exchange-correlation energy. While the electrostatic term could be easily expressed explicitly, the other terms are much more complex. The method of choice here is the orbital method developed by Kohn and Sham, which uses the one-particle Schroedinger equation with effective potential to describe the kinetic term,

$$\left(-\frac{\hbar^2}{2m}\nabla^2 + v_{eff}\right)\psi_i = \epsilon_i\psi_i, \tag{1}$$

such that $n = \sum_{i=1}^{N}|\psi_i|^2$ holds for the electronic density n. The effective potential v_{eff} then satisfies

$$v_{eff} = v - e\phi + v_{xc}, \tag{2}$$

where v is the external potential, $\phi = -e\int dr'n(r')/|r-r'|$ the electrostatic potential and v_{xc} the exchange correlation potential. The used Kohn Sham orbitals thus approximate the electron density, though they do not coincide with the electron wave functions.

Technically, the physical properties are calculated by iteratively optimizing the electron density distribution of a structure within the so-called self-consistent field method to attain the ground state geometry. Therefore, v_{eff} determines the electronic density n in Eq. 1, and vice versa in Eq. 2. The number of electrons and the external potential are given, the chemical potential is set to zero. In combination with an explicit approximation of the exchange correlation energy E_{xc} and the resulting exchange correlation potential $v_{xc} = \delta E_{xc}/\delta n$, the equations listed here allow for the calculation of the electron density n and the ground state energy for a system of N interacting particles.

Efficiency and accuracy are achieved through the employment of the implemented pseudopotentials based on the projector augmented wave (PAW) method. Nevertheless, such calculations on the atomistic scale are computationally very demanding since some of the calculation algorithms scale with N^3 where N is the number of atoms in the cell.

Phonopy [27] is a post-processing tool written to read specific data from the output of the ab initio code in order to calculate dynamical (phonon) properties. Its framework includes functions for fitting the equation of state and calculation routines for deriving results in the quasi-harmonic approximation. The actual computationally demanding part are the ab initio calculations for obtaining atomic response forces for the derivation of the phonon properties. The calculation of these forces based on the finite difference method requires the fully relaxed crystal structure as input to generate supercells with symmetry-distinct atomic displacements. The force constants are computed by calculating the atomic response forces and computing the ratio between the force differences and the absolute displacements,

$$k = \frac{\partial^2 E_{pot}(R)}{\partial u^2} \cong -\frac{F(R + \triangle u) - F(R)}{\triangle u} \quad . \tag{3}$$

In the harmonic oscillator model the force constants relate to the phonon frequencies in the following way:

$$\omega^2 = \frac{k}{m} \Leftrightarrow f = \frac{1}{2\pi}\sqrt{\frac{k}{m}} \quad . \tag{4}$$

Therefore, this provides the means to obtain the phonon spectrum. It enables the computation of the depending phonon properties based on the harmonic phonon free energy. We calculate phonon properties in the quasi-harmonic approximation. For further details on this method we refer the reader to the work of Shang et al. [26].

For the elastic description of the system, we used the method of Le Page and Saxe to calculate the elastic tensors. With this method the elastic tensor is determined by performing six finite distortions of the lattice and deriving the elastic constants from the stress-strain relationship [14].

3   Results

The phonon dispersion curve along the high symmetry points in the Brillouin zone Γ, T and LD corresponding to the 3a (Li), 3b (Co) and 6c (O) sites, is shown exemplarily for LiCoO2 in Fig. 1. The absence of imaginary frequencies indicates a stable and well converged crystal structure geometry and its respective thermodynamic stability. The total phonon density of states of $LiCoO_2$ is in good agreement with that calculated by Du et al. [6]. Bulk modulus and thermal expansion coefficients from 0 to $600\,K$ are obtained from the fits to the third-order Birch-Murnaghan equation of state within the quasi-harmonic approximation and are shown exemplary for $LiCoO_2$ in Fig. 2. Reference data on these physical properties with respect to the $LiCoO_2$ compound are scarce. From our survey we could find that our calculated bulk modulus of 139.8 GPa at 0K and 134 GPa at 300 K compares well to calculations by Wang et al. [28] obtained for 0 K and to experimental data with values of 142.9 GPa and 149 GPa, respectively. A compilation of data including our own calculations is presented in Table 1. Based on the data about $LiCoO_2$ it can be confirmed that

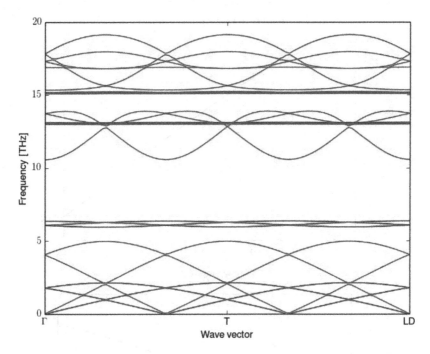

Fig. 1. Phonon dispersion curve of $LiCoO_2$ along the high symmetry points Γ, T and LD. No imaginary frequencies in the whole spectrum evidence that the structure is well converged (phonopy presents imaginary frequencies as negative frequencies).

Table 1. Parameters obtained from the fit of the third-order Birch-Murnaghan equation of state to the energy-volume data given for $LiCoO_2$. Comparison is given with respect to the data by Wang et al. [28] for $LiCoO_2$.

Method	$V_0/\text{Å}^3$	B_0/GPa	B_0'
LDA	30.471	168.5	4.67
GGA	32.946	142.9	4.51
Experimental	32.16	149.2	4.13
GGA (this work)	33.17	140.2	4.48

there is a reasonable agreement. The small differences in our results when compared to Wang et al. may be attributed to the fact that they employed a lower energy cutoff of 500 eV as opposed to 520 eV in our case.

For the Li_xCoO_2 compounds the obtained phonon densities of states and the isobaric heat capacities are compiled in Fig. 3. The decrease of the heat capacity with decreasing lithium content is physically plausible due to the reduced mass. As can be seen from the heat capacity curves the overall trend is modelled correctly although there is some deviation of the calculated results from the experimental data by Ménétrier et al. [18] and Jankovsky et al. [10].

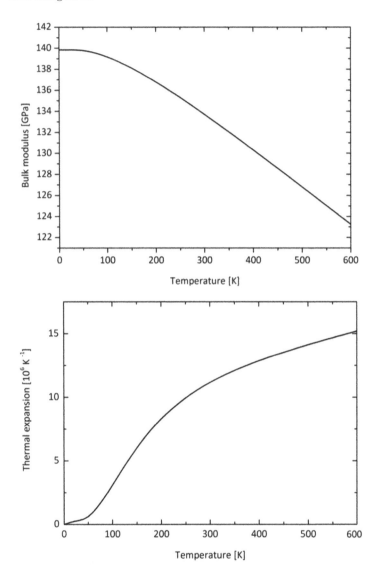

Fig. 2. Bulk modulus and thermal expansion coefficient of LiCoO$_2$ as a function of temperature as derived from the fit to the third-order Birch-Murnaghan equation of state in the framework of the quasi-harmonic approximation.

The deviation between the calculated and the experimental heat capacity at $T = 298K$ amounts to $\approx 6.8\%$. This may be attributed to the fact that the phonon calculations are based on a single-crystal model whereas the experimental data is obtained for a polycrystalline sample, which lowers the compounds density relative to the calculated model structure due to grain boundaries. A further source of error may be linked to the calculated force constants based on the employed projector-augmented wave potential and might be worth reinvestigating with other alternative PAW potentials.

Concerning the elastic properties of Li_xCoO_2, the computed single crystal elastic constants of the three stoichiometries as obtained from VASP as well as the elastic aggregate properties (polycrystalline) bulk modulus B, shear modulus G and their respective ratios B/G derived on the basis of the formulae as outlined by Hector et al. [7] are compiled in Table 2. The Youngs moduli Y_H and Poisson ratios ν are estimated as

$$Y_H = \frac{9BG}{3B + G},$$ (5)

$$\nu = \frac{3B - 2G}{6B + 2G},$$

which means we use the isotropic elasticity approximation. Since for scales above one micron the electrode particles are typically polycrystalline already, this pragmatically motivated simplification is legitimate here. The elastic stability conditions for the hexagonal symmetry as taken from Mouhat and Coudert [20] are fulfilled for all calculated structures:

$$\left\{ \begin{array}{l} C_{11} > \|C_{12}\|; 2C_{13}^2 < C_{33}(C_{11} + C_{12}) \\ C_{44} > 0; C_{66} > 0 \end{array} \right\}$$

According to the stability conditions, negative eigenvalues such as in $Li_{0.5}CoO_2$ do not imply physical implausibility. On the contrary, it simply suggests elongation upon compressive stress for specific deformational modes. We included the only reference of elastic properties for $LiCoO_2$ that we are aware of in Table 1, which are based on DFT calculations with a hybrid functional approach by Qi et al. [24]. It should be noted that their calculated elastic tensor for $LiCoO_2$ possesses the wrong symmetry most likely due to a misprint. In a hexagonal cell the elastic constants are only isotropic within the basal plane so that solely $C_{55} = C_{66}$. However, their tensor satisfies $C_{44} = C_{55} = C_{66}$. Further comparison reveals that the tensor by Qi et al. generally displays larger elastic constants, e.g., their C_{11}/C_{22} and their C_{33} values are larger by 26% and 12% respectively. This can be attributed to the employment of a hybrid functional instead of the GGA-PBE functional used in this work. The C_{55}/C_{66} values corresponding to the shearing parallel to the oxygen layers show an even more significant deviation (37% lower). These results are to be expected, since the GGA-PBE functional is known to underestimate elastic properties [13,22]. As a result, the derived elastic aggregate properties like bulk and shear modulus (G, B) are lower as well (12% and 21% respectively). The ratio of bulk to shear modulus can be evaluated according to Pughs criterion [23], which postulates ductile materials for B/G > 1.75 and brittle materials for B/G < 1.75. In this respect, the analysis suggests brittle behavior for stoichiometries of $x >$ 0.67 and therefore implies that integrity loss of the compound is more likely to occur during cycling at higher lithiated states due to brittle crack propagation. In addition, we employed a universal elastic anisotropy index A^U for arbitrary

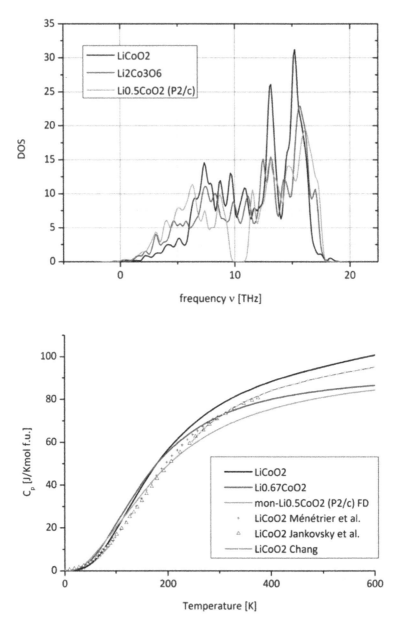

Fig. 3. The phonon density of states and derived heat capacities at constant pressure for LiCoO$_2$, Li$_{0.67}$CoO$_2$ and Li$_{0.5}$CoO$_2$ compared to available literature data.

Table 2. Elastic properties of $LiCoO_2$, $Li_{0.67}CoO_2$ and $Li_{0.5}CoO_2$ computed with GGA-PBE exchange correlation functionals showing elastic tensor components C_{ij}, bulk modulus B, shear modulus G, B/G ratio, Young's modulus Y_H, Poisson ratio ν and anisotropy index A^U. The indices V, R, H correspond to the different approaches of the Voigt-Reuss-Hill homogenisation scheme.

Structure	C_{ij}						B[GPa]	G[GPa]	$\frac{B_H}{G_H}$	Y_H	ν	A^U
$LiCoO_2{}^1$	422	106	62	0	0	0	$B_V : 171$	$G_V : 115$	1.5	264	0.32	-
	106	422	163	0	0	0	$B_H : 163$	$G_H : 107$				
	62	65.4	239	0	0	0	$B_R : 156$	$G_R : 98.6$				
	0	0	0	68.1	0	0						
	0	0	0	0	68.1	0						
	0	0	0	0	0	68.1						
$LiCoO_2$	334.2	100.7	65.4	0	-7.1	0	$B_V : 149.5$	$G_V : 104$	1.64	220.4	0.25	2.2
	100.7	334.2	65.4	0	7.1	0	$B_H : 145$	$G_H : 88.4$				
	65.4	65.4	213.7	0	0	0	$B_R : 140.5$	$G_R : 72.8$				
	0	0	0	116.8	0	-7.1						
	-7.1	7.1	0	0	49.5	0						
	0	0	0	-7.1	0	49.5						
$Li_{0.67}CoO_2$	312.6	95.2	35.8	4.7	-6.7	-2.8	$B_V : 122.3$	$G_V : 79.6$	1.90	140.4	0.28	8.5
	95.2	329.2	35.4	9.6	7.8	0.8	$B_H : 104.7$	$G_H : 55.0$				
	35.8	35.4	126.2	-0.4	-8.7	15.0	$B_R : 87.0$	$G_R : 30.3$				
	4.7	9.6	-0.4	115.7	-1.8	-5.2						
	-6.7	7.8	-8.7	-1.8	17.3	0.3						
	-2.8	0.8	15.0	-5.2	0.3	17.0						
$Li_{0.5}CoO_2$	270.2	97.9	51.7	8.1	-6.4	50.7	$B_V : 111.9$	$G_V : 58.1$	2.40	96.7	0.32	14.7
	97.9	288.0	36.4	7.3	-30.6	13.3	$B_H : 88.2$	$G_H : 36.7$				
	51.7	36.4	77.2	-13.2	7.5	-13.0	$B_R : 64.5$	$G_R : 15.3$				
	8.1	7.3	-13.2	90.1	18.7	-9.6						
	-6.4	-30.6	7.5	18.7	19.0	-10.8						
	50.7	13.3	-13.0	-9.6	-10.9	31.6						

[1] from Qi et al. [24]

crystal symmetry as proposed by Ranganathan et al. [25]:

$$A^U = 5\frac{G_V}{G_R} + \frac{B_V}{B_R} - 6 \geq 0, \tag{6}$$

which accounts for both shear and bulk moduli to quantify the single-crystal anisotropy. For locally isotropic single crystals $A^U = 0$ since $G_V = G_R$ and $B_V = B_R$. As observable from Table 2, the anisotropy increases by a factor of 6.7 in the course of delithiation from $LiCoO_2$ to $Li_{0.5}CoO_2$. This observation is supported by the much higher values of C_{11}, C_{22} and C_{44} relative to the other elastic constants indicating brittle properties specifically along the direction perpendicular to the oxygen layers. Fractures due to cycling-induced stress may therefore particularly originate from shear stress arising in the a-b-plane (basal plane) and normal stress parallel to the basal plane leading to cleavage perpendicular to the layers as illustrated in Fig. 4.

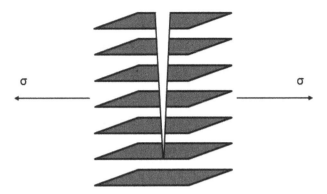

Fig. 4. Illustration of brittle fracture occurring perpendicular to the layers of Li_xCoO_2 based on the evaluated elastic tensors.

4   Summary and conclusions

In this paper we derived key properties for lithium ion battery electrode materials from first principles. The calculated isobaric heat capacities are in good agreement with available experimental data and therefore demonstrate that the quasi-harmonic approximation is a robust method to yield data particularly for delithiated $LiCoO_2$, which is difficult to obtain via an experimental approach. The obtained data for the delithiated stoichiometries could be used to enhance models in computational fluid dynamics simulations for a more accurate evaluation of the heat distribution in cells in pursuit of the identification of hot spots. The comparison of the elastic properties of $LiCoO_2$ to available literature data yields discrepancies, which can be attributed to the employed GGA exchange-correlation functional in this work. In this respect, the bulk and the shear moduli of $LiCoO_2$ obtained are calculated to be 12% and 21% lower than the reference, respectively. Qualitatively, the evaluation of the bulk to shear modulus ratio (B/G) suggests brittle behavior for stoichiometries with $0.67 < x < 1$ and ductile behavior when $0.5 < x < 0.67$. In this context the elastic tensors indicate that brittle fracture and crack propagation may occur specifically perpendicular to the basal plane in the direction of which the compound is much less ductile than parallel to the basal plane, as indicated experimentally.

Acknowledgements. This work is supported by the BMBF project Meet Hi-EnD II.

References

1. Beaulieu, L., Beattie, S., Hatchard, T., Dahn, J.: The electrochemical reaction of lithium with tin studied by in situ AFM. J. Electrochem. Soc. **150**(4), A419–A424 (2003)
2. Cheng, Y.T., Verbrugge, M.W.: Evolution of stress within a spherical insertion electrode particle under potentiostatic and galvanostatic operation. J. Power Sources **190**(2), 453–460 (2009)

3. Christensen, J., Newman, J.: Stress generation and fracture in lithium insertion materials. J. Solid State Electrochem. **10**(5), 293–319 (2006)
4. Dahn, J.: Phase diagram of Li x C 6. Phys. Rev. B **44**(17), 9170 (1991)
5. Deshpande, R., Cheng, Y.T., Verbrugge, M.W.: Modeling diffusion-induced stress in nanowire electrode structures. J. Power Sources **195**(15), 5081–5088 (2010)
6. Du, T., Xu, B., Wu, M., Liu, G., Ouyang, C.: Insight into the vibrational and thermodynamic properties of layered lithium transition-metal oxides LiMO2 (M= Co, Ni, Mn): a first-principles study. J. Phys. Chem. C **120**(11), 5876–5882 (2016)
7. Hector, L., Herbst, J., Capehart, T.: Electronic structure calculations for LaNi 5 and LaNi 5 H 7: energetics and elastic properties. J. Alloy Compd. **353**(1), 74–85 (2003)
8. Huggins, R., Nix, W.: Decrepitation model for capacity loss during cycling of alloys in rechargeable electrochemical systems. Ionics **6**(1–2), 57–63 (2000)
9. Imai, Y., Watanabe, A.: Energetics of compounds related to Mg 2 Si as an anode material for lithium-ion batteries using first principle calculations. J. Alloy Compd. **509**(30), 7877–7880 (2011)
10. Jankovsky, O., Kovarik, J., Leitner, J., Rzicka, K., Sedmidubsky, D.: Thermodynamic properties of stoichiometric lithium cobaltite LiCoO 2. Thermochim. Acta **634**, 26–30 (2016)
11. Kevorkov, D., Schmid-Fetzer, R., Zhang, F.: Phase equilibria and thermodynamics of the Mg-Si-Li system and remodeling of the Mg-Si system. J. Phase Equilibr. Diffus. **25**(2), 140–151 (2004)
12. Kresse, G., Furthmüller, J.: Software VASP, vienna (1999). Phys. Rev. B **54**(11), 169 (1996)
13. Kurth, S., Perdew, J.P., Blaha, P.: Molecular and solid-state tests of density functional approximations: LSD, GGAs, and meta-GGAs. Int. J. Quant. Chem. **75**(4–5), 889–909 (1999)
14. Le Page, Y., Saxe, P.: Symmetry-general least-squares extraction of elastic coefficients from ab initio total energy calculations. Phys. Rev. B **63**(17), 174103 (2001)
15. Li, Y., Cheng, Y.T.: Studies of metal hydride electrodes using an electrochemical quartz crystal microbalance. J. Electrochem. Soc. **143**(1), 120–124 (1996)
16. Liu, H., Hu, C., Wu, S.: Ab initio study on the lithiation mechanism of Mg 2 Si electrode. In: 2011 International Conference on Materials for Renewable Energy & Environment (ICMREE), vol. 1, pp. 683–685. IEEE (2011)
17. Ma, D., Cao, Z., Hu, A.: Si-based anode materials for Li-ion batteries: a mini review. Nano-Micro Lett. **6**(4), 347–358 (2014)
18. Menetrier, M., Carlier, D., Blangero, M., Delmas, C.: On really stoichiometric LiCoO2. Electrochem. Solid-State Lett. **11**(11), A179–A182 (2008)
19. Moriga, T., Watanabe, K., Tsuji, D., Massaki, S., Nakabayashi, I.: Reaction mechanism of metal silicide Mg 2 Si for Li insertion. J. Solid State Chem. **153**(2), 386–390 (2000)
20. Mouhat, F., Coudert, F.X.: Necessary and sufficient elastic stability conditions in various crystal systems. Phys. Rev. B **90**(22), 224104 (2014)
21. Park, C.M., Kim, J.H., Kim, H., Sohn, H.J.: Li-alloy based anode materials for Li secondary batteries. Chem. Soc. Rev. **39**(8), 3115–3141 (2010)
22. Perdew, J.P., Ruzsinszky, A., Csonka, G.I., Vydrov, O.A., Scuseria, G.E., Constantin, L.A., Zhou, X., Burke, K.: Restoring the density-gradient expansion for exchange in solids and surfaces. Phys. Rev. Lett. **100**(13), 136406 (2008)
23. Pugh, S.: XCII. relations between the elastic moduli and the plastic properties of polycrystalline pure metals. Lond. Edinb. Dublin Philos. Mag. J. Sci. **45**(367), 823–843 (1954)

24. Qi, Y., Hector, L.G., James, C., Kim, K.J.: Lithium concentration dependent elastic properties of battery electrode materials from first principles calculations. J. Electrochem. Soc. **161**(11), F3010–F3018 (2014)

25. Ranganathan, S.I., Ostoja-Starzewski, M.: Universal elastic anisotropy index. Phys. Rev. Lett. **101**(5), 055504 (2008)

26. Shang, S.L., Hector, L.G., Shi, S., Qi, Y., Wang, Y., Liu, Z.K.: Lattice dynamics, thermodynamics and elastic properties of monoclinic Li 2 CO 3 from density functional theory. Acta Materialia **60**(13), 5204–5216 (2012)

27. Togo, A., Tanaka, I.: First principles phonon calculations in materials science. Scr. Mater. **108**, 1–5 (2015)

28. Wang, X., Loa, I., Kunc, K., Syassen, K., Amboage, M.: Effect of pressure on the structural properties and Raman modes of LiCoO 2. Phys. Rev. B **72**(22), 224102 (2005)

Overlapping of Communication and Computation in `nb3dfft` for 3D Fast Fourier Transformations

Jens Henrik Göbbert[1(✉)], Hristo Iliev[2,3], Cedrick Ansorge[4], and Heinz Pitsch[5]

[1] Jülich Supercomputing Centre, Forschungszentrum Jülich GmbH, Jülich, Germany
`j.goebbert@fz-juelich.de`
[2] JARA-HPC, 52074 Aachen, Germany
[3] IT Center, RWTH Aachen University, Aachen, Germany
[4] Institut für Geophysik und Meteorologie, University of Cologne, Cologne, Germany
[5] Institut für Technische Verbrennung, RWTH Aachen University, Aachen, Germany

Abstract. For efficiency and accuracy of Direct Numerical Simulations (DNS) of turbulent flows pseudo-spectral methods can be employed, where the governing equations are solved partly in Fourier space. The inhouse-developed 3d-FFT library `nb3dfft` is optimized to the special needs of pseudo-spectral DNS, particularly for the scientific code `psOpen`, used by the Institute for Combustion Technology at RWTH Aachen University. In this paper we discuss the method of overlapping communication and computation of multiple FFTs at the same time.

Keywords: 3D-FFT · Overlapping communication and computation · Turbulence · Pseudo-spectral · Numerical simulation · HPC

1 Introduction

Highly optimized libraries for 3D Fast Fourier Transformations (3d-FFT) are needed for pseudo-spectral Direct Numerical Simulation (DNS) codes.

Several platform-independent parallel 3d-FFT libraries, capable of 1d and 2d domain decomposition, are available as open-source software for single and double precision data, e.g. P3DFFT [8] and 2DECOMP&FFT [5], which are developed to run on large supercomputers. But, taking the specific properties of the entire DNS algorithm into account, a new 3d-FFT library was developed for even more optimized performance and scaling.

This 3d-FFT library for pseudo-spectral DNS called `nb3dfft` [7] was developed to take advantage of two optimization techniques. Firstly, this library reduces the data to be sent between the MPI processes significantly. This has been discussed in detail in [2]. Secondly, it provides the ability to compute multiple 3d-FFTs simultaneously. In the following this approach is discussed in detail.

The basic algorithm for massive-parallel 3d fast Fourier transformations is very communication intensive and requires a global and time consuming redistribution of the data between all MPI processes. But, while data are being sent and

© Springer International Publishing AG 2017
E. Di Napoli et al. (Eds.): JHPCS 2016, LNCS 10164, pp. 151–159, 2017.
DOI: 10.1007/978-3-319-53862-4_13

received over the network, the CPUs are often idle as they are waiting for data to process. Therefore masking the communication can have a major impact on the overall performance. The technique for multiple 3d-FFTs of `nb3dfft` significantly optimize the 3d-FFT algorithm for pseudo-spectral DNS by introducing methods for overlapping computation and communication phases.

2   Pseudo-spectral Algorithm

Understanding turbulence remains a big challenge of major importance to both science and engineering. Turbulence is a strongly nonlocal and nonlinear continuum field phenomenon and is governed by the Navier-Stokes equations. For incompressible flows these can be written as follows:
continuity

$$\nabla \cdot \boldsymbol{v} = 0, \tag{1}$$

momentum

$$\frac{\partial \boldsymbol{v}}{\partial t} + \boldsymbol{\omega} \times \boldsymbol{v} = -\nabla p_0 + \nu \nabla^2 \boldsymbol{v}, \tag{2}$$

where $\boldsymbol{v}$, p_0 and ν denote the velocity vector, the static pressure and the kinematic viscosity, respectively, and $\boldsymbol{\omega} = \nabla \times \boldsymbol{v}$ is the vorticity vector.

DNS of turbulent flows can be solved by various iterative numerical methods, but for simple geometries pseudo-spectral methods [1] lead to the most accurate results compared to finite-difference and finite-volume methods.

A pseudo-spectral algorithm for decaying isotropic homogeneous turbulence as an incompressible flow in a cubed $(2\pi)^3$ domain with periodic boundaries represents the use case for the need of highly optimized 3d-FFT. The iterative algorithm works on a 3d computational domain of $N_x \times N_y \times N_z$ grid points in real space and $K_x \times K_y \times K_z$ wave numbers in spectral space as a superposition of plane waves.

The incompressible Navier-Stokes equations for momentum (Eq. 2) is Fourier transformed to

$$\frac{\partial \hat{\boldsymbol{v}}}{\partial t} = -(\delta_{ij} - \frac{k_i k_j}{k^2})(\widehat{\boldsymbol{\omega} \times \boldsymbol{v}})_j + \nu k^2 \hat{\boldsymbol{v}}, \tag{3}$$

in spectral space by applying incompressibility and introducing $\hat{p}_0 = \frac{i\boldsymbol{k}}{k^2} \cdot \widehat{\boldsymbol{\omega} \times \boldsymbol{v}}$ as the transformed Poisson equation and δ_{ij} as the Kronecker delta.

The linear term $\nu k^2 \hat{\boldsymbol{v}}$ and the time integration is computed in spectral space, but the nonlinear product $(\widehat{\boldsymbol{\omega} \times \boldsymbol{v}})_j$ is a highly computationally expensive convolution in spectral space and is better computed in real space. Therefore, while stepping forward in time with each iteration, three backward in-place 3d-FFTs, three backward and out-of-place 3d-FFTs and three forward and in-place 3d-FFTs have to be computed as shown in the Algorithm 1. Here 'backward' refers to a transformation from spectral to real space in contrast to 'forward', while 'in-place' refers to overwriting the input values with the result in contrast to 'out-of-place'.

Algorithm 1. Outline of the efficient algorithm of the pseudo-spectral algorithm for iterating the velocity of homogeneous isotropic forced turbulence and a passive scalar in a periodic domain. The required 13 3d-FFTs are computed by two `nb3dfft` calls in blocks of seven and six 3d-FFTs and benefit from overlapping communication and computation. It requires memory for 22 scalars values (numbered by the lower index) per grid point and computes 13 3d-FFTs in each iteration.

1: **procedure** ITERATE VELOCITY $(n \to [n+1])$, PASSIVE SCALAR $([n-1] \to n)$

2:    **input (velocity):** $\widehat{u}^n_{1|2|3}$, $\widehat{G}^{n-1}_{4|5|6}$, $\widehat{f}^{n-1}_u$

3:    **input (passive scalar):** $\widehat{\phi}^{n-1}_{17}$, J^{n-1}_{19}, $\widehat{J}^{n-2}_{18}$, $\widehat{u}^{n-1}_{16}$

4:    **for all** wave numbers (κ) **do:**   ▷ compute vorticity

5:        $\widehat{\omega}^n_{x,10} \leftarrow \kappa_z \widehat{u}^n_{y,2} - \kappa_y \widehat{u}^n_{z,3}$

6:        $\widehat{\omega}^n_{y,11} \leftarrow \kappa_x \widehat{u}^n_{z,3} - \kappa_z \widehat{u}^n_{x,1}$

7:        $\widehat{\omega}^n_{z,12} \leftarrow \kappa_y \widehat{u}^n_{x,1} - \kappa_x \widehat{u}^n_{y,2}$

8:    $\omega^n_{10|11|12} \xleftarrow{\mathcal{F}+3/2 \text{ filter}} \widehat{\omega}^n_{10|11|12}$ ▷ 3x in-place backward 3d-FFT

9:    $u^n_{7|8|9} \xleftarrow{\mathcal{F}+3/2 \text{ filter}} \widehat{u}^n_{1|2|3}$ ▷ 3x out-of-place backward 3d-FFT

10:    $\widehat{J}^{n-1}_{19} \xleftarrow{\mathcal{F}+3/2 \text{ filter}} J^{n-1}_{19}$ ▷ 1x in-place forward 3d-FFT

11:    **for all** wave numbers (κ) **do:**   ▷ advance passive scalar

12:        $\widehat{\phi}^n_{17} \leftarrow \mathrm{F}_{\mathrm{adv}}(\widehat{\phi}^{n-1}_{17}, \widehat{J}^{n-1}_{19}, \widehat{J}^{n-2}_{18}, \widehat{u}^{n-1}_{16})$

13:    $\widehat{J}^{n-1}_{19} \overset{\text{zero copy}}{\rightleftharpoons} \widehat{J}^{n-2}_{18}$ ▷ swap memory

14:    **for all** grid points (N) **do:**   ▷ compute $G^n = \omega^n \times u^n$

15:        $G^n_{x,13} \leftarrow u^n_{y,8} \cdot \omega^n_{z,12} - u^n_{z,9} \cdot \omega^n_{y,11}$

16:        $G^n_{y,14} \leftarrow u^n_{z,9} \cdot \omega^n_{x,10} - u^n_{x,7} \cdot \omega^n_{z,12}$

17:        $G^n_{z,15} \leftarrow u^n_{x,7} \cdot \omega^n_{y,11} - u^n_{y,8} \cdot \omega^n_{x,10}$

18:    $\widehat{\nabla\phi}^n_{10|11|12} \leftarrow \widehat{\phi}^n_{17}$ ▷ 3x compute derivatives

19:    $\widehat{G}^n_{13|14|15} \xleftarrow{\mathcal{F}+3/2 \text{ filter}} G^n_{13|14|15}$ ▷ 3x in-place forward 3d-FFT

20:    $\nabla\phi^n_{20|21|22} \xleftarrow{\mathcal{F}+3/2 \text{ filter}} \widehat{\nabla\phi}^n_{20|21|22}$ ▷ 3x in-place backward 3d-FFT

21:    $J^n_{19} \leftarrow u^n_{7|8|9} \cdot \nabla\phi^n_{20|21|22}$ ▷ compute convective term

22:    $\widehat{G}^n_{13|14|15} \overset{\text{zero copy}}{\rightleftharpoons} \widehat{G}^{n-1}_{4|5|6}$ ▷ swap memory

23:    $\widehat{u}^n_{16} \overset{\text{zero copy}}{\rightleftharpoons} \widehat{u}^n_2$ ▷ swap memory

24:    $\widehat{f}^n_u \leftarrow \mathrm{F}(\widehat{f}^{n-1}_u)$ ▷ compute forcing energy

25:    **for** wave numbers $(|\kappa_{\mathrm{ijk}}| < k_f = 2\sqrt{2})$ **do:**   ▷ add forcing energy

26:        $\widehat{u}^{\mathrm{force}}_{1|2|3} \leftarrow \mathrm{F}_{\mathrm{force}}(\widehat{u}^n_{1|16|3}, \widehat{f}^n_u)$

27:    **for all** wave numbers (κ) **do:**   ▷ advance velocity

28:        $\widehat{u}^{\mathrm{step1}}_{1|2|3} \leftarrow \mathrm{F}_{\mathrm{step1}}(\widehat{u}^{\mathrm{force}}_{1|2|3}, \widehat{G}^n_{4|5|6}, \widehat{G}^{n-1}_{13|14|15})$

29:    **for all** wave numbers (κ) **do:**   ▷ apply projection tensor

30:        $\widehat{u}^{n+1}_{1|2|3} \leftarrow \mathrm{F}_{\mathrm{step2}}(\widehat{u}^{\mathrm{step1}}_{1|2|3})$

31:    $\langle \widehat{u}^{n+1}_{1|2|3} \rangle = 0$ ▷ set mean velocity to zero

32:    **output (velocity):** $\widehat{u}^{n+1}_{1|2|3}$, $\widehat{G}^n_{4|5|6}$, $u^n_{7|8|9}$, $\widehat{u}^n_{16}$

33:    **output (passive scalar):** $\widehat{\phi}^n_{17}$, J^n_{19}, $\widehat{J}^{n-1}_{18}$

3   Overlapping Communication and Computation

For a 3d-FFT library without the technique of overlapping computation and communication the following can be said: While the communication phase is active and data is exchanged between the MPI processes no calculations can be performed outside the MPI library. Computation and communication do not overlap. Therefore, the two communication phases require the fraction f_{comm} of the time to compute a complete 3d-FFT while the three computation phases occupy the fraction f_{calc}. Both sum up to $f_{\mathrm{calc}} + f_{\mathrm{comm}} = 1$. This situation is sketched in Fig. 1a. Here six individual 3d-FFTs for different input data are computed one after the other. The computation phases are shown in orange and the communication phases in green. For each 3d-FFT all five phases are sequentially executed.

As each phase depends on the previous one it is takes some extra effort and compute time to overlap communication and computation for a single 3d-FFT [9]. This can be avoided if multiple 3d-FFTs have to be computed at the same time: here computation phases and communication phases of different 3d-FFTs can overlap.

In 2012, MPI-3.0 introduced non-blocking collective MPI calls. This included the all-to-all communication pattern as functions of the `MPI_IAlltoall()` family. But even though those functions return immediately after being called, the data is not actually sent in the background for large message sizes because of the way most MPI libraries are implemented. Without special hardware support for communication offloading and MPI envelope matching, the library has to actively participate in the data transfer and therefore the non-blocking collective is progressed entirely by a second MPI call like `MPI_Wait()` or `MPI_Test()`, which has to be executed before the result is needed. The result is that, in comparison to the blocking collective MPI function `MPI_Alltoall()`, the communication time shifts to `MPI_Wait()` / `MPI_Test()` and no overall speedup could be measured for a 3d-FFT algorithm by simply switching from `MPI_Alltoall()` to `MPI_Ialltoall()` combined with `MPI_Wait()` / `MPI_Test()`. Some MPI implementations try to overcome the aforementioned limitation by introducing asynchronous progression threads. While providing true background data transfer, this mechanism increases the message passing latency and is rarely enabled by default. Wittmann et al. [10] suggest calling MPI repeatedly in a separate user thread, which requires MPI thread support level of MPI_THREAD_MULTIPLE and that is known to not work given certain combinations of MPI implementations and communication hardware, e.g. Open MPI and InfiniBand. A solution that works in all cases and does not rely on the asynchronous progression or MPI_THREAD_MULTIPLE is thus required.

`nb3dfft` has been developed to overcome this issue and follows an approach based on two OpenMP threads per MPI process for the two different types of computation and communication phases (Fig. 1b). The communication thread executes all MPI function calls of the communication phases, while the compute thread is responsible for the computation phases. If nested OpenMP is supported multiple threads can be used to support the compute thread. This two-threaded

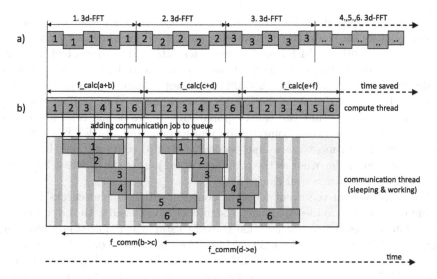

Fig. 1. Schematic re-organization of non-blocking 3d-FFT algorithm in nb3dfft for overlapping computation and communication for the example of six 3d-FFTs. (a) shows the standard implementation where the computation (orange) and the communication (green) is called sequentially. (b) shows the algorithm used in nb3dfft which masks any communication by the communication thread, which flips between sleeping and working sequentially. In the optimal case the compute thread has not to wait at any time for the communication to be finished. The index a-f refers to Fig. 2 in [2]. (Color figure online)

approach utilizes modern CPUs in a convenient way and is particularly efficient on systems, which have more logical than physical CPUs (this is the case for the JUQUEEN [3] as well as for Intel architecture) as the communication thread is sent to sleep for most of the time.

Dependencies between the different phases ensure, that they are executed at any time in the right order. But these dependencies only exist between phases of the same 3d-FFT. If multiple 3d-FFTs are requested to be computed nb3dfft can overlap computation and communication phases of different 3d-FFTs as shown in Fig. 1b. It efficiently re-organizes computation and communication to utilize the network over significant parts of the process.

First the communication thread is started and loops through its event loop waiting and sleeping until communication jobs are added to its job queue. The first computation phase of all 3d-FFTs is then executed one after the other by the compute thread. After each of these phases has finished a communication job is passed to the job queue of the communication thread instead of calling MPI_Alltoall() directly. Depending on a successfully finished communication job the compute thread executes the corresponding subsequent second computation phases and passes again a communication job to the job queue of the communication thread for each finished phase. Finally the last computation phases are executed by the compute thread if the second communication job has finished.

If any communication job has not been completed when the computation thread requests the data, the computation thread will continue with phases to process for any other 3d-FFT and comes back later. Therefore, nb3dfft only optimizes the dependencies between phases and not the order with which phases of different 3d-FFTs are called. nb3dfft does not require that communication jobs, which are added first to the job queue are completed first. This way it is for example possible that the third computation phase of the first 3d-FFT is computed, while the second computation phase of another 3d-FFT has not even started yet. But in most cases first, second and third computation phases are executed one after the other as the communication jobs of the different 3d-FFTs are consuming the same wall clock time.

For each cycle of the event loop the communication thread checks for new communication jobs in the job queue. The information passed with the communication job enables the communication thread to start the required non-blocking collective MPI function MPI_IAlltoall(). Then all active connections started in a previous cycle are tested by MPI_Test(). This function call passes compute time to MPI library, which can process some more operations to proceed with the data transfer. It does not necessarily mean that all data has been sent after the first call to MPI_Test(). If the test function returns with success, the status of this communication job is set to finished. Depending on the MPI library the number of simultaneous non-blocking collective operations is limited. For JUQUEEN it is limited to a maximum of six. The communication thread will therefore not process more than six communication jobs at the same time on JUQUEEN.

Ideally, the time required for the computation phases is equal or larger than the time for the communication phases. In a real-world setup this is rarely the case. But the more 3d-FFTs are computed simultaneously by nb3dfft, the better the communication can be masked. Hence, the algorithms order of 3d-FFT-execution has been re-organized to optimally benefit from overlapping communication and computation with nb3dfft.

In the example of the Algorithm 1 nb3dfft has only to be called once for seven 3d-FFTs and once for six 3d-FFTs. This means, that the algorithm has only two synchronization points when using nb3dfft with overlapping communication and computation instead of $2 \cdot 13 = 26$ (2 synchronization points for 2 MPI_Alltoall() per 3d-FFT, times $7 + 6 = 13$ 3d-FFTs).

4   Results

For highly parallel production runs nb3dfft is used in the DNS code psOpen on the system JUQEEN. Hence performance and scaling results are measured for this system here.

Comparing the optimized Algorithm 1 with the same setup, but without overlapping communication & computation when calculating the 3d-FFTs, psOpen shows a speedup of up to 29.63% (Table 1). Depending on the grid points per core the result differs from 15.50% with 65 536 grid points per core to 29.63%

Table 1. Performance increase on JUQUEEN by overlapping communication & computation in the simulation code `psOpen` using the Algorithm 1 with `nb3dfft` for different domain sizes from 1024^3 up to 6144^3. Because of the memory requirement of `psOpen` certain configurations could not be tested.

N^3	1024^3	2048^3	4096^3	6144^3
16 384 cores	15.50 %	21.60 %	-	-
32 768 cores	-	26.63 %	**29.63 %**	-
65 536 cores	-	17.70 %	19.78 %	-
131 072 cores	-	11.64 %	22.69 %	17.53 %

with 2 097 152 grid points per core. Larger message sizes on the same number of cores show a larger speedup, except for the 6144^3 grid on 131 072 cores.

This speedup is on-top of the speedup achieved by optimizations by better MPI mapping and data reduction using implicit filtering [2]. Figure 2b shows the estimated compute time required for `psOpen` on JUQUEEN to simulate homogeneous isotropic turbulence on a 6144^3 grid until statistical steady state with 16 384 compute nodes (262 144 cores). Here, overlapping communication &computation saves 13.4 million core-h of compute time.

Hiding the time for communication has great impact on the scaling of `psOpen`. Strong scaling of `psOpen` for four grid sizes between 2048^3 and 8192^3 grid points on 458 752 cores (1 835 008 compute threads) is shown in Fig. 2a on BlueGene/Q (JUQUEEN). It can be seen that this hiding of time for communication is successful almost up to 16 384 compute nodes for a 6144^3 grid, but not beyond.

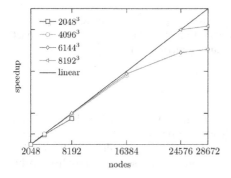
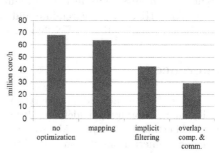

Fig. 2. (a) Strong scaling of psOpen for four grid sizes between 2048^3 and 8192^3 grid points on 458 752 cores (1 835 008 compute threads) on BlueGene/Q (JUQUEEN) Linear scaling is shown for reference. psOpen exhibits an almost linear speedup for up to 16 384 compute nodes for a 6144^3 grid. (b) Estimated compute time required for `psOpen` on JUQUEEN to simulate homogeneous isotropic turbulence on a 6144^3 grid until statistical steady state with 16 384 compute nodes with 262 144 cores.

5   Conclusion

Developing pseudo-spectral codes for DNS that scale on large systems are challenging. Especially the time consuming and communication intensive 3d-FFT is difficult to optimize to a large number of cores because 3d-FFTs require `MPI_alltoall()` calls, which cannot be avoided.

With `nb3dfft` the 3d-FFTs can be optimized, as they are not thought as single operations, but as part of the algorithm. Calling multiple 3d-FFT for different fields at the same time allows overlapping of communication and computation and results in a performance gain of $\simeq 20\%$. At the same time the message sizes and the number of messages of the `MPI_alltoall()` call is not changed. Additionally the number of synchronization points of an algorithm can dramatically be lowered, as shown for algorithm 1 (from 26 to 2) This enables `psOpen` using `nb3dfft` to scale to large number of cores on BlueGene/Q (JUQUEEN).

The technique and benefits of overlapping computation and communication by `nb3dfft` are in general independent of the specific 3d-FFT algorithm. They can be used for any algorithm with alternating computation and communication phases. Hence, `nb3dfft` was adopted by the algorithm used for the DNS code `tlab2015` developed by Juan-Pedro Mellado and Cedrick Ansorge at the Max-Planck Institut of Meterology in Hamburg for Intel x86 and IBM BlueGene/Q architecture. This DNS code is based on compact schemes [4] to compute spatial derivatives, which require the same kind of global transposes as known from 3d-FFT. It was possible to overlap computations of significant parts of the numerical algorithm with communications required by the global transposes for the compact scheme. A speedup by up to 40% (depending on the configuration) was achieved on JUQUEEN.

Acknowledgments. The authors gratefully acknowledge the computing time granted by the JARA-HPC Vergabegremium and provided on the JARA-HPC Partition part of the supercomputer JUQUEEN [3] at Forschungszentrum Jülich.

References

1. Canuto, C., Hussaini, M.Y., Quarteroni, A., Zang, T.A.: Spectral Methods in Fluid Dynamics. Springer, Heidelberg (1988). Technical report
2. Goebbert, J.H., Gauding, M., Ansorge, C., Hentschel, B., Kuhlen, T., Pitsch, H.: Direct numerical simulation of fluid turbulence at extreme scale with psOpen. Adv. Parallel Comput. **27**, 777–785 (2016)
3. JUQUEEN: Jülich Blue Gene/Q (2012–2015). http://www.fz-juelich.de/ias/juqueen. Accessed 01 Aug 2015
4. Lele, S.K.: Compact finite difference schemes with spectral-like resolution. J. Comput. Phys. **103**(1), 16–42 (1992)
5. Li, N., Laizet, S.: 2DECOMP & FFT-A highly scalable 2D decomposition library and FFT interface. In: 2010 Conference Cray User Group, pp. 1–13 (2010)
6. Mellado, J.P., Ansorge, C.: tlab - Tools to simulate and analyze different configurations of 2D and 3D turbulent flows. https://github.com/turbulencia/tlab. Accessed 07 Dec 2015

7. nb3dfft: non-blocking 3d-fft library (2014–2016). https://gitlab.version.fz-juelich.de/goebbert/nb3dfft. Accessed 30 Oct 2016

8. Pekurovsky, D.: P3DFFT: A framework for parallel computations of fourier transforms in three dimensions. SIAM J. Sci. Comput. **34**(4), C192–C209 (2012)

9. Song, S., Hollingsworth, J.K.: Designing and auto-tuning parallel 3-D FFT for computation-communication overlap. ACM SIGPLAN Not. **49**(8), 181–192 (2014)

10. Wittmann, M., Hager, G., Zeiser, T., Wellein, G.: Asynchronous MPI for the masses (2013). arXiv:1302.4280

Towards Simulating Data-Driven Brain Models at the Point Neuron Level on Petascale Computers

Till Schumann$^{(\boxtimes)}$, Csaba Erő, Marc-Oliver Gewaltig,
and Fabien Jonathan Delalondre

BBP, Geneva, Switzerland
Till.Schumann@epfl.ch

Abstract. We present a solution to two important problems that arise in the simulation of large data-driven neural networks: (a) efficient loading of network descriptions and (b) efficient instantiation of the network by executing the model specification. To address the first problem, we present a general data-format PointBrainH5, to store the network information along with the parallel-distributed RTC algorithm to efficiently load and instantiate a network model. We test data-format and algorithm on a data-driven simulation of the size of a full mouse brain on 4 racks of a IBM Blue Gene/Q. The model comprised 75 million neurons with 664 billion synapses and occupied 15 TB on disk. Loading and instantiation of the network on 4 racks of the BlueGene/Q took 30 min. We observe good scaling for up to 16,384 nodes.

Keywords: Data-driven simulation · Parallel I/O · Spiking neural network models · Supercomputer · Threading · MPI

1 Introduction

In recent years, considerable progress has been made in simulating large neuronal networks, representing brain regions or entire brains, on super-computers. In 2008, Ishikevich and Edelman published a model consisting of one million neurons and almost half a billion connections, based on DT imaging data [8]. In 2009, Rajagopal Ananthanarayanan et al. published a model of the scale of a cat cortex with 10 billion neurons and 100 trillion synapses [9]. In 2013, Diesmann et al. were able to simulate a network, containing 1.73 billion nerve cells connected by 10.4 trillion synapses on the K computer [4]. All these simulations have in common that the network or brain model is described in probabilistic terms: The properties of the neurons and their connections are defined by a relatively small number of probability density functions, resulting in very compact network descriptions that are negligible compared to the size of the network when it is instantiated in the computer memory. Thus, from a computer science perspective, the main challenges of simulating these networks lied in

© Springer International Publishing AG 2017
E. Di Napoli et al. (Eds.): JHPCS 2016, LNCS 10164, pp. 160–169, 2017.
DOI: 10.1007/978-3-319-53862-4_14

(i) efficiently instantiating the network model, based on its algorithmic definition and (ii) efficiently simulating the model on massively parallel computers. In the course of the Human Brain Project, a new type of network model is arising where many of the network properties are explicitly specified by anatomical and electrophysiological data. These networks are sometimes called *data-driven models* or *digital reconstructions*. For these models it is no longer possible to describe the network by a (relatively) small number of probability density functions. One example is the digital reconstruction of a neocortical column, developed by the Blue Brain Project [5]. This network has a comparatively small number of 31,000 neurons with 8 million connections. However due to the explicit specification of neuronal morphologies and connectivity, the specification of the network reaches the size of 27 GB on disk. We can therefore imagine that the explicit specification of a network at the scale of a mouse brain will occupy substantial amount of space on disk. If we consider a mouse brain with 75 million neurons and 10,000 connections per neuron, a fully specified network, that is a network where every connection is explicitly defined, will occupy several TB of disk space. To simulate such a network on a supercomputer, we must (a) efficiently load the network description from a distributed file-system and (b) efficiently instantiate the neurons and their connections by executing the model specification. Here we present results of our efforts to address these two steps. We present a new data-format, based on HDF5 [11], to store the network information along with a parallel-distributed algorithm to efficiently load and instantiate a network model. The algorithm is implemented as an extension to the neural simulation tool NEST [1].

2   Contribution

In this paper, we describe an extension to the neural simulation tool NEST [14] that allows to efficiently load and instantiate large-scale data-driven network models such as the prototype model of a mouse brain. As concrete starting point, we used a prototype model of a mouse brain [13] that is based on aggregated data from the Allen Mouse Brain Atlas [2] and Blue Brain Project [5]. The model consists of 75 million adaptive exponential integrate-and-fire neurons [6] and their 3D positions with around 10,000 conductance based synapses per neuron. Each synapse obeys the Tsodyks-Markram short-term dynamics [7] which yields 5 parameters per synapse. We describe a novel file format to the store an explicitly defined neural model network model of point neurons on disk and an import module to load the model from file into the simulator. It enables to exclude the model generation from NEST and generate therefore the model with our own scripts. This is a major change to common simulations with NEST. The flexibility to generate the model with our own scripts allow us to realize complex generation algorithms. Thus, we are able to generate a mouse brain model by combining data from the Allen Mouse Brain Atlas and Blue Brain Project and simulate it with NEST. On the full scale, the model has around 75 million neurons with 660 billion synapses. Because of the large amount of synapses, an efficient data layout of the file format and optimal I/O are crucial. To overcome

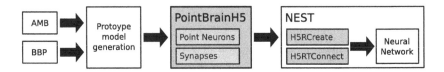

Fig. 1. Illustration of the workflow of the generation of the mouse brain prototype model. The workflow encapsulates the model *generation* from the simulator *NEST*. The generation uses data from the Allen Mouse Brain Atlas (*AMB*) and the Blue Brain Project (*BBP*). In between the generation and the simulator the *neural network* is stored on disk in the presented PointBrainH5 format. The parts of the workflow, which are presented in this paper have a grey background.

the limitation of markup languages, we store our model definition in the presented PointBrainH5 data format. The simulator NEST does not support the import from PointBrainH5. Therefore, we extended NEST with an import module to support it. We tested a first approach of our HDF5 import module at the JUQUEEN Extreme Scaling Workshop 2016 [12].

3 Methods

We present a file format to store an explicitly defined neural network model of point neurons on disk. We extend NEST with import modules to support the presented data format. Therefore, we develop an algorithm to efficiently load synaptic connectivity data from the data format and transpose it according to the internal data structure of NEST. Combing it with an implementation of the model generation, we get a workflow to run simulations of explicitly defined brain-scale models with NEST (see Fig. 1).

3.1 PointBrainH5

We choose self-descriptive HDF5 [11] files as a container for the neural network model. The entities of our neural network are neurons and synapses. Two different file layouts are used to store both: The neuron file encapsulates all neuron parameters. Each parameter has its dataset (C_m, $Delta\_T$, ...). The length of each dataset defines the number of neurons. The synapse file encapsulates connection information and synapse parameters. The synapses are grouped by pre-synaptic neurons. Therefore, all pre-synapic neuron ids (*id*) with references to the syn dataset (*syn_n* and *syn_ptr*) are stored in the neuron dataset (*neuron*). In the *syn* dataset, all related post-synaptic neuron IDs (*target*) and the synapse parameters (*delay, weight, U0, TauRec, TauFac*) are stored (Fig. 2).

3.2 Implementation

We implement an extension in NEST that allows to efficiently load the Point-BrainH5 data-format and instantiate the model in the data structure of NEST.

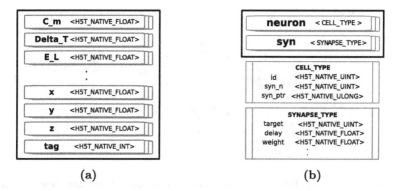

Fig. 2. (a) The neurons are stored in one HDF5 file. Each dataset in the HDF5 file represents one neuron parameter. H5RCreate supports the loading of parameters from datasets with a floating point data type. An additional dataset with the data type *int* can be used to tag and group neurons. The neuron groups can be accessed by the SLI interface to interact with only parts of neurons. (b) The synapses are stored in a different HDF5 file. Each HDF5 file has two datasets: *neuron* and *syn*. Each dataset has its own compound data type: *CELL_TYPE* and *SYNAPSE_TYPE*. The synapse import module permits differences of the *SYNAPSE_TYPE* type: The float values *delay*, *weight*, ... can be removed, replaced or extended by different float values.

Due to the splitting of the model in neuron and synapse information, we implement the import modules H5RCreate for neurons and H5RTConnect for synapses. The internal C++ API of NEST allows the creation and manipulation of the neural network model. The API is mainly developed to work as an interface between the internal structure and the user interface. Our implementation accesses the C++ functions directly to avoid overhead. Both import modules load parts of the HDF5 files and store them in the NEST data structure. H5RCreate loads only the neurons from PointBrainH5 per MPI rank, which are needed on the MPI rank. NEST distributes all neurons based on a modulo function. Thus, we know in advance, which parts have to be loaded on which MPI rank. For synapses, it is more complex: Because of memory optimizations, the synapses are only stored on the post-synaptic MPI rank [4]. This means that the synapse information is stored on the MPI rank where the post-synaptic neuron is located. The data delivered by the model generation orders the synapses based on the pre-synaptic neuron. Thus, a transformation of the synapse data is necessary. Preprocessing of the input data should be avoided in order to maintain its original PointBrainH5 format for future changes in the model generation. Therefore, we transpose the data during the import with the RTC algorithm.

3.3   RTC Algorithm

The RTC algorithm transposes the synaptic connectivity information iteratively (see Fig. 3). The algorithm reads synaptic connectivity from PointBrainH5 files

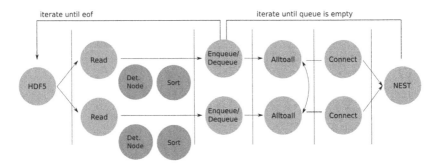

Fig. 3. Illustration of the RTC algorithm. RTC can be divided into five steps, which are separated in two loops. *Read* reads a set of synapses from file into a buffer. *Det. Node*, *Sort* and *Alltoall* transpose the synapses across the MPI ranks. *Connect* extracts the synapses from the buffer and stores them into the NEST data structure. The steps *Read*, *Det. Node* and *Sort* are called in the enqueue loop. Afterwards, the second dequeue loop calls *Alltoall* and *Connect*. The red steps are executed on the master thread. The blue steps are executed in OpenMP tasks on idle threads. The two rows represent the parallel execution of the steps. The arrow between both *Alltoall* represent collective communication between MPI ranks. *Alltoall* contains a collective MPI operations (all other steps are executed independently by the MPI ranks). (Color figure online)

in parallel and transposes the read synapses across the MPI processes. Therefore, it makes use of MPI and shared memory parallelism. We derived RTC from the synapse import algorithm tested at the JUQUEEN Extreme Scaling Workshop 2016 [12]. Our introduced enhancements are a better load balancing and a better utilizations of available OpenMP threads. RTC balances the mount of data read per MPI rank. As in common systems, the available I/O bandwidth is balanced between the MPI ranks, each MPI rank reads the same amount of data. The system and the parallel file system take care of an equal distribution of the bandwidth. In practice, the distribution of the bandwidth is closer to a normal distribution. Thus, the wall-clock times of the read operations differ between the MPI ranks, even though all MPI ranks read the same amount of data. This means, the read operation produces imbalance, which results in waiting times in subsequent collective operations. Therefore, a better load balancing is achieved by performing the read and the necessary collective operations consecutively. Hence, the algorithm iterates twice over all synapses (Fig. 5a illustrates the synapses in memory). In a first loop, all synapses are read block-wise from file and enqueued. Once each block of synapses is read, a parallel thread assigns the target MPI rank to each synapse and sorts the synapses in the block by target MPI rank. In a second loop, the synapses are transferred to the target MPI ranks in a collective *MPI_Alltoall* operation. From there, they are passed to the *connect* function from the NEST internal C++ API and stored in the NEST data structure function.

4   Performance Results

The I/O performance of the model import and the memory footprint of the model in NEST effect mainly the usability of brain-scale data-driven simulations. From the model import, the synapse import plays the major role, as it has to load 10,000 more data than the neuron import module. Thus, we negligible the neuron import module performance and present the I/O performance results from our H5RTConnect implementation (RTC algorithm). Benchmarks on different scales on JUQUEEN [3] should give detailed information about the reached performance. The tested implementation is available on GitHub [15]. It is forked from the NEST repository [16]. For the HDF5 interface, we used the HDF5 version *1.8.15*, which is given as a module on JUQUEEN. As performance metrics, we use the I/O bandwidth and the connection frequency, which corresponds to the pass-through of synapses per time interval. Both metrics are linear related. Thus, both metrics are directly comparable. For benchmarks, we measured the number of created synapses, the according bytes and the wall-clock time of different parts of our implementation. From this we calculate the connection frequency per second and the corresponding bandwidth [GB/s]. Figure 4b shows the metrics for different runs over the number of used ranks. In Fig. 4b, *Read* corresponds to bandwidth of the HDF5 read operation, *Connect* corresponds to the connection frequency of the whole algorithm and *Rearrange* corresponds to the connection frequency with the *Connect* step excluded. The bandwidth of *Read* matches approximately the theoretical I/O performance of the system. Thus, the used read operation utilizes the available bandwidth. By additionally rearranging the synapses (*Rearrange*), the performance drops. Due to the collective operation in the *Alltoall* step, we lose most of the performance. I/O read calls produce imbalance, which result in waiting times during the first *Alltoall* step. Taking additionally the *Connect* step into account, the resulted connection frequency reaches around 10% of the I/O bandwidth. Figure 4a shows the performance in comparison to our implementation, tested at the JUQUEEN Extreme Scaling Workshop 2016. We reach better performance by having the collective after and not in between the I/O read operations (see Fig. 3 and algorithm description in [12]). By performing the sequential read operations consecutively, we have less imbalance caught by the collective operations. Additionally, we want to know how many racks of IBM Blue Gene/Q we need to simulate a mouse brain scale model. We expect that the simulation is memory bound. We extend our implementation with a memory logger and run simulations on different scales. We observe during the loading the memory usage of each compute node. Figure 5b shows the observed values for a simulation on full Blue Brain IV [10]. The *4 racks* and *4 racks opt* represent two different runs with different configurations. In contrast to the 4 racks, 4 racks opt uses 4g kernel synapses [4] and reduced floating point precision for the synapse parameters. The optimized synapse objects reduce the memory footprint for each stored synapse. Thus, the *4 racks opt* run succeed to load the whole model into memory. However, the *4 racks* run crashes into the memory wall, before the whole model is loaded.

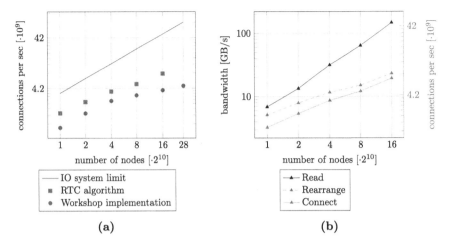

Fig. 4. (a) Performance comparison of the Workshop implementation and the RTC algorithm on different scales on JUQUEEN. The theoretical line shows the approximate peak connection frequency, bounded by the I/O bandwidth of the system. The red squares and the blue dots show the measured connection frequencies from benchmarks of the RTC algorithm and the Workshop implementation, respectively. The Workshop implementation is the implementation of the algorithm, tested at JUQUEEN Extreme Scaling Workshop 2016. The RTC algorithm is the implementation of the presented algorithm (see Fig. 3). (b) Performance of the RTC algorithm in detail. The performance of different parts of our implementation over the number of racks are shown: *Read*, *Rearrange* and *Connect*. The parts contain following steps of the algorithm description in Fig. 3. *Read*: *Read*; *Rearrange*: *Read*, *Det. Node*, *Sort* and *Alltoall*; *Connect*: *Read*, *Det. Node*, *Sort*, *Alltoall* and *Connect*. As performance metrics bandwidth (gigabyte per second) and connection frequency (giga connections per second) are used. Both metrics are linear related. The relation is factored by the scales of the vertical axis. (Color figure online)

5   Functionality

The presented NEST extension can load neural network models from PointBrainH5 into the simulator. PointBrainH5 supports any explicitly defined neural network model of point neurons. We used the NEST extension to run first simulations of the prototype of the mouse brain model. Initial experiments gave us insights of the model behavior. For further experiments, we wanted to perturb the parameter of the synapses. To avoid regeneration of the whole model, we integrated the possibility to adapt parameters during the import for both neurons and synapses. Each neuron and synapse is defined by a set of parameters $(p_1, ..., p_m)$. A manipulation kernel k can be used to operate on each parameter set $(p_1, ..., p_m) = k((x_1, ..., x_n))$ before the parameters are stored in the NEST data structure. We implemented basic functions: E.g. the multiplication kernel enables to strengthen all synapse weights with a factor S: $(p_1, p_2, ..., p_m) = (x_1, Sx_2, ..., x_n)$. New kernels can be implemented easily to customize the model.

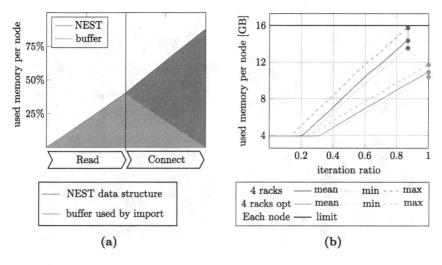

Fig. 5. (a) Theoretical memory usage of RTC algorithm over iterations. First, *Read* reads the synapse files and stores the data in a queue in a first loop. Afterwards, a second loop dequeues the synapses and stores them in the NEST data structure using *Connect* function of NEST. The enqueuing iterations fill up the buffer used by the import module. During dequeuing the buffer is emptied and the synapses are passed to the NEST data structure. (b) Used memory per node over iterations ratio (loading progress) for importing mouse brain scale model in NEST. The solid, dotted and dashed lines represent the mean, minimum and maximum used memory per node, respectively. The *4 racks* lines show the observed used memory from a standard configuration run plotted over the loading progress. The *4 racks opt* shows the same for an optimized configuration. Both runs are executed on 4 racks of IBM Blue Gene/Q.

6   Summary

In this paper we presented a solution to two important problems that arise in the simulation of large data-driven networks: First, we must (a) efficiently load the network description from a distributed file-system and (b) we must efficiently instantiate the neurons and their connections by executing the model specification. To address the first problem, we presented the data-format Point-BrainH5, based on HDF5, to store the network information along with the parallel-distributed RTC algorithm to efficiently load and instantiate a network model. PointBrainH5 enables to store an explicitly defined neural network model of point neurons in HDF5 files on disk. Thus, we are able to run a data-driven simulation of the size of a full mouse brain on 4 racks of IBM Blue Gene/Q machines (see Fig. 5b). The data-format is currently very general. Further optimizations will require a specialization of the format to the characteristics of the particular computer and storage architecture. Having a general data-format for explicit network definitions offers the additional advantage that the network becomes available for off-line analysis and visualization (see Fig. 6), independent of the computer system that is used for simulation. To load and instantiate

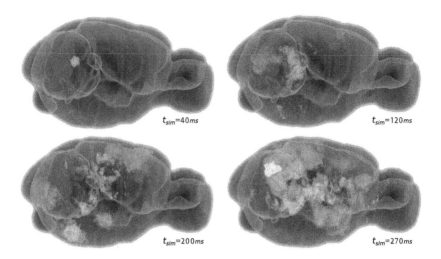

Fig. 6. Visualized spiking activity of the mouse brain model prototype. The figures show active neurons in four different time steps (from top left to bottom right: 40 ms, 120 ms, 200 ms, 270 ms). Only active neurons are shown. The color represent the region of each neuron given by the Allen Mouse Brain Atlas [2]. (Color figure online)

large-scale data-driven networks we devised the parallel-distributed RTC algorithm and implemented it an extension to the neural simulation tool NEST. We tested the algorithm on a prototype model of the whole mouse brain. This model comprised 75 million neurons with 664 billion synapses. Using our data format, the model description occupied 15 TB on disk. Using all 4 racks of the BlueGene/Q it was possible to load and instantiate this network in 30 min. Our benchmark simulations showed good scaling for up to 16384 nodes.

Acknowledgement. The authors of this paper would like to gratefully thank both the HPC and the Visualization teams of the Blue Brain Project, for the many discussions and feedback provided. This work has been funded by both the EPFL Blue Brain Project (funded by the Swiss ETH board) and the European Union Seventh Framework Program (FP7/20072013) under grant agreement no. 604102 (HBP).

References

1. Gewaltig, M.-O., Diesmann, M.: NEST (neural simulation tool). Scholarpedia **2**(4), 1430 (2007)
2. Jones, A.R., Overly, C.C., Sunkin, S.M.: The Allen brain atlas: 5 years and beyond. Nat. Rev. Neurosci. **10**(11), 821–828 (2009)
3. Stephan, M., Docter, J.: JUQUEEN: IBM Blue Gene/Q Supercomputer system at the Jlich supercomputing centre. J. Large-Scale Res. Facil. JLSRF **1**, 1 (2015)
4. Kunkel, S., et al.: Spiking network simulation code for petascale computers. Front. Neuroinformatics **8**, 78 (2014)

5. Markram, H., Muller, E., Ramaswamy, S., Reimann, M.W., Abdellah, M., Sanchez, C.A., Ailamaki, A., Alonso-Nanclares, L., Antille, N., Arsever, S., et al.: Reconstruction and simulation of neocortical microcircuitry. Cell **163**(2), 456–492 (2015)
6. Brette, R., Gerstner, W.: Adaptive exponential integrate-and-fire model as an effective description of neural activity. J. Neurophysiol. **94**(5), 3637–3642 (2005)
7. Fuhrmann, G., Segev, I., Markram, H., Tsodyks, M.: Coding of temporal information by activity-dependent synapses. J. Neurophysiol. **87**(1), 140–148 (2002)
8. Izhikevich, E.M., Edelman, G.M.: Large-scale model of mammalian thalamocortical systems. Proc. Natl. Acad. Sci. **105**(9), 3593–3598 (2008)
9. Ananthanarayanan, R., et al.: The cat is out of the bag: cortical simulations with 109 neurons, 1013 synapses. In: Proceedings of the Conference on High Performance Computing Networking, Storage and Analysis. IEEE (2009)
10. Blue Brain Project. Blue Brain 4 (2016). http://www.cscs.ch/computers/blue_brain_4/index.html
11. The HDF Group Hierarchical Data Format, version 5 (2016). http://www.hdfgroup.org/HDF5
12. Schumann, T., Delalondre, F.: HDF5 import module for the spiking neuronal simulator NEST. In: JUQUEEN Extreme Scaling Workshop, no. FZJ-2016-01816, pp. 43–48 (2016)
13. Eroe, C., et al.: Estimation of neuron numbers and densities of the mouse brain (in preparation)
14. Bos, H., et al.: NEST 2.10.0. Zenodo (2015). doi:10.5281/zenodo.44222
15. Schumann, T.: Nest-simulator, branch:h5kernel (2016). GitHub repository. https://github.com/tillschumann/nest-simulator/tree/h5kernel
16. Bos, H., et al.: Nest-simulator, ref:4b0f360 (2016). GitHub repository. https://github.com/nest/nest-simulator

Parallel Adaptive Integration in High-Performance Functional Renormalization Group Computations

Julian Lichtenstein[1]($\boxtimes$), Jan Winkelmann[2], David Sánchez de la Peña[1], Toni Vidović[3], and Edoardo Di Napoli[2,4,5]

[1] Institute for Theoretical Solid State Physics, RWTH Aachen University,
52074 Aachen, Germany
lichtenstein@physik.rwth-aachen.de
[2] Aachen Institute for Advanced Study in Computational Engineering Science,
RWTH Aachen University,
52072 Aachen, Germany
[3] Department of Mathematics, Faculty of Science, University of Zagreb,
10000 Zagreb, Croatia
[4] Jülich Supercomputing Centre, Forschungszentrum Jülich GmbH,
52425 Jülich, Germany
[5] JARA–HPC, 52425 Jülich, Germany

Abstract. The conceptual framework provided by the functional Renormalization Group (fRG) has become a formidable tool to study correlated electron systems on lattices which, in turn, provided great insights to our understanding of complex many-body phenomena, such as high-temperature superconductivity or topological states of matter. In this work we present one of the latest realizations of fRG which makes use of an adaptive numerical quadrature scheme specifically tailored to the described fRG scheme. The final result is an increase in performance thanks to improved parallelism and scalability.

Keywords: Adaptive quadrature · Functional renormalization group · Interacting fermions · Hybrid parallelization · Shared memory parallelism

1 Introduction

In this paper we report on the algorithmic and performance improvements resulting from the collaboration between High-Performance Computing (HPC) experts and domain scientists in the specific field of functional Renormalization Group (fRG). In particular, we focus on an adaptive implementation of a two-dimensional numerical quadrature algorithm tailored to the evaluation of a large number of integrals within a recently developed fRG method. The result of such an effort is the Parallel Adaptive Integration in two Dimensions (PAID) library. PAID requires approximately an order of magnitude fewer operations for

© Springer International Publishing AG 2017
E. Di Napoli et al. (Eds.): JHPCS 2016, LNCS 10164, pp. 170–184, 2017.
DOI: 10.1007/978-3-319-53862-4_15

the computation of the numerical integrals and translates this reduction into a substantial gain in parallel performance.

The Renormalization Group (RG) is a powerful method describing the behavior of a physical system at different energy and length scales. RG techniques allow smooth interpolation between well studied models at a given energy scale and complicated emergent phenomena at lower energy scales. In what is known as *RG flow*, physical quantities are computed iteratively with respect to variation of an auxiliary scale parameter by solving a system of coupled ordinary integro-differential equations. In its application to interacting electrons on a lattice at low temperatures, fRG methods are commonly used to detect transitions of the metallic state towards some ordered state [1,2]. At the initial energy scale of the flow, the physical system is in a well understood metallic state, where weakly correlated electrons interact pairwise through Coulomb repulsion. Lowering the scale, a second order phase transition may take place at some critical temperature, in which some form of order (e.g. magnetism or superconductivity) spontaneously emerges.

fRG methods passed through many refinements over the years [3–6] in the form of specific approximation schemes. While each of these schemes has its strength, the improvement of their accuracy (e.g. on predictions for critical temperatures) is still underway. In the current work, we illustrate the *Truncated Unity* scheme (TUfRG) [7] and its parallel implementation. One of the computational advantages of this scheme stems from the insertion of truncated partitions of unity in the flow equations. The resulting numerical integration becomes less challenging at the expense of having extra operations to perform (so-called inter-channel projections). At each step of the equations' flow one ends up computing multiple independent integrals parametrized by three indices, namely l, m, and n. In the original TUfRG code all these integrals are distributed over a large number of threads where each one is computed sequentially by a single thread using the adaptive DCUHRE library [8]. Since computing such integrals accounts for around 80% of the total computational time, they are the ideal candidate for an HPC optimization.

While recent implementations have shown increased performance and scalability through parallel quadrature schemes [9,10], we follow a different path by tailoring the numerical quadrature to the needs of the TUfRG algorithm. In PAID, the subset of all integrals corresponding to one value of l are collected in a container and computed adaptively. All the integrals in the container become tasks which are executed under just one parallel region over the shared memory of a compute node. With this approach we intend to gain better control over the global quadrature error and minimize load imbalance while increasing scalability. Our results show that PAID scales as well as the trivial parallelization using DCUHRE. In addition, PAID's adaptivity over the indexes m and n of the integrals consistently yields a speedup from 2× up to 4×. In Sect. 2 we give a brief account of the method at the base of the TUfRG scheme. In the following section we present the basic notion of adaptive integration and the algorithm underlying the PAID library. In Sect. 4 we describe the parallel implementation in more detail. We conclude with a section on numerical results and future work.

2   The fRG Method and the Truncated Unity Approach

In this section we provide a short introduction to the mathematical framework of the TUfRG scheme. This is by no means an exhaustive description and we refer the reader to [7] for a detailed presentation. As several other fRG methods, TUfRG focuses on interacting electrons on 2D lattice systems. These systems exhibit strong correlations at low energy, which results in a rich diversity of ordered ground states. At the mathematical level, the effective two-particle coupling function $V(k_{0,1}, \mathbf{k_1}; k_{0,2}, \mathbf{k_2}; k_{0,3}, \mathbf{k_3})$ contains essential information on the properties of the electronic ground state. V depends on both three frequencies (k_0) and three momenta $(\mathbf{k})$, while the fourth ones are fixed due to conservation of energy and momentum respectively. In favor of a short notation, we sum up the dependence on frequency and momentum of one particle into a combined index $k = (k_0, \mathbf{k})$ and write $V(k_1, k_2, k_3)$.

The fRG calculation is based on the insertion of a control parameter Ω, which is an artificial energy scale. It is used for tuning the system from an easily solvable starting point to a system that includes the physically important features. For a given value of the control parameter, the strong correlations at energies below Ω are excluded from V. Starting from a high enough Ω results in a well-defined initial value for V, which corresponds to an interaction between two isolated charges. By decreasing Ω, we successively include correlation effects into the effective two-particle coupling. From a mathematical point of view, the calculation of V at lower energy scales can be seen as an *initial value problem*, where the value of V at a high energy scale is the initial value. In order to obtain the resulting two-particle coupling function at lower values of Ω, one needs to integrate a first order ordinary differential equation extracted from a so-called level-2 truncation of the fRG equation hierarchy [1] and from neglecting self-energies. Such an equation can be written as

$$\dot{V}(k_1, k_2, k_3) = \mathcal{T}_{\text{pp}}(k_1, k_2, k_3) + \mathcal{T}_{\text{ph}}^{\text{cr}}(k_1, k_2, k_3) + \mathcal{T}_{\text{ph}}^{\text{d}}(k_1, k_2, k_3), \qquad (1)$$

where the dependence on Ω of all quantities is implicit and the dot above V denotes the first derivative with respect to the artificial energy scale. The right-hand side is divided in three main contributions: a particle-particle

$$\mathcal{T}_{\text{pp}} = -\int dp \, [\partial_\Omega G(p) \, G(k_1 + k_2 - p)] \, V(k_1, k_2, p) \, V(k_1 + k_2 - p, p, k_3), \quad (2)$$

a crossed particle-hole

$$\mathcal{T}_{\text{ph}}^{\text{cr}} = -\int dp \, [\partial_\Omega G(p) \, G(p + k_3 - k_1)] \, V(k_1, p + k_3 - k_1, k_3) \, V(p, k_2, p + k_3 - k_1) \qquad (3)$$

and three direct particle-hole terms summarized in $\mathcal{T}_{\text{ph}}^{\text{d}}$ as

$$\mathcal{T}_{\text{ph}}^{\text{d}} = \int dp \, [\partial_\Omega G(p) \, G(p + k_2 - k_3)] \, [2V(k_1, p + k_2 - k_3, p) \, V(p, k_2, k_3)$$
$$- V(k_1, p + k_2 - k_3, k_1 + k_2 - k_3) \, V(p, k_2, k_3)$$
$$- V(k_1, p + k_2 - k_3, p) \, V(p, k_2, p + k_2 - k_3)]. \qquad (4)$$

All five summands that appear as integrands are quadratic in both V and the function $G(k) = \frac{\theta(k)}{ik_0 - \epsilon(\mathbf{k})}$, which is the propagator of the system containing non-interacting particles. The regulator function θ implements the exclusion of correlation effects from the system at energies below Ω. In this paper we use $\theta(k) = \theta(k_0) = \frac{k_0^2}{k_0^2 + \Omega^2}$ as regulator, which suppresses G for Ω much larger than all relevant energy scales of the system. In the limit of $\Omega \to 0$ the structure of G is recovered and we regain the physical system. The energy dispersion $\epsilon(\mathbf{k})$—which appears in the denominator of G—contains the energy spectrum of the single-particle problem. Since in this paper we are dealing with a t-t' Hubbard model on a square lattice, the dispersion is

$$\epsilon(\mathbf{k}) = -2\,t\,(\cos(k_x) + \cos(k_y)) - 4\,t'\,\cos(k_x)\,\cos(k_y) - \mu \qquad (5)$$

where t and t' describe the kinetics of the particles and μ is the chemical potential controlling the total number of particles in the system.

The calculation of the two-particle coupling V using a direct implementation of Eqs. (1)–(4) is numerically challenging. Even if the dependence on the external frequencies $k_{0,1}$, $k_{0,2}$ and $k_{0,3}$ is neglected—as we will do in the following—the scaling of the number of differential equations with respect to the number of momentum sampling points is cubic. Using frequency independent two-particle couplings, the frequency integrals from Eqs. (2)–(4) involve just the Ω derivative of a product of two fermionic propagators and can be performed analytically. The result of this shows sharp structures as function of momentum at small values of Ω (see Fig. 1). As mentioned above, at low energy scales the system can get close to a phase transition, which is indicated by a strong increase of specific components of V. Thus a product of two strongly peaked two-particle couplings and sharp structured propagators constitutes the integrands of the momentum integrals in Eqs. (2)–(4).

In order to change Eqs. (1)–(4) in the direction of a numerically easier treatment, accompanied by the introduction of quantities with a more direct physical interpretation, we perform modifications that can be classified in three steps[1]. First, the initial part $V^{(0)}$ is separated from the two-particle coupling and the rest is split into three single-channel coupling functions Φ^P, Φ^C and Φ^D. Their derivatives with respect to Ω are given by $\mathcal{T}_{pp}$, $\mathcal{T}_{ph}^{cr}$ and $\mathcal{T}_{ph}^d$ respectively. This is motivated by the fact that V develops strong dependencies on the external momentum combinations appearing in Eqs. (2)–(4) respectively, denoted by $\mathbf{l}$ in the following. In a second step, the remaining weak momentum dependencies of each channel are expanded in a complete set of orthonormal functions $\{f_n\}$—so-called form-factors. Since we can only use a finite number of basis functions while doing numerics, we restrict the basis to slowly oscillating functions to achieve a good description of weak momentum dependencies of the channels. This latter step can be interpreted as a sort of discretization with $\Phi_{\mathbf{l},\mathbf{k},\mathbf{k'}}^P \to P_{m,n}(\mathbf{l})$—and

---

[1] See Ref. [7] for a more detailed derivation and an example application of the scheme.

equivalently for the C and D channels—where $\mathbf{k}$ and $\mathbf{k}'$ are replaced by form-factor indices m and n. As a consequence of implementing the first two steps in Eqs. (1)–(4), the scaling of the number of coupled differential equations respect to the number of momentum sampling points is reduced to a linear relation. Moreover, the scaling respect to the number of form-factors is less important in most cases, since a good description can be achieved even using a small number of form-factors.

In a third and final step we change the form of the RHS of the resulting differential equations by inserting two partitions of unity of the form-factor basis set. The fermionic propagators can then be separated from the two-particle coupling terms and the differential Eq. (1) now takes the form of three separate equations

$$\dot{\mathbf{P}}(1) = \mathbf{V}^P(1)\,\dot{\boldsymbol{\mathcal{X}}}^{\mathrm{pp}}(1)\,\mathbf{V}^P(1)\,, \tag{6}$$

$$\dot{\mathbf{C}}(1) = -\mathbf{V}^C(1)\,\dot{\boldsymbol{\mathcal{X}}}^{\mathrm{ph}}(1)\,\mathbf{V}^C(1)\,, \tag{7}$$

$$\dot{\mathbf{D}}(1) = 2\mathbf{V}^D(1)\,\dot{\boldsymbol{\mathcal{X}}}^{\mathrm{ph}}(1)\,\mathbf{V}^D(1) - \mathbf{V}^C(1)\,\dot{\boldsymbol{\mathcal{X}}}^{\mathrm{ph}}(1)\,\mathbf{V}^D(1) - \mathbf{V}^D(1)\,\dot{\boldsymbol{\mathcal{X}}}^{\mathrm{ph}}(1)\,\mathbf{V}^C(1)\,, \tag{8}$$

where

$$\mathcal{X}^{\mathrm{pp}}_{m,n}(1) = \int d\mathbf{p}\left[\int dp_0\, G\left(p_0, \frac{1}{2}+\mathbf{p}\right) G\left(-p_0, \frac{1}{2}-\mathbf{p}\right)\right] f_m(\mathbf{p})\, f_n(\mathbf{p})\,, \tag{9}$$

$$\mathcal{X}^{\mathrm{ph}}_{m,n}(1) = \int d\mathbf{p}\left[\int dp_0\, G\left(p_0, \mathbf{p}+\frac{1}{2}\right) G\left(p_0, \mathbf{p}-\frac{1}{2}\right)\right] f_m(\mathbf{p})\, f_n(\mathbf{p})\,. \tag{10}$$

$\mathbf{V}^P$, $\mathbf{V}^C$ and $\mathbf{V}^D$ are two-particle couplings with two momenta replaced by form-factor indices, and can be computed from P, C, and D in the aforementioned inter-channel projections. The inserted partitions of unity are also truncated by ignoring strongly oscillating form-factors. Inner integrals from Eqs. (9) and (10) can be treated analytically, while the calculation of the outer (momentum) integrals requires a sophisticated numerical integration scheme. Due to the last modification, we call the scheme described in Eqs. (6)–(10) *Truncated Unity fRG* (TUfRG).

Numerically, this scheme is implemented in four steps organized in a loop mimicking the flow of the ODE for decreasing values of Ω. Within the loop, the most intensive part of the computation is given by the numerical integration. In the current C++ implementation of TUfRG, the numerical integration is parallelized using the MPI+OpenMP paradigm. Each MPI process receives a subset of values of l indices while an OpenMP `parallel for` pragma encapsulates the actual computation of the integrals for all m and n values. Each integral is then assigned to a thread and computed sequentially using the DCUHRE library [8].

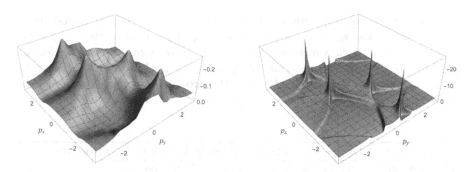

Fig. 1. The value of the integrand is plotted against the two-dimensional momentum **p** for $\Omega = 1.0$ (left plot) and $\Omega = 0.1$ (right plot). In this example case the external momentum **l** is set to $(3.14, 0.78)$ and both form-factor indices label the lowest order function, which is constant in momentum space.

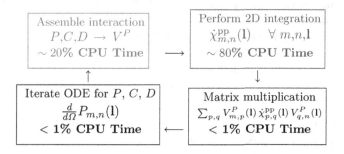

Using example values of **l**, m and n, Fig. 1 shows the integrand from Eq. (9) at a high and a low value of Ω. This example illustrates a general characteristic of the integrands: While at high Ω values the variations in momentum space are smooth, sharp edges and peaks emerge as the energy scale is lowered. This means in terms of numerical integration that the density of sampling points in momentum space should be chosen adaptively and separately for every integration. As the data from Fig. 1 suggest, the adaptive routine used should furthermore be able to refine the grid of sampling points using strongly local criteria in order to reduce the inaccuracies caused by sharp structures and to save time when flat regions are considered. In the next section we show how such a target is achieved by Algorithm 2, and give an account of its parallel implementation.

3 Adaptive Integration A-La Clenshaw-Curtis

The main target of adaptive integration is to decrease the error in a consistent and controlled fashion over relatively low-dimensional domains [11]. A possible choice to increase accuracy is to increase the number of integration points for a given integration method. Alternatively one can fix the number of integration points and instead partition the integration domain. Numerical integration with the same number of integration points is then performed on each subdomain. The latter method is known as *adaptive integration*. One of the most accurate variations of such a method computes the error across the whole domain [12, Chap. 6]. If some estimate for the global error is above a given threshold, one iteratively subdivides and integrates the sub-domain with the largest local error. Algorithm 1 shows the typical structure of such an adaptive integration scheme.

Algorithm 1. Adaptive integration on domain $\mathcal{D}$ with global error criterion

---

1: **function** ADAPTIVE(Integrand ϕ, Domain $\mathcal{D}$, Target Error ε)
2:     Compute integrals $Q(\phi, \mathcal{D}, n_1)$ and $Q(\phi, \mathcal{D}, n_2)$
3:     $\text{ERR}[\phi] = |Q_{n_1}\phi - Q_{n_2}\phi|$
4:     Store domain $\mathcal{D}$ and $\text{ERR}[\phi]$
5:     **while** $\text{ERR}[\phi] > \varepsilon$ **do**
6:         Take the sub-domain $\mathcal{D}^s$ with largest error
7:         Subdivide it into parts $\mathcal{D}^{s_1}, \ldots, \mathcal{D}^{s_d}$
8:         **for** $a = 1 : d$ **do**
9:             Compute $Q(\phi, \mathcal{D}^{s_a}, n_1)$ and $Q(\phi, \mathcal{D}^{s_a}, n_2)$
10:            $\text{ERR}^{s_a}[\phi] = |Q_{n_1}^{s_a}\phi - Q_{n_2}^{s_a}\phi|$
11:            Store domain $\mathcal{D}^{s_a}$ and $\text{ERR}^{s_a}[\phi]$
12:        **end for**
13:        $\text{ERR}[\phi] = \sum_s \text{ERR}^s[\phi]$
14:    **end while**
15:    **return** VALUE $= \sum_s Q(\phi, \mathcal{D}^s, n_2)$
16: **end function**

In the current work we compute the numerical integrals (and also the estimate for the error) using the Clenshaw-Curtis Quadrature (CCQ) formula[2]. Starting with n_1 integration points, we settle for a formula with $n_2 \geq n_1$ as the more accurate estimate [14]. With this choice the error estimate is equal to

$$\text{ERR}[\phi] = |Q_{n_1}\phi - Q_{n_2}\phi|,$$

where with $Q_n\phi = Q(\phi, \mathcal{D}, n)$ we indicate the computation of the integral $\Phi = \int_{\mathcal{D}}\phi$ over the domain $\mathcal{D}$ through numerical quadrature with n integration points[3]. When n_2 is proportional to n_1, the advantage of the CCQ scheme—compared to Gauss for instance—is the reuse of the n_1 points as a subset of the n_2 points. In the rest of this work we set $n_1 = N$ and $n_2 = 2n_1$.

---

[2] For a review of Clenshaw-Curtis and a comparison with Gauss quadrature rules we refer to the excellent review [13].
[3] We use the conventional notation indicating with the capital symbol the integral (Φ) and with the corresponding small cap symbol (ϕ) its integrand.

The schematic description in Algorithm 1 should be applied to the computations of the integral on the RHS of the flow Eqs. (2)–(4). After discretizing and projecting (using a truncated partition of unity), the RHS of such equations are split in multiplications of two-particle couplings $\mathbf{V}^i$ ($i = P, C, D$) and susceptibility factors $\mathcal{X}^j$ ($j = \mathrm{pp}, \mathrm{ph}$), only the latter expressed in terms of integrals. Despite the fact that now the integrals seem limited to the RHS of Eqs. (9)–(10), the adaptive approach has to encompass the whole set of integrals labeled by the indices m and n. Moreover, the original integrals included also the values of the couplings $\mathbf{V}^i$ in the integrand, so these quantities play an active role in the computation of the global error. Let us clarify this point by considering just the particle-particle channel Eq. (2), and formally evaluating it using a generic quadrature formula

$$Q_N \; \tau_{\mathrm{pp}} = - \sum_{\ell=1}^{N} w_\ell \left[\partial_\Omega G(p_\ell) \, G(k_1 + k_2 - p_\ell) \right] V(k_1, k_2, p_\ell) \, V(k_1 + k_2 - p_\ell, p_\ell, k_3) \, , \tag{11}$$

where the w_ℓ are the weights associated with the quadrature points p_ℓ. After some rearrangements and the introduction of the truncated partition of unity, the RHS of this equation is transformed into $\sum_{p,q} V^P_{m,p} \left(Q_N \, \dot{\chi}^{\mathrm{pp}}_{p,q} \right) V^P_{q,n}$ where we made explicit the m and n indices and suppressed, for the moment, the dependence on the l index. Despite the fact that now this quantity is the sum of distinct quadratures $Q_N \, \dot{\chi}^{\mathrm{pp}}_{p,q}$, the global error should be thought as defined by the original expression $|Q_N \, \tau_{\mathrm{pp}} - Q_{2N} \, \tau_{\mathrm{pp}}|$, leading to the following expression

$$\mathrm{ERR}[\dot{P}_{m,n}] = \left| \sum_{p,q} \left[V^P_{m,p} \left(Q_N \, \dot{\chi}^{\mathrm{pp}}_{p,q} \right) V^P_{q,n} - V^P_{m,p} \left(Q_{2N} \, \dot{\chi}^{\mathrm{pp}}_{p,q} \right) V^P_{q,n} \right] \right|$$
$$\leq \left\| V^P_{m,:} \right\|_\infty \left\| V^P_{:,n} \right\|_\infty \sum_{p,q} \left| Q_N \, \dot{\chi}^{\mathrm{pp}}_{p,q} - Q_{2N} \, \dot{\chi}^{\mathrm{pp}}_{p,q} \right| , \tag{12}$$

where $x = V_{m,:}$ is the vector made by all column entries corresponding to the mth row and $\|x\|_\infty = \max_j |x_j|$.

We can think of the entire numerical integration as the union of the quadratures $Q_n \, \dot{\chi}^{\mathrm{pp}}_{p,q}$ on the same domain $\mathcal{D}$ for each value of the indices p and q. While each adaptive quadrature labeled by p and q returns its own VALUE, the absolute error is computed globally over all indices (p, q). We further simplify the definition of the error by dropping the terms proportional to $\|V\|_\infty$. This last step may seem arbitrary but it is in part justified by the fact that, in the actual computation, we are only interested in the error relative to the value of the function. In order to maintain generality we define with $\phi^{i,j,k} = \mathbf{V}^i \dot{\chi}^j \mathbf{V}^k$ and the associated global relative error as

$$\mathrm{ERR}[\phi^{i,j,k}] = \sum_{p,q} \mathrm{ERR}[\dot{\chi}^j_{p,q}].$$

Algorithm 2. Parallel adaptive integration of TUfRG with global error

1: **for all** i, j, k, l **do**
2:     **function** ADAPTIVE(Integrand $\phi^{i,j,k}$, Domain $\mathcal{D}$, Target Error ε)
3:         done $= false$
4:         **while** done $\neq true$ **do**
5:             Take the domain $\mathcal{D}^s \subseteq \mathcal{D}$ and indices (p, q) with largest error
6:             Subdivide it into parts $\mathcal{D}^{s_1}, \ldots, \mathcal{D}^{s_4}$
7:             **for** $a = 1 : 4$ **do**
8:                 Compute $Q(\chi^j_{p,q}, \mathcal{D}^{s_a}, N)$ and $Q(\chi^j_{p,q}, \mathcal{D}^{s_a}, 2N)$
9:                 $\mathrm{ERR}^{s_a}[\chi^j_{p,q}] = |Q^{s_a}_N \chi^j_{p,q} - Q^{s_a}_{2N} \chi^j_{p,q}|$
10:                Store domain $\mathcal{D}^{s_a}$, indices (p, q) and $\mathrm{ERR}^{s_a}[\chi^j_{p,q}]$
11:            **end for**
12:            $\mathrm{ERR}[\phi^{i,j,k}] = \displaystyle\sum_{s,p,q} \mathrm{ERR}^s[\chi^j_{p,q}]$
13:            **if** $\mathrm{ERR}[\phi^{i,j,k}] < \varepsilon$ **then** done $= true$ **end if**
14:        **end while**
15:        **return** $(\mathrm{VALUE})^j_{p,q} = \displaystyle\sum_s Q(\chi^j_{p,q}, \mathcal{D}^s, 2N)$
16:    **end function**
17: **end for**

We kept the index l still implicit so as to avoid cluttering the notation, but it is understood that all definitions above depend implicitly on it. With these definitions in mind we end up with the adaptive quadrature scheme illustrated in Algorithm 2.

4   Parallel Implementation

In this work, we describe a parallel implementation of the ADAPTIVE function of Algorithm 2 over one computing node using OpenMP pragmas, and leave the outer **for** loops—identified by indices i, j, k, and l—distributed over MPI processes. Each elementary integration is encoded as a `task`, which can be imagined as a struct type. Each `task` has the following members: an `id` field that corresponds to distinct values of the p and q indices, a `domain`, the two values `val_N` and `val_2N` computed according to the CCQ method, and an estimate of the error `err`.

The adaptive integration scheme requires the tasks with the largest error to be scheduled first. Such an approach is not easily expressible with the OpenMP task construct. Although OpenMP tasks have recently gained support for task priorities, the allowed priority values are limited to non-negative scalars. As a result PAID cannot make use of OpenMP tasks.

The container into which the tasks are placed is a heap data structure that uses the `err` as the sorting key. A heap structure allows cheap en- and dequeuing of tasks. The heap is initialized at the beginning of the program.

Listing 1. Initialization of the task queue container

```
1   ERR[φ] := 0.0
2   for all (p, q)
3       task.id := (p, q) and task.domain := D
4       task.val_N := Q_N χ and task.val_2N := Q_2N χ
5       task.err := |Q_N χ − Q_2N χ|
6       container.PUSH(task)
7       ERR[φ] += task.err
8   HEAPIFY(container, key = task.err)
```

The heap structure of the container guarantees that task extraction is done in a way that refines regions with larger error estimates first, independent of which pair of indices (p, q) they belong to. In a way this algorithm can be seen as adaptive integration with starting regions defined by both D and (p, q). Due to the adaptivity based on the global error, the OpenMP parallel block has to enclose the domain D as well as the indices (p, q). As previously stated, PAID cannot make use of OpenMP's more advanced work sharing constructs. Instead, Algorithm 2 parallelizes the main part of the routine from line 4 to 14 using just the **parallel** directive (see line 4 of Listing 5). Access to the queue in lines 5 and 10 requires exclusive access in order to avoid race conditions. For queues that are not thread-safe a mutex is required (**critical** directive). This may decrease parallel performance as threads may need to wait for access to the queue. For this reason we implement bulk extraction and insertion into a thread-local container: Each thread can extract a MaxTask number of tasks, whose value is set by the user. Care has to be taken in choosing MaxTask; Its optimal value is a trade-off between maintaining acceptable levels of parallel performance and avoiding unnecessary adaptive refinements.

Listing 2. Extract tasks with maximal error from the queue

```
1   #PRAGMA OMP CRITICAL {
2   for n = 1 : MaxTask
3       local_container[n] = EXTRACT-MAX(container)
4   }
```

This results in a work sharing construct, as each task returned from the heap is different. Tasks are processed by partitioning their domain once in each dimension, which yields four new tasks. Before the new tasks can be inserted into the heap an error estimate is required, which in turn requires evaluation of the integrals.

Listing 3. Divide domains and evaluate new tasks

```
1   for n = 1 : MaxTask
2       evaltask[n, 1 : 4] := Divide local_container[n].domain into 4 parts
3       for a = 1 : 4
4           evaltask[n, a].domain := part a of local_container[n].domain
5           Compute evaltask[n, a].val_N and evaltask[n, a].val_2N
6           Compute evaltask[n, a].err
```

Eventually, the global error is updated within the mutex. Each thread then inserts the new tasks, together with their relative sub-domain, and `id` in the heap.

Listing 4. Update error and insert new tasks in the queue

```
1  #PRAGMA OMP CRITICAL {
2  for n = 1 : MaxTask
3      ERR[φ] −= local_container[n].err
4      for a = 1 : 4
5          ERR[φ] += evaltask[n, a].err
6          INSERT(evaltask[n, a] ⇒ container)
7  }
```

The termination criterion need only be checked by a single thread at the end of its block of refinements. This implies that the termination criterion is checked not sooner than after MaxTask refinements. When the global error is lower than the required threshold, all other threads are instructed to exit the while loop via the **done** flag. The entire program, which includes all previous Listings, is illustrated in Listing 5.

Listing 5. Full program

```
1   Program PAID(φ, D, ε)
2       done := false
3       Initialize  the task queue container              (Listing 1)
4       #PRAGMA OMP PARALLEL {
5       while done ≠ true do
6           Extract tasks with max error from container   (Listing 2)
7           Divide the domain and evaluate new tasks      (Listing 3)
8           Update ERR[φ] and insert new tasks in the queue  (Listing 4)
9           #PRAGMA OMP MASTER {
10          if ERR[φ] < ε then done := true
11          }
12      }
13      forall distinct task.id = (p, q)
14          return (VALUE)_{(p,q)} := ∑_{task.domain} task.val_2N
```

5   Results and Conclusions

In order to illustrate the effectiveness of PAID within the TUfRG code, we present a number of numerical tests, run on the JURECA computing cluster located at the Jülich Supercomputing Centre. Each node of the cluster is equipped with 2 Intel Xeon E5-2680 v3 Haswell CPUs. All tests were run with a single MPI rank per compute node. Node level parallelism is exclusively due to the shared memory parallelization of the adaptive quadrature implementation described in Algorithm 2.

In the following we draw a comparison between the previous implementation using DCUHRE and the newly developed implementation based on PAID. As both adaptivity and parallel efficiency play an important role in terms of performance, we conducted the comparative analysis in terms of these two aspects separately, before we compare the runtimes.

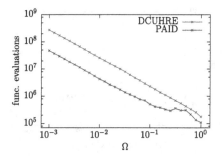 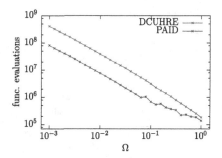

Fig. 2. The number of function evaluations needed for calculating all integrals of a fixed l value is plotted against Ω. We use a form-factor expansion that results in 45 independent integrals for each external momentum l, which is fixed to $(1.57, 1.31)$ (left plot) and $(2.88, 0.26)$ (right plot) respectively. The results of both implementations—the one using DCUHRE (red) and the one using PAID (blue)—are shown in the same plot in favor of a direct comparison. In order to use the same number of evaluations per subregion as in DCUHRE, we set the PAID parameter N to 4. Further we use MaxTask $= 10$. (Color figure online)

Figure 2 shows that the number of function evaluations needed by PAID is smaller than the one needed by DCUHRE at all values of the scale parameter, especially at low scales where most of the computation time is used[4]. As a smaller number of evaluations implies a more efficient partition of the integration domain, this number can be seen as an inverse measure for the adaptivity of the implementation provided by PAID, especially at low scales where the integrands tend to blow up. The difference in adaptivity between the both schemes can be understood as a consequence of the error estimation. DCUHRE computes the errors of the integrals labeled by p and q in isolation so that each error fulfills the same termination criterion independently. The PAID scheme treats all integrals as *one* task which in practice prioritizes computation over the most difficult partitions of the domain. As the major part of the computation time is used by the low-Ω integration domains, a code that is more efficient in this region of the parameter space pays off in terms of total runtime.

The second performance analysis addresses the parallel efficiency of PAID. Figure 3 shows that the speedup is close to ideal for any thread number up to 24[5]. Using SMT—up to 48 threads—still increases the speedup compared to the one using 24, but the curves in Fig. 3 show a slower increase in performance. This result suggests that the code is compute bound and can not profit highly from a larger memory bandwidth per core. Although the shared memory parallelization of the implementation of TUfRG using DCUHRE is much simpler—as described in Sect. 2—, we find a speedup which is as high as the one we achieve using PAID. We verified that the runtimes of the integrals for distinct p and q within a fixed

---

[4] Notice that the fRG flow in the current setup starts at high Ω values and successively reduces this scale during the flow.

[5] The granularity of the affinity is set to 'compact,core,1'.

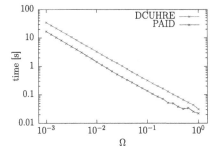
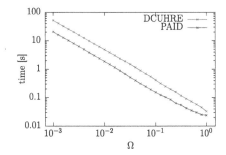

Fig. 3. These plots show the speedup at $\Omega = 10^{-3}$ against the number of threads for the implementation based on PAID. For thread numbers up to 24 each compute core executes only a single thread. At 48 threads each compute core processes two threads at a time using simultaneous multithreading. The l-values are chosen as in Fig. 2 and there are 325 integrals to calculate per l. For this analysis we use the PAID parameters that result in the best performance: $N = 6$ and MaxTask $= 18$.

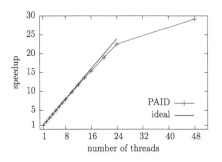
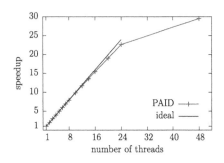

Fig. 4. The computation time needed for calculating all integrals of a fixed l value using 48 threads is plotted against Ω. We use a form-factor expansion that results in 325 independent integrals for each l, which takes the same values as in Fig. 2. For reasons of comparison we use $N = 4$ in PAID as in the analysis shown in Fig. 2. Further, MaxTask is set to 7.

value of l do not vary much in serial execution. In such a case the parallelization over the p and q values does not suffer from load imbalances and results in a close to ideal speedup.

In a third set of tests—possibly the most relevant to a user of TUfRG—we compared the runtimes that are needed by DCUHRE and PAID to perform all the integrations within a fixed value of l. As illustrated in Fig. 4, PAID needs less compute time than DCUHRE at all scales and is about 2–3 times faster at low Ω values.

In conclusion the TUfRG code greatly benefits from the proposed adaptive integration algorithm both in terms of load balancing and adaptivity. The result is a good exploitation of the node-level parallelism at any stage of the flow equation without the need of ad-hoc parameter choices. Comparing the new integration scheme with the one provided by DCUHRE shows that the PAID algorithm exhibits a higher level of adaptivity which in turn leads to shorter runtimes. In addition, the use of standard OpenMP pragmas ensures performance portability over clusters other than JURECA with the potential for off-loading to many-cores platforms with minimal effort. In the future, we envision to expand the internal parallelism of PAID to distributed memory. Such an extension could replace the currently used distribution of the l values over the MPI ranks and would prevent load imbalances that limit the number of accessible nodes in the current implementation.

Acknowledgements. Financial support from the Jülich Aachen Research Alliance–High Performance Computing, and the Deutsche Forschungsgemeinschaft (DFG) through grants GSC 111, RTG 1995 and SPP 1459 is gratefully acknowledged. We are thankful to the Jülich Supercomputing Centre (JSC) for the computing time made available to perform the numerical tests. Special thanks to JSC Guest Student Programme which sponsored the research internship of one of the authors.

References

1. Metzner, W., Salmhofer, M., Honerkamp, C., Meden, V., Schönhammer, K.: Functional renormalization group approach to correlated fermion systems. Rev. Mod. Phys. **84**, 299–352 (2012)
2. Platt, C., Hanke, W., Thomale, R.: Functional renormalization group for multiorbital fermi surface instabilities. Adv. Phys. **62**(4–6), 453–562 (2013)
3. Zanchi, D., Schulz, H.J.: Weakly correlated electrons on a square lattice: a renormalization group theory. EPL (Europhysics Letters) **44**(2), 235 (1998)
4. Salmhofer, M., Honerkamp, C.: Fermionic renormalization group flows: technique and theory. Progress Theoret. Phys. **105**(1), 1–35 (2001)
5. Husemann, C., Salmhofer, M.: Efficient parametrization of the vertex function, Ω scheme, and the t, t' hubbard model at van hove filling. Phys. Rev. B **79**, 195125 (2009)
6. Wang, W.S., Xiang, Y.Y., Wang, Q.H., Wang, F., Yang, F., Lee, D.H.: Functional renormalization group and variational monte carlo studies of the electronic instabilities in graphene near $\frac{1}{4}$ doping. Phys. Rev. B **85**, 035–414 (2012)
7. Lichtenstein, J., Sánchez de la Peña, D., Rohe, D., Di Napoli, E., Honerkamp, C., Maier, S.A.: High-performance functional renormalization group calculations for interacting fermions. arXiv:1604.06296, April 2016
8. Berntsen, J., Espelid, T.O., Genz, A.: Algorithm 698: DCUHRE: an adaptive multidimensional integration routine for a vector of integrals. ACM Trans. Math. Softw. **17**(4), 452–456 (1991)
9. DApuzzo, M., Lapegna, M., Murli, A.: Practical aspects and experiences - Scalability and load balancing in adaptive algorithms for multidimensional integration. Parallel Comput. **23**(8), 1199–1210 (1997)
10. Laccetti, G., Lapegna, M.: PAMIHR. A parallel FORTRAN program for multidimensional quadrature on distributed memory architectures. Euro-Par 1999 Parallel Processing (1999)
11. Cools, R.: Advances in multidimensional integration. J. Comput. Appl. Math. **149**(1), 1–12 (2002)

12. Krommer, A.R., Ueberhuber, C.W. (eds.): Numerical Integration on Advanced Computer Systems. LNCS, vol. 848. Springer, Heidelberg (1994)
13. Trefethen, L.N.: Is gauss quadrature better than clenshaw-curtis? SIAM Rev. **50**(1), 67–87 (2008)
14. Berntsen, J.: Practical error estimation in adaptive multidimensional quadrature routines. J. Comput. Appl. Math. **25**(3), 327–340 (1989)

Performance Portability

It can be challenging to develop scientific simulations flexible enough to perform well across the diverse set of modern HPC architectures. The spectrum of High-Performance Computing (HPC) systems varies greatly from specialized massively-parallel RISC architectures, such as IBM Blue Gene, through clusters of commodity hardware, to heterogeneous combinations of traditional CPUs and accelerator devices such as GPGPUs. The network and systems interconnects span a similarly wide spectrum. Taking full advantage of a specific kind of HPC system requires intricate low-level knowledge and specialized programming, which then results in software that does not run efficiently on other kinds of HPC hardware. Therefore, the development of adaptive algorithms and methods, which allow for the efficient porting of scientific simulations across HPC systems while trying to maintain their performance characteristics, is of paramount interest.

The papers presented in this section offer different views on the topic of achieving performance portability that complement and complete each other. They cover a) novel methods for visualization of performance data, which allow the quick identification and filtering of relevant performance information, b) the re-engineering of existing parallel codes and the integration into them of modern portable high-performance numeric libraries, and c) experiences from filling the "gaps" in scientific and engineering software development by bridging HPC expertise with domain science through on-demand collaboration.

Performance Optimization of Parallel Applications in Diverse On-Demand Development Teams

Hristo Iliev[1,2]([✉]), Marc-André Hermanns[3,4], Jens Henrik Göbbert[4],
René Halver[4], Christian Terboven[1,2], Bernd Mohr[3,4], and Matthias S. Müller[1,2]

[1] JARA-HPC, 52074 Aachen, Germany
[2] Chair for High Performance Computing, IT Center, RWTH Aachen University,
Seffenter Weg 23, 52074 Aachen, Germany
{iliev,terboven,mueller}@itc.rwth-aachen.de
[3] JARA-HPC, 52425 Jülich, Germany
[4] Jülich Supercomputing Centre, Forschungszentrum Jülich GmbH,
52425 Jülich, Germany
{m.a.hermanns,j.goebbert,r.halver,b.mohr}@fz-juelich.de

Abstract. Current supercomputing platforms and scientific application codes have grown rapidly in complexity over the past years. Multi-scale, multi-domain simulations on one hand and deep hierarchies in large-scale computing platforms on the other make it exceedingly harder to map the former onto the latter and fully exploit the available computational power. The complexity of the software and hardware components involved calls for in-depth expertise that can only be met by diversity in the application development teams. With its model of simulation labs and cross-sectional groups, JARA-HPC enables such diverse teams to form on demand to solve concrete development problems. This work showcases the effectiveness of this model with two application case studies involving the JARA-HPC cross-sectional group "Parallel Efficiency" and simulation labs and domain-specific development teams. For one application, we show the results of a completed optimization and the estimated financial impact of the combined efforts. For the other application, we present results from an ongoing engagement, where we show how an on-demand team investigates the behavior of dynamic load balancing schemes for an MD particle simulation, leading to a better overall understanding of the application and revealing targets for further investigation.

Keywords: Software development · Parallel efficiency · Performance optimization · On-demand teams · Diversity

1 Introduction

In the past decade, concurrency in supercomputing platforms has risen exponentially. With increasing transistor density resulting in new multi- and many-core processor node architectures and large-scale networks, such as multi-dimensional

© Springer International Publishing AG 2017
E. Di Napoli et al. (Eds.): JHPCS 2016, LNCS 10164, pp. 187–199, 2017.
DOI: 10.1007/978-3-319-53862-4_16

tori and variations of fat-tree architectures, users are faced with deep NUMA hierarchies on the node and complex network topologies. Reasoning about application performance in such environments becomes increasingly more difficult and requires more and more expertise. Homogeneous development teams comprised of scientists of the same domain easily reach the boundaries of their expertise.

Simulation codes have undergone a similar transformation in complexity. The ever increasing computing power available to simulation scientists has led to unprecedented detail with multi-scale, multi-domain simulations that expose a complexity inaccessible to most developers outside that specific domain. Modifications to such complex codes can often only be performed by the core developers of a specific simulation component.

From this status quo arises the need for scientific development teams with a diverse knowledge base, in order to sustain scientific productivity and code maintainability. However, such requirements are often not attainable by small to mid-sized development teams, common to university research groups. Moreover, not all expertise is needed all the time during the application life cycle. As such, much of the available expertise is left untapped during the development process. Furthermore, the synergism between domain and HPC experts is claimed to be an often overlooked means to reducing the operating costs of institutions providing computing services [1].

JARA-HPC addresses this problem by establishing two different types of research groups: (1) domain-specific research groups (simulation labs) focused on a specific domain, its approaches, and algorithms; and (2) cross-sectional groups in fields of expertise needed by all of the simulation labs. Simulation labs serve as beacons for a specific community, assisting research groups from their respective fields at RWTH Aachen University and Forschungszentrum Jülich, i.e., smaller research groups can call on a simulation lab's expertise and manpower for a specific problem. Likewise, the cross-sectional groups assist simulation labs and research groups in the area of their scientific field.

2   Mission Statement

The mission of the cross-sectional group "Parallel Efficiency" is the creation and dissemination of methods and tools in the area of software engineering of massively parallel applications that enable the efficient use of HPC resources. One of the core ideas is a synergistic exchange of knowledge between the cross-sectional group and developers of scientific simulation software. The former brings in the existing tools and expertise in parallel efficiency while the close collaboration leads to concrete insights on how the tools are used, how existing functionality can be improved, and which functionality is needed to investigate a specific application scenario.

2.1   Related Activities

Activities similar in spirit to the JARA-HPC cross-sectional groups and simulation labs also exist in scientific communities around the world. Major US national labs implement so-called computational end stations, such as the Climate-science Computational End Station (CCES) [15] or the Performance Evaluation and Analysis Consortium (PEAC) End Station. In comparison to the cross-sectional group, PEAC focuses more on the proliferation of scalable performance tool support and is less directly engaged in explicit optimization efforts of other end stations. However, end stations, such as CCES, have kept close ties to individual members of the PEAC group to drive the optimization of the community codes on large-scale systems, as in the context of the G8 project ECS, targeting climate simulations at exascale [3].

The Hessian Competence Center for High Performance Computing (Hessisches Kompetenzzentrum für Hochleistungsrechnen, HKHLR) provides specific performance optimization support for the users of their systems [11]. With acknowledging the need for specific in-depth knowledge of HPC environments and performance tools and establishing the respective expertise within their HPC user support, they now serve as an available contact for HPC user groups throughout the German federal state of Hesse.

While the cross-sectional group focuses on collaboration with other JARA-HPC groups, performance optimization is needed not only within the scientific community, but also within the commercial and industry sectors. This prompted the creation of the EU Horizon 2020 center of excellence Performance Optimization and Productivity (POP) [4], which targets performance analysis and optimization of third-party application codes on a broader European scale. The main goal of the center is the development of a unified set of performance metrics, a collection of structured methods and workflows for performance analysis and optimization, and a standard set of reports for presenting the results to the end user. POP offers several levels of involvement ranging from performance audits of the user code to proof-of-concept modifications that improve the performance and scalability of the code. The cross-sectional group shares many of POP's goals and therefore actively collaborates with its members.

3   Case Study: psOpen

As a first example of a successful optimization work performed by a team assembled on demand, we present the performance optimization of the simulation code *psOpen*. The team in that case consisted of one performance analyst from the cross-sectional group and one core developer of the target application; the duration of the collaboration was one month. The target was to improve the performance of *psOpen* on the RWTH Compute Cluster, which consists of compute nodes with two Intel Westmere processors each (12 cores per node) connected via a non-blocking QDR InfiniBand network.

psOpen [7] is a parallel Navier-Stokes solver for the time evolution of incompressible fluid flows with high Reynolds numbers that uses a pseudo-spectral direct numerical simulation (DNS) method [9]. The software is developed by the Institute for Technical Combustion (ITV) of RWTH Aachen University and is currently a member of the High-Q Club of extremely scalable applications that run on the IBM Blue Gene/Q system JUQEEN at the Jülich Supercomputing Centre (JSC) of Forschungszentrum Jülich (Jülich, Germany).

Spectral methods [2] solve systems of differential equations in the inverse space spanned by the eigenvectors of the differential operators. In such basis the costly numerical differentiations reduce to point operations, which simplifies the solution. Not all equations can be solved efficiently in inverse space alone since any non-linear term containing field products transforms into an expensive convolution in inverse space. A possible solution is to compute such products in real space while the rest of the computations are performed in inverse space, which gives rise to pseudo-spectral methods.

The point operations in *psOpen* are simple loops with independent iterations and have been extensively tuned to make use of the available vectorization capabilities of the system compiler. Therefore, the main optimization efforts were focused on analyzing the forward and backward 3D Fourier transforms as they take a significant amount of time in each step of the time-integration loop. *psOpen* uses the open-source *P3DFFT* library [10], which implements the 3D Fast Fourier Transform (3D-FFT) and is parallelized with the Message Passing Interface (MPI). Both slab (1D) and pencil (2D) domain decompositions are supported and in both cases the MPI all-to-all operations MPI_ALLTOALL and MPI_ALLTOALLV are used to perform the global array transpose needed by the 3D-FFT algorithm. The pencil domain decomposition technique needs two all-to-all operations, one before the FFT in the Y direction and one before the FFT in the Z direction, while the slab decomposition needs a single all-to-all operation before the FFT in the Z direction, therefore the pencil decomposition might seem more appealing from a performance point of view. As the typical simulation domain is a cube of certain number of points N along each dimension, that number determines the maximum scalability in terms of MPI ranks that can be used: (1) up to N MPI ranks for the slab (1D) decomposition, or (2) up to N^2 MPI ranks for the pencil (2D) decomposition.

The optimization task consisted of two parts, each involving specific knowledge of the scientific problem and the implementation of MPI on the specific hardware respectively. In the first part, knowledge about the use of the results from the 3D-FFT was applied to reduce the amount of data processing and exchange. Since the real space multiplication introduces spurious frequency components (spectral aliasing), once the result has been forward Fourier transformed, a dealiasing step is performed where a low-pass cut-off filter removes the upper third of the spectrum in each spatial dimension. As a result, 70,4% of the transformed data gets discarded. Since a 3D-FFT is a combination of three independent 1D-FFTs in each dimension with a global transpose between each and since the transform itself is linear, the filtering step can be interleaved with the 1D-FFTs, which can be expressed using right-associative operator notation as:

$$f \circ \mathcal{F} = f_z \circ \mathcal{F}_z \circ f_y \circ \mathcal{F}_y \circ f_x \circ \mathcal{F}_x, \tag{1}$$

where $\mathcal{F}_i$ and f_i denote the 1D-FFT and the low-pass filter in direction i respectively. Once part of the spectrum has been zeroed out, it is not necessary to

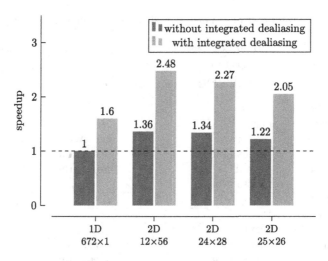

Fig. 1. Speed-up of with three different pencil (2D) domain decompositions relative to the slab (1D) decomposition for a domain of size 1024^3. Results without (left) and with integrated dealiasing (right) are shown.

carry the filtered data into the further steps. Consequently, the following 1D Fourier transforms have less data to work on. This reduces both the number of 1D Fourier transforms by 30% and the amount of data for the first global transform by 33% and for the second global transform by 56% [8].

In the second part of the optimization task, the lock-step ring implementation of MPI_ALLTOALL and MPI_ALLTOALLV in Open MPI 1.6.5 was studied in detail and a model for the execution time of the global data transpose for each of the two domain decompositions was derived. Given the same number of MPI ranks, it can be shown that the number of message exchanges for the pencil decomposition is substantially lower than for the slab decomposition, which reduces the total latency. It also allows for optimized process mappings that take advantage of the communication structure of the 3D-FFT algorithm to minimize the amount of data sent over slower network links. One such mapping is a pencil decomposition of size $N \times M$, where N equals the number of cores on each node of the cluster, in which case one of the two all-to-all operations involves communication only within groups of processes that reside on the same compute node. With the integrated filtering procedure described above, the second all-to-all operation involves less data and it is therefore beneficial to select a mapping which results in inter-node communication during that operation only. No changes to the source code of *psOpen* or the supporting libraries were made during this part of the optimization project.

The performance of the modified version of the filtered 3D-FFT routine in transformations per second when running on 56 compute nodes (672 MPI ranks in total) is shown in Fig. 1. All values are normalized to the case of slab (1D) decomposition with separate 3D-FFT and filtering steps. The figure also shows

Table 1. Total cost of ownership analysis for a domain size of 2048^3.

Setup	1D (672×1) separate dealiasing	2D (12×56) integrated dealiasing
Hardware costs	250,000 EUR	
Electricity	0.14 EUR/kWh	
Scenario 1		
Fixed no. 3D-FFTs	$1 \cdot 10^8$	
3D-FFTs/kWh	152	277
Energy to solution	658 MWh	361 MWh
Energy cost	92,105 EUR	50,525 EUR
Personnel costs	0 EUR	10,000 EUR
Savings	31,580 EUR	
Scenario 2		
Fixed lifetime	5 years	
3D-FFTs/hour	2273	4215
Energy used	657 MWh	666 MWh
Energy cost	91,980 EUR	93,206 EUR
3D-FFTs/EUR	291	523
Efficiency improvement	+80%	

that having process distribution that matches the topology of the computing system (in that particular case, 12×56) becomes even more relevant for the case with integrated dealiasing.

An important aspect of any kind of collaboration is justifying funding it, therefore we quantified the financial impact of the optimization efforts by performing a simplified total cost of ownership (TCO) analysis in two ideal scenarios, comparing the original unoptimized version and the optimized version, including the best domain decomposition. To remove the dependency on the specific input data and the different physics models associated with it, the analysis covers only the 3D-FFT kernel as it is the most time consuming part of the simulation and is also reusable by other projects. In both scenarios we considered the acquisition cost for a part of the RWTH Compute Cluster used exclusively by ITV, the cost of the electricity, and the personnel costs involved in optimizing the application as summarized in Table 1. The personnel costs are based on 2 person-months with scientific employees at the typical for doctoral and postdoctoral researchers in Germany pay grade TV-L E13, which totals to 10,000 EUR [6]. This is a simplified TCO analysis based on the method of Wienke et al. [16].

First, a use case with 100 million 3D-FFTs was considered, which corresponds to performing a fixed number of studies with a specified statistical significance of the simulation results. A managed power distribution unit (PDU) was used to measure the power use of the system while performing a fixed number of 3D-FFTs, then the energy to solution value was obtained by a linear extrapolation. Assuming that the price of electricity remains constant for the entire period, performing the specified number of 3D-FFTs with the optimized version uses

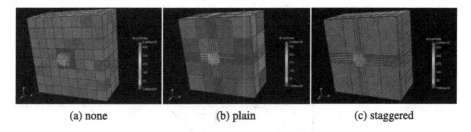

(a) none   (b) plain   (c) staggered

Fig. 2. Different levels of load balancing available in MP2C. Without load balancing the size of the simulation domain is constant across all processes, leading to imbalance during particle interaction. Plain load balancing allows dimensions to be adjusted, yet the borders remain on a single plain cutting through the entire simulation box. Staggered load balancing allows further to shift individual borders, influencing the number of neighbors a process can have during the simulation.

361 MWh of electrical power and costs 50,525 EUR compared to 658 MWh and 92,105 EUR for the unoptimized version. Subtracting the personnel costs from the difference of the two values, one arrives at the cost savings of 31,580 EUR. While the number was derived in a highly idealized scenario, it serves to show that investing in performance optimization can have a significant overall financial impact on certain scientific projects.

The second use case covers running simulations for the entire lifetime of the cluster system. A value of 5 years was chosen as it is typical for many computing centers. The unmodified version of the 3D-FFT kernel achieves 2,273 transforms per hour for a total of 99.6 million transforms for the entire lifetime of the compute cluster. The consumed electrical power will total to 657 MWh or 91,980 EUR. The TCO in that case will be 342 thousand EUR and the cost efficiency, defined as the number of 3D-FFTs per EUR, will be 291 transforms/EUR. The optimized version achieves 4,215 transforms per hour for a total of 184.6 million transforms for the entire lifetime of the compute cluster. It uses slightly more energy, 666 MWh, resulting in TCO of 353.2 thousand EUR, which also includes the personnel costs. The cost efficiency of the optimized version is 523 transforms/EUR. Therefore, more research can be done during the lifetime of the computer cluster with 80% better cost efficiency.

4 Case Study: MP2C

As a second example of successful engagements of the cross-sectional group and a simulation lab, we present the ongoing investigation of the load balancing mechanisms present in the Massively Parallel Multi-Particle Collision Dynamics simulation code (MP2C) [14]. The team in this case consisted of one performance analyst from the cross-sectional group and one core developer of the simulation code.

MP2C is a particle based parallel solver in the field of mesoscopic hydrodynamics. It combines Multi Particle Collision Dynamics (MPC) with Molecular

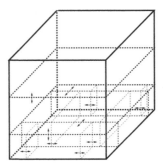

Fig. 3. Geometry of the staggered load-balance scheme: (1) the work of one Cartesian plane is collected and the border between neighboring planes adjusted according to the differences in work load between them; (2) the procedure is repeated for Cartesian columns and (3) for individual cells. This leads to a staggered grid, as the columns of neighboring planes are likely to be shifted against each other, as are the cells of neighboring columns.

Dynamics (MD) to simulate solute systems, such as polymers embedded in a fluid. The parallelization approach is based on a domain decomposition where data is exchanged via the Message Passing Interface (MPI). For data intensive applications, a highly-scalable parallel I/O library, SIONlib [5], developed at Jülich Supercomputing Centre (JSC) is available. The code is developed by the simulation laboratory *Molecular Systems* [13] at JSC and has successfully run at extreme scale on the IBM Blue Gene/Q system JUQUEEN of Forschungszentrum Jülich [12], as well as on other architectures, e.g. CRAY XT4/XT5. The 3D domain-decomposition relies on disjunct spatial sub-domains which are administered by individual processes. Due to the dynamic nature of the simulated systems, the particles are free to move between domains, which demands for data exchange between the processors. While the fluid fills the simulation box almost homogeneously, the embedded particle systems can cluster, which may create load imbalances in the MD computations. To tame the performance degradation due to load imbalance, MP2C implements different load-balancing strategies to adapt to these dynamically changing work loads using (1) plain and (2) staggered domain geometries. Figure 2 shows the decomposition of a part of the simulation box, with no (Fig. 2a), plain (Fig. 2b), and staggered (Fig. 2c) load balancing enabled. The former implements load balancing along a regular three-dimensional Cartesian grid, while the latter hierarchically adjusts the load within the cells as is shown in Fig. 3. This may lead to irregular neighborhood relationships among processes, i.e., some processes having a larger neighborhood than others.

Both of these load-balancing strategies have their own advantages and disadvantages, e.g. the adjustment of work is better for the staggered scheme, as the cells can be fitted to clusters of work in a more optimal way than in the plain scheme. This advantage comes at the price of a much more complex communication scheme, as the number of neighbors for each cell can increase in a

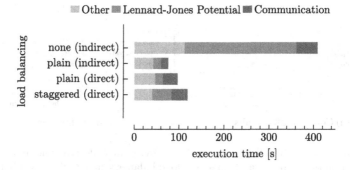

Fig. 4. Total execution time in seconds—broken down in communication, computation of the Lennard-Jones potential during particle interaction, and other computation—for no, plain, and staggered load balancing. Plain load balancing is shown for both direct and indirect communication. Any load balancing clearly outperforms no load balancing, yet the plain load balancing strategies perform best overall.

non-predictable way, while for the plain scheme the number of neighbors is conserved. The static number of neighbor processes allows for more sophisticated communication algorithms to be used with the plain load-balancing scheme. Instead of exchanging messages directly with every neighbor (direct communication), processes send data for all processes in one dimension to one process, to have it distribute the relevant portions to the others on its behalf (indirect communication).

To investigate the performance, we conducted pure particle simulations, i.e. without inclusion of the solvent, on 4,096 processes on JUQUEEN, an IBM Blue Gene/Q system at Forschungszentrum Jülich. The simulation was configured for 50,000 particles and 50,000 iterations. Furthermore, we investigated the simulation using no load-balancing with indirect communication; plain load balancing with either indirect and direct communication; and staggered load balancing with direct communication.

Figure 4 shows that any load balancing strategy exceeds the simulation performance without load balancing by far. Furthermore, the plain load-balancing scheme, with either direct and indirect communication schemes, achieves better results in terms of runtime than the staggered version, which is currently only implemented using direct communication.

The goal of this specific collaboration between the cross-sectional group *Parallel Efficiency* and the simulation laboratory *Molecular Systems* is to identify the cause for this difference and to locate optimization targets in the staggered load-balancing scheme, as previous measurements on static domains indicate the superiority of the staggered over the plain load-balancing scheme due to its finer adaption capabilities.

The initial working hypothesis assumed a rise in communication complexity as the culprit for the increase in simulation time. Performance screening confirmed the increase in communication complexity, as Figs. 5a and b show.

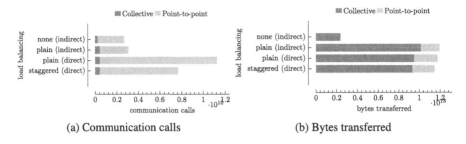

Fig. 5. Communication calls and transferred bytes in collective and point-to-point communication for no, plain, and staggered load balance scheme. Plain load balancing is shown for both direct and indirect communication. Indirect communication clearly cuts down on the number of calls overall, yet, also the improved neighborhood decomposition of the staggered scheme is able to reduce the number of calls.

However, comparing the available load balancing options, it becomes clear that the additional overhead in communication calls is actually due to the requirement to use direct communication for the staggered case, as enabling direct communication for the plain load balancing already increases the number of point-to-point communication calls by a factor of 4. The staggered load balancing strategy is able to reduce this to a factor of 2.7. Direct communication also seems to cut down on the overall bytes transferred. Revisiting the time spent for communication in the investigated load-balancing schemes in Fig. 4 indicates that although the communication itself seems to be more complex, the overall time spent in point-to-point communication does not depend on the load-balancing scheme itself, but on the use of direct versus indirect communication. Surprisingly even for the MP2C developers, the time spent in computing the Lennard-Jones potential during particle interaction—a section void of any communication, but highly dependent on the number of particles per process and in the neighborhood— differs significantly between plain and staggered load balancing. This suggests suboptimal load balance. In summary, the increase in communication complexity is not introduced by the staggered load balancing itself, but by its requirement of direct communication among the neighbor processes. The total amount of increase in simulation time, however, is much more influenced by the particle distribution, i.e., the quality of the load balancing.

To confirm the difference in adoption speed between the plain and staggered load-balancing scheme, we conducted further measurements, to get iteration-based information of the time spent in the particle interaction. To keep instrumentation overhead low, we configured the measurement to aggregate the performance metrics of the individual call paths of the main loop—including the computation of the Lennard-Jones potential—for every 100 iterations. Based on those measurements, Fig. 6 confirms different adaption speeds for the plain and the staggered load-balancing schemes. Moreover, the staggered load balancing seems to adapt much worse after the collapse of the particle cloud around the 20,000-th iteration, where the slope of the curve of the staggered load balancing

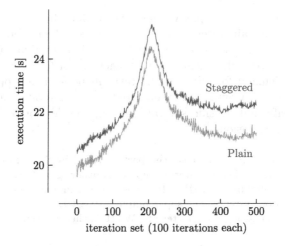

Fig. 6. Computation time of the Lennard-Jones potential during particle interaction for 500 iteration sets with 100 iterations each. Each iteration set value comprises the aggregated values of the maximum time spent by a process across all processes in each iteration. As load balancing is enabled each 10 iterations, each iteration set comprises 10 balancing steps.

flattens out much earlier than the plain load balancing. Also surprising and worthy of further investigation is the fact that the staggered load balancing seems to experience another increase of imbalance in the system around the 40,000-th iteration.

The resulting working hypothesis for future investigations now assumes the difference in mesh-adaption speed between the two load-balancing strategies to play a significant role in the overall simulation performance of dynamic particle systems. Future work will therefore focus on 1. developing adequate performance metrics to investigate the particle distribution over time, 2. identify key components in the load-balancing strategies that influence the adaption speed, and 3. explore potential optimization targets for either load-balancing scheme.

5   Conclusion

Diverse development teams are needed to meet the challenges of the ever increasing complexity of modern high-performance computing infrastructures and simulation codes. While maintaining such diverse teams over the full application life cycle is often unfeasible, drawing from a set of existing domain-specific groups to form such teams on demand for specific development tasks is feasible. In this work, we have shown two examples of application optimization performed by such teams. In one example, we have also shown through total-cost-of-ownership analysis that funding such environments is economically justified, as their work pays off and can greatly impact the overall code efficiency in terms of cost per simulation. In the other example, we have shown that the combination of complementing set of domain-specific knowledge increases the understanding of the overall application, and can generate valuable insights into dynamic application behavior at scale. We will continue our engagement of forming small development teams on demand for very specific tasks in performance optimization of scientific simulations. Contact between cross-sectional groups and simulation labs may intensify and subside several times in the development cycle of an application or its extensions.

Acknowledgments. This work has been partly funded by the Excellence Initiative of the German federal and state governments. The authors gratefully acknowledge the computing time granted by the JARA-HPC Vergabegremium and provided on the two JARA-HPC Partition systems—the supercomputer JUQUEEN at Forschungszentrum Jülich and the RWTH Compute Cluster at RWTH Aachen University.

References

1. Bischof, C., an Mey, D., Iwainsky, C.: Brainware for green HPC. Comput. Sci. Res. Dev. **27**(4), 227–233 (2012). http://dx.doi.org/10.1007/s00450-011-0198-5
2. Canuto, C., Hussaini, M.Y., Quarteroni, A., Zang, T.A.: Spectral Methods. Springer, Heidelberg (2006)
3. Cappello, F., Wuebbles, D.: G8 ECS: Enabling climate simulation at extreme scale, 2012. In: G8 Exascale Projects Workshop, 12 November 2012
4. CoE Performance Optimisation and Productivity (2016). https://pop-coe.eu/
5. Freche, J., Frings, W., Sutmann, G.: High throughput parallel-I/O using SIONlib for mesoscopic particle dynamics simulations on massively parallel computers. In: Chapman, B., Desprez, F., Joubert, G.R., Lichnewsky, A., Peters, F.J., Priol, T. (eds.) Parallel Computing: From Multicores and GPU's to Petascale. Advances in Parallel Computing, vol. 19, pp. 371–378. IOS Press, Amsterdam (2010)
6. German Science Foundation (DFG): Personalmittelsätze der DFG für das Jahr 2013 (2013)
7. Göbbert, J.H.: psOpen (2015). http://www.fz-juelich.de/ias/jsc/EN/Expertise/High-Q-Club/psOpen/_node.html. Accessed 4 July 2016
8. Goebbert, J.H., Gauding, M., Ansorge, C., Hentschel, B., Kuhlen, T., Pitsch, H.: Direct numerical simulation of fluid turbulence at extreme scale with psOpen. Adv. Parallel Comput. **27**, 777–785 (2016)
9. Orszag, S.A.: Analytical theories of turbulence. J. Fluid Mech. **41**(2), 363–386 (1970)
10. Pekurovsky, D.: P3DFFT: A framework for parallel computations of Fourier transforms in three dimensions. SIAM J. Sci. Comput. **34**(4), C192–C209 (2012)
11. Sitt, R., Feith, A., Sternel, D.C.: Parallel code analysis in HPC user support. In: Knüpfer, A., Hilbrich, T., Niethammer, C., Gracia, J., Nagel, W.E., Resch, M.M. (eds.) Tools for High Performance Computing 2015, pp. 127–133. Springer, Cham (2016). http://dx.doi.org/10.1007/978-3-319-39589-0_10
12. Sutmann, G.: MP2C (2015). http://www.fz-juelich.de/ias/jsc/EN/Expertise/High-Q-Club/MP2C/_node.html. Accessed 4 July 2016
13. Sutmann, G.: Simulation lab Molecular Systems (2015). http://www.fz-juelich.de/ias/jsc/EN/AboutUs/Organisation/ComputationalScience/Simlabs/slms/_node.html. Accessed 4 July 2016

14. Sutmann, G., Westphal, L., Bolten, M.: Particle based simulations of complex systems with MP2C: Hydrodynamics and electrostatics. AIP Conf. Proc. **1281**(1), 1768–1772 (2010). http://scitation.aip.org/content/aip/proceeding/aipcp/10.1063/1.3498216

15. Washington, W.M., Drake, J., Buja, L., Anderson, D., Bader, D.C., Dickinson, R., Erickson, D., Gent, P., Ghan, S., Jones, P., Jacob, R.L.: The use of the Climate-Science Computational End Station (CCES) development and grand challenge team for the next IPCC assessment: An operational plan, December 2007

16. Wienke, S., an Mey, D., Müller, M.S.: Accelerators for technical computing: is it worth the pain? A TCO perspective. In: Kunkel, J.M., Ludwig, T., Meuer, H.W. (eds.) ISC 2013. LNCS, vol. 7905, pp. 330–342. Springer, Heidelberg (2013). doi:10. 1007/978-3-642-38750-0_25

Hybrid CPU-GPU Generation of the Hamiltonian and Overlap Matrices in FLAPW Methods

Diego Fabregat-Traver[1(✉)], Davor Davidović[2], Markus Höhnerbach[1], and Edoardo Di Napoli[1,3,4]

[1] AICES, RWTH Aachen, 52062 Aachen, Germany
{fabregat,hoehnerbach}@aices.rwth-aachen.de
[2] RBI, 10040 Zagreb, Croatia
davor.davidovic@irb.hr
[3] JARA-HPC, 52425 Jülich, Germany
[4] Jülich Supercomputing Center, Forschungszentrum Jülich, 52425 Jülich, Germany
e.di.napoli@fz-juelich.de

Abstract. In this paper we focus on the integration of high-performance numerical libraries in ab initio codes and the portability of performance and scalability. The target of our work is FLEUR, a software for electronic structure calculations developed in the Forschungszentrum Jülich over the course of two decades. The presented work follows up on a previous effort to modernize legacy code by re-engineering and rewriting it in terms of highly optimized libraries. We illustrate how this initial effort to get efficient and portable shared-memory code enables fast porting of the code to emerging heterogeneous architectures. More specifically, we port the code to nodes equipped with multiple GPUs. We divide our study in two parts. First, we show considerable speedups attained by minor and relatively straightforward code changes to off-load parts of the computation to the GPUs. Then, we identify further possible improvements to achieve even higher performance and scalability. On a system consisting of 16-cores and 2 GPUs, we observe speedups of up to 5× with respect to our optimized shared-memory code, which in turn means between 7.5× and 12.5× speedup with respect to the original FLEUR code.

Keywords: DFT · High-performance computing · Performance portability · Heterogeneous architectures · FLAPW method · FLEUR

1 Introduction

Many legacy codes in scientific computing have grown over time with an eye on functionality, but little emphasis on portable performance and scalability. Often, these codes are a direct translation of mathematical formulae, and lack proper engineering (i.e. modularity, code reuse, etc.). One such example is FLEUR, a software for electronic structure calculations developed at the Jülich Research

E. Di Napoli et al. (Eds.): JHPCS 2016, LNCS 10164, pp. 200–211, 2017.
DOI: 10.1007/978-3-319-53862-4_17

Center during the last two decades [3]. In previous work by Di Napoli et al. [2], the authors made the effort of reengineering a portion of FLEUR's code base in an attempt to demonstrate the value of writing the computational bottlenecks in terms of kernels provided by standardized and highly-tuned libraries. There, they show an increase in performance and anticipate its portability beyond multi-core architectures. In this paper, we confirm that the reengineering process indeed guarantees quick portability and high-performance on emerging heterogeneous architectures, as in the case of multi-core CPUs equipped with one or more coprocessors such as GPUs.

In times where massively-parallel heterogeneous architectures have become the most common computing platform, legacy scientific code has to be modernized. New software is often designed with portable efficiency and scalability in mind, and some old code is undergoing major rewriting to adapt to the newest architectures. However, there is still a lot of reluctance to undergo through the rewriting process since it requires a vast initial effort and may incur in validation issues. While it is understandable that domain scientists are hesitant to introduce major changes into a code developed and tested in the course of many years, legacy codes that do not go through this process are destined to be marginalized.

A critical insight in writing long-lasting scientific code is to have a modular design where, at the bottom layers, the computational bottlenecks are written in terms of kernels available from standardized and highly-tuned libraries. Examples of such kernels are fast Fourier transforms, matrix products, and eigensolvers, provided by a number of commercial as well as academic libraries. The most prominent example of standard and optimized scientific library is the Basic Linear Algebra Subprograms (BLAS). This library has its roots in the early realization of the necessity for portable performance. Today, BLAS kernels, which include matrix products and linear systems, are the building blocks for a multitude of libraries, so much that BLAS is the first library to be ported to and optimized for every new architecture. Therefore, writing code on top of BLAS and other standardized and broadly available libraries constitutes a first and essential step in the modernization of scientific software.

In this paper we follow the same approach illustrated in [2], where the authors made a major effort to address the computational bottlenecks of the FLEUR's code base: the generation of the so-called Hamiltonian and Overlap matrices. In generating such matrices, the main goal of the original FLEUR code was the minimization of memory usage. Furthermore there is no notion of abstraction and encapsulation, and the different modules are tightly coupled. At this point, low-level optimizations were unfeasible, and the authors opted for a clean slate approach: starting from the mathematical formulation behind the code, they cast it in terms of matrix operations supported by the BLAS and LAPACK libraries. As presented in their results, despite lacking some mathematical insight that reduced the amount of computation in the FLEUR code, HSDLA (the new code) outperformed the original one with speedups between 1.5× and 2.5×. Most importantly, the authors claim that HSDLA could be easily ported to other architectures.

In this paper, we continue their work, and illustrate how such an initial reengineering effort enables a quick port to heterogeneous architectures consisting of multi-core CPUs and one or more GPUs. More specifically, we quantify the minimal effort required in terms of additional code to attain substantial speedups. When running on a system equipped with two GPUs, we observe speedups of up to 5× with respect to HSDLA and about one order of magnitude with respect to the corresponding FLEUR code. Moreover, we identify the additional work required to attain close-to-optimal efficiency and scalability, and partially implement it to illustrate the idea. Finally, beyond the results specific to the case of FLEUR, the main contribution of this paper is to demonstrate that, despite the major initial effort, a reengineering of legacy codes is not only worth it but imperative in order to obtain long-lasting portable performance and scalability.

This paper is organized as follows. Section 1.1 provides the background on Density Functional Theory (DFT) and the math behind the computation to generate the Hamiltonian and Overlap matrices. Section 2 gives an overview of the optimized algorithm behind HSDLA for the generation of these matrices. In Sect. 3 we discuss the porting of the code to heterogeneous architectures, including a review of the available BLAS libraries for GPUs and a simple analysis of the computation to decide which portions of the code to off-load to the GPUs. Section 4 presents experimental results for 1, 2 and 4 GPUs, and points at potential improvements to the hybrid code. Finally, Sect. 5 draws conclusion and discusses future research directions.

1.1   DFT, FLAPW and the H and S Matrices

The FLEUR code is based on the widely accepted framework of Density Functional Theory (DFT). In the last decade, Density Functional Theory (DFT) [6,7] has become the "standard model" in Materials Science. Within the DFT framework, it is possible to simulate the physical properties of complex quantum mechanical systems made of few dozens up to few hundreds of atoms. The core of the method relies on the simultaneous solution of a set of Schrödinger-like equations. These equations are determined by a Hamiltonian operator $\hat{H}$ containing an effective potential $V_0[n]$ that depends functionally on the one-particle electron density $n(\mathbf{r})$. In turn, the solutions of the equations $\psi_i(\mathbf{r})$ determine the one-particle electron density $n(\mathbf{r})$ used in calculating the effective potential V_0.

$$\hat{H}\psi_i(\mathbf{r}) = \left(-\frac{\hbar^2}{2m}\nabla^2 + V_0(\mathbf{r})\right)\psi_i(\mathbf{r}) = \epsilon_i\psi_i(\mathbf{r}) \quad ; \quad \epsilon_1 \leq \epsilon_2 \leq \ldots$$
$$n(\mathbf{r}) = \sum_i^N |\psi_i(\mathbf{r})|^2 \tag{1}$$

In practice, this set of equations, also known as Kohn-Sham (KS) [5], is solved self-consistently; an initial guess for $n_0(\mathbf{r})$ is used to calculate the effective potential V_0 which, in turn, is inserted in Eq. (1) whose solutions, $\psi_i(\mathbf{r})$, are used to compute a new charge density $n_1(\mathbf{r})$. Convergence is checked by comparing the new density to the starting one. When convergence is not reached, an opportune mixing of the two densities is selected as a new guess, and the process is repeated. This is properly called a Self-Consistent Field (SCF) iteration.

In principle, the theory only requires as input the quantum numbers and the positions of the atoms that are part of the investigated system. In practice, there is a plethora of DFT methods which depends on the *discretization* used to parameterize the KS equations. The discretization in the Full-potential Linearized Augmented Plane Wave (FLAPW) method [4, 10] is based on plane wave expansion of $\psi_{\mathbf{k},\nu}(\mathbf{r})$, where the momentum vector $\mathbf{k}$ and the band index ν replace the generic index i. The $\mathbf{k}$-point wave function $\psi_{\mathbf{k},\nu}(\mathbf{r}) = \sum_{|\mathbf{G}+\mathbf{k}| \leq \mathbf{K}_{max}} c_{\mathbf{k},\nu}^{\mathbf{G}} \varphi_{\mathbf{G}}(\mathbf{k},\mathbf{r})$ is expanded in terms of a basis set $\varphi_{\mathbf{G}}(\mathbf{k},\mathbf{r})$ indexed by the vectors $\mathbf{G}$ lying in the lattice reciprocal to configuration space up to a chosen cut-off value $\mathbf{K}_{max}$. In FLAPW, the physical (configuration) space of the simulation cell is divided into spherical regions, called Muffin-Tin (MT) spheres, centered around atomic nuclei, and interstitial areas between the MT spheres. The basis set $\varphi_{\mathbf{G}}(\mathbf{k},\mathbf{r})$ takes a different expression depending on the region

$$
\varphi_{\mathbf{G}}(\mathbf{k},\mathbf{r}) \propto \begin{cases} e^{i(\mathbf{k}+\mathbf{G})\mathbf{r}} & \text{Interstitial} \\ \sum_{l,m} \left[A_{l,m}^{a,\mathbf{G}}(\mathbf{k}) u_l^a(r) + B_{l,m}^{a,\mathbf{G}}(\mathbf{k}) \dot{u}_l^a(r) \right] Y_{l,m}(\hat{\mathbf{r}}_a) & a^{th} \text{ Muffin Tin} \end{cases} \tag{2}
$$

where the coefficients $A_{l,m}^{a,\mathbf{G}}(\mathbf{k})$ and $B_{l,m}^{a,\mathbf{G}}(\mathbf{k})$ are determined by imposing continuity of $\varphi_{\mathbf{G}}(\mathbf{k},\mathbf{r})$ and its derivative at the boundary of the MTs. Due to this expansion the KS equations naturally translate to a set of generalized eigenvalue problems $\sum_{\mathbf{G}'} [H_{\mathbf{G},\mathbf{G}'}(\mathbf{k}) - \lambda_{\mathbf{k}\nu} S_{\mathbf{G},\mathbf{G}'}(\mathbf{k})] c_{\mathbf{k},\nu}^{\mathbf{G}'} = 0$ for the coefficients of the expansion $c_{\mathbf{k},\nu}^{\mathbf{G}'}$ where the Hamiltonian and Overlap matrices H and S are given by multiple integrals and sums

$$
\{H(\mathbf{k}), S(\mathbf{k})\}_{\mathbf{G},\mathbf{G}'} = \sum_a \iint \varphi_{\mathbf{G}}^*(\mathbf{k},\mathbf{r}) \{\hat{H}, I\} \varphi_{\mathbf{G}'}(\mathbf{k},\mathbf{r}) d\mathbf{r}. \tag{3}
$$

Since the set of basis functions in Eq. (2) is implicitly labeled by the values the variable $\mathbf{k}$ takes in the Brillouin zone, there are multiple Hamiltonian and Overlap matrices, one for each independent $\mathbf{k}$-point.

Without loss of generality, we can abstract from the $\mathbf{k}$-point index and recover an explicit formulation of the $H_{\mathbf{G},\mathbf{G}'}$ and $S_{\mathbf{G},\mathbf{G}'}$ matrices by substituting Eq. (2) in (3) and carrying out the multiple integration. The computation is particularly complex within the MT regions where the initialization of the Hamiltonian and Overlap matrices is by far the most computationally intensive task. By exploiting the properties of the basis functions, the H and S matrices are directly expressed as functions of the set of A and B coefficients.

$$
(S)_{\mathbf{G}',\mathbf{G}} = \sum_{a=1}^{N_A} \sum_{l,m} \left(A_{l,m}^{a,\mathbf{G}'} \right)^* A_{l,m}^{a,\mathbf{G}} + \left(B_{l,m}^{a,\mathbf{G}'} \right)^* B_{l,m}^{a,\mathbf{G}} \|\dot{u}_l^a\|^2 \tag{4}
$$

$$
(H)_{\mathbf{G}',\mathbf{G}} = \sum_{a=1}^{N_A} \sum_{L',L} \left(\left(A_{L'}^{a,\mathbf{G}'} \right)^* T_{L',L;a}^{[AA]} A_L^{a,\mathbf{G}} \right) + \left(\left(A_{L'}^{a,\mathbf{G}'} \right)^* T_{L',L;a}^{[AB]} B_L^{a,\mathbf{G}} \right)
$$

$$
+ \left(\left(B_{L'}^{a,\mathbf{G}'} \right)^* T_{L',L;a}^{[BA]} A_L^{a,\mathbf{G}} \right) + \left(\left(B_{L'}^{a,\mathbf{G}'} \right)^* T_{L',L;a}^{[BB]} B_L^{a,\mathbf{G}} \right). \tag{5}
$$

Notice that in Eq. (5) for convenience we have compacted the indexes l, m into L, and expressed the range of the index a over all the distinct atom types N_A. The new matrices $T^{[\dots]}_{L',L;a} \in \mathbb{C}^{N_L \times N_L}$ are dense and their computation involves multiple integrals between the basis functions and the non-spherical part of the potential V_0 (See [2, Appendix A.2] for details). Due to the non-orthornormality of the basis function set (2), the matrix S is non-diagonal, dense, and generically positive definite with the exception of having few very small singular values. On the opposite H is always non-definite and both matrices are either complex Hermitian or real symmetric.

2   Algorithm

As a first step towards using the BLAS and LAPACK libraries, all the involved objects in Eqs. (4) and (5) are expressed in matrix form, dropping indexes L, L', G, and G'. Assuming the coefficient objects A and B as well as the T matrices as input, matrices H and S can be computed as follows:

$$H = \sum_{a=1}^{N_A} \underbrace{A_a^H T^{[AA]} A_a}_{H_{AA}} + \underbrace{A_a^H T^{[AB]} B_a + B_a^H T^{[BA]} A_a + B_a^H T^{[BB]} B_a}_{H_{AB+BA+BB}} \qquad (6)$$

$$S = \sum_{a=1}^{N_A} A_a^H A_a + B_a^H U_a^H U_a B_a, \qquad (7)$$

where A_a and $B_a \in \mathbb{C}^{N_L \times N_G}$, $T_a^{[\dots]} \in \mathbb{C}^{N_L \times N_L}$, H and $S \in \mathbb{C}^{N_G \times N_G}$, and $U \in \mathbb{C}^{N_L \times N_L}$ is a diagonal matrix. Typical for the matrix sizes are $N_A \sim \mathcal{O}(100)$, $N_G \sim \mathcal{O}(1000)$ to $\mathcal{O}(10000)$, and $N_L \sim \mathcal{O}(100)$.

Algorithm 1 illustrates the algorithm used to compute Eqs. (6) and (7) in HSDLA. Two main insights drive the design of the algorithm. First, it exploits symmetries to reduce the computational cost; then, it casts the computation in terms of BLAS and LAPACK kernels. Furthermore, when possible, multiple matrices are stacked together to allow for larger matrix products, which in general results in higher performance.

The computation of H is split into two parts, $H_{AB+BA+BB}$ and H_{AA}. The computation of $H_{AB+BA+BB}$ corresponds to lines 4 through 10. The key idea behind the calculation is to rewrite the expression as

$$\sum_{a=1}^{N_A} B_a^H (T^{[BA]} A_a) + (A_a^H T^{[AB]}) B_a + \frac{1}{2} B_a^H (T^{[BB]} B_a) + \frac{1}{2} (B_a^H T^{[BB]}) B_a,$$

noting that $T^{[BA]}$ is the Hermitian transpose of $T^{[AB]}$ and that $T^{[BB]}$ is itself Hermitian. The operations in parentheses are computed one at a time for each i. Then, the results are aggregated into single large matrices for a large product.

The computation of H_{AA} corresponds to lines 17 through 29. The algorithm first attempts a Cholesky factorization of $T^{[AA]}$ ($C_a C_a = T^{[AA]}$), which requires the matrix to be Hermitian positive definite (HPD). While, in theory, $T^{[AA]}$ is HPD, in practice, due to numerical considerations, the factorization may fail. Depending on the success or failure of each individual factorization, the results of operations in lines 21 and 24 are stacked on different temporary operands to then compute H_{AA} in two steps (lines 28 and 29).

The computation of S (lines 13 through 15) is more straightforward. First, the product $A^H A$ is computed as a single large product. Then B is updated with the norms stored in U and a second large product $B^H B$ completes the computation.

Algorithm 1. Computation of the H and S matrices in HSDLA.

1. Create A, B		
2. Backup $\hat{A} = A$, $\hat{B} = B$		
3. // First part of H		
4. **for** $a := 1 \to N_A$ **do**		
5. $\quad Z_a = T_a^{[BA]} A_a$	$\triangleright$ (**zgemm**: $8N_L^2 N_G$ Flops)	
6. $\quad Z_a = Z_a + \frac{1}{2}T_a^{[BB]} B_a$	$\triangleright$ (**zhemm**: $8N_L^2 N_G$ Flops)	
7. $\quad$ Stack Z_a to Z		
8. $\quad$ Stack B_a to B		
9. **end for**		
10. $H = Z^H B + B^H Z$	$\triangleright$ (**zher2k**: $8N_A N_L N_G^2$ Flops)	
11. Restore $A = \hat{A}$, $B = \hat{B}$		
12. // S		
13. $S = A^H A$	$\triangleright$ (**zherk**: $4N_A N_L N_G^2$ Flops)	
14. $B = UB$	$\triangleright$ (**scaling**: $2N_A N_L N_G$ Flops)	
15. $S = S + B^H B$	$\triangleright$ (**zherk**: $4N_A N_L N_G^2$ Flops)	
16. // Second part of H		
17. **for** $a := 1 \to N_A$ **do**		
18. $\quad$ **try:**		
19. $\qquad C_a = Cholesky(T_a^{[AA]})$	$\triangleright$ (**zpotrf**: $\frac{4}{3}N_L^3$ Flops)	
20. $\quad$ **success:**		
21. $\qquad Y_a = C_a^H A_a$	$\triangleright$ (**ztrmm**: $4N_L^2 N_G$ Flops)	
22. $\qquad$ Stack Y_a to Y_{HPD}		
23. $\quad$ **failure:**		
24. $\qquad X_a = T_a^{[AA]} A_a$	$\triangleright$ (**zhemm**: $8N_L^2 N_G$ Flops)	
25. $\qquad$ Stack X_a to $X_{\neg\mathrm{HPD}}$		
26. $\qquad$ Stack A_a to $A_{\neg\mathrm{HPD}}$		
27. **end for**		
28. $H = H + A_{\neg\mathrm{HPD}}^H X_{\neg\mathrm{HPD}}$	$\triangleright$ (**zgemm**: $8N_{A_{\neg\mathrm{HPD}}} N_L N_G^2$ Flops)	
29. $H = H + Y_{\mathrm{HPD}}^H Y_{\mathrm{HPD}}$	$\triangleright$ (**zherk**: $4N_{A_{\mathrm{HPD}}} N_L N_G^2$ Flops)	

---

3   Software Re-engineering and Performance Portability

In this section we set the focus on the porting of the multi-core implementation of Algorithm 1 to heterogeneous architectures consisting of one multi-core node equipped with one or more GPUs. We perform a quick analysis of the computation to determine how to split the computation between CPU and GPU(s) with minimal modifications to the code, and illustrate how with these minor modifications one can already benefit considerably from the combined computational power of CPU and GPUs.

Given the characteristic values for N_A, N_L, and N_G observed in our test cases, at least 97% of the computation is performed by the operations in lines 10, 13, 15, 28 and 29. Thanks to the aggregation of many small matrix products into single large ones, all these 5 operations are large enough to be efficiently computed on the GPUs. Therefore, the first step is to off-load these computations to the GPU making sure that relatively high efficiency is attained.

All five calls correspond to BLAS kernels; we thus look into available BLAS implementations for GPUs. There exists a range of GPU libraries that offer BLAS functionality, both academic and commercial, such as cuBLAS [1], cuBLAS-XT, MAGMA [8], and BLASX [9]. The first two are commercial and developed by NVIDIA, the other two are academic efforts. From the point of view of programmability, the most convenient alternatives are cuBLAS-XT and BLASX, since they require minor or no changes to the calls to BLAS routines and take also care of the data transfers between CPU and GPU transparently. While BLASX offers certain advantages from the programmability perspective and claims higher performance and scalability (see [9]), we encountered some problems in the integration and opted for using cuBLAS-XT for our initial study.

Since cuBLAS-XT does not abide to the BLAS standard interface, three wrappers, of about 15 lines of code each, around the calls to zherk, zher2k and zgemm are required to ensure the code works seamlessly in both CPU-only and CPU-GPU(s) modes. An example for zgemm follows:

```
void gpu_zgemm_( char *transa, char *transb, int *m,  int *n, int *k,
                 std::complex<double> *alpha,  std::complex<double> *A,  int *lda,
                 std::complex<double> *B,  int *ldb,
                 std::complex<double> *beta, std::complex<double> *C,  int *ldc )
{
    cublasOperation_t cu_transa = transa[0] == 'N' ? CUBLAS_OP_N :
                                  transa[0] == 'T' ? CUBLAS_OP_T : CUBLAS_OP_C;
    cublasOperation_t cu_transb = transb[0] == 'N' ? CUBLAS_OP_N :
                                  transb[0] == 'T' ? CUBLAS_OP_T : CUBLAS_OP_C;
    cublasXtZgemm( handle, cu_transa, cu_transb, *m, *n, *k,
                   (cuDoubleComplex *)alpha, (cuDoubleComplex *)A, *lda,
                                             (cuDoubleComplex *)B, *ldb,
                   (cuDoubleComplex *)beta,  (cuDoubleComplex *)C, *ldc );
}
```

In addition, two routines for proper initialization and cleanup of the cuda runtime and the devices are needed. Finally, for the data transfers between CPU and GPU to be efficient, memory for the matrices involved must be pinned (page-locked).

With these minor modifications, about 100 lines of extra coding, the program is ready to off-load most of the computation to multiple GPUs and attain n-fold speedups. It is important to highlight that this simple extension is only possible thanks to the initial effort in rewriting the initial FLEUR code in terms of matrix

(BLAS/LAPACK) operations. At that point the efficiency and scalability of the code may be easily ported to more complex architectures. Had the original FLEUR code not undergone the reengineering process, the coding of efficient low level routines for the GPUs would be a much more complex and time-consuming effort.

4 Experimental Results

We turn now our attention to experimental results. We compare the performance of our hybrid CPU-GPU implementation of Algorithm 1 with the performance of the multi-core (CPU only) HSDLA. As test cases we use two input systems describing two distinct physical systems, to which we refer as NaCl and AuAg, respectively. By including both an insulator and a conductor, these systems represent a heterogeneous sample with different physical properties. The tests generate the matrices H and S for one single **k**-point, and different K_{max} values. The actual problem sizes, that is, the values for N_A, N_L, and N_G in each case are given in Table 1.

Table 1. Problem sizes for NaCl and AuAg and for a variety of K_{max} values. The value of N_G varies with K_{max}.

Test case	N_A	N_L	$N_G : K_{max} = 2.5$	$K_{max} = 3.0$	$K_{max} = 3.5$	$K_{max} = 4.0$
NaCl	512	49	2256	3893	6217	9273
AuAg	108	121	3275	5638	8970	13379

We ran our experiments in two different compute nodes, which we will refer to as RWTH and JURECA. The RWTH node consists of two eight-core Sandy Bridge E5-2650 processors, running at a nominal frequency of 2.0 GHz, and 2 NVIDIA Tesla K20Xm GPUs. The node is equipped with 64 GBs of RAM. The combined peak performance for the 16 CPU cores in double precision is of 256 GFlops, while the peak performance for double precision of each GPU is of 1.3 TFlops, for a total of 2.6 TFlops. The JURECA node consists of two twelve-core Haswell E5-2680v3 processors, running at a nominal frequency of 2.5 GHz, and 2 NVIDIA K80 GPUs (each of which consists of two K40 GPU devices). The node is equipped with 128 GBs of RAM. The combined peak performance for the 24 CPU cores in double precision is of 960 GFlops, while the peak performance for double precision of each GPU device is of about 1.45 TFlops, for a total of 5.8 TFlops. In all cases, the code was linked to Intel MKL version 11.3.2 for the BLAS and LAPACK routines on the CPU; the GPU code was linked to NVIDIA cuBLAS-XT version 7.5.

RWTH. Table 2 collects the timings for the NaCl test case for the three scenarios of interest (CPU only, CPU + 1 GPU, CPU + 2 GPUs). The speedup with respect to HSDLA is given in parentheses. As expected, the considerable gap in performance between CPU and GPU is reflected in the observed large speedups: up to 2.76× and 4.04× for 1 and 2 GPUs, respectively.

Similar results are presented in Table 3 for the AuAg test case, but in this case the observed speedups are even larger. The reason for this is that, while MKL is already close to its peak performance for the matrix sizes of NaCl, cuBLAS-XT still has room for improvement and benefits from the larger matrices in AuAg. In fact, one can expect still better speedups for larger systems.

Table 2. Timings and speedup (in parentheses) for the NaCl test case for varying K_{max}. Results for the RWTH node.

Setup	$K_{max} = 2.5$	$K_{max} = 3.0$	$K_{max} = 3.5$	$K_{max} = 4.0$
CPU only	18.27s	39.84s	91.52s	189.53s
CPU + 1 GPU	8.03s (2.28×)	15.87s (2.51×)	35.64s (2.57×)	68.59s (2.76×)
CPU + 2 GPUs	6.51s (2.81×)	12.37s (3.22×)	24.39s (3.75×)	46.97s (4.04×)

Table 3. Timings and speedup (in parentheses) for the AuAg test case for varying K_{max}. Results for the RWTH node.

Setup	$K_{max} = 2.5$	$K_{max} = 3.0$	$K_{max} = 3.5$	$K_{max} = 4.0$
CPU only	15.64s	46.23s	104.25s	215.98s
CPU + 1 GPU	7.52s (2.08×)	16.16s (2.86×)	35.62s (2.93×)	71.35s (3.03×)
CPU + 2 GPUs	5.62s (2.78×)	11.28s (4.10×)	23.10s (4.51×)	43.54s (4.96×)

JURECA. Results for the JURECA node are presented in Tables 4 and 5 for NaCl and AuAg, respectively. In this case we show timings and speedups for up to 4 GPUs. The maximum observed speedups are 1.77×, 2.76× and 4.26× for 1, 2 and 4 GPUs, respectively. Given that the increase in computational power in each case is of 2.4×, 3.9× and 6.8×, respectively, these numbers are quite satisfactory.

Table 4. Timings and speedup (in parentheses) for the NaCl test case for varying K_{max}. Results for the JURECA node.

Setup	$K_{max} = 2.5$	$K_{max} = 3.0$	$K_{max} = 3.5$	$K_{max} = 4.0$
CPU only	9.33s	23.29s	41.50s	74.73s
CPU + 1 GPU	6.47s (1.44×)	14.50s (1.61×)	32.73s (1.27×)	66.55s (1.12×)
CPU + 2 GPUs	5.00s (1.87×)	10.38s (2.24×)	21.84s (1.90×)	42.58s (1.76×)
CPU + 4 GPUs	4.72s (1.98×)	8.76s (2.66×)	15.45s (2.69×)	26.58s (2.81×)

4.1 Fine-Tuning for Performance and Scalability

The observed speedups are substantial. Yet, one could expect even better results, especially in the case of the RWTH node where the computational power of the two GPUs combined is ten times larger than that of the CPUs. This potential for improvement comes as no surprise, since this is only a basic port to illustrate

Table 5. Timings and speedup (in parentheses) for the AuAg test case for varying K_{max}. Results for the JURECA node.

Setup	$K_{max} = 2.5$	$K_{max} = 3.0$	$K_{max} = 3.5$	$K_{max} = 4.0$
CPU only	9.10s	22.68s	57.31s	100.19s
CPU + 1 GPU	6.14s (1.48×)	14.47s (1.57×)	32.34s (1.77×)	68.91s (1.45×)
CPU + 2 GPUs	4.38s (2.08×)	9.70s (2.34×)	20.80s (2.76×)	42.24s (2.37×)
CPU + 4 GPUs	3.53s (2.58×)	6.69s (3.39×)	13.46s (4.26×)	25.36s (3.95×)

how far one can get with minimal code modifications; to attain close-to-optimal performance further work is required. For ideal results, a hybrid and highly-tuned BLAS as well as a GPU-accelerated version of the computation in the loops are needed.

In order to have a more tangible discussion, we provide in Table 6 a break-down of the timings for the NaCl ($K_{max} = 4.0$) test case running in the RWTH node with two K20x GPUs. The bottom rows correspond to the large BLAS operations off-loaded to the two GPUs; the top rows correspond to the rest of the code (both loops and the application of the U norm) executed on the CPU only. The efficiency is measured with respect to the combined performance of CPU plus GPUs.

Table 6. Breakdown of timings for NaCl ($K_{max} = 4.0$) together with the respective attained performance and efficiency.

Section (line(s))	Time	Performance	Efficiency
Loop 1 (4–9)	2.27 s	80.35 GFlops/s	0.03
Loop 2 (17–27)	2.62 s	34.81 GFlops/s	0.01
U norm (14)	0.23 s	1.01 GFlops/s	0.00
S1 (13)	4.37 s	1974.63 GFlops/s	0.69
S2 (15)	4.41 s	1956.72 GFlops/s	0.68
H1 (10)	9.49 s	1818.57 GFlops/s	0.63
H2 (28)	2.32 s	1859.72 GFlops/s	0.65
H3 (29)	4.75 s	1816.66 GFlops/s	0.63

Three main messages can be extracted from Table 6:

1. NVIDIA's cuBLAS-XT does a good job attaining an efficiency between 63% and 69%.
2. Yet, these operations may attain about 90% of the peak if the matrices are large enough and the code is highly optimized and hybrid. This would mean attaining around 2.5 TFlops/s, that is, an extra 25% speedup for these heavy computations.

3. When the target architecture offers massive parallelism, minor portions of code that do not scale may become a bottleneck. In our case, the 3% of the computation that was not off-loaded to the GPUs becomes non-negligible. In fact, the weight of these operations in our experiments may account for up to 35% of the time to solution, and compromise the overall scalability.

Due to the size of the matrices involved in these operations (between 50×50 and 100×100 for the T matrices in our test cases), these products do not scale well, especially on GPUs.

Specialized code is required to mitigate their impact in the overall time to solution.

5   Conclusions and Future Work

We concentrated on the benefits of rewriting scientific code in terms of standardized libraries for portable performance and scalability. As use case we considered a portion of the FLEUR code base, a software for electronic structure calculations.

We demonstrated that major efforts in re-engineering part of the original FLEUR code, and writing it in terms of the BLAS and LAPACK libraries, enables a fast porting that exploits the vast computational power of emerging heterogeneous architectures such as multi-core CPUs combined with multiple GPUs. Most importantly, the porting only required less than 100 new lines of code. The resulting implementation attains speedups of up to $3\times$ and $5\times$ for simulations run on a system equipped with two K20x GPUs, respectively, and speedups of up to $1.8\times$, $2.8\times$ and $4.3\times$ for runs with 1, 2 and 4 GPUs, respectively, on a system equipped with two K80 GPUs (each consisting of two K40 GPUs).

While satisfactory, these results highlight room for improvement. In the future, we aim at developing more efficient hybrid CPU-GPU routines for the major matrix products in the code as well as attaining sufficient scalability of the rest of the code to ensure a uniform overall scalability.

Acknowledgements. This work was partially funded by the Ministry of Science and Education of the Republic of Croatia and the Deutsche Akademische Austauschdienst (DAAD) from funds of the Bundesministeriums für Bildung und Forschung (BMBF) through project "PPP Kroatien" ID 57216700. Financial support from the Jülich Aachen Research Alliance-High Performance Computing and the Deutsche Forschungsgemeinschaft (DFG) through grant GSC 111 is also gratefully acknowledged. Furthermore, the authors thank the RWTH IT Center and the Jülich Supercomputing Centre for the computational resources.

References

1. cuBLAS: The NVIDIA CUDA Basic Linear Algebra Subroutines. https://developer.nvidia.com/cublas
2. Di Napoli, E., Peise, E., Hrywniak, M., Bientinesi, P.: High-performance generation of the hamiltonian and overlap matrices in FLAPW methods. Comput. Phys. Commun. **211**, 61–72 (2016). doi:10.1016/j.cpc.2016.10.003
3. FLEUR: The Jülich FLAPW code family, October 2016. http://www.flapw.de/pm/index.php
4. Jansen, H.J.F., Freeman, A.J.: Total-energy full-potential linearized augmented-plane-wave method for bulk solids - electronic and structural-properties of tungsten. Phys. Rev. B **30**(2), 561–569 (1984)
5. Kohn, W., Sham, L.J.: Self-consistent equations including exchange and correlation effects. Phys. Rev. **140**, A1133–A1138 (1965)
6. Nogueira, F., Marques, M.A.L., Fiolhais, C.: A Primer in Density Functional Theory. Lecture Notes in Physics. Springer, Heidelberg (2003)
7. Sholl, D., Steckel, J.A.: Density Functional Theory: A Practical Introduction. Wiley, New York (2011)
8. Tomov, S., Nath, R., Ltaief, H., Dongarra, J.: Dense linear algebra solvers for multicore with GPU accelerators. In: Proceedings of the IEEE IPDPS 2010, pp. 1–8. IEEE Computer Society, Atlanta, GA, 19–23 April 2010. doi:10.1109/IPDPSW.2010.5470941
9. Wang, L., Wu, W., Xu, Z., Xiao, J., Yang, Y.: BLASX: A high performance level-3 BLAS library for heterogeneous multi-GPU computing. In: Proceedings of the 2016 International Conference on Supercomputing, ICS 2016, pp. 20:1–20:11. ACM, New York (2016)
10. Wimmer, E., Krakauer, H., Weinert, M., Freeman, A.J.: Full-potential self-consistent linearized-augmented-plane-wave method for calculating the electronic-structure of molecules and surfaces - O2 molecule. Phys. Rev. B **24**(2), 864–875 (1981)

Visualizing Performance Data
with Respect to the Simulated Geometry

Tom Vierjahn[1,2]($\boxtimes$), Torsten W. Kuhlen[1,2], Matthias S. Müller[1,3],
and Bernd Hentschel[1,2]

[1] JARA-HPC, 52064 Aachen, Germany
[2] Visual Computing Institute, RWTH Aachen University, 52064 Aachen, Germany
`vierjahn@vr.rwth-aachen.de`
[3] Chair for High-Performance Computing, RWTH Aachen University,
Seffenter Weg 23, 52064 Aachen, Germany

Abstract. Understanding the performance behaviour of high-performance computing (HPC) applications based on performance profiles is a challenging task. Phenomena in the performance behaviour can stem from the HPC system itself, from the application's code, but also from the application domain. In order to analyse the latter phenomena, we propose a system that visualizes profile-based performance data in its spatial context in the application domain, i.e., on the geometry processed by the application. It thus helps HPC experts *and* simulation experts understand the performance data better. Furthermore, it reduces the initially large search space by automatically labelling those parts of the data that reveal variation in performance and thus require detailed analysis.

Keywords: Performance measures · Applications · Visualization

1 Introduction

Optimizing an application to use the compute power efficiently that is offered by a modern high-performance computing (HPC) system requires powerful tools for performance analysis. With the exponentially growing number of cores in HPC systems the acquired performance data grows and gets more complex. While visual exploration of this data is a valuable asset for developers to form an in-depth understanding of an application's run-time behaviour, straightforward means of visualization easily break down for large core counts. Furthermore, retrieving relevant information that actually fosters a deeper understanding, by manually browsing the large amounts of performance data easily becomes a challenging task in itself.

Annotating the individual performance metrics and functions in their execution contexts, i.e., call paths, with their performance data, e.g., execution time, gives an overview of an application's behaviour (Fig. 1). However, this does only provide an impression on the average load. Potential imbalances cannot be represented that way.

© Springer International Publishing AG 2017
E. Di Napoli et al. (Eds.): JHPCS 2016, LNCS 10164, pp. 212–222, 2017.
DOI: 10.1007/978-3-319-53862-4_18

Severity	Self		Performance Metric
9.7e+07	6.93e-12	sec	▼ Time
3.46e+07	6.36e+06	sec	▼ Execution
2.82e+07	3.13e-12	sec	▼ MPI
156	0	sec	▶ Synchronization
1.24e+07	-3.2e-12	sec	▶ Communication
0	0	sec	File I/O
1.59e+07	1.59e+07	sec	Init/Exit
6.24e+07	6.24e+07	sec	Overhead
5.23e+09	5.23e+09	occ	Visits
1.97e+05	0	occ	▶ Synchronizations
2.61e+09	0	occ	▶ Communications

(a) Performance metrics

	Severity ▼	Self		Code Region
■	9.7e+07	4.56e+04	sec	▼ driver
■	7.83e+07	22.7	sec	▶ task_init
▪	1.87e+07	1.78	sec	▼ inner_auto
■	1.87e+07	965	sec	▼ inner
■	1.6e+07	5.55e+06	sec	▼ sweep
■	9.73e+06	4.3e+03	sec	▶ rcv_real
	7.58e+05	4.82e+03	sec	▶ snd_real
	11.7	11.7	sec	octant
▫	1.87e+06	4.56	sec	▶ global_int_sum
	7.29e+05	7.29e+05	sec	source
	2.83e+04	2.83e+04	sec	▶ flux_err

(b) Call paths

Fig. 1. Annotating the performance metrics (a) and the call paths (b) with their overall performance.

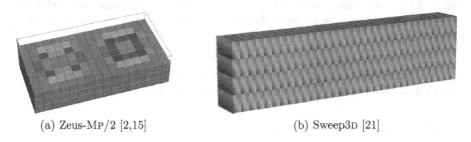

(a) Zeus-MP/2 [2,15]   (b) Sweep3D [21]

Fig. 2. Visualizing performance in an HPC system's topology may reveal the underlying geometry in small cases (a), but obscures it in larger cases (b).

Visualizing performance data on the process or thread level with respect to the HPC system's topology (Fig. 2) clearly shows such imbalances. It thus helps HPC experts and performance analysts understand an application's performance behaviour better. However, it does not clearly reveal performance phenomena that stem from the application domain that are for instance due to a sub-optimal domain decomposition.

In simple cases, an analyst might be able to infer the geometry in the application domain from the visualization in the HPC system's topology: in case of Fig. 2(a) a sphere, cut in half and then mapped to the HPC system's nodes. For larger cases the application domain can hardly be inferred: in case of Fig. 2(b) a 2D gradient, cut several times.

Thus, in order to provide complete insight into an application's performance behaviour, analysis tools ought to visualize the available data also with respect to the geometry in the application domain (cf. Fig. 3). Only then, HPC experts, performance analysts, *and* simulation experts can understand the performance data better. However, only few tools take the application domain into account, and if they do they restrict it, e.g., to regular grids.

Therefore, we propose a tool that facilitates visualizing performance data in its spatial context on an arbitrary geometry in the application domain, e.g., a triangle mesh, provided there is a mapping from the computing resources to the geometry. In order to help the analyst find meaningful views on the data that

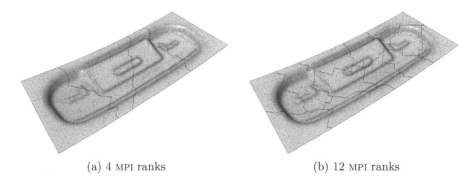

(a) 4 MPI ranks   (b) 12 MPI ranks

Fig. 3. Two finite-element meshes from a sheet-metal forming simulation and their domain decomposition. The triangle edges are rendered light gray, the blocks' outlines are rendered dark.

are good indicators of performance bottlenecks, the tool automatically identifies and suggests views that reveal variation in performance.

2   Related Work

Isaacs et al. give an overview of the state of the art in performance visualization [6]. Several tools exist that are able to visualize performance data in the HPC system's topology. Boxfish, for instance, visualizes network activity on 3D-torus [7] and on 5D-torus network topologies [8] using a set of 3D visualizations and 2D projections. Similarly, VizTorus [14] uses a set of linked projections to visualize communication in high-dimensional torus networks. The TAU [12] parallel performance system provides extensive 3D exploration support for profile-based performance data, including mapping the data to the network topology in ParaProf [13]. Finally, the Cube performance profile browser [4] also allows for the mapping of profile data onto Cartesian network topologies in a pseudo-3D projection.

Yet, very few techniques exist that are considering the application domain. Nevertheless, Schulz et al. stress the importance of taking the application domain into account during performance analysis [11]. Wylie and Geimer use Cartesian grids [20] in the Cube performance profile browser in order to visualize performance with respect to the application domain. For a visualization in Cube, the application domain can be higher-dimensional. However, then the complete domain will be displayed as separate 2D slices. A recent visual-analytics approach automatically identifies relevant and similar sections of profile-based performance data in 2D application domains, only [10]. Huck et al. [5] coupled the visualisation tool VisIt [3] to the TAU [12] parallel performance system, demonstrating the usefulness of visualizing performance data in the context of the application domain.

In this work, we propose a tool that is similar in spirit to the Cube performance profile browser. Similar to the said VisIt-TAU combination, it enables visualizing performance data on arbitrary geometry, however in an integrated tool. To this end, it extends our prior approach [16] and complements our performance-visualization toolkit that before only operated in the HPC system's domain [17,18].

3 Nomenclature: Performance Profiles, Severity Views

Profiling is a common technique in performance analysis. A profile summarizes performance data over an application's complete run-time. Data is collected according to *performance metrics* $m \in \mathcal{M}$, e.g., execution time, for the *call paths* $c \in \mathcal{C}$ of the application's functions executed on the *system resources* $s \in \mathcal{S}$, i.e., processes or threads. During analysis, by selecting a pair of metric m and call path c, analysts specify a *severity view*

$$v_{m,c} : \mathcal{S} \mapsto \mathbb{R},$$

with $v_{m,c}(s)$ yielding the severity of a user-selected pair (m,c) on a system resource s.

Instead of analysing performance on a thread or process level, this work focuses on the individual MPI ranks $r_i \in \mathcal{S}_{\mathrm{MPI}}$ that each execute a set $\mathcal{S}_{r_i} \subseteq \mathcal{S}$ of processes or threads, so that

$$\mathcal{S} = \bigcup_{r_i \in \mathcal{S}_{\mathrm{MPI}}} \mathcal{S}_{r_i} \quad \text{and} \quad \forall_i \forall_{j \neq i} \mathcal{S}_{r_i} \cap \mathcal{S}_{r_j} = \emptyset.$$

Therefore, the severities measured for the individual processes or threads need to be aggregated in order to compute the severity for the i-th MPI rank r_i:

$$\sum\nolimits_{s \in \mathcal{S}_{r_i}} v_{m,c}(s).$$

Slightly abusing the notation we use the shorthand

$$v_{m,c}(r_i) := \sum\nolimits_{s \in \mathcal{S}_{r_i}} v_{m,c}(s),$$

with $v_{m,c}(r_i)$ denoting the severity of, e.g., execution time, for a user-selected pair (m,c) on the i-th MPI rank r_i. Since we require the performance data to include a mapping from the MPI ranks to the individual parts of the geometry in the simulation domain, $v_{m,c}(r_i)$ also denotes the severity for the part of the geometry that is computed by the i-th MPI rank r_i.

4 Detecting Large-Impact, Large-Variation Views

Visualizing the severity $v_{m,c}(r_i)$ for the individual MPI ranks may provide valuable insight for finding root causes of performance bottlenecks. However, such a detailed visualization is only sensible if there is a certain amount of variation in performance across the MPI ranks. Otherwise, a single number representing the accumulated severity

$$\sum_{r_i \in S_{\text{MPI}}} v_{m,c}(r_i)$$

in the selected performance metric would do.

In order to identify those severity views that have the greatest impact on an application's performance, our system first identifies those $v_{m,c}$ for which the above accumulated severity exceeds a certain threshold $\tau'_{\Sigma v}$. This threshold is set to a fraction $\tau_{\Sigma v}$ of the accumulated severity for the whole application in the currently selected metric, for instance the complete execution time:

$$\tau'_{\Sigma v} = \tau_{\Sigma v} \sum_{r_i \in S_{\text{MPI}}} v_{m,0}(r_i).$$

According to the feedback provided by HPC experts, a fraction of $\tau_{\Sigma v} = 0.01$, i.e., detecting those severity views that represent 1% of the application's performance, turned out to be a sensible default. However, $\tau_{\Sigma v}$ can be interactively adjusted by the analyst.

In order to identify large-variation severity views, our system uses the variation coefficient

$$q_{m,c} = \frac{\sigma_{m,c}}{\mu_{m,c}}$$

as an indicator. Here, $\mu_{m,c}$ denotes the mean severity of the MPI ranks in the selected severity view $v_{m,c}$, and $\sigma_{m,c}$ denotes the standard deviation, with

$$\mu_{m,c} = \frac{\sum_{r_i \in S_{\text{MPI}}} v_{m,c}(r_i)}{|S_{\text{MPI}}|}$$

and

$$\sigma_{m,c} = \frac{\sum_{r_i \in S_{\text{MPI}}} \left(v_{m,c}(r_i) - \mu_{m,c}\right)^2}{|S_{\text{MPI}}|}.$$

According to the feedback provided by HPC experts, a threshold of $\tau_q = 0.01$ turned out to be sensible for detecting severity views of interest with $q_{m,c} \geq \tau_q$. However, τ_q can be adjusted by the analyst.

Our tool automatically identifies those severity views that exceed both thresholds. They are indicated to the performance analyst for further inspection in the application domain.

The performance data may contain a certain amount of variation that is caused by specific, intentional execution patterns. These are due to performance trade-offs like using only every second hardware thread in order to efficiently utilize the available CPU caches. Since these are intentional, such variations are considered to be already known at the time of analysis. In order to exclude them from the automatic variation-detection mechanism and thus in order to detect new variation, we included filtering capabilities [18].

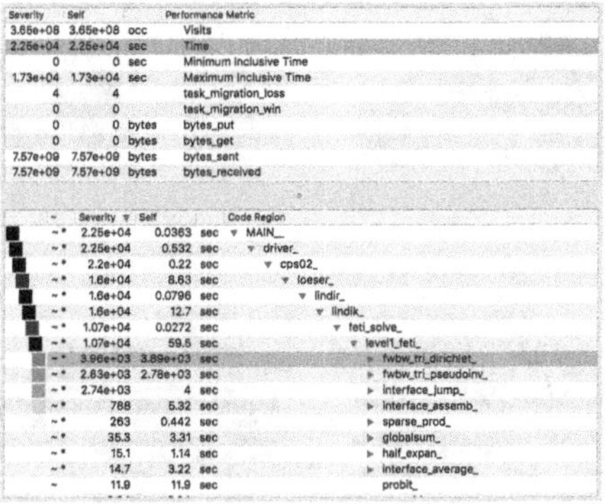

Fig. 4. Proposed user interface: the performance metrics (top) and the call-paths (bottom) are arranged in tree-view widgets.

5   Interactive Visualizations

The proposed system provides several visualizations that have been developed according to requirements posed by HPC experts. These facilitate interactive analysis of profile-based performance data in a top-down fashion in order to find and analyse severity views of interest that reveal performance phenomena.

5.1   Performance Metrics and Call-Path Tree Widgets

The hierarchies of the metrics and call paths are visualized in tree widgets on the left of the user interface (Fig. 4). For each entry the total severity including the descendants (column "Severity") and the net severity of only the entry itself (column "Self") are printed. Both widgets can be sorted by total or net severity.

When the analyst selects a metric, the severities in the call-path tree widget are updated accordingly. When they select a pair of metric and call path, that severity view gets visualized in the remaining parts of the user interface. The columns "Severity" and "Self" can be swapped in any of the two tree widgets. The leftmost determines whether total or net severity is being visualized.

A glyph in the leftmost column of the call-path tree widget guides the analyst to the call paths with the largest severity by colour-encoding the severity relative to the respective parent's severity. The colour map can be user-defined. A linear black (100% relative severity) to transparent (0%) map is used by default. A tilde printed in the second column of the call-path tree widget indicates a large-variation severity view for detailed evaluation. If a severity view in the descendants of a call path exposes large variation, an asterisk is printed in order to speed up finding that severity view. Note that the presented data set contains much variation in every visible view (cf. Sect. 6).

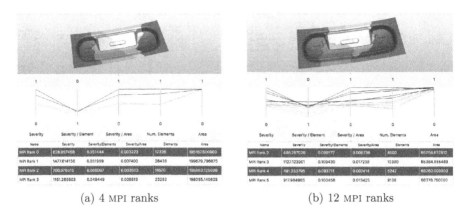

(a) 4 MPI ranks   (b) 12 MPI ranks

Fig. 5. Proposed user interface: the severity of "Time/Execution" in "fwbw_tri_dirichlet_" (Fig. 4) is visualized on the geometry (top). The data from the table (bottom) is visualized by parallel coordinates (middle). The geometry for different MPI ranks is selected.

5.2 Visualizing Performance Data in Its Spatial Context

The 3D viewport in the upper right part of the user interface (Fig. 5) renders the geometry in the application domain. The severity for each MPI rank is visualized colour-coded on the respective part of the geometry. The colour map can be user-defined. A linear black (0% severity) to light grey (100%) map is used by default. The simulation domain can be explored by moving a virtual camera with five degrees of freedom using keyboard and mouse. Elevation is limited to ±90°, and rotation around the viewing direction is locked in order to keep orientation intuitive and to prevent the analyst from losing track of the perspective.

The table in the lower part of the user interface (Fig. 5) lists the severities for each MPI rank alongside the properties of the associated part of the geometry, i.e., the number of finite elements and their surface area. In addition, the severity is related to these properties by, for instance, presenting the severity per surface area. A parallel coordinates plot in the middle of the user interface (Fig. 5) presents the same data as the table for a better, concise overview. This is particularly helpful for simulations using many MPI ranks Fig. 5(b). Each axis is normalized from zero to the respective maximum, and it can be flipped. That way the performance data can be inspected for meaningful structures when related to the geometry.

The views are linked: a geometry part or the associated MPI rank can be selected in the 3D view or the table. Selected geometry and the related information are then highlighted in all three views.

Table 1. Data sets, system topology sizes, and search-space reduction by limiting minimum severity ($\geq$1%) and by suggesting large-variation severity views.

| Code | System topology | | | # Views | | # Suggested, τ_q = | | | | |
	# Dims.	# Thr.	Excl.	$\neq$0	$\geq$1%	0.01	0.02	0.03	0.04	0.05
Sheet-metal f. (4 R.)	3	64	None	29,482	7,360	7,354	7,349	7,344	7,336	7,318
			Thread			5,888	5,538	5,229	4,886	4,530
Sheet-metal f. (12 R.)	3	240	None	46,909	7,652	7,651	7,649	7,645	7,643	7,627
			Thread			7,522	7,476	7,431	7,371	7,218
Sweep3D	3	65,536	None	842	393	252	245	232	168	166

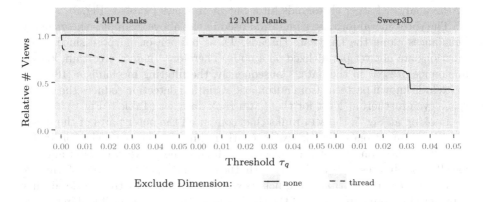

Fig. 6. Search space reduction without (solid) and with dimension exclusion (dashed): relative number of views being suggested for detailed evaluation, normalized to the number of views that exceed 1% of total performance measured in the respective metric. Results for the sheet-metal forming simulation using 4 (left) and 12 MPI ranks (middle), and for Sweep3D as a reference (right).

6   Results

We have evaluated our system with two performance data sets. They have been created by Score-P [9], instrumenting a sheet-metal forming simulation. The simulation was executed

– on 4 thin nodes of SuperMuc (Phase 1) [1], executing 1 MPI rank each, and
– on 6 fat nodes of SuperMuc (Phase 1), executing 2 MPI ranks each.

The simulated geometry has been stored to disk by each MPI rank at the end of the simulation. The mapping from the MPI ranks to the geometry is implicitly provided by the file naming convention in use. For reference, we include a measurement of the benchmark code Sweep3D executed on an IBM(R) System Blue Gene(R)/P [21].

The automatic suggestion mechanism effectively sieves out those views that have a low impact on the overall performance and that expose only low variation in performance across the individual MPI ranks. Filtering out low-impact views reduces the overall search space by between 53% and 84% for the used datasets (Table 1). The reduction rates for additionally filtering out low-variation views, however, are highly application-dependent: they depend on the amount of variation present in the performance data, i.e., on the performance behaviour of the application's code, and to a great deal on the distribution of the simulated data and thus on the domain decomposition. The results for the sheet-metal forming datasets serve as an example where the proposed large-variation detection system can hardly filter out any severity views since variation is large in most of them. However, the results for Sweep3D serve as a proof of concept (Table 1). In general, $\tau_q = 0.01$ serves as a sensible default that can be interactively adjusted by the analyst. Larger thresholds filter out more views (Table 1, Fig. 6).

The sheet metal forming simulation used in the above examples shows many imbalances along the hardware threads. These happen on purpose since many functions are not yet parallelized on a node. Therefore, there is a certain, known imbalance present in the data. Consequently, the filtering mechanism [18] used to exclude known patterns from automatic variation detection reduces the search space even further, at least for the 4 MPI rank data set (Table 1, Fig. 6).

Looking at Fig. 5, the MPI ranks that computed the outer parts of the mesh, i.e., the selected ones, had lowest execution time. In the parallel coordinates view these form an almost separate class. Having the 3D visualization and the parallel coordinates plots available, both, the domain expert and the performance analyst can clearly see that this quicker execution is caused by the less detail that is present in these outer parts of the simulated mesh – no matter if looking at the 4 MPI rank data set or the 12 MPI rank one. In fact, in most of the simulation's functions MPI ranks simulating the inner blocks of the mesh required most CPU-time. The 3D visualization clearly points out that these MPI ranks are computing high-detail parts of the geometry. With our tool, simulation experts were able to relate the observed performance phenomenon to a disadvantageous domain decomposition that did not consider the forming tool's shape.

7   Conclusion and Future Work

We have presented a system that maps performance data to the simulated geometry in the application domain. Our system helps analysts evaluate an HPC application's performance behaviour based on profiles by greatly reducing the search space: low-impact severity views and ones that do not expose variation in performance are sieved out. Glyphs representing the severity of and labels indicating large-variation severity views quickly guide analysts down the application's call hierarchy towards *important* severity views. Relating the performance data to the simulation domain provides valuable insight. This is accessible even to pure domain experts. Our tool directed them to the domain decomposition as the cause for a performance phenomenon in the presented example. However, tests with improved decompositions and significantly more compute nodes are left for future work.

Currently, the provided system maps data to triangle meshes in the application domain. Applying the presented technique to other, arbitrary geometries remains for future work. Then, additional tools for examining the application domain, like brushing and filtering, need to be integrated.

We have made the current implementation of our system publicly available [19] to get broader feedback and to facilitate integration into established performance analysis tools.

Acknowledgements. This work has been partially funded by the German Federal Ministry of Research and Education (BMBF) under grant number 01IH13001D (Score-E), and by the Excellence Initiative of the German federal and state governments.

References

1. SuperMUC petascale system. https://www.lrz.de/services/compute/supermuc/systemdescription/
2. Böhme, D., Geimer, M., Wolf, F., Arnold, L.: Identifying the root causes of wait states in large-scale parallel applications. In: Proceedings of the 39th International Conference on Parallel Processing, pp. 90–100. IEEE Computer Society, September 2010
3. Childs, H., Brugger, E., Whitlock, B., Meredith, J., Ahern, S., Pugmire, D., Biagas, K., Miller, M., Weber, G.H., Krishnan, H., Fogal, T., Sanderson, A., Garth, C., Bethel, E.W., Camp, D., Rübel, O., Durant, M., Favre, J., Navratil, P.: VisIt: an end-user tool for visualizing and analyzing very large data. In: High Performance Visualization—Enabling Extreme-Scale Scientific Insight, pp. 357–372, November 2012
4. Geimer, M., Saviankou, P., Strube, A., Szebenyi, Z., Wolf, F., Wylie, B.J.N.: Further improving the scalability of the Scalasca toolset. In: Jónasson, K. (ed.) PARA 2010. LNCS, vol. 7134, pp. 463–473. Springer, Heidelberg (2012). doi:10.1007/978-3-642-28145-7_45
5. Huck, K.A., Potter, K., Jacobsen, D.W., Childs, H., Malony, A.D.: Linking performance data into scientific visualization tools. In: Proceedings of the 1st Workshop on Visual Performance Analysis, pp. 50–57 (2014)
6. Isaacs, K.E., Giménez, A., Jusufi, I., Gamblin, T., Bhatele, A., Schulz, M., Hamann, B., Bremer, P.T.: State of the art of performance visualization. In: EuroVis - STARs (2014)
7. Landge, A.G., Levine, J.A., Bhatele, A., Isaacs, K.E., Gamblin, T., Schulz, M., Langer, S.H., Bremer, P.T., Pascucci, V.: Visualizing network traffic to understand the performance of massively parallel simulations. IEEE Trans. Vis. Comput. Graph. 18(12), 2467–2476 (2012)
8. McCarthy, C.M., Isaacs, K.E., Bhatele, A., Bremer, P.T., Hamann, B.: Visualizing the five-dimensional torus network of the IBM Blue Gene/Q. In: Proceedings of the 1st Workshop on Visual Performance Analysis, pp. 24–27 (2014)
9. an Mey, D., Biersdorff, S., Bischof, C., Diethelm, K., Eschweiler, D., Gerndt, M., Knüpfer, A., Lorenz, D., Malony, A.D., Nagel, W.E., Oleynik, Y., Rössel, C., Saviankou, P., Schmidl, D., Shende, S.S., Wagner, M., Wesarg, B., Wolf, F.: Score-P: a unified performance measurement system for petascale applications. In: Bischof, C., Hegering, H.G., Nagel, W., Wittum, G. (eds.) Competence in High Performance Computing 2010, pp. 85–97. Springer, Heidelberg (2012)

10. von Rüden, L., Hermanns, M.A., Behrisch, M., Keim, D., Mohr, B., Wolf, F.: Separating the wheat from the chaff: identifying relevant and similar performance data with visual analytics. In: Proceedings of the 2nd Workshop on Visual Performance Analysis, pp. 4:1–4:8 (2015)
11. Schulz, M., Levine, J.A., Bremer, P.T., Gamblin, T., Pascucci, V.: Interpreting performance data across intuitive domains. In: Proceedings of the 40th International Conference on Parallel Processing (2011)
12. Shende, S.S., Malony, A.D.: The TAU parallel performance system. Int. J. High Perform. Comput. Appl. **20**(2), 287–311 (2006)
13. Spear, W., Malony, A.D., Lee, C.W., Biersdorff, S., Shende, S.: An approach to creating performance visualizations in a parallel profile analysis tool. In: Alexander, M., et al. (eds.) Euro-Par 2011. LNCS, vol. 7156, pp. 156–165. Springer, Heidelberg (2012). doi:10.1007/978-3-642-29740-3_19
14. Theisen, L., Shah, A., Wolf, F.: Down to earth: how to visualize traffic on high-dimensional torus networks. In: Proceedings of the 1st Workshop on Visual Performance Analysis, pp. 17–23 (2014)
15. Vernaleo, J.C., Reynolds, C.S.: Agn feedback and cooling flows: problems with simple hydrodynamic models. Astrophys. J. **645**, 83–94 (2006)
16. Vierjahn, T., Hentschel, B., Kuhlen, T.W.: Geometry-aware visualization of performance data. In: Isenberg, T., Sadlo, F. (eds.) EuroVis 2016 - Posters, pp. 37–39 (2016)
17. Vierjahn, T., Hermanns, M.A., Mohr, B., Müller, M.S., Kuhlen, T.W., Hentschel, B.: Correlating sub-phenomena in performance data in the frequency domain. In: LDAV 2016 - Posters (2016)
18. Vierjahn, T., Hermanns, M.A., Mohr, B., Müller, M.S., Kuhlen, T.W., Hentschel, B.: Using directed variance to identify meaningful views in call-path performance profiles. In: Proceedings of the 3rd Workshop Visual Performance Analysis, pp. 9–16 (2016)
19. Virtual Reality and Immersive Visualization, RWTH Aachen University: pvt performance visualization toolkit. https://devhub.vr.rwth-aachen.de/VR-Group/pvt. Accessed 28 Oct 2016
20. Wylie, B.J.N., Geimer, M.: Large-scale performance analysis of PFLOTRAN with Scalasca. In: Proceedings of the 53rd Cray User Group meeting. Cray User Group Inc. (2011)
21. Wylie, B.J.N., Geimer, M., Mohr, B., Böhme, D., Szebenyi, Z., Wolf, F.: Large-scale performance analysis of Sweep3D with the Scalasca toolset. Parallel Process. Lett. **20**(4), 397–414 (2010)

Provenance Tracking

Traditionally, method and data tracking in science was accomplished using the venerable lab notebook where every step of an experiment was noted, result tables were added, and finally every page was numbered and dated. This approach has been extended for computational simulations and analyses with careful usage of revision control systems for code, unique scripts for every production run, and annotated file names, often cross-referenced to spreadsheet tables. However, as the size of simulations and analyses in HPC centers continue to grow, these manual systems are no longer scalable. The provenance of results – linking final output files with the original input files and the pipelines used to construct them – requires the same level of HPC engineering as the underlying codes, if we hope to ensure reproducibility.

In domains like neuroscience and earth sciences, data sets have grown to the order of tens of terabytes, while pipelines can span multiple HPC centers to take advantage of advanced computing architectures. Data sharing has become a requirement for many funding agencies, creating a need to be able to identify raw original files and the processes needed to reproduce end files for HPC projects that otherwise would drown in data intermediates. Developers of visualization and data search front-ends need data provenance to allow the hierarchical investigation of data from end product back to source, as well as enabling data mining operations by linking analyses, raw data, experimental conditions and analytical methods.

As "Big Data" and "Big Simulation" become everyday tools in the scientific community, the same standards of care for data used in the experimental lab is coming to bear to the curation of data produced through supercomputing. The papers in this section tackle these scaling issues which don't involve more traditional HPC concerns of new hardware and computer science algorithms – but which are crucial for the application of HPC in science. They cover data sharing in the geosciences, automatic tracking of data flows and operations within and across HPC centers, and the construction of large scale frameworks for collaboration in neuroscience.

Framework for Sharing of Highly Resolved Turbulence Simulation Data

Bastian Tweddell[1], Jens Henrik Göbbert[1(✉)], Michael Gauding[2], Benjamin Weyers[3], and Björn Hagemeier[1]

[1] Jülich Supercomputing Centre, Forschungszentrum Jülich GmbH, Jülich, Germany
j.goebbert@fz-juelich.de
[2] CORIA - CNRS UMR 6614, Saint-Étienne-du-Rouvray, France
[3] Visual Computing Institute, Virtual Reality and Immersive Visualization Group,
RWTH Aachen University, Aachen, Germany

Abstract. The growing computational capabilities of nowadays super-computers have made highly resolved turbulence simulations possible. The large data-sets and tremendous amount of required compute resources create serious new challenges when attempting to share the data between different research groups. But even more difficult to solve is the incompatibility of the data formats and numerical approaches used for turbulence simulations, which in detail are often only known to the simulation code developer. In this paper a framework for sharing data of large scale simulations is presented, which simplifies the access and further post-processing even beyond a single supercomputing center. It combines established services to provide an easy to manage-and-extend software setup without the need to standardize a database or -format. Beside other advantages, it enables the use of direct file outputs from simulation runs which are often archived anyway.

Keywords: Data sharing · Framework · Turbulence

1 Introduction

Small scale turbulence continues to be one of the unsolved problems of classical physics [13]. The turbulent motion of fluids is a highly complex phenomenon and the statistical description and modeling is challenging. Turbulence is involved in many natural and engineering processes like turbulent mixing, multi-phase flow, turbulent combustion, plasma physics or astrophysics and also in environmental processes like cloud formation and precipitation, or sea-ice melting. Therefore, the understanding of the physics behind turbulence is of both fundamental and practical importance.

Turbulence is a continuum field phenomenon with in principle infinite dimensions. The main difficulties regarding the understanding of turbulent flows originates from its strong non-locality and non-linearity of the governing equations,

© Springer International Publishing AG 2017
E. Di Napoli et al. (Eds.): JHPCS 2016, LNCS 10164, pp. 225–232, 2017.
DOI: 10.1007/978-3-319-53862-4_19

namely the Navier-Stokes equations (or similar the equations for magnetohydro-dynamics (MHD)). Although the Navier-Stokes equations are formally deter-ministic, turbulence dynamics are by no means the same.

A solution of turbulent flows can be obtained by numerical methods. The growing computational capabilities of nowadays supercomputers have made sim-ulations of highly resolved turbulent flows an indispensable tool in computa-tional fluid dynamics (CFD). But the memory and computational requirements of direct numerical simulations (DNS) dramatically increase with the Reynolds number, which is the most important non-dimensional number to characterize turbulent flows. Turbulent flows usually have high Reynolds numbers and there-fore a numerical solution must be carried out by fast supercomputers and result in large data-sets.

Preparing and running such a simulation requires substantial expertise in parallel computing and turbulence research and, even more important, access to a supercomputing facility. The large data-sets and tremendous amount of required compute resources create serious new challenges when attempting to translate the simulation results into meaningful knowledge.

To gain deeper insight it is required to share and discuss simulation results with domain experts from other research groups world-wide. How can we improve this process and simplify the steps needed to share large-scale simulation data?

As an answer to this challenge we developed a software for easy and flexible setup of a data sharing framework for canonical cases of highly resolved turbu-lence simulations. It is our intention to simplify the access to high-quality, world-class turbulence DNS data computed at supercomputing centres to researches in physics, engineering and environmental sciences who might not have access to supercomputing facilities.

2 State-of-the-Art and Motivation

With a similar intention in mind the 'Johns Hopkins Turbulence Databases' (JHTDB) [12] has been started in 2008. It currently provides access to over 20 TiB for isotropic turbulence data, 56 TiB for MHD data, 130 TiB for channel flow data and 27 TiB for homogeneous buoyancy driven turbulence data (in 10/2016). These data can be accessed [8] via a web service and C, Fortran and Matlab interfaces. Subsets of the data can be downloaded in hdf5 file format. Beyond the raw data itself it allows to calculate spatial differentiation using various order approximations (up to 8th order) and filtering. A focus of the database is on particle tracking, which can be performed both forward and backward in time using a second order accurate Runge-Kutta integration scheme. The JHTDB project is funded by the US National Science Foundation.

As a Data Pilot Community of EUDAT [11] the 'Direct simulation data of turbulent flows' (DATATURB) [2] started to archives raw data and share it in a more standardised and stable way for public access using the tools and services EUDAT provides. It is based on the idea of a meta-data for the community to reach a standard that allows easy and fluent data exchange between different

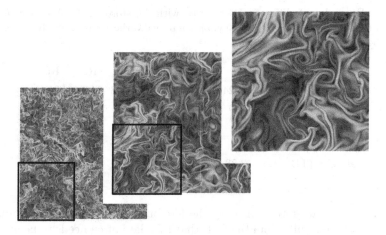

Fig. 1. Slice of instantaneous scalar dissipation of a DNS of homogeneous isotropic turbulence on a 2048^3 grid. It shows the fine filamented structures of the turbulent flow field. The scalar dissipation is a highly intermittent quantity.

research groups. EUDAT receives funding from the European Union's Horizon 2020 research and innovation programme (Fig. 1).

JHTDB is already used since years by a wide range of turbulence researchers and is successful with its centralized infrastructure. After registration any researcher can have access to its large and well-documented database. The infrastructure of JHTDB is not intended to allow other researchers to add easily their own data-sets to the database. In contrast to this DATATURB is open in both directions: researchers can access the provided data, but can also add new data to the database. This is possible, because DATATURB is based on common meta-data for the community and standardize the data format.

In this paper we describe a framework developed to avoid the need for standardization of data formats and centralization of services as much as possible. This main motivations are driven by the the following practical experiences.

For high performance simulation codes developed for DNS of turbulent flows a common file format did not come accepted until now by the community even though attempts have been made (e.g. the CFD General Notation System). This partly originates from the need for best I/O performance on different supercomputers and the special advantages of each I/O strategy in combination with the simulation code and -algorithm. Therefore, output files are written today using I/O libraries like HDF5 [14], NetCDF [15], SIONlib [3] or with MPI-I/O or POSIX. But using the same file format does not specify any semantic meaning to the stored data. In addition to a common file format a general notation would be required, too. Nowadays, the turbulence community faces a multitude of file formats and notations, which do not even need to be convertable into each other. The details of these file formats are often only known by the simulation code developers. Hence, the development to extract data from these different file formats must be left to the simulation code developers.

Table 1. Examples of different DNS cases with M stored data files, which have been conducted on JUQUEEN [9]. Reynolds number variation between $Re_\lambda = 88$ and $Re_\lambda = 754$.

	R0	R1	R2	R3	R4	R5	R6
N^3	512^3	1024^3	1024^3	2048^3	2048^3	4096^3	4096^3
Re_λ	88	119	184	215	331	529	754
File size (GB)	8	64	64	512	512	4096	4096
M	189	62	61	10	10	6	11
Data size (TB)	1.5	3.88	3.81	5	5	24	44

An additional advantage of using the file format of each specific simulation code as data base results from the fact, that this data often needs to be archived for future restart of the simulation and post-processing anyway. Even if possible to convert the data to a common file format, this would mean to store the same data a second time on the storage system. Especially for the large amount of data generated by turbulence simulations this would be not desirable.

Avoiding centralization of services is the second main motivation for this framework. A framework for sharing highly resolved data must allow communities or small groups and institutes to build-up and manage online share points in short time for their simulation data world-wide. Each research domain needs to collect special information to understand the request of a user asking for data. Therefore these forms can only be defined by the domain experts themselfs. If the framework integrates nicely into a large number internet sites without requiring deep knowledge of specific web technology, the domain experts can setup their web pages for sharing data on their own. This is faster to setup, more flexible and less error-prone than leaving it to someone else.

3   Highly Resolved Turbulence Simulation

The temporal and spatial evolution of turbulent flows is governed by the Navier-Stokes equations. Direct Numerical Simulation (DNS) solves these governing equations for all scales down to the viscous cut-off length and provides a complete description of the flow, where the three-dimensional flow fields are known as function of space and time.

The simulation data is of general interest since the fine-scales of high Reynolds number turbulence become universal. But DNS of high Reynolds number turbulence is computationally very expensive. The number of required grid points N^3 to resolve the finest scales increases rapidly with Reynolds number, i.e.

$$N^3 \propto Re_\lambda^{9/2}, \qquad (1)$$

where Re_λ denotes the Taylor based Reynolds number. Due to Eq.(1) DNS of fine-scale turbulence results in huge data files. The handling and storage of the DNS data is very demanding and requires reliable supercomputers.

First data sets of the data sharing framework are results of simulations listed in Table 1. Several publications are based on these simulations, cf. [1,4,6,7] and [5].

DNS can be understood as a numerical experiment yielding an exact flow representation. The DNS can be used as reference for further studies and to validate fundamental results from turbulence theory. Hence, novel questions and methods arising in turbulence theory can be addressed by the reuse of the same DNS data already available.

4   Data Sharing Framework

To simplify this reuse of available DNS data we developed a data handling and sharing concept written in Python 3, which is described in the following.

The framework is sketched in Fig. 2. It is subdivided into three layers of services. The top layer includes the web services (WS), the middle layer the data exchange services (DES) and the bottom layer the data process services (DPS).

To receive data from the turbulence database the user first (Fig. 2-(1)) fills a web form provided on a web page. This form is defined by the turbulence domain experts and can be hosted on any web server independent of the location of the other services or the data. A suitable place could be the web site of the research group or institute the domain expert belongs to. It queries all information in a key-value style required to clearly define the requested data set. As most web sites are build on top of a content management system, which provide extensions

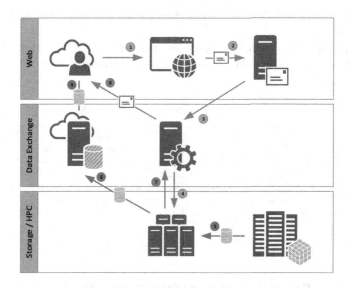

Fig. 2. Sketch of the Data Sharing Framework: User → Website → Mail-Server → Management Server → Data Access Server → Storage → Data Server

to generate mail forms (like Typo3/PowerMail [10]) it is easy to implement. The request and the required information about the user (e.g. name, affiliation, email) are send via email (Fig. 2-(2)) from the web server to a mail server for temporary storage.

The middle layer provides the Management Server, which runs the Python script for requests management (Fig. 3). It provides a queuing system with processing slots which can handle requests in parallel. Each time an empty processing slot becomes available after a request has been fully processed it checks for a new request (Fig. 2-(3)) from the mail server. Then, at first the mail is translated back to a key-value representation and then checked for plausibility. If it passes this test a response mail is send to the user to inform that the request is processed. The key-value pairs are used to generate command line arguments for a specialized data processing script (Fig. 3) - in this case called h5hypers - provided by the domain experts.

The data processing can have certain hardware requirements depending on data size, locality and compute requirements and is not executed on the Management Server but as close to the data as possible. The data processing command enters the bottom layer when it is scheduled (Fig. 2-(4)) to be executed on one of the Data Access Servers. These servers have fast access to the main storage servers (Fig. 2-(5)) and are set up to process large data files. The requested data is processed and stored on the Data Server (Fig. 2-(6)) as a single file.

The Management Server is informed about the successful copying of the requested data (Fig. 2-(7)) and sends the user an email with all required information including a download link (Fig. 2-(8)) if the data processing has be successfully finished. In any other case the user gets informed about the failure and its reason.

The user can now follow the link and download the data (Fig. 2-(9)) until a certain date.

Different advantage can be named for this approach. The three layers of services allow to distribute the responsibilities to experts of each field.

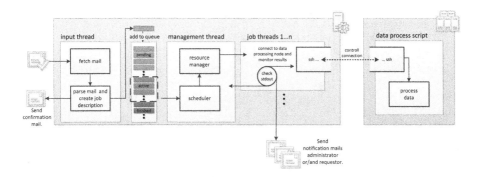

Fig. 3. Structure of the requests management script written in Python 3.

The web services (WS) in the top layer can be located on any web server and integrated into any web page independent of the data exchange services (DES) or the data process services (DPS). A web form can nowadays easily be set up on static or dynamic web pages or any popular content management systems. Storing the submitted requests on a mail server decouples the top layer from the middle layer. The reliability of the top layer is designed to be high as it is based on the individual web and mail services, which are in general of high reliability each.

The management services in the middle layer is under control of the supercomputing center. It bear the responsibility of scheduling the requests depending on the available resources.

The data processing in the bottom layer uses available resources of the supercomputing center and do not require additional services installed. The developer to the simulation code can be responsible to interpret the incoming commands as key-value-pairs and to read/write the requested data packages. This is possible because the data sharing framework consequent decouples the web interface and data processing from the request management.

5   Conclusion

In this paper, a modular framework for sharing data of large scale simulations is presented, which is based on established protocols/services (Email, HTTP, SSH) and simplifies the access to HPC simulation results, especially for turbulence.

At the Jülich Supercomputing Centre each research groups has their established workflows, which are based on the data-/file format of their simulation code they use. The input/output routines of a simulation code are based on different IO libraries like HDF5 [14], NetCDF [15], SionLib [3] or even use pure MPI-IO for reading and writing data to/from disk and are tuned for an HPC system. Even if every group has the time and the intention to change their simulation codes and workflows, it would take a large effort to find a data format which suites all research groups. Special numerical methods and their computational grids can often not be represented by just one data format and any definition of a standard data format limits the developers of HPC simulation codes.

Beside this, each research domain has their own requests they ask on the data. It is important, that the web interface (and therefore the possible requests/key-value pairs) are defined by the domain experts and the data processing script is written by the domain experts.

The data sharing framework decouples the web interface and data processing from the request management and allows domain experts to manage their web interface and data processing script on their own. It is easy to integrate in existing infrastructure and is independent of a special research domain. The framework scales to high loads if needed with its support for multiple web interfaces and data access servers and allows collaboration of multiple supercomputing centers.

Our intention is to enhance the data handling and sharing between research groups world-wide. In future this shall not only include sharing of the DNS data files, but also sharing of post-processing results, and the codes. This might be achieved by a central revision system or by establishing web-based collaborative tools.

Acknowledgements. The authors gratefully acknowledge the computing time granted by the John von Neumann Institute for Computing (NIC) and provided on the supercomputer JURECA at Jülich Supercomputing Centre (JSC) in the context of the Scientific Big Data Analytics (SBDA) project No. 006.

References

1. Boschung, J., Schaefer, P., Peters, N., Meneveau, C.: The local topology of stream- and vortex lines in turbulent flows. Phys. Fluids (1994-present) **26**(4), 045107 (2014)
2. DataTurb: Direct simulation data of turbulent flows. https://eudat.eu/communities/dataturb-direct-simulation-data-of-turbulent-flows.   [Accessed 30 Nov 2016]
3. Frings, W., Wolf, F., Petkov, V.: Scalable massively parallel i/o to task-local files. In: Proceedings of the Conference on High Performance Computing Networking, Storage and Analysis, pp. 1–11. IEEE (2009)
4. Gampert, M., Goebbert, J.H., Schaefer, P., Gauding, M., Peters, N., Aldudak, F., Oberlack, M.: Extensive strain along gradient trajectories in the turbulent kinetic energy field. New J. Phys. **13**(4), 043012 (2011)
5. Gauding, M., Goebbert, J.H., Hasse, C., Peters, N.: Line segments in homogeneous scalar turbulence. Physics of Fluids (1994-present) **27**(9), 095102 (2015)
6. Gauding, M., Wick, A., Peters, N., Pitsch, H.: Generalized scale-by-scale energy budget equations for large-eddy simulations of scalar turbulence at various schmidt numbers. J. Turbul. (2014)
7. Goebbert, J.H., Gauding, M., Gampert, M., Schaefer, P., Peters, N.: A new view on geometry and conditional statistics in turbulence. Inside: Innovatives Super- computing in Deutschland (2011)
8. JHTDB: Johns hopkins turbulence database. http://turbulence.pha.jhu.edu (2008–2016). [Accessed 30 Nov 2016]
9. JUQUEEN: Jülich blue gene/q. http://www.fz-juelich.de/ias/juqueen (2012– 2015). [Accessed 01 Aug 2015]
10. Kellner, A.: Typo3/powermail. https://docs.typo3.org/typo3cms/extensions/ powermail (2005–2016). [Accessed 30 Nov 2016]
11. Lecarpentier, D., Wittenburg, P., Elbers, W., Michelini, A., Kanso, R., Coveney, P., Baxter, R.: Eudat: a new cross-disciplinary data infrastructure for science. Int. J. Digit. Curation **8**(1), 279–287 (2013)
12. Li, Y., Perlman, E., Wan, M., Yang, Y., Meneveau, C., Burns, R., Chen, S., Szalay, A., Eyink, G.: A public turbulence database cluster and applications to study lagrangian evolution of velocity increments in turbulence. J. Turbul. (9), N31 (2008)
13. Shraiman, B.I., Siggia, E.D.: Scalar turbulence. Nature **405**(6787), 639–646 (2000)
14. The HDF Group: Hierarchical data format version 5. http://www.hdfgroup.org/ HDF5 (2000–2016). [Accessed 30 Nov 2016]
15. UCAR/Unidata: Network common data format. http://www.unidata.ucar.edu/ software/netcdf (1989–2016). [Accessed 30 Nov 2016]

UniProv: A Flexible Provenance Tracking System for UNICORE

André Giesler[1(✉)], Myriam Czekala[1], Björn Hagemeier[1], and Richard Grunzke[2]

[1] Forschungszentrum Jülich GmbH, 52425 Jülich, Germany
a.giesler@fz-juelich.de
[2] Technische Universität Dresden, Dresden, Germany
http://www.fz-juelich.de/ias/jsc

Abstract. In this paper we present a flexible provenance management system called UniProv. UniProv is an ongoing development project providing provenance tracking in scientific workflows and data management particularly in the field of neuroscience, thus allowing users to validate and reproduce tasks and results of their experiments.

The primary goal is to equip the commonly used Grid middleware UNICORE [1] and its incorporated workflow engine with the provenance capturing mechanism of UniProv. We also explain an approach for using predefined patterns to ensure compatibility with the W3C PROV [2] Data Model and to map the provenance information properly to a neo4j graph database.

Keywords: Scientific workflows · Reproducibility · Interoperability · Provenance

1 Introduction

In the past few years, scientific workflows have been often used to automatize and execute a range of experiments in many domains. However, reproducibility and validation of workflows did not get the same attention in that context. As scientific workflows often comprises joint effort, there is a growing demand for a repository that allows everyone involved to store and query provenance information of executed workflows having produced relevant data results. Here, it is particularly important that such a repository must support an interoperable data model, since provenance may be collected from various systems. Moreover, the storage of provenance must also be considered in terms of maintenance and an efficient query processing.

This paper presents UniProv which addresses three main requirements: (i) enabling the traceability of scientific workflows exemplarily in the domain of neuroimaging by designing a flexible provenance management system that can be conveniently integrated in the existing UNICORE workflow system; (ii) building an interoperable framework so that further potential provenance information providers can make use of the system; (iii) and designing a suitable storage management system, so that the provenance graph can be mapped efficiently and

© Springer International Publishing AG 2017
E. Di Napoli et al. (Eds.): JHPCS 2016, LNCS 10164, pp. 233–242, 2017.
DOI: 10.1007/978-3-319-53862-4_20

arbitrary analytics on its data can be performed. We met the first requirements by implementing a modular architecture of UniProv that allows to connect different provenance providers mapping proprietary source information to the framework by making use of a predefined set of provenance patterns applying the emerging W3C PROV standard and addresses the interoperability requirement. Finally, we chose the scalable neo4j graph database [3] that supports Cypher, an expressive query language. Furthermore, neo4j provides a convenient web interface to query and visualize the tracked provenance data.

This paper starts with a description of provenance in scientific workflows in general and related work in that area. Additionally, the UNICORE software suite and its integrated workflow management system which is particularly used in neuroimaging studies is briefly examined. It then explains the concept and implementation of the UniProv provenance management system which we are currently working on, and concludes with an evaluation of UniProv's ability to enhance reproducibility of scientific workflows and its extension capabilities regarding further potential areas of provenance capturing.

2   Workflows and Provenance

In this section we describe the relation of provenance and scientific workflow systems, show the existing shortcomings, and provide an overview of related work to solve them. At the end of the section we present a particular example which is using UNICORE and requires a flexible provenance management.

2.1   Scientific Workflow Systems

State of the art scientific workflow management systems provide programming environments for composing and executing complex computational processes commonly referred to as scientific workflows. Main objectives include providing an easy-to-use environment for scientists, providing interactive tools to view results in real-time, and simplifying the process of sharing and reusing workflows between scientists.

Another motive for abstracting several computations in one workflow is to enable an integrated and seamless provenance tracking of the derived data products [4]. Without the possibility to check lineage information, a resulting data set could be regarded useless from the scientific point of view. This implies to capture the processing information, to store it efficiently, and to allow queries over it. The first part of the problem, capturing provenance information, has been made considerably easier by using scientific workflow management systems. In such environments, provenance data is often automatically captured in the form of execution traces. However, these systems often rely on proprietary formats hampering the interchange of provenance information.

2.2   Related Work

The need for provenance management in scientific workflows has been widely acknowledged and has been investigated in many systems and studies. However, most of these implementations are in a manner specific to their application domain or using specific concepts and technologies. Only a few research projects exist addressing generic provenance management systems. Here, we concentrate on those supporting especially the handling of scientific workflows. Apache Taverna [5] is a scientific workflow system for combining web services and local tools. Taverna records provenance of workflow runs, intermediate values and even user interactions, and exports that pieces in a workflow data bundle which is a ZIP archive that relies on the concept of Research Object bundles [6]. The archive contains additionally a PROV formatted trace of the workflow execution. For later debugging or reproducibility issues that bundle can be downloaded from an appropriate server and reused in the Taverna system.

Other workflow systems extended to capture provenance information are Kepler [7] and VisTrails [8]. Kepler provides an interactive provenance browser for viewing and navigating workflow data and computations. The PROV-man toolkit [9] is a more general approach to capture, manage, and store provenance data permanently. PROV-man is compliant to standard PROV and consists of a programming interface (API) and a configurable database that can be used to create and store provenance information. It is however limited to the integration in Java programming environments and relational database systems.

2.3   Neuroimaging Workflows with UNICORE

UNICORE is an open source middleware that facilitates access to supercomputing resources and allows to perform scientific workflows on them. It offers integrated workflow support that is used to control the execution of multiple compute jobs at one or multiple sites, dealing with dependencies between jobs and handling any required data movement. The workflow engine offers a wide range of control constructs which can be nested to any depth. Workflow variables can be defined, modified, and used in scripts. A full-featured graphical workflow editing and monitoring is part of the UNICORE Rich Client (URC) [10].

A significant demand for provenance-enabled scientific workflows exists in neuroimaging communities. Thus, scientists at the Institute for Neuromedicine (INM-1) at Forschungszentrum Jülich investigate the connectivity of brain regions by using techniques such as Three-dimensional Polarized Light Imaging (3D-PLI) which make it possible to study the complex nerve fiber architectures across human brains at the micrometer level [11]. Images of brain slices are processed with a chain of tools for calibration, independent component analysis, stitching and segmentation. These tools have been integrated in a UNICORE workflow to achieve an automated and accelerated image processing [12]. The PLI workflow contains a lot of parametrization in its integrated tools, so that provenance recording of these variables would be a significant benefit to the scientists in order to enhance the repeatability of their experiments.

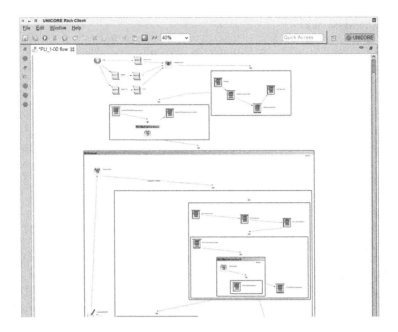

Fig. 1. Partial screenshot of UNICORE Client showing 3D-PLI workflow control flow diagram

Figure 1 shows a section of the control diagram of the PLI workflow in the UNI-CORE Rich Client.

Beyond addressing the individual 3D-PLI use case, UNICORE based work-flows are becoming increasingly important in neuroscience by deploying the middleware in the Human Brain Project [13]. UNICORE will be a core element of the project's so called Collaboratory which is a web platform for executing applications and workflows on HPC resources [14]. Additionally, coarse-grained metadata based on W3C PROV can be registered in the Collaboratory and domain specific PROV conform provenance data as tracked by UniProv could be attached to the HBP provenance repository.

3   UniProv Provenance Management

Besides the need to facilitate experiments by making use of scientific workflows, the availability of provenance information is as important as the results of the scientific analysis itself [15]. The latter aspect is covered by UniProv which is designed as a provenance management system for scientific analysis. The first milestone of UniProv is to support provenance tracking of scientific workflows designed in UNICORE. UniProv aims to represent both prospective and retro-spective provenance of workflows and to link them in a searchable repository [16]. Thus, UniProv captures firstly the "recipe" of the workflow including the

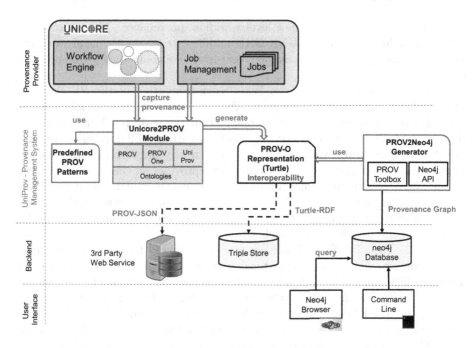

Fig. 2. Architecture of UniProv

workflow model, scripts of single tasks, dependencies between them, and static user annotations [17]. Additionally, each single workflow execution will be tracked adding information about runtime variables, input data, results, and other resources. UniProv receives all required information, prospective and retrospective, from the provenance information providers (i.e. UNICORE in case of this study). Figure 2 shows the dataflow and architecture of the UniProv provenance management system.

3.1 Implementation

The UNICORE middleware acts as a provenance provider and supplies all required information to UniProv. The Unicore2PROV module of the UniProv system captures at first the raw data from UNICORE server components. While the workflow logic, for instance the sequence of jobs, workflow variables, or data staging between supercomputers, is captured directly from the UNICORE workflow engine, detailed information about single compute job resources is tracked from the UNICORE job management services. The latter provenance information includes, among other things, used supercomputing resources, scripts and input data, environment variables, user annotations, user information, and also references to the resulting output of the computations. The recorded provenance information from the job level is transferred together with other related output files to the workflow engine and, subsequently, after the whole workflow has finished, merged with the higher level workflow provenance. This reflects the federated architecture of the UNICORE middleware where a central workflow service can manage several job management instances controlling geographically distributed supercomputers.

UniProv is built based on the W3C recommendation of the PROV Data Model (PROV-DM) which is a rich vocabulary describing provenance information in a standardized way. The mapping from the captured UNICORE raw data to the W3C PROV-DM has been realized with OWL2 ontologies [18] and the Apache Jena framework API [19]. The ontology approach guarantees the interoperable exchange of provenance data and provides an efficient opportunity to specialize the existing semantics to model provenance information for different applications and domains. The basic set of classes, properties, and relations is already defined in the PROV Ontology (PROV-O) representing the OWL2 encoding of the PROV Data Model.

Since the basic PROV-DM does not provide semantics for the processing logic of workflows, a suitable ontology extension model was needed to be integrated in UniProv. Different PROV extension models were analyzed during the evaluation phase of UniProv with regard to their suitability for UNICORE based workflows. With *wfdesc* and *wfprov*, the Wf4Ever Research Object model [20] provides suitable vocabularies describing the static model and the trace of workflows. While the Wf4ever model is embedded in a higher level research object and is in general more oriented towards data preservation, another PROV extensions, the specialised ProvONE [21] ontology, was chosen as a suitable model description for the directed acyclic graphs of UNICORE workflows. Figure 3 shows the conceptual ProvONE model as a UML diagram. For example, the Controller class of the ProvONE ontology allows to specify the execution of a given program which is controlled by another program. In this manner sequential logic and conditions in UNICORE workflows as if-else branches and loop constructs can be optimally implemented by specializing the Controller class.

An additional PROV-O extension is required to describe some UNICORE specific semantics and features. Accordingly, UniProv supports user annotations in job and workflow scripts. For that reason PROV-O has been extended with an appropriate collection class and object relation so that annotations can be related to workflow scripts. Furthermore, UNICORE compute jobs allow the definition of properties for the required supercomputing resources like the number of needed cores, memory, and maximum wall times. Even the total execution time of the complete workflow and single jobs must be tracked. Appropriate parameters have also been added to the OWL2 encoded PROV-O extension which has been serialized as the UniProv ontology. Based on the three provenance ontologies, PROV-O and its extensions ProvOne and UniProv, the Jena framework API maps the captured provenance information from UNICORE to a PROV modeled output in the compact RDF Turtle syntax. Figure 4 shows a visual representation of a simple UNICORE job's provenance output including used environment resources and variables as well as output data generated by the executed job script.

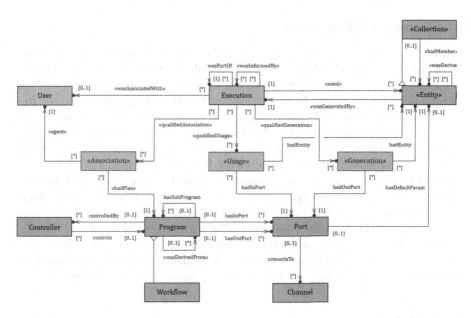

Fig. 3. Workflow provenance model for UniProv: ProvONE UML diagram

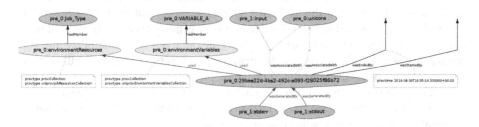

Fig. 4. Visualized UniProv provenance output of a single UNICORE job

3.2 Flexible Extensibility

UniProv has been designed to be able for the integration of different provenance providers beyond the UNICORE middleware. Each application connected to UniProv must be capable to map the captured proprietary provenance information to the W3C PROV standard model and, in case of workflow information, in its extension ProvONE. To ensure that provenance providers generate a well-formed and compatible mapping to PROV and its extensions, UniProv has also implemented a common repository of predefined patterns based on PROV-TEMPLATE [22] separating the tracking of information from the construction of provenance. This approach has the additional advantage that patterns which are often repeated in one or more applications are stored in one central location and can be re-used by providers which want to store provenance information in UniProv.

3.3   Provenance Repository

UniProv stores the collected provenance data using the neo4j graph database. The choice of a graph database was mainly attributed to the much more natural mapping from a directed acyclic provenance graph to the property graph data model as offered by neo4j. In order to store PROV information in neo4j, the PROV representation of the data is mapped to the property graph model. In UniProv this is performed by the PROV2Neo4j-Generator. Furthermore, with Cypher, neo4j offers a declarative, SQL-inspired query language for describing patterns in graphs. Queries can be formulated conveniently in the neo4j browser interface to submit graph traversals to the underyling database. Additionally, this web interface is able to visualize the requested results in a customized manner so that users can easily browse through the captured provenance data. Alternatively, the PROV formatted provenance information could be stored directly in a triple store if the users prefer RDF databases. The interoperable PROV representation also allows to convert the data conveniently in lightweight notations like JSON for interchanging it with third party provenance processing services.

4   Conclusion

The main purpose of the UniProv provenance management system is to enable the back-tracking of experimental data which has either not been possible so far or could only be realised at considerable costs. This means that UniProv will help researchers struggling with information tracking, analysis reproducibility and the verification of scientific output. So for example, end users of UniProv will be able to query the provenance system in order to receive all execution traces within a specific time frame that utilized a particular version of an application which seemed to be incorrect. In general, any possible query about the provenance information of a workflow will be supported by the repository.

Since UniProv is built upon interoperable standards it therefore guarantees both the exchange of provenance data and the extensibility of the provenance management system to various provenance information providers.

At present, UniProv is still work in progress. So the practicality of its design and implementation will be proven in the near future. Especially tests in environments with large collections of traces remain to be carried out.

5   Future Work

Currently, the implementation of UniProv is concentrated on supporting the provenance tracking of UNICORE based scientific workflows. However, UniProv has been designed to be able to adapt various provenance information providers. If one regards data life cycles in science, it becomes apparant that not every processing task is managed within workflows. There is ingestion of raw data in laboratories, annotation of data, transfers to storages and computation clusters, and pre- and post-processing of data outside of controlled workflow executions.

In future, these tasks could also be captured by UniProv in order to achieve a complete provenance graph of the data life cycle. One way for keeping track of datasets in such environments is presented by the PROB tool [23] where provenance information is captured by the version control system GIT and metadata is converted to W3C PROV by using Git2PROV [24]. For UniProv, the adaption of provenance information of distributed version control systems which maintain the revisions of data storages could also provide a promising approach. Another focus will be the integration with the MASi [25] research data repository. Here, data processed by UNICORE shall by ingested and managed by MASi and enriched with provenance information that UniProv provides.

Acknowledgments. The authors thank the German Helmholtz Association's LSDMA [26] project for supporting the specification of UniProv. Furthermore, we would like to thank the DFG for funding the MASi (NA711/9-1) project.

References

1. Streit, A., Bala, P., Beck-Ratzka, A., Benedyczak, K., et al.: UNICORE 6 - recent and future advancements. Ann. Telecommun. - annales des Télécommunications **65**, 757–762 (2010). Springer
2. Moreau, L., Missier, P. (eds.): PROV-DM: The PROV Data Model, 30 April 2013. W3C Recommendation. http://www.w3.org/TR/2013/REC-prov-dm-20130430/
3. Neo4j graph database. http://neo4j.com
4. Deelman, E., Gil, Y.: NSF Workshop on Challenges of Scientific Workflows. Technical report, NSF (2006)
5. Wolstencroft, K., Haines, R., Fellows, D., Sufi, S., Goble, C., et al.: The Taverna workflow suite: designing and executing workflows of web services on the desktop, web or in the cloud. Nucleic Acids Res. **41**(W1), W557–W561 (2013). doi:10.1093/nar/gkt328
6. Soiland-Reyes, S., Gamble, M., Haines, R.: Research Object Bundle 1.0. researchobject.org Specification (2014). https://w3id.org/bundle/2014-11-05. doi:10.5281/zenodo.12586
7. The Kepler Project. http://kepler-project.org
8. The VisTrails Project. http://www.vistrails.org
9. Benabdelkader, A., van Kampen, A.H.C., Olabarriaga, S.D.: PROV-man: a PROV-compliant toolkit for provenance management. PeerJ PrePr. **3**, e1102 (2015)
10. Demuth, B., Schuller, B., Holl, S., Daivandy, J., Giesler, A., Huber, V., Sild, S.: The UNICORE Rich Client: facilitating the automated execution of scientific workflows. In: 2010 IEEE Sixth International Conference on e-Science (e-Science), pp. 238–245 (2010)
11. Amunts, K., Bücker, O., Axer, M.: Towards a multiscale, high-resolution model of the human brain. In: Grandinetti, L., Lippert, T., Petkov, N. (eds.) Brain-Comp 2013. LNCS, vol. 8603, pp. 3–14. Springer, Heidelberg (2014). doi:10.1007/978-3-319-12084-3_1
12. Hagemeier, B., Giesler, A., Saini, R., Schuller, B., Buecker, O.: A workflow for polarized light imaging using UNICORE workflow services. In: UNICORE Summit, Poznan, Poland (2014)
13. The Human Brain Project. http://www.humanbrainproject.eu

14. BerndSchuller: UNICORE in the Human Brain Project (2016). http://neuralensemble.org/media/slides/UNICORE_HBP.pdf

15. Miles, S., Groth, P., Deelman, E., Vahi, K., Mehta, G., Moreau, L.: Provenance: the bridge between experiments and data. Comput. Sci. Eng. **10**, 38–46 (2008). AIP Publishing

16. Zhao, Y., Wilde, M., Foster, I.: Applying the virtual data provenance model. In: Moreau, L., Foster, I. (eds.) IPAW 2006. LNCS, vol. 4145, pp. 148–161. Springer, Heidelberg (2006). doi:10.1007/11890850_16

17. McPhillips, T., Bowers, S., Belhajjame, K., Ludäscher, B.: Retrospective provenance without a runtime provenance recorder. In: Proceedings of TAPP 2014 (2015)

18. OWL 2 Web Ontology Language. https://www.w3.org/TR/owl2-overview/

19. The Apache Jena Project. http://jena.apache.org/

20. Wf4Ever Research Object Model (2013). http://wf4ever.github.io/ro/

21. ProvONE: A PROV Extension Data Model for Scientific Workflow Provenance (2014). http://purl.org/provone

22. PROV-TEMPLATE: A Template System for PROV Documents. https://provenance.ecs.soton.ac.uk/prov-template/

23. Korolev, V., Joshi, A., Korolev, V., Grasso, M.A., Joshi, A., et al.: PROB: a tool for tracking provenance and reproducibility of big data experiments. In: Reproduce 2014, HPCA 2014, vol. 11, pp. 264–286 (2014)

24. De Nies, T., Magliacane, S., Verborgh, R., Coppens, S., Groth, P., Mannens, E., Van de Walle, R.: Git2PROV: exposing version control system content as W3C PROV. In: Proceedings of the 2013th International Conference on Posters & Demonstrations Track, vol. 1035, pp. 125–128 (2013)

25. Project: MASI - Metadata Management for Applied Sciences. https://tu-dresden.de/zih/forschung/projekte/masi

26. LSDMA Project: Large-Scale Data Management and Analysis. https://www.helmholtz-lsdma.de/

A Collaborative Simulation-Analysis Workflow for Computational Neuroscience Using HPC

Johanna Senk[1(✉)], Alper Yegenoglu[1(✉)], Olivier Amblet[2], Yury Brukau[2], Andrew Davison[3], David Roland Lester[4], Anna Lührs[5], Pietro Quaglio[1], Vahid Rostami[1], Andrew Rowley[4], Bernd Schuller[5], Alan Barry Stokes[4], Sacha Jennifer van Albada[1], Daniel Zielasko[6,7], Markus Diesmann[1,8,9], Benjamin Weyers[6,7], Michael Denker[1], and Sonja Grün[1,10]

[1] Institute of Neuroscience and Medicine (INM-6) and Institute for Advanced Simulation (IAS-6) and JARA-BRAIN Institute I, Forschungszentrum Jülich, Jülich, Germany
{j.senk,a.yegenoglu}@fz-juelich.de
[2] Human Brain Project, École Polytechnique Fédérale de Lausanne, Geneva, Switzerland
[3] Unité de Neurosciences, Information et Complexité (UNIC), Centre National de la Recherche Scientifique, Gif-sur-Yvette, France
[4] Department of Computer Science, University of Manchester, Manchester, UK
[5] Jülich Supercomputing Centre (JSC), Forschungszentrum Jülich, Jülich, Germany
[6] Visual Computing Institute, RWTH Aachen University, Aachen, Germany
[7] JARA-HPC, Aachen, Germany
[8] Department of Psychiatry, Psychotherapy and Psychosomatics, Medical Faculty, RWTH Aachen University, Aachen, Germany
[9] Department of Physics, Faculty 1, RWTH Aachen University, Aachen, Germany
[10] Theoretical Systems Neurobiology, RWTH Aachen University, Aachen, Germany

Abstract. Workflows for the acquisition and analysis of data in the natural sciences exhibit a growing degree of complexity and heterogeneity, are increasingly performed in large collaborative efforts, and often require the use of high-performance computing (HPC). Here, we explore the reasons for these new challenges and demands and discuss their impact with a focus on the scientific domain of computational neuroscience. We argue for the need of software platforms integrating HPC systems that allow scientists to construct, comprehend and execute workflows composed of diverse data generation and processing steps using different tools. As a use case we present a concrete implementation of such a complex workflow, covering diverse topics such as HPC-based simulation using the NEST software, access to the SpiNNaker neuromorphic hardware platform, complex data analysis using the Elephant library, and interactive visualization methods for facilitating further analysis. Tools are embedded into a web-based software platform under development by the Human Brain Project, called the Collaboratory. On the basis of this implementation, we discuss the state of the art and future challenges in constructing large, collaborative workflows with access to HPC resources.

E. Di Napoli et al. (Eds.): JHPCS 2016, LNCS 10164, pp. 243–256, 2017.
DOI: 10.1007/978-3-319-53862-4_21

Keywords: High-performance computing · Workflows · Collaboration · Reproducibility · Provenance tracking · Simulation · Neuromorphic hardware · Comparative data analysis · Visualization

1   Introduction

Workflows in the natural sciences that deal with the acquisition and analysis of experimental or simulated data often comprise an intricate sequence of processing steps, each of which requires the use of diverse software tools. The resulting heterogeneity in terms of both the composition of steps of the workflows and the diversity of tools employed generates a substantial degree of complexity that increases with the number of researchers involved. The situation is compounded if the tools themselves add an additional level of complexity, for instance requiring scientists to be trained in using the software. In particular, in interdisciplinary settings, users need to know how to integrate the various tools that may be unfamiliar to them in terms of practical usage and/or the scientific processing step they perform. A commonly encountered scenario where this holds are workflows and tools that rely on the capabilities of high-performance computing (HPC) systems, but where the access to and usage of such systems is complicated for less experienced users. Another problem dimension is added if requirements such as reproducibility or reusability are considered, for example in terms of version control of code and data or provenance tracking of the analysis. Ad hoc approaches are bound to fail as the complexity of the workflow increases. Instead, the heterogeneity and the emerging complexity of such workflows call for user-friendly standards and software tools that meet and integrate such requirements.

Interdisciplinary workflows in computational neuroscience are facing these problems. Computational neuroscience entails integrating and analyzing experimental data, building network models for brain simulations, and using theory to develop concepts concerning neuronal information processing. Datasets obtained from both experiments and simulations are highly diverse in their internal structure and content. Analysis tools are therefore often adapted to the specifics of the experiment or the simulation study. Moreover, the analysis tools employ methods with a different focus depending on the source of the data. For instance, while simulation studies often exploit the fact that data are controlled and can be acquired over long durations and large ensembles, experimentally obtained data are often analyzed with respect to the inherent non-stationarity of the data and the behavioral protocols. Thus, in the attempt to bring experiment and simulation closer together, a large array of heterogeneous data standards and tools exist. These need to be merged and linked into workflows for analysis, in particular for comparison of data from model and experiment. Moreover, workflows typically consist of complex chains of processing steps that often require the use of HPC systems for expensive computations, e.g., to run large-scale network simulations, to process extensive data records, or to perform parameter scans. At the same time, they necessitate the option of exploratory analysis in an interactive fashion (cf. [9]).

To propose a solution for this problem domain, this work presents an example of such an interdisciplinary and heterogeneous workflow in computational neuroscience. We describe in the following a realistic research question, derive its concrete challenges, and provide a possible approach to tackle them. The research question addressed is to what extent different simulators produce comparable results as they differ, for instance, in the biological detail they can represent, their underlying architecture, performance, flexibility, or other design goals like application in robotics. We here compare two simulators, NEST and SpiN-Naker, relying on two different types of digital hardware, and outline a workflow which is conceptually applicable for the comparison of other simulators as well. Both simulators aim at simulations of large networks of simple spiking neuron models which are currently gaining significant relevance in the field of computational neuroscience [2]. The simulator NEST (NEural Simulation Tool[1], see [11,15]) is optimized to efficiently use existing HPC infrastructure and allows for exact and reproducible simulations. It combines ease of use (Python interface) and runtime performance (C++ kernel, multi-threading, and MPI-parallelism). Recent development of NEST has notably reduced the memory requirements [17], thus further facilitating large-scale simulations. In contrast, SpiNNaker (Spiking Neural Network Architecture[2], see [12,20]) is a specific neuromorphic hardware designed for biological real-time operation, low power consumption, and scalability. The architecture of the SpiNNaker Neuromorphic Computing Platform itself is inspired by biological neuronal networks. A large number of low-powered and thus energy-efficient computation units are highly connected together by an asynchronous communication network.

Since there are by design major differences in how NEST and SpiNNaker operate, it remains to be evaluated to what extent simulation results are comparable at all. This suggests the refined research question (cf. above):

If a simulation of the same neural network model is run both on an HPC system using NEST and on the neuromorphic hardware system SpiNNaker, are the results the same?

When investigating the implications of this question in detail, the following distinct challenges emerge. First of all, access to HPC systems and the neuromorphic hardware is required. It must also be guaranteed that the same network model is simulated on both systems to enable a direct comparison of the simulation results; this calls for a model description valid for both systems. The model development itself needs to be performed under version control and the source code must be accessible to all scientists involved. Assuming that both simulations have been run successfully, the simulation output must be validated and compared using a suitable analysis tool. In order to evaluate the recorded series of spike times of each simulated neuron, i.e., the spike trains, and to assess whether the results from both simulations can be considered "the same", a tool for statistical data analysis is needed. A prerequisite for the analysis is that the simulation output is readily accessible, for example after transferring it to the

---

[1] http://nest-simulator.org/
[2] http://apt.cs.manchester.ac.uk/projects/SpiNNaker/

same data storage, and that the data is available in the same format. It is further desirable to have the possibility of an interactive data analysis and a more sophisticated one relying on HPC. Finally, visualization techniques are needed in order to convey a more intuitive understanding of the expectedly complex analysis results.

In summary, the initially posed research problem can be broken down into a list of separate demands which encompass the collaboration of experts from different scientific disciplines as well as a series of consecutive tasks that depend on access to and usage of specific tools. On first sight, one could argue that solutions for the isolated problems already exist. To give an example, there are web-based repository hosting services like GitHub[3] for source code management and version control which allow sharing repositories among researchers of different institutions. Sumatra[4] allows for automated tracking of scientific computations. For the field of neuroscience, in particular, there are platforms to facilitate access, storage, analysis, and exchange of data, such as the G-Node Data Portal[5]. Resources for computational models of neural systems are Open Source Brain[6] and ModelDB[7]. The Neuroscience Gateway[8] provides an opportunity for neuroscientists to use HPC resources. When using such independent solutions, however, one faces major problems in terms of provenance tracking. If there are no links between the individual components, it will quickly become untraceable who did what, why, and when. Since scientific progress is rarely straightforward, but includes trial and error, repetitions, and iterative improvement, it is crucial to keep track of all steps involved and their history. Here, we suggest integrating such components into one collaboration platform in order to establish a stable and reproducible workflow.

In this study, we demonstrate how such a workflow can be implemented addressing the aforementioned problems by integrating established and emerging software tools using a web-based infrastructure. We will describe the workflow consisting of the following steps: (i) simulate the activity generated by a model of a cortical microcircuit [18] using the NEST simulator, (ii) simulate the same network model with identical parameters using the SpiNNaker system, (iii) pool data on the centralized storage of the integrative software infrastructure, (iv) compare the resulting activity data using Elephant (Electrophysiology Analysis Toolkit, see [21,22]), and (v) interactively visualize the analysis results. In the following, the individual steps comprising this workflow will be briefly highlighted, before we discuss the benefits and shortcomings of the currently available implementation of this workflow based on an integrative software architecture that is developed in the European FET Flagship "Human Brain Project" (HBP).

---

[3] https://github.com/

[4] http://neuralensemble.org/sumatra/

[5] http://www.g-node.org/

[6] http://opensourcebrain.org/

[7] https://senselab.med.yale.edu/modeldb/

[8] https://www.nsgportal.org/

2 Workflow

The principal layout of the workflow that we defined and implemented to compare the activity data coming from the classical NEST-based simulations, and the neuromorphic SpiNNaker-based simulations is depicted in Fig. 1. The workflow comprises a collaboration of different laboratories with different expertises (marked by colored dots): HPC, neural network simulation, neuromorphic hardware, data analysis, and visualization. Each of the five steps in Fig. 1 is defined by a set of methods and tools specific to these individual areas of expertise, and needs to be integrated into a common infrastructure that makes them accessible for cooperative work. All components integrated in the workflow are based on or accessible via Python, a programming language which is becoming commonly used in computational neuroscience for both simulation and data analysis [6]. Furthermore, we incorporate tools like NEST and Elephant which follow standardized development processes in software engineering, e.g., test-driven development and continuous integration.

We embedded our workflow into an integrative software platform called the "HBP Collaboratory"[9]. The Collaboratory is a web-based portal which provides a common entry point to facilitate collaboration by providing a shared project space (termed the "Collab") for groups of scientists. Specifically, for our project we created the "NEST SpiNNaker Elephant Demo" Collab[10], which enables us to share simulation data and analysis results through the centralized "Collab storage", to use all relevant applications including access to HPC infrastructures and neuromorphic hardware, and to document the workflow. For interactive Python programming, the Collaboratory provides Jupyter Notebooks[11] that run directly in the Collab and have NEST and Elephant preinstalled by default. The HPC resources required for simulations and analyses are launched via the Collaboratory's internal task framework as jobs ("tasks") which are sent to predefined compute clusters or supercomputers. Finally, the Collaboratory offers basic provenance tracking, providing the ability to reenact an already executed task.

The specific network we simulate is a full-scale neural network model of a cortical microcircuit [18]. Full-scale means that the natural density of neurons and synapses of the biological circuit is preserved. The microcircuit represents $1 \, \text{mm}^2$ of cortex and contains around $80,000$ spiking leaky integrate-and-fire point neurons connected by around 0.3 billion synapses in four cortical layers (L2/3, L4, L5, L6). Each layer comprises an excitatory and an inhibitory neuron population which are interconnected with cell-type- and layer-specific connection probabilities derived from experimental data on early sensory cortex. The model is well-suited for our workflow for two reasons: First, it is of neuroscientific interest since it is a minimal microcircuit that combines a realistic number of synapses per neuron with sparse network connectivity as found in cortex, exhibits realistic spiking

---

[9] http://collab.humanbrainproject.eu/

[10] https://collab.humanbrainproject.eu/#/collab/507/nav/6326

[11] http://jupyter.org/

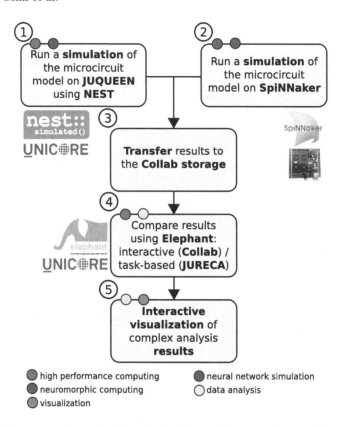

Fig. 1. Workflow overview: A network simulation of a cortical microcircuit model is run using both NEST (**1**) and SpiNNaker (**2**). Simulation results are transferred to a common storage (**3**) and compared utilizing functionalities of the Elephant library (**4**). Complex analysis results are visualized to gain further insight (**5**). The middleware UNICORE is used to access HPC systems. Colored dots on top of each box indicate the disciplines involved. For example, supercomputers (red dots) are used to run a NEST simulation and to compare results using Elephant. (Color figure online)

activity, and serves as a prototype for larger networks (see [19] for an example). Second, it fits onto both systems in terms of computational resources. More precisely, the network size indicates HPC for the NEST simulations, although it is still considered to present a small workload for HPC systems. For SpiNNaker, the model is an interesting use case because it requires the parallel use of multiple boards [1]. For comparability of the simulation results, we use a common model implementation based on PyNN and develop the source code using the version control system git[12]. PyNN is a Python API for simulator-independent neuronal network model specification [5,7,8]. The PyNN API enables writing generic code to control different simulators such as NEST, NEURON, Brian and

---

[12] https://git-scm.com/

also neuromorphic hardware [4], including the SpiNNaker platform. In the case of SpiNNaker, a software library is used to break down the Python network description into small chunks each of which can be run on a core, and to route communications between the parts of the network.

As the first step of the workflow (Fig. 1, Step 1) we run the microcircuit simulation on an HPC system using NEST. We established two ways to access HPC resources from within the Collaboratory: using the task framework or interactively from a Jupyter Notebook running within the Collab. Specific simulation and network parameters such as the simulation duration (in our case: 10 s) can be configured via a Jupyter Notebook before submitting the job. Both the task framework and the Jupyter Notebooks use UNICORE[13] as middleware that yields secure and seamless access to supercomputing and data resources from a web-based environment such as the Collaboratory. UNICORE provides a wide range of features for HPC job submission and management as well as data transfer and handling. Concretely, the microcircuit simulation runs on JUQUEEN[14], a supercomputer with an IBM BlueGene/Q architecture at the Jülich Supercomputing Centre (JSC), Forschungszentrum Jülich, Germany and is one of the fastest supercomputers in Europe and worldwide. Gathered simulation results, i.e., a down-sampled set of spike data from 100 excitatory and 100 inhibitory neurons from each of the four simulated cortical layers (800 neurons in total), are automatically copied from the supercomputer to the central Collab storage (Step 3).

In the second step of the workflow (Step 2), the simulation is run on (a part of) the half-million-core SpiNNaker machine located in Manchester, UK, with identical parameters. The Collaboratory integration in this case is implemented via the Neuromorphic Job Manager App. This allows users to submit PyNN scripts directly, through a git repository, or as a compressed archive of files using a webpage-based user interface. It is also possible to submit jobs directly from a Python script through the hbp_neuromorphic_platform library[15]. Jobs for execution on SpiNNaker are periodically retrieved and run on a virtual machine cluster situated close to the SpiNNaker machine. Results are then retrieved from the machine, stored locally, and finally transferred to the Collab storage via the Job Manager App when requested (Step 3).

In order to compare the simulation results of the two systems and to characterize potential differences, we analyze the statistical features of the two datasets using the Elephant library (Step 4). Elephant is a community-centered, open-source Python library for analyzing multi-scale data on brain dynamics from experiments and simulations. The focus is on tools for the analysis of electrical activity, such as single-unit or massively parallel spike train data and local field potentials (LFP). The scope of the library covers the analysis of analog signals (including time-domain and frequency-domain methods), spike-based analysis (e.g., spike train correlation, spike pattern analysis), and methods combining

---

[13] https://www.unicore.eu/

[14] http://www.fz-juelich.de/ias/jsc/EN/

[15] https://pypi.python.org/pypi/hbp_neuromorphic_platform/

both signal types (e.g., spike-triggered averaging of an LFP signal). We first execute a task on the Collab to convert the data into the HDF5[16] format and save the result. This data format is compatible with the Neo library [13,14] which serves as a foundation of Elephant. The internal structure of the HDF5 file complies with the Neo architecture[17] introduced in version 0.2 and is created using the Neo HDF5 I/O[18].

Next, we compare the two simulation results in an interactive fashion using the Elephant library within a Jupyter Notebook. In particular, we consider features that are typically analyzed in neuroscience, such as the irregularity of the individual spike trains and correlations between pairs of neurons. A first visual impression (Step 5) of the firing behavior of individual neurons and the neuronal populations is provided by dot displays as shown for NEST in Fig. 2**A** and for SpiNNaker in Fig. 2**B**. Each spike is represented as a dot at the time of its occurrence. Multiple neurons are displayed below each other in different lines. The summed population activity is shown in the histogram below the dot display of the respective layer. On the right, the average firing rates of the individual neurons are depicted. The visualized spiking activity of NEST and SpiNNaker is qualitatively comparable. As we compare different network realizations on NEST and SpiNNaker, the neurons do not correspond one-to-one between the two systems, and hence, statistical measures for comparison are needed.

To capture properties of the coordination between individual neurons, we also computed Pearson correlation coefficients, i.e., the zero-delay correlation coefficients between all pairs of neurons in each population. Their distributions are visualized in Fig. 3**A** and **B**. The shapes of the distributions agree between the two types of simulations–except for a remarkable difference for the layer four (L4) neurons (second row of Fig. 3). In the process of tracking down the origin of this variation, a slight improvement in the simulation and recording routine of SpiNNaker was made. With respect to the dot displays, the dataset resulting from this iteration step, shown in Fig. 2**C**, does not exhibit striking differences to the initial results that are noticeable by eye. However, the distribution of correlation coefficients, Fig. 3**C**, approaches the ones from the NEST simulation in Fig. 3**A** in L4 much better.

We hence see that rather simple analysis methods already suffice to reveal prominent differences between the simulation results. To access the subtle differences, however, we aimed to uncover the full correlation structure of the activity using more sophisticated techniques. Since these demand HPC resources due to expensive surrogate generation and multiple hypothesis testing, we execute a task that uses UNICORE to send the data to the HPC system JURECA, located at the Forschungszentrum Jülich, and to parallelize the analysis (Step 4).

After completion, the results are again transferred to the Collab storage. Due to the complicated nature of the resulting data, we decided to visualize them using a special tool designed to interactively probe the correlation structure in

---

[16] https://www.hdfgroup.org/hdf5/

[17] http://neo.readthedocs.io/en/0.4.1/core.html#grouping-objects

[18] http://neo.readthedocs.io/en/0.4.1/io.html#neo.io.NeoHdf5IO

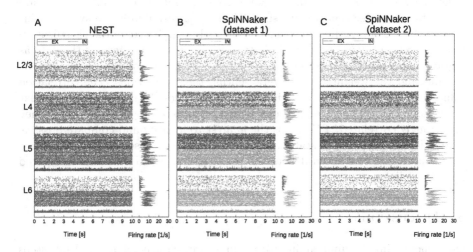

Fig. 2. The data obtained from the NEST (**A**) and the first (**B**) and second (**C**) iteration of the SpiNNaker simulations are presented as raster displays. Each dot indicates a spike at its time of occurrence and each line represents the firing activity of a neuron. Neurons are grouped into different cortical layers (L2/3, L4, L5, L6) and sorted by neuron type, i.e., excitatory (EX) and inhibitory (IN). The histograms at the bottom and right side show the population activity and the firing rate of the neurons, respectively.

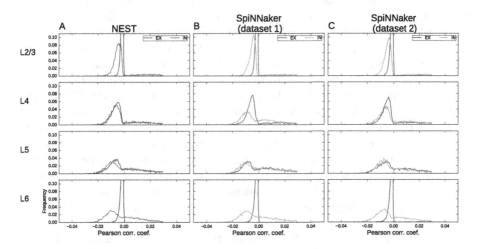

Fig. 3. The distributions of Pearson correlation coefficients are shown for the NEST (**A**) and and the two SpiNNaker (**B** and **C**) simulations. The correlation coefficients were computed for all pairs of recorded neurons of the same layer and neuron type. The y-axis is truncated for comparability between the different neuron populations.

order to obtain an overview and to gain further insight. To this end, the data are staged to a visualization server using dCache[19], a distributed file system. This enables the use of high-fidelity visualization tools, e.g., based on the visualization toolkit ViSTA (Virtual Reality Toolkit[20]). Such a tool can interpret the data as a graph and render it as a node-link diagram, with the nodes representing the neurons and the weighted edges representing the correlations. The correlation value serves as attraction criterion in a force-directed layout algorithm that results in visual clusters of neurons where neurons are spatially close if they are strongly correlated. This helps the analyst to identify and compare possible correlation patterns in the statistical data. Using a web-based streaming library, the visualization tool could deliver the rendered images to a website integrated into the Collab.

3   Discussion

Our general aim is to map an interdisciplinary workflow involving multiple steps and tools to a common platform and to address major problems emerging from this setting: heterogeneous data, diverse knowledge of the participants in the workflow, the involvement of complex tools and infrastructures as well as aspects such as reproducibility, reusability and iterative refinement. The requirements for such a platform are to provide a collaborative environment which allows one to integrate and easily access software tools, libraries, and data, as well as HPC systems which are needed for demanding simulations and analyses. As an example, we demonstrated a concrete working solution implemented in the HBP Collaboratory and responded to the list of challenges identified in the introduction. From within the Collaboratory, we established access to the HPC systems JUQUEEN and JURECA by means of the middleware UNICORE. Likewise, a connection to a SpiNNaker machine was realized via the Neuromorphic Job Manager App. PyNN provides an interface to NEST and SpiNNaker and hence allows for a common model description, developed under version control with git. The simulation output from both systems was obtained in the HDF5 data format and, once transferred to the common Collab storage, it was read by the Elephant library which offers a variety of analysis methods. Jupyter Notebooks in the Collab were used for interactive Python programming and, as a last point, analysis results were visualized. In summary, our workflow comprises a variety of tools and resources which themselves are widely used within the communities involved. Our Collab is public within the Collaboratory, i.e., other users can inspect the developed tasks and Jupyter Notebooks as documented there or integrate them into their own Collabs.

Using a common framework usually restricts the user to available tools, but a versatile structure allows for adaption and extension if requested by the user. For example, a continuous exchange between us (computational neuroscientists

---

[19] https://www.dcache.org/

[20] http://www.itc.rwth-aachen.de/cms/IT-Center/Forschung-Projekte/Virtuelle-Realitaet/Infrastruktur/~fgmo/ViSTA-Virtual-Reality-Toolkit/?lidx=1

as users and software engineers as developers of the Collaboratory) resulted in the integration of Jupyter Notebooks into the portal. This shows the importance of a bilateral communication between developers and users for a successful and ongoing development of a collaboration platform. Use cases based on the daily practice of the users are a main component of this development. During the implementation of the workflow into the Collaboratory, we not only aimed at the full integration of tools like Jupyter Notebooks, but also at establishing interfaces to tools outside the portal, for example by making supercomputers accessible via the middleware UNICORE. Furthermore, we accounted for different data types and formats with a conversion task to enable applying the same analysis functions to data obtained from different sources.

In addition to the inherent heterogeneity of workflow components, reproducibility and reusability are considered. For single workflow steps, we use tools that fulfill criteria of quality assurance, e.g., continuous integration and test-driven development. The task framework of the Collaboratory already allows provenance tracking to some extent, but the whole workflow is not fully traceable, yet. Thus, we envision that all individual steps of the workflow can be tracked from the beginning of the simulations to the end of the visualization The workflow can be improved through an iterative adjustment of single steps and parameters. Therefore, we need a flexible workflow implementation that allows for easy integration of individual parts.

Transparency of the workflow is an important property of a successful integration since it allows collaborators to comprehend and even carry out different steps of the workflow. The web interface of the Collaboratory serves as a common access point for collaboration where we collect documentation together with code, data, and results, as well as provenance information. However, a complete representation of how individual steps of the workflow are connected within the Collab is still ongoing work.

A possible next step is to set up a test battery to quantify detailed differences in results complementing the visual inspection in the interactive analysis. Furthermore, having common metadata (e.g., layer of neuron) for the data simulated by the two systems is important for the follow-up analysis tools. Here, we aim to make use of the odML metadata framework which is also used for experimental data [16,23]. We seek a shared terminology which allows for easy handling and manipulation of the data, and avoids misinterpretations of vocabulary.

In contrast to well-established groupware solutions, such as BSCW [3] for project management and file sharing or Moodle [10] used in the context of academic teaching, the Collaboratory offers a domain-specific integration of tools and middleware. It concentrates on content-based communication (e.g., sharing data and documentation) instead of direct communication using video or audio conference tools and therefore offers a single point of access for tools and data used in the neurosciences. The latter makes it especially useful for this scientific community and thus differentiates it from existing more general solutions.

Taken together, we believe that the workflow implementation presented in this work provides a promising vista of how a collaborative system such as the

HBP Collaboratory, supported by a chain of compatible software tools, can help scientists to come together in large, interdisciplinary, and collaborative research endeavors. Indeed the availability of technologies that allow for large collaborative research endeavors is expected to become an indispensable asset as neuroscience moves towards questions that can no longer be handled by a single person. Considering the diversity of approaches and data types in the field of neuroscience, even the workflow presented here, consisting of a collaborative effort of eighteen researchers distributed over six institutes, may be considered a small collaboration in the future. These developments are expected to produce new challenges, e.g., the need for more dynamic ways of setting up workflows, better visualizations of the provenance information for generated data, or the ability to control more heterogeneous HPC environments required by the individual components of the workflows.

Acknowledgments. This project has received funding from the Helmholtz Portfolio Supercomputing and Modeling for the Human Brain (SMHB), the European Union's Horizon 2020 research and innovation programme under grant agreement No 720270 (HBP SGA1), and the DFG SPP Priority Program 1665 (GR 1753/4-1 and DE 2175/1-1).

References

1. van Albada, S.J., Rowley, A.G., Hopkins, M., Schmidt, M., Senk, J., Stokes, A.B., Galluppi, F., Lester, D.R., Diesmann, M., Furber, S.B.: Full-scale simulation of a cortical microcircuit on SpiNNaker. In: Frontiers in Neuroinformatics Conference Abstract: Neuroinformatics 2016 (2016). http://dx.doi.org/10.3389/conf.fninf.2016.20.00029
2. van Albada, S.J., Helias, M., Diesmann, M.: Scalability of asynchronous networks is limited by one-to-one mapping between effective connectivity and correlations. PLoS Comput. Biol. **11**(9), e1004490 (2015). http://dx.doi.org/10.1371/journal.pcbi.1004490
3. Appelt, W.: WWW based collaboration with the BSCW system. In: Pavelka, J., Tel, G., Bartošek, M. (eds.) SOFSEM 1999. LNCS, vol. 1725, pp. 66–78. Springer, Heidelberg (1999). doi:10.1007/3-540-47849-3_4
4. Brüderle, D., Petrovici, M.A., Vogginger, B., Ehrlich, M., Pfeil, T., Millner, S., Grübl, A., Wendt, K., Müller, E., Schwartz, M.O., de Oliveira, D.H., Jeltsch, S., Fieres, J., Schilling, M., Müller, P., Breitwieser, O., Petkov, V., Muller, L., Davison, A.P., Krishnamurthy, P., Kremkow, J., Lundqvist, M., Muller, E., Partzsch, J., Scholze, S., Zühl, L., Mayr, C., Destexhe, A., Diesmann, M., Potjans, T.C., Lansner, A., Schüffny, R., Schemmel, J., Meier, K.: A comprehensive workflow for general-purpose neural modeling with highly configurable neuromorphic hardware systems. Biol. Cybern. **104**(4–5), 263–296 (2011). http://dx.doi.org/10.1007/s00422-011-0435-9
5. Davison, A.P., Brüderle, D., Kremkow, J., Muller, E., Pecevski, D., Perrinet, L., Yger, P.: PyNN: a common interface for neuronal network simulators. Front. Neuroinformatics **2**(11), 204 (2009). http://dx.doi.org/10.3389/neuro.11.011.2008
6. Davison, A.P., Hines, M.L., Muller, E.: Trends in programming languages for neuroscience simulations. Front. Neurosci. **3**(3), 374–380 (2009). http://dx.doi.org/10.3389/neuro.01.036.2009

7. Davison, A.P., Yger, P., Muller, E., Kremkow, J., Brüderle, D., Perrinet, L., Eppler, J., Pecevski, D., Debeissat, N., Djurfeldt, M., Schmuker, M., Kaplan, B., Natschlaeger, T., Ray, S., Zaytsev, Y., Gravier, A.: PyNN 0.7.5. https://pypi.python.org/pypi/PyNN/0.7.5

8. Davison, A.P., Yger, P., Muller, E., Kremkow, J., Brüderle, D., Perrinet, L., Eppler, J., Pecevski, D., Debeissat, N., Djurfeldt, M., Schmuker, M., Kaplan, B., Natschlaeger, T., Ray, S., Zaytsev, Y., Antolik, J., Gravier, A., Close, T., Breitwieser, O., Schücker, J., Schmidt, M.: PyNN 0.8.0 (2015). https://github.com/NeuralEnsemble/PyNN/releases/tag/0.8.0

9. Denker, M., Grün, S.: Designing workflows for the reproducible analysis of electrophysiological data. In: Amunts, K., Grandinetti, L., Lippert, T., Petkov, N. (eds.) BrainComp 2015. LNCS, vol. 10087, pp. 58–72. Springer, Cham (2016). doi:10.1007/978-3-319-50862-7_5

10. Dougiamas, M., Taylor, P.: Moodle: Using learning communities to create an open source course management system. In: World Conference on Educational Multimedia, Hypermedia and Telecommunications (EDMEDIA) (2003). http://research.moodle.net/id/eprint/33

11. Eppler, J.M., Pauli, R., Peyser, A., Ippen, T., Morrison, A., Senk, J., Schenck, W., Bos, H., Helias, M., Schmidt, M., Kunkel, S., Jordan, J., Gewaltig, M.O., Bachmann, C., Schuecker, J., Albada, S., Zito, T., Deger, M., Michler, F., Hagen, E., Setareh, H., Riquelme, L., Shirvani, A., Duarte, R., Deepu, R., Plesser, H.E.: Nest 2.8.0 (2015). https://doi.org/10.5281/zenodo.32969

12. Furber, S.B., Lester, D.R., Plana, L.A., Garside, J.D., Painkras, E., Temple, S., Brown, A.D.: Overview of the SpiNNaker system architecture. IEEE Trans. Comput. **62**(12), 2454–2467 (2013). http://dx.doi.org/10.1109/TC.2012.142

13. Garcia, S., Davison, A.P., Rodgers, C., Yger, P., Mahnoun, Y., Estabanez, L., Sobolev, A., Brizzi, T., Jaillet, F., Rautenberg, P., Wachtler, T., Dejean, C., Pröpper, R., Guarino, D.: Neo 0.4.1. https://github.com/NeuralEnsemble/python-neo/releases/tag/0.4.1

14. Garcia, S., Guarino, D., Jaillet, F., Jennings, T., Pröpper, R., Rautenberg, P.L., Rodgers, C.C., Sobolev, A., Wachtler, T., Yger, P., Davison, A.P.: Neo: an object model for handling electrophysiology data in multiple formats. Front. Neuroinformatics 8, 10 (2014). http://dx.doi.org/10.3389/fninf.2014.00010

15. Gewaltig, M.O., Diesmann, M.: NEST (NEural Simulation Tool). Scholarpedia 2(4) (2007). http://dx.doi.org/10.4249/scholarpedia.1430

16. Grewe, J., Wachtler, T., Benda, J.: A bottom-up approach to data annotation in neurophysiology. Front. Neuroinformatics 5 (2011). http://dx.doi.org/10.3389/fninf.2011.00016

17. Kunkel, S., Schmidt, M., Eppler, J.M., Plesser, H.E., Masumoto, G., Igarashi, J., Ishii, S., Fukai, T., Morrison, A., Diesmann, M., Helias, M.: Spiking network simulation code for petascale computers. Front. Neuroinformatics **8**(78), 1 (2014). http://dx.doi.org/10.3389/fninf.2014.00078

18. Potjans, T.C., Diesmann, M.: The cell-type specific cortical microcircuit: relating structure and activity in a full-scale spiking network model. Cereb. Cortex **24**(3), 785–806 (2014). http://dx.doi.org/10.1093/cercor/bhs358

19. Schmidt, M., Bakker, R., Shen, K., Bezgin, G., Hilgetag, C.C., Diesmann, M., van Albada, S.J.: Full-density multi-scale account of structure and dynamics of macaque visual cortex (2015). arXiv preprint https://arxiv.org/abs/1511.09364

20. Stokes, A.B., Rowley, A.G.D., Knight, J., Lester, D.R., Rast, A., Hopkins, M.W., Davidson, S., Temple, S., Plana, L., Davies, S., Sharpe, T., Patterson, C., Furber, S.B.: sPyNNaker 3.0.0 (2016). https://github.com/SpiNNakerManchester/sPyNNaker/releases/tag/3.0.0

21. Yegenoglu, A., Denker, M., Phan, L., Holstein, D., Chorley, P., Ito, J., Jennings, T., Meyes, R., Quaglio, P., Rostami, V., Sprenger, J., Torre, E., Davison, A., Grün, S.: Elephant - open-source tool for the analysis of electrophysiological data sets. In: Bernstein Conference 2015: Abstract Book, p. W-05 (2015). http://dx.doi.org/10.12751/nncn.bc2015.0126

22. Yegenoglu, A., Davison, A.P., Holstein, D., Muller, E., Torre, E., Hagen, E., Gosmann, J., Sprenger, J., Ito, J., Denker, M., Chorley, P., Yger, P., Quaglio, P., Meyes, R., Rostami, V., Ray, S., Pröpper, R., Gerkin, R.C., Telenczuk, B.: Elephant 0.3.0. https://github.com/NeuralEnsemble/elephant/releases/tag/0.3.0

23. Zehl, L., Jaillet, F., Stoewer, A., Grewe, J., Sobolev, A., Wachtler, T., Brochier, T.G., Riehle, A., Denker, M., Grün, S.: Handling metadata in a neurophysiology laboratory. Front. Neuroinformatics 10 (2016). http://dx.doi.org/10.3389/fninf.2016.00026

Author Index

Aeberhard, Urs   111
Amblet, Olivier   243
Ansorge, Cedrick   151

Bale, Rahul   13
Behr, Marek   24
Berger, Sandrine   3
Berger, Sven   70
Bode, Mathis   96
Brukau, Yury   243

Celino, Massimo   111
Czaja, Philippe   111
Czekala, Myriam   233

Dang, Siaufung O.   139
Davidović, Davor   200
Davidovic, Marco   96
Davison, Andrew   243
Degirmenci, Niyazi Cem   58
Delalondre, Fabien Jonathan   160
Denker, Michael   243
Di Napoli, Edoardo   170, 200
Diesmann, Markus   243
Duchaine, Florent   3
Duda, Benjamin   48

Erő, Csaba   160

Fabregat-Traver, Diego   200
Fares, Ehab   48
Finsterbusch, Martin   139

Gauding, Michael   225
Gewaltig, Marc-Oliver   160
Gicquel, Laurent   3
Giesler, André   233
Giusepponi, Simone   111
Göbbert, Jens Henrik   151, 187, 225
Grün, Sonja   243

Grunzke, Richard   233
Gusso, Michele   111

Hagemeier, Björn   225, 233
Halver, René   187
Hasse, Christian   82
Hentschel, Bernd   212
Hermanns, Marc-André   187
Hoffman, Johan   58
Höhnerbach, Markus   200
Houzeaux, Guillaume   37
Hunkel, Martin   125
Hüter, Claas   125, 139

Iliev, Hristo   151, 187

Jansson, Johan   58
Jansson, Niclas   13, 58

Kuhlen, Torsten W.   212

Larcher, Aurélien   58
Lester, David Roland   243
Lichtenstein, Julian   170
Lin, Mingxuan   125
Lintermann, Andreas   70
Lührs, Anna   243

Meinke, Matthias   70
Mira, Daniel   37
Mohr, Bernd   187
Müller, Matthias S.   187, 212

Onishi, Keiji   13

Pauli, Lutz   24
Pitsch, Heinz   96, 151
Popp, Sebastian   82
Prahl, Ulrich   125
Prill, Marco   139

Quaglio, Pietro   243

Rostami, Vahid   243
Rowley, Andrew   243

Sánchez de la Peña, David   170
Schicchi, Diego   125
Schlottke-Lakemper, Michael   70
Schröder, Wolfgang   70
Schuller, Bernd   243
Schumann, Till   160
Senk, Johanna   243
Spatschek, Robert   125, 139
Spühler, Jeannette Hiromi   58
Staffelbach, Gabriel   3
Stokes, Alan Barry   243

Terboven, Christian   187
Tsubokura, Makoto   13
Tweddell, Bastian   225

van Albada, Sacha Jennifer   243
Vázquez, Mariano   37
Vidović, Toni   170
Vierjahn, Tom   212
Vilela De Abreu, Rodrigo   58

Weikamp, Marc   125
Weise, Steffen   82
Weyers, Benjamin   225, 243
Winkelmann, Jan   170

Yegenoglu, Alper   243
Yu, Hans   70

Zavala-Aké, Miguel   37
Zielasko, Daniel   243

Printed in the United States
By Bookmasters